PROFESSIONAL PRACTICE IN ARTIFICIAL INTELLIGENCE

IFIP – The International Federation for Information Processing

IFIP was founded in 1960 under the auspices of UNESCO, following the First World Computer Congress held in Paris the previous year. An umbrella organization for societies working in information processing, IFIP's aim is two-fold: to support information processing within its member countries and to encourage technology transfer to developing nations. As its mission statement clearly states,

> *IFIP's mission is to be the leading, truly international, apolitical organization which encourages and assists in the development, exploitation and application of information technology for the benefit of all people.*

IFIP is a non-profitmaking organization, run almost solely by 2500 volunteers. It operates through a number of technical committees, which organize events and publications. IFIP's events range from an international congress to local seminars, but the most important are:

- The IFIP World Computer Congress, held every second year;
- Open conferences;
- Working conferences.

The flagship event is the IFIP World Computer Congress, at which both invited and contributed papers are presented. Contributed papers are rigorously refereed and the rejection rate is high.

As with the Congress, participation in the open conferences is open to all and papers may be invited or submitted. Again, submitted papers are stringently refereed.

The working conferences are structured differently. They are usually run by a working group and attendance is small and by invitation only. Their purpose is to create an atmosphere conducive to innovation and development. Refereeing is less rigorous and papers are subjected to extensive group discussion.

Publications arising from IFIP events vary. The papers presented at the IFIP World Computer Congress and at open conferences are published as conference proceedings, while the results of the working conferences are often published as collections of selected and edited papers.

Any national society whose primary activity is in information may apply to become a full member of IFIP, although full membership is restricted to one society per country. Full members are entitled to vote at the annual General Assembly, National societies preferring a less committed involvement may apply for associate or corresponding membership. Associate members enjoy the same benefits as full members, but without voting rights. Corresponding members are not represented in IFIP bodies. Affiliated membership is open to non-national societies, and individual and honorary membership schemes are also offered.

PROFESSIONAL PRACTICE IN ARTIFICIAL INTELLIGENCE

IFIP 19th World Computer Congress, TC 12: Professional Practice Stream, August 21-24, 2006, Santiago, Chile

Edited by

John Debenham
University of Technology, Sydney, Australia

Professional Practice in Artificial Intelligence

Edited by J. Debenham

p. cm. (IFIP International Federation for Information Processing, a Springer Series in Computer Science)

ISSN: 1571-5736 / 1861-2288 (Internet)

ISBN: 13: 978-1-4419-4189-3

eISBN: 10: 0-387-34749-6
e-ISBN: 13: 978-0-387-34749-3

Printed on acid-free paper

9 8 7 6 5 4 3 2 1
springer.com

Preface

The Second Symposium on Professional Practice in AI 2006 is a conference within the IFIP World Computer Congress 2006, Santiago, Chile. The Symposium is organised by the IFIP Technical Committee on Artificial Intelligence (Technical Committee 12) and its Working Group 12.5 (Artificial Intelligence Applications). The First Symposium in this series was one of the conferences in the IFIP World Computer Congress 2004, Toulouse France.

The conference featured invited talks by Rose Dieng, John Atkinson, John Debenham and Max Bramer. The Symposium was a component of the IFIP AI 2006 conference, organised by Professor Max Bramer. I should like to thank the Symposium General Chair, Professor Bramer for his considerable assistance in making the Symposium happen within a very tight deadline.

These proceedings are the result of a considerable amount of hard work. Beginning with the preparation of the submitted papers, the papers were each reviewed by at least two members of the international Program Committee. The authors of accepted papers then revised their manuscripts to produce their final copy. The hard work of the authors, the referees and the Program Committee is gratefully acknowledged.

The IFIP AI 2006 conference and the Symposium are the latest in a series of conferences organised by IFIP Technical Committee 12 dedicated to the techniques of Artificial Intelligence and their real-world applications. Further information about TC12 can be found on our website http://www.ifiptc12.org.

John Debenham

Acknowledgements

Symposium Organising Committee

Symposium General Chair

Max Bramer (University of Portsmouth, United Kingdom)

Symposium Program Chair

John Debenham (University of Technology, Sydney, Australia)

Program Committee

Agnar Aamodt (Norwegian University of Science and Technology, Norway)
Analia Amandi (ISISTAN Research Institute, Argentina)
Lora Aroyo (Eindhoven University of Technology, The Netherlands)
Stefania Bandini (University of Milan, Italy)
Max Bramer (University of Portsmouth, UK)
Krysia Broda (Imperial College London, United Kingdom)
Zdzislaw Bubnicki (Wroclaw University of Technology, Poland)
Luigia Carlucci Aiello (Università di Roma La Sapienza, Italy)
Monica Crubezy (Stanford University, USA)
John Debenham (University of Technology, Sydney, Australia)
Joris Deguet (CNRS - IMAG Institute, France)
Evangelos Dellis (Inst. of Informatics & Telecommunications, NCSR, Athens, Greece)
Yves Demazeau (CNRS - IMAG Institute, France)
Vladan Devedzic (University of Belgrade, Serbia and Montenegro)
Tharam Dillon (University of Technology, Sydney, Australia)
John Domingue (The Open University, United Kingdom)
Anne Dourgnon-Hanoune (EDF, France)
Gintautas Dzemyda (Institute of Mathematics and Informatics, Lithuania)
Henrik Eriksson (Linköping University, Sweden)
Matjaz Gams (Slovenia)
Ana Garcia-Serrano (Technical University of Madrid, Spain)
Daniela Godoy (ISISTAN Research Institute, Argentina)
Fedja Hadzic (University of Technology, Sydney, Australia)
Andreas Harrer (University Duisburg-Essen, Germany)
Timo Honkela (Helsinki University of Technology, Finland)
Werner Horn (Medical University of Vienna , Austria)
Tony Jan (University of Technology, Sydney, Australia)
Kostas Karpouzis (National Technical University of Athens, Greece)
Dusko Katic (Serbia and Montenegro)
Ray Kemp (Massey University, New Zealand)
Dr. Kinshuk (Massey University, New Zealand)
Joost N. Kok (Leiden University, The Netherlands)

Stasinos Konstantopoulos (Inst. of Informatics & Telecommunications, NCSR, Athens, Greece)
Jasna Kuljis (Brunel University, United Kingdom)
Daoliang Li (China Agricultural University, Beijing)
Ilias Maglogiannis (University of Aegean, Samos, Greece)
Suresh Manandhar (University of York, UK)
Ramon Lopez de Mantaras (Spanish Council for Scientific Research)
Brian Mayoh (University of Aarhus, Denmark)
Dimitri Melaye (CNRS - IMAG Institute, France)
Eunika Mercier-Laurent (KIM, France)
Tanja Mitrovic (University of Canterbury, Christchurch, New Zealand)
Riichiro Mizoguchi (Osaka University, Japan)
Zsolt Nagy (Budapest University of Technology and Economics, Hungary)
Pavol Navrat (Slovak University of Technology in Bratislava, Slovakia)
Erich Neuhold (RSA-DME)
Bernd Neumann (University of Hamburg, Germany)
Daniel O'Leary (University of Southern California, USA)
Andrea Omicini (Alma Mater Studiorum–Università di Bologna, Italy)
Mihaela Oprea (University of Ploiesti, Romania)
Stavros Perantonis (Inst. of Informatics & Telecommunications, NCSR, Athens, Greece)
Guillaume Piolle (CNRS - IMAG Institute, France)
Alun Preece (University of Aberdeen, UK)
Abdel-Badeeh M. Salem (Ain Shams University, Egypt)
Demetrios Sampson (University of Piraeus & CERTH, Greece)
M Sasikumar (C-DAC, Mumbai, India)
Silvia Schiaffino (ISISTAN Research Institute, Argentina)
Mauricio Solar (Chile)
Constantine Spyropoulos (Inst. of Informatics & Telecommunications, NCSR, Athens, Greece)
Steffen Staab (University of Koblenz, Germany)
Olga Stepankova (Czech Technical University in Prague, Czech Republic)
Péter Szeredi (Budapest University of Technology and Economics, Hungary)
Vagan Terziyan (University of Jyvaskyla, Finland)
Nicolas Kemper Valverde (National Autonomous University of Mexico)
Wiebe van der Hoek (University of Liverpool, United Kingdom)
Marie-Helene Verrons (CNRS - IMAG Institute, France)
Virginia Daniela Yannibelli (ISISTAN Research Institute, Argentina)
Zdenek Zdrahal (The Open University, United Kingdom)
Jianhan Zhu (Open University, United Kingdom)

Contents

Applications

Applications

Detection of Breast Lesions in Medical Digital Imaging Using Neural Networks

Gustavo Ferrero, Paola Britos and Ramón García-Martínez

Software & Knowledge Engineering Center. Graduate School. Buenos Aires Institute of Technology
Intelligent Systems Laboratory. School of Engineering. University of Buenos Aires.

rgm@itba.edu.ar

Abstract. The purpose of this article is to present an experimental application for the detection of possible breast lesions by means of neural networks in medical digital imaging. This application broadens the scope of research into the creation of different types of topologies with the aim of improving existing networks and creating new architectures which allow for improved detection.

1. Introduction

Breast cancer has been determined to be the second leading cause of cancer death in women, and the most common type of cancer in women; there are no official statistics in the Argentine Republic, but it is estimated that 22 in 100,000 women are affected by this illness, similarly to what is observed in other Western countries [Mols *et al*, 2005]. The mammography is the best method of diagnosis by images that exists at the present time to detect minimum mammary injuries, fundamentally small carcinomas that are shown by micro calcifications or tumors smaller than 1cm. of diameter that are not palpated during medical examination. [Antonie *et al*, 2001]. Currently, joint efforts are being made in order to be able to detect tissue anomalies in a timely fashion, given that there are no methods for breast cancer prevention. Early detection has proved an essential weapon in cancer detection, since it helps to prolong patients' lives. Physicians providing test results must have diagnostic training based on mammography, and must issue a certain number of reports annually. Double reading of reports increases sensitivity for detection of minimal lesions by about 7%, though at a high cost. The physician shall then interpret these reports and determine according to his/her best judgment the steps to be taken for the proper diagnosis and treatment of the patient. for this reason, physicists, engineers, and physicians are in search of new tools to fight cancer, which would also allow physicians to obtain a second opinion [Gokhale *et al*, 2003, Simoff *et al*, 2002]. The American College of Radiology having approved the use of new digital mammographs, digital photos have begun to be stored in databases together with the patient's information, for later processing via different methods [Selman, 2000]. Different methods have been used to classify and/or detect anomalies in medical images, such as wavelets, fractal

Please use the following format when citing this chapter:

Ferrero, G., Britos, P., García-Martínez, R., 2006, in IFIP International Federation for Information Processing, Volume 218, Professional Practice in Artificial Intelligence, eds. J. Debenham, (Boston: Springer), pp. 1–10.

theory, statistical methods and most of them used features extracted using image-processing techniques. In addition, some other methods were presented in the literature based on fuzzy set theory, Markov models and neural networks. Most of the computer-aided methods proved to be powerful tools that could assist medical staff in hospitals and lead to better results in diagnosing a patient [Antonie *et al*, 2001].

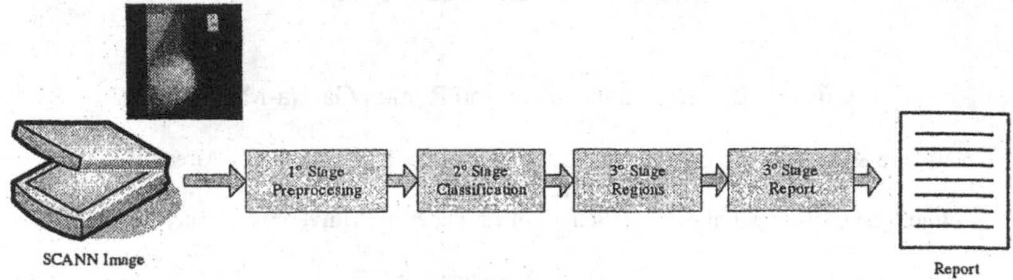

Fig. 1. Processing Steps

Different studies on using data mining in the processing of medical images have rendered very good results using neural networks for classification and grouping. In recent years different computerized systems have been developed to support diagnostic work of radiologists in mammography. The goal of these systems is to focus the radiologist's attention on suspicious areas. They work in three steps: i. analogic mammograms are digitized; ii. images are segmented and preprocessed; iii. Regions of Interests (ROI) are found and classified by neural networks [Lauria *et al*, 2003].

2. Proposed Method

Radiologists do not diagnose cancer versus benign nodules; they detect suspicious regions and send them for additional work up [Baydush *et al*, 2001]. Bearing in mind the way medical imaging specialists work, the system works as follows: i. capturing medical image, ii. storing image on the data base, iii. starting up processing, iv. generating report, v. validating report. The first and last steps generate information which provides a work environment where system users are given the ability to create new network topologies in order to validate the results obtained.

2.1. Mammography Processing

Figure 1 shows the stages that have been adopted for the image processing of a mammography. Stage 1: image pre-processing; this stage begins by acquiring the image, which is delivered to the following stage containing only the region of interest. Stage 2: image classification to determine whether or not it contains malignant lesions that require in-depth examination by specialists. Stage 3: if the classifier determines that the image shows malignant lesions, suspicious areas are scanned for. Stage 4: mammography processing report generated.

2.2 Mammography Pre-processing

The first stage contains a set of steps which as a group serve the purpose of eliminating all information which is irrelevant for the classification. Step 1. Using median filter. Step 2. Cropping margins. Step 3. Eliminating isolated regions. Step 4. Equalizing. Order filters are based on a specific treatment of image statistics called order statistics. These filters operate in the neighborhood of a certain pixel, known as window, and they replace the value of the central pixel. Order statistics is a technique that organizes all pixels in a window in sequential order, on the basis of their grey level [Liew *et al*, 2005]. The M mean in a set of values is such that half of the values in the set are smaller than M and half of the values are greater than M. In order to filter the mean in the area around the neighborhood, we ranked the intensities in the neighborhood, we determined the mean, and assigned the latter to the intensity of the pixel. The main purpose of mean filtering is to cause the points with very different intensities to become similar to their neighbors, thus eliminating any isolated intensity peaks that appear in the area of the filter mask. The median filter is a nonlinear filter, used in order to eliminate the high-frequency filter without eliminating the significant characteristics of the image. A 3x3 mask is used, which is centered on each image pixel, replacing each central pixel by the mean of the nine pixels covering the mask. The window size allows the characteristics of the image to me preserved while at the same time eliminatinng high frequencies [Díaz, 2004]. Next the automatic cropping is performed. The purpose of this step is to focus the process exclusively on the relevant breast region, which reduces the possibility for erroneous classification by areas which are not of interest. Image segmentation is an important step in several image applications. A host of techniques and algorithms usually fall into this general category as a starting point for edge detection, region labelling, and transformations. All these techniques, region labelling, and analyses, are relatively simple algorithms that have been used for many years to isolate, measure, and identify potential regions [Jankowski and Kuska, 2004]. A stack method is used for region labelling, as it is one of the fastest and simplest to implement. After labelling, those areas which are not of interest to the study are eliminated. It is known that the surface covered by the breast is over 80%; therefore, isolated areas with surfaces smaller than 1% do not belong to the breast and are eliminated through the creation of masks obtained from neighboring pixels. Lastly, a uniform equalization is performed, which will essentially help enhance image contrast.

$$F(g) = [\, g_{max} - g_{min}]\, P_p(g) + g_{min}$$

Where g_{max}, and g_{min} correspond to the maximum and minimum intensity values in the range of grey values of the image. Figure 2 shows the results of image pre-processing.

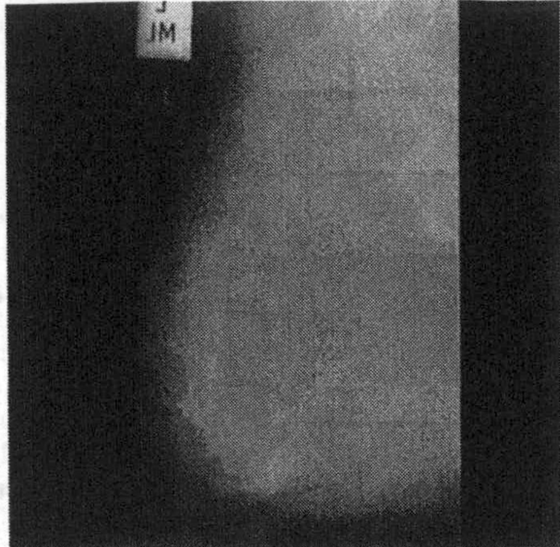

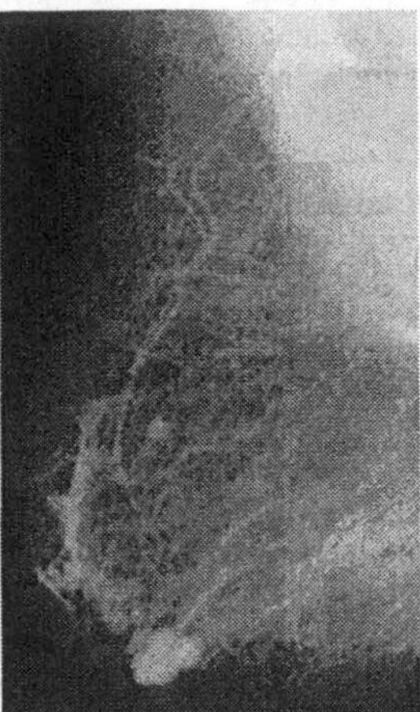

Fig. 2. Automatic Pre-processing

2.3 Classification

Neural networks are models which attempt to emulate the behavior of the brain. As such, they perform simplification, identifying the relevant elements in the system. An adequate selection of their features coupled with a convenient structure constitutes the conventional procedure utilized to build networks which are capable of performing a given task [Hertz *et al,* 1991]. Artificial neural networks offer an attractive paradigm for the design and analysis of adaptive, intelligent systems for a wide range of applications in artificial intelligence [Fiszelew *et al,* 2003]. Artificial neural networks are based on a rather simple model of a neuron. Most neurons have three parts, a dendrite which collects inputs from other neurons (or from an external stimulus); a soma which performs an important nonlinear processing step; finally an axon, a cable-like wire along which the output signal is transmitted to other neurons is called synapse [W. Gestner, NA]. Neurons are grouped in layers; these interconnected layers form a neural network, thus each neural network is composed of N number of layers (Figure 3). Depending on how these components (layers) are connected, different architectures may be created (feed forward NN, recurrent NN, etc.). The topology or architecture of a neural network refers to the type, organization, and arrangement of neurons in the network, forming layers or clusters. The topology of a multilayered neural network depends on the number of variables in the input layer, the number of hidden neuron layers, the number of neurons per each hidden layer, and the number of output variables in the last layer. All these factors are important when determining network configuration [Zurada, 1995].

Thus, neural network structures can be defined as collections of parallel processors interconnected in the form of an oriented lattice, arranged in such a way that the network structure is appropriate for the problem under consideration. The connections between neurons in a neural network have an associated weight, which is what allows the network to acquire knowledge. The most commonly used learning écheme for the MLP is the back-propagation algorithm. The weight updating for the hidden layers adopts the mechanism of back-propagated corrective signal from the output layer.

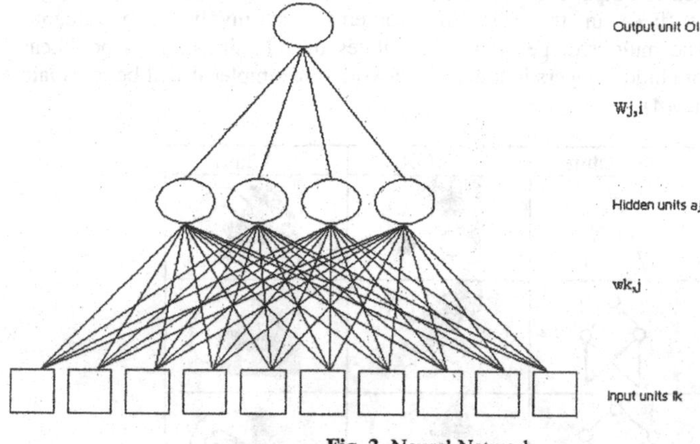

Fig. 3. Neural Network

It has been shown that the MLP, given flexible network/neuron dimensions, offers an asymptotic approximation capability. It was demonstrated that two layers (one hidden only) perceptrons should be adequate as universal approximators of any nonlinear functions [Kung *et al*, 1998]. A multilayer perceptron is structured as follows:

- Function signal: the signal that propagates from the input to output.
- Error signal: generated by output neurons and it backpropagates as an adjustment to the synaptical connections towards the input in order to adjust the output obtained to the expected output as faithfully as possible.

Thus all output neurons and those in the hidden layer are enabled to perform two types of calculations according to the signal they receive: If it is a function signal, it will be a forward calculation (forward pass); if it is an error signal, it will be a backward calculation (backward pass). The rule of propagation for neurons in the hidden layer is the weighted sum of the outputs with synaptic weights wji, then, a sigmoid transference function is applied to that weighted sum and is limited in the response. Basically, the backpropagation algorithm is based on error minimization by means of a traditional optimization method called gradient descent. That is, the key point consists in calculating the proper weights of the layers from the errors in the output units; the secret lies in evaluating the consequences of an error and dividing the value among the weights of the contributing network connections. Neural network learning can be specified as a function approximation problem where the goal is to learn an unknown function ?:RN ? R (or a good approximation of it) from a set of input-output pairs $S = \{(x^N, y) \mid x^N \in R^N, y \in R\}$ [Parekh, *et al*, 2000]. Pattern classification is a special case of function approximation where the function's output y is restricted to one of M (M ≥ 2) discrete values (or classes). A neural network for solving classification problems typically has N input neurons and M output neurons. The kth output neuron (1 ≤ K ≤ M) is trained to output one (while all the other output neurons are trained to output zero) for patterns belonging to the kth class. A single output neuron suffices in the case of problems that involve two category classifications. The multilayer perceptron facilitates the classification of nonlinear problems; the more hidden layers in a neural network, the simpler it will be to isolate the problem (Figure 4).

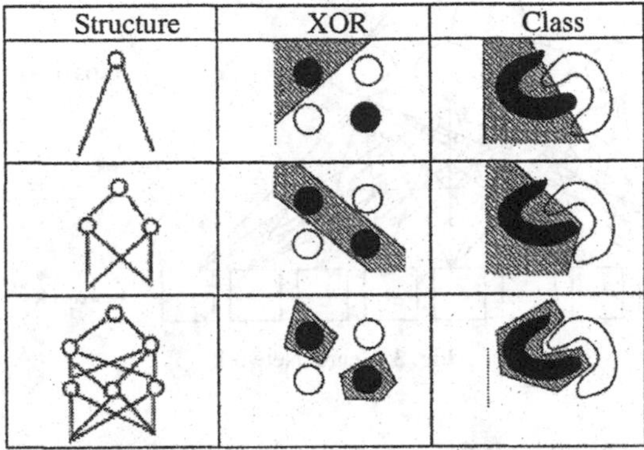

Fig. 4. Geometric Interpretation of the Role of Hidden Layers

2.4. Image Features

A radiological image is formed by tissue absorption when exposed to Roentgen radiation. Depending on the amount of radiation absorbed, an object (tissue) may be radiopaque (RO), radiolucid (RL), or radiotransparent (RT).

- When a low amount of X-ray radiation is absorbed by the object, virtually all the rays reach the film; the color appears dark and it is a radiotransparent body (air cavities).
- When a moderate amount of radiation is absorbed by the object, the color appears grey and it is a radiolucid body (noncalcified organic tissue).
- When a large amount of X-ray radiation has been absorbed or it has been completely absorbed, the color appears light or white and it is a radiopaque body (inorganic tissue, calcified tissue).

The range of colors is related to and depends on the extent of X-ray absorption by the tissue. The more radiation that is absorbed by the tissue, the less radiation will reach the film, signifying that the body is radiopaque; the less radiation that is absorbed by the tissue, the more radiation will reach the film, signifying that the body is radiolucid. This feature of X-ray images will be taken into account and will be used in order to obtain information about the sample tissues. The input layer is formed by K input neurons; this value is obtained by considering: the regions defined for the image (image subdivisions), the amount of statistical operations applied to those regions, plus one neuron according to the position of the breast (left or right) and a set of three neurons according to the type of tissue (dense, dense-glandular, and glandular). The characteristics of each of the regions are obtained from the information provided by the tissues represented in the pixels. Data extraction in the regions is carried out via the following statistical procedures:

Mean: it is the mean data value.
Bias: it is the systemic error which frequently occurs.
Kurtosis: it measures whether the distribution values are relatively concentrated around the mean values of the sample.
Variance: it measures the existing distance between the values and the mean.

The mean is defined by the following function:

$$\bar{X} = \frac{\sum x_i}{n}$$

Bias is defined:

$$bias = \frac{n}{(n-1)(n-2)} \sum \left(\frac{(x_i - X)}{s} \right)^3$$

Kurtosis is defined by the following formula:

$$k = \frac{n * (n-1)}{(n-1)(n-2)(n-3)} \sum \left(\frac{(x_i - X)}{s} \right)^4 - \frac{3 * (n-1)^2}{(n-2)(n-3)}$$

Lastly, variance is given by:

$$s = \frac{\sum (x_i - X)^2}{(n-1)}$$

The system offers the possibility of creating different topologies for multilayer networks ($N \geq 3$, where N is the number of layers). This feature allows the user to research new architectures. As it has been mentioned before, image information (regions) is entered in the network, for instance; for an image divided into 16 regions, there are 69 (16 * 4 + 1 + 3 + 1) neurons including the independent term; the output layer may have only one or two neurons.

2.5. Training

Supervised learning is characterized by a controlled training by an external agent (supervisor or teacher) who determines the response to be generated by the network from a certain input. The supervisor verifies the network output and in case it does not match the expected output, connection weights are to be modified, in order to obtain an output as close as possible to the expected one [Hertz *et al*, 1991]. The proposed method for the system is learning by trial and error, which consists in adjusting the weights of the connections according to the distribution of the quadratic error among the expected responses r_q and the appropriate current responses O_q.

$$E_q = \frac{1}{2} \sum_{q=1}^{N_q} \left(r_q - O_q \right)^2$$

Training data are mammographies obtained by Mammographic Image Analysis Society (MIAS); they consist in 322 images from which 55 are to be analyzed in order to obtain further information, which shall be used to train the neural network.
The following information is necessary for neural network training:

Stop error: it is the acceptable output error for training, below this error, training is brought to a halt and weights are said to converge.

Number of cycles: it sets the maximum number of cycles that need to be learned by the network.

Momentum: each connection is given a certain inertia or momentum, in such a way that its tendency to change direction with a steeper descent be averaged with the "tendencies" for change of direction that were previously obtained. The momentum parameter must be between 0 and 1 [Zurada, 1995].

Learning ratio: it is a value between 0 and 1 used in error distribution (delta rule).

The training procedure is evaluated every thousand cycles, obtaining information about the last ten cycles, performing an evaluation of the mean, in a way that the speed of network convergence can be determined, thus allowing to conclude training and start with a new set of weights.

3. Experimenting with the System

The system allows for the generation of different architectures, for which reason different networks are evaluated, bearing in mind certain factors, whenever a new architecture is created. The performance (and cost) of a neural network on any given problem is critically dependent, among other things, on the network's architecture and the particular learning algorithm used. [Fiszelew *et al*, 2003]. Too small networks are unable to adequately learn the problem well while overly large networks tend to over fit the training data and consequently result in poor generalization performance [Parekh, *et al*, 2000]. With varying numbers of hidden layers, the following configuration has yielded the best results: 69 Neurons in the input layer. 16 Neurons in the hidden layer, one for each region the image was divided into. 4 Neurons in the following hidden layer, one for each operation performed on the regions. 2 Output neurons, one for each possible direction (right and left). In addition, two networks have been set up for use depending on the location of the breast (left or right), since the initial results obtained using one single network for both were very poor. Training times were also reduced using this modality, thereby increasing the convergence speed. The single network trained for both sides was able to classify correctly with a 30% success rate, whereas the networks trained for a specific side have a 60% success rate. In addition, the former took over 4 hours to converge, while the second did so in less than 60 minutes. Further research will be done to identify the appropriate neural network that will allow classifications to be obtained with 80% certainty.

4. Related Work

In this research the neural net architecture is trained to distinguish malignant nodules from benign ones. It differs from the CALMA project approach [Lauria *et al*, 2003] which has tools that identify micro calcification clusters and massive lesions.
The proposed architecture deals with mammography images in image formats (JPG, BMP, TIFF, GIF), which differs from standard data mining approach based on image parameters sets provided by the community [UCIMLR. 2006a.; 2006b].

5. Conclusions

This project has been an attempt to provide an environment for the continued investigation of new neural network models that will achieve better results in the classification of medical images. The project is open source, allowing access to the source code so that others may study, improve, expand and distribute it, so that healthcare institutions may have access to tools they can use to improve breast cancer detection.
The goal of the project is to improve the detection of areas suspected of containing some type of lesion. The results obtained are very different from our initial expectations, although the initial results obtained are promising. The future will bring improvements to this application as well as the possibility of inputting additional statistical data that will enhance the reading of the images.
Next research steps are: (a) to compare results of the proposed architecture in this paper with others provided by vector machines based classifiers [Fung and Mangasarian, 1999; Lee *et al.*, 2000; Fung and Mangasarian, 2003]; and (b) to study specific filters that recognize structures in mammography images.

6. Bibliography

Antonie M., Zaïene O., Coman A. (2001). *Application of data mining techniques for medical image classification.* Proceedings of the Second International Workshop on Multimedia Data Mining. San Francisco.

Baydush A., Cararious D., Lo J., Abbey C., Floyd C. (2001). *Computerized classification of suspicious regions in chest radiographs using subregion hotelling observers.* American Association of Physicists in Medicine. Vol 28 (12).

Diaz, S. (2004). *Detección de microcalcificaciones en imágenes de mamografías usando diferencias de filtro gaussianos optimizados*. Universidad Nacional de Ingeniería. Facultad de Ingeniería Industrial y de Sistemas. Lima. Perú.

Egmont-Petersen M., de Ridder D., Handels H. (2002). *Image processing with neural networks. The Journal of the pattern recognition society*. Vol. 35 (10).

Fiszelew, A., Britos, P. , Perichisky, G. & García-Martínez, R. (2003). *Automatic Generation of Neural Networks based on Genetic Algorithms*. Revista Eletrônica de Sistemas de Informação, 2(1): 1-7.

Fung, G. and Mangasarian, O. 1999. Semi-Supervised Support Vector Machines for Unlabeled Data Classification. Optimization Methods and Software Vol. 15, pp. 29-44.

Fung, G. and Mangasarian, O. 2003. *Breast Tumor Susceptibility to Chemotherapy via Support Vector Machines*. Data Mining Institute Technical Report 03-06, November 2003. Computational Management Science.

Gerstner W. (1998). *Supervised learning for neural networks: A tutorial with Java Exercises*. Technical Report. Laboratory of Computational Neuroscience at the Swiss Federal Institute of Technology Lausanne.

Hertz J., A. Krogh y R. Palmer 1991. *Introduction to the Theory of Neural Computation*. Reading, MA: Addison-Wesley.

Jankowski M., Kuska J. (2004). *Connected components labelling – algorithms in Mathematica, Java, C++ and C#*. IMS2004.

Kung S., Hwang J. (1998). *Neural network for intelligent multimedia processing*. Proceedings of the IEEE. Vol 86 (6).

Lauria A., Palmiero R., Forni G., Cerello P., Golosio B., Fauci F., Magro R., Raso G, Tangaro S., Indovina P. (2003). *The CALMA system: an artificial neural network for detecting masses and microcalcifications in digitalized mammograms*. 9th Pisa Meeting on Advanced Detector. La Biodola, Isola d'Elba, Italy.

Lee, Y., Mangasarian, O. and Wolberg, W.2000. *Breast Cancer Survival and Chemotherapy: A Support Vector Machine Analysis*. DIMACS Series in Discrete Mathematics and Theoretical Computer Science, Vol. 55, pp. 1-10.

Liew, A., Yan, H. and Yang, M.(2005). *Pattern Recognition techniques for the emerging field of bioinformatics: A review*. Pattern Recognition 38(11): 2055-2073

Mols, F., Vingerhoets, A., Coebergh, J. and Poll-Franse, L. (2005). *Quality of life among long-term breast cancer survivors: A systematic review*. European Journal of Cancer 41(17): 2613-2619.

Parekh R., Yang J., Honavar V. (2000) *Constructive neural-network learning algorithms for pattern classification*. IEEE Transactions on neural networks. Vol. 11 (2).

Selman, S. (2000). *Data Mining of Digital Mammograms Will Aid in War against Cancer*. www.gatech.edu Página vigente al 17/08/2003.

Simoff, S., Djeraba, C., y Zaïane, O. *Multimedia Data Mining between Promise and Problems*. 3rd Edition of the International Workshop on Multimedia Data Minig. Pages 118-121. SIGKDD Explortions.

UCIMLR. 2006a. *Breast Cancer Database*. UCI Machine Learning Repository. http://www.ics.uci.edu/~mlearn/MLSummary.html

UCIMLR. 2006b. *Wisconsin Breast Cancer Databases*. UCI Machine Learning Repository. http://www.ics.uci.edu/~mlearn/MLSummary.html

Zurada, J. (1995). *Introduction to Artificial Neural Systems*. West Publishing Company.

Identification of Velocity Variations in a Seismic Cube Using Neural Networks

Dario Sergio Cersósimo, Claudia Ravazoli, Ramón García-Martínez

PhD Program & Geophisic Group of the Astronomic & Geophisic Science School. University of La Plata
PETROBRAS ENERGÍA Exploración ARGENTINA
Software & Knowledge Engineering Center. Graduate School. Buenos Aires Institute of Technology
Intelligent Systems Laboratory. School of Engineering. University of Buenos Aires.
rgm@itba.edu.ar

Abstract. . This research allow to infer that from seismic section and well data it is possible to determine velocity anomalies variations in layers with thicknesses below to the seismic resolution using neuronal networks.

1. Introduction

The intelligent systems [Holland *et al.*, 1987; Towell & Shavlik, 1994; García-Martinez & Borrajo, 2000, Grosser *et al.*, 2005] have shown to be very useful in prospective problems in which other approaches have failed. The neuronal networks as a particular case of intelligent systems [Hertz *et al.*, 1991; Rich & Knight, 1991; Setiono & Liu, 1996; Yao & Liu, 1998], have given promising results in fields like: modeling, analysis of time series, patterns recognition among others [Dow & Sietsma, 1991; Gallant, 1993; Back *et al.*, 1998]. In the field of the geosciences this type of systems has contributed with conventional and no conventional developments of interpretation and processing [Heggland *et al.*, 1999a; 1999b; 2000; An & Moon, 1993; Johnston, 1993; Wang & Huang, 1993; Ping, 1994; Cai, 1994; Huang & Williamson, 1994; Zhang *et al.*, 1995a; 1995b, Sun *et al.*, 2001; Deker *et al.*, 2001; Chengdang, 1993].
One open issue in high resolution inversion is that there is no way to obtain from seismic data the top and the base of a geologic formation with a thickness under 15 meters (approximately). Considering that the observed seismic trace can be seen as the real component of a complex trace, attributes as envelope amplitude, phase and frequency can be separated and calculated. Each one of these attributes and the combination of them could show the characteristics and petrophisical variations of the rock.
One of the petrophysical characteristics is the lateral velocity variation. These velocity variations can be inferred through a neuronal network having as input wells synthetic data and the calculation of the trace attributes as envelope amplitude, phase and frequency on an interpreted seismic horizon.

Please use the following format when citing this chapter:

Cersósimo, D.S., Ravazoli, C., García-Martínez, R., 2006, in IFIP International Federation for Information Processing, Volume 218, Professional Practice in Artificial Intelligence, eds. J. Debenham, (Boston: Springer), pp. 11–19.

2. Treatment of the Data

For the experimental treatment it has been started from a synthetic geologic model. From this synthetic geologic model it has been calculated a synthetic seismic section (direct method). A synthetic geologic model of parallel layers was used. Gas velocity and petroleum velocity have been assigned to some of these layers. As it is observed in Figure 1, we have five layers, the third layer (yellow) is around ten meters of thickness. This layer has lateral and vertical velocities variation (Table 1).

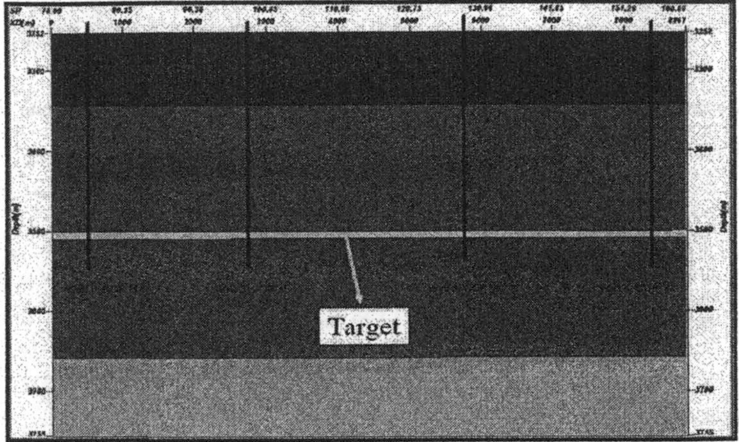

Fig. 1. Geological Model

NAME	PATTERN	DIST	VTOP	VBOT	DTOP	DBOT
C1		0.00	3500.00	3500.00	2375.724	2375.724
		8866.80	3500.00	3500.00	2375.724	2375.724
C2		0.00	3500.00	3500.00	2375.724	2375.724
		8866.80	3500.00	3500.00	2375.724	2375.724
C3		0.00	3467.00	3467.00	2370.104	2370.104
CDP 11	Well 1	2000.00	3467.00	3467.00	2370.104	2370.104
		2500.00	3380.00	3467.00	2355.093	2370.104
CDP 31	Well 2	3000.00	3380.00	3467.00	2355.093	2370.104
		3500.00	3467.00	3467.00	2370.104	2370.104
		5000.00	3467.00	3467.00	2370.104	2370.104
		5500.00	3380.00	3467.00	2355.093	2370.104
CDP 51	Well 3	6000.00	3380.00	3467.00	2355.093	2370.104
		6500.00	3467.00	3467.00	2370.104	2370.104
CDP 72	Well 4	8866.80	3467.00	3467.00	2370.104	2370.104
C4		0.00	3800.00	3800.00	2425.073	2425.073
		8866.80	3800.00	3800.00	2425.073	2425.073
C5		0.00	3900.00	3900.00	2440.873	2440.873
		8866.80	3900.00	3900.00	2440.873	2440.873

Table 1. Velocity field

In Table 1 DIST is the distance from the origin, VTOP is the velocity of the top of layer, VBOT is the velocity of the base of layer, DTOP is the density of the top of the layer and DBOT is the density of the base of the layer. The involved densities has been calculated with Gardner equation [Gardner *et al.*, 1974]. This geological model is used in the sinthetic sismic section calculation. (Figure 2).

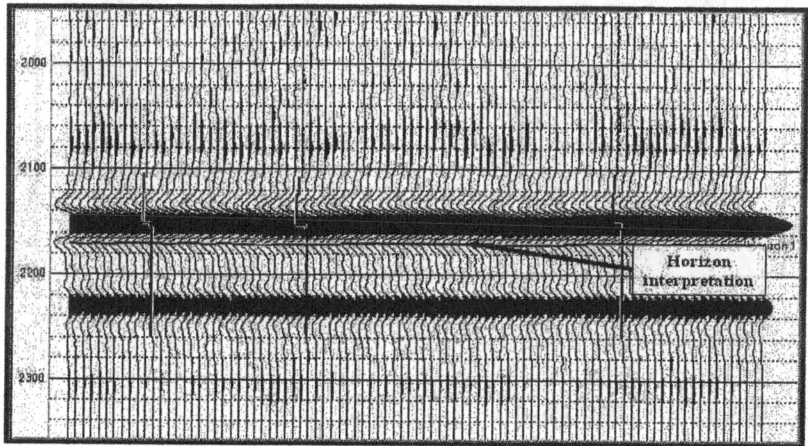

Fig. 2. Synthetic Seismic Section

The used parameters for the processing of the synthetic seismic section and for wavelets calculation are showed in Table 2. Due to the frequency content in the synthetic seismic section, it is impossible to determine the top and the base of the objective horizon. The velocity variation on the real horizon is in Fig. 3.

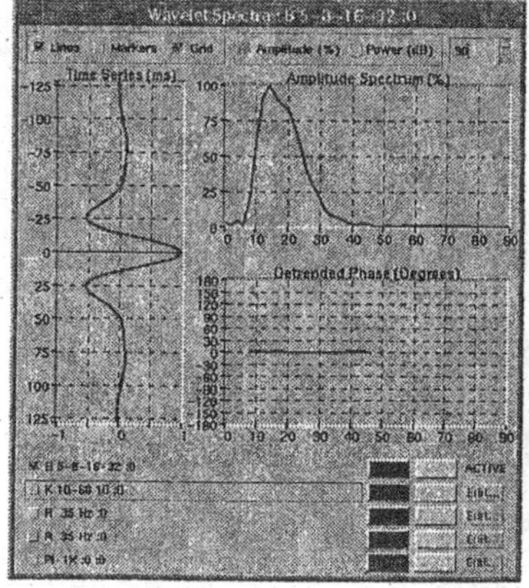

Start Trace	1
End Trace	91
Trace Increment	1
Trace Amplitude	1.00
Sample Rate	2.00
Start Shot Pt.	70.00
End Shot Pt.	160.00
Shot Pt. Space	98.52
Shot Pt. Incr.	1.00
Wavelet	ORMSBY
Frecuency 1	5.0
Frecuency 2	8.0
Frecuency 3	16.0
Frecuency 4	32.0
Phase (M=min)	0.0

Table 2. Wavelette and parameters used in the calculation of the Synthetic Seismic Section

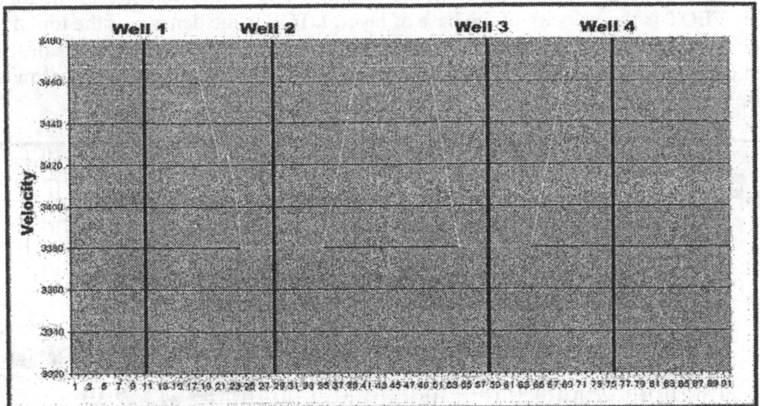

Fig. 3. Velocity variation on the Real Horizon

3. Model Based Inversion

In model based inversion [Russell, 1988; Treitel *et al.*, 1993; 1995; Stewart *et al.*, 1984], the synthetic seismic data and the data of three wells (Well 1, Well 3 and Well 4) was process in a conventional way to calculate an initial velocities model. The initial model (Figure 4) has been taken from a seismic interpretation over a horizon near the target.

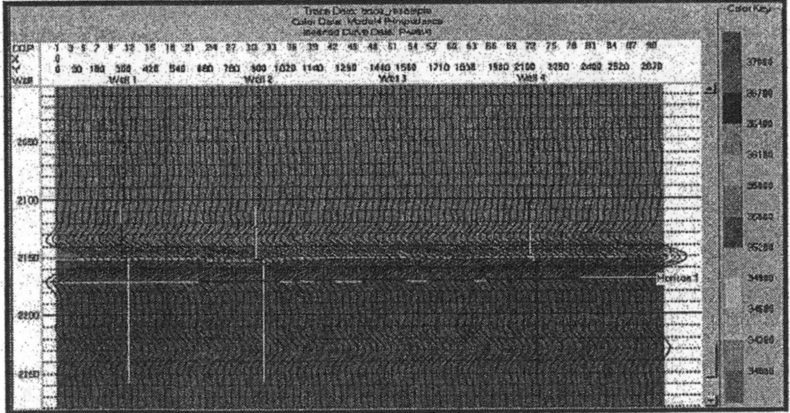

Fig. 4. Inicial Model

When the initial velocities model is finished, this model trace would differ from the original seismic trace (fig. 2). Then least squares optimization makes the difference between the original trace and the model as small as possible. The result shown in figure 5 was reached after 50 iterations. This figure shows the velocity variation given by the model-based inversion in the target horizon. The result show that the model based inversion discriminates two low velocity zones in well2 and well3 (2150 mseg.).

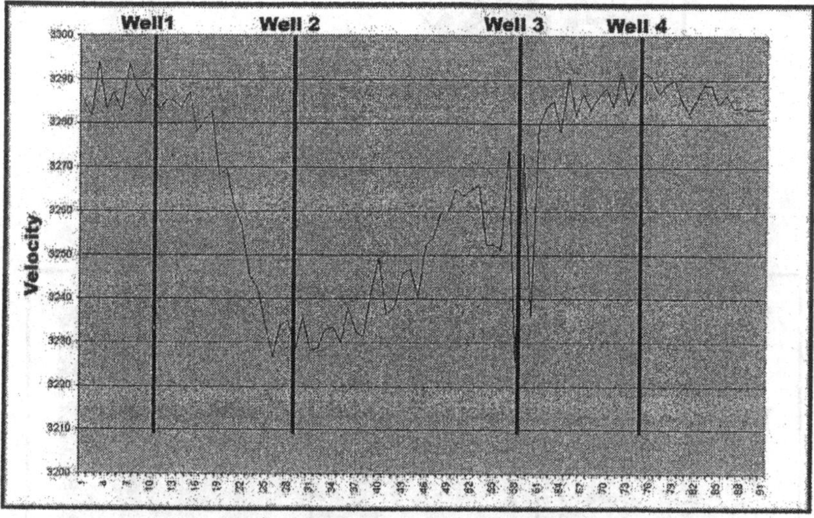

Fig. 5. Velocity variation on the target Horizon (Model Based Inversion)

4. Artificial Neuronal Network Based Inversion

In this approach an artificial neuronal network was applied to an interpreted horizon with a Feed Forward Back Propagation algorithm [Freeman & Skapura; 1991, Haykin, 1998], defined with nine neurons of input, a hidden layer of five neurons and one neuron of output. The neuronal network design can be appreciated in figure 6 with their inputs and outputs.

The input data include the seismic interpretation, seismic attributes calculated from the interpreted horizon. The desired data was the velocity of the Wells from "Well1", "Well2" and "Well4" (the same input data than the model based inversion). In order to calculate the velocity in each trace with less than 1% error and 1000 iterations, the neuronal network has been trained with the three mentioned wells. The velocity as a Shot Point function (SP) and CDP´s has been represented in figure 7.

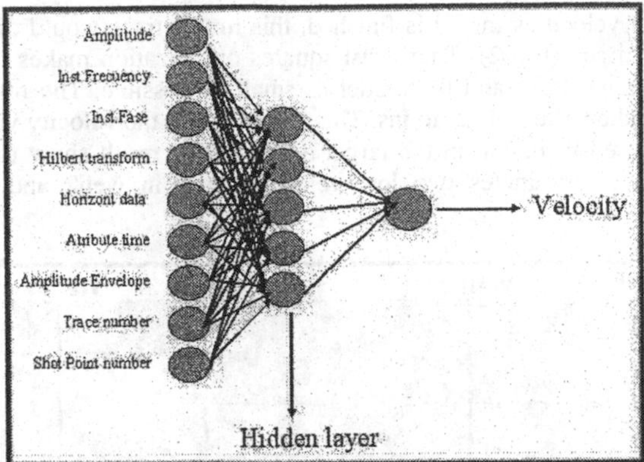

Fig. 6. Artificial Neuronal Network Design

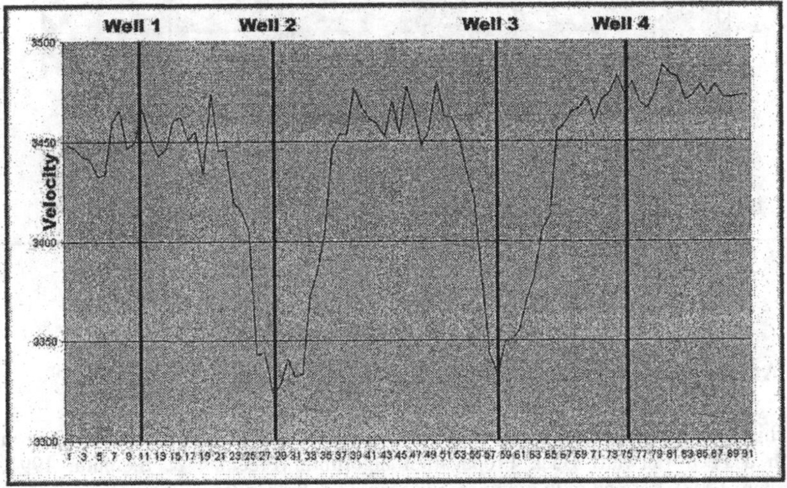

Fig. 7. Velocity variation on the target Horizon according to Artificial Neuronal Networks

It has been compared the velocity variation calculated from Model based inversion versus the one processed from artificial neuronal networks (figure 8), it is possible to observe that the neural net has been able to discriminate two low velocity zones. First one is between CDP's 22 and 37, corresponding the Well 2, and second between CDP's 52 and 70, corresponding the Well 3. It is important to emphasize that this last zone has been predicted by the neural network successfully because the Well3 has not been used for the training of the network, this can be corroborated observing the field of velocities given in Table 1. The intervals between 2500m to 3000m and 5500m to

6000m, the top velocity of the yellow horizon it is 3380m/seg, associated to the Wells2 and Well3 respectively.

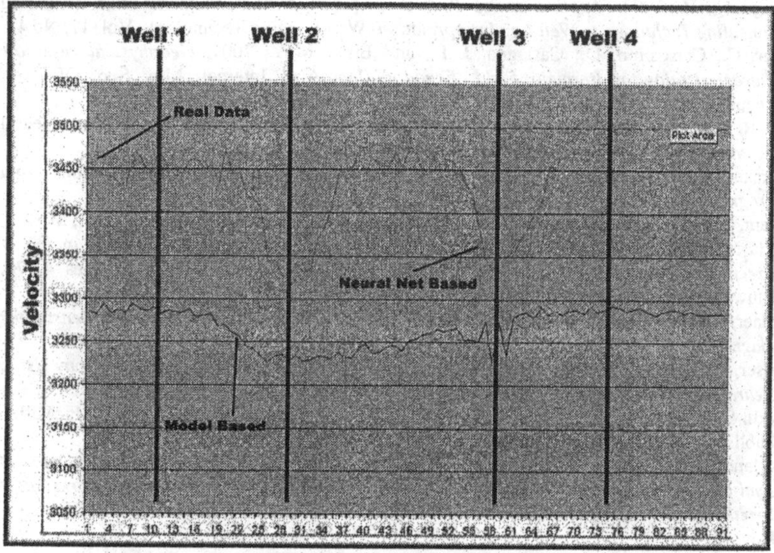

Fig. 8. Comparison of Velocity variation on the target horizon

5. Conclusions

The experimental goal was to obtain the velocity variation with: [a] the data of the seismic interpretation, [b] the calculated seismic attributes in the interpreted seismic horizon (amplitude, instantaneous frequency, instantaneous phase, transformed hilbert, amplitude envelope, seismic trace) and [c] the well data. The neural net was able to discriminate better the low velocity as is observed in the Well3. This result allow us to infer that it is possible to discriminate velocity variations, acoustic impedances or any other well curve throughout a section of seismic cube using neural net.

6. References

An, P. and Moon, W. 1993. *Reservoir characterization using feedforward neural networks.* 63rd Annual Internat. Mtg., Soc. Expl. Geophys., Expanded Abstracts, , 93, 258-262.

Back, B., Sere, K., & Vanharanta, H. 1998. *Managing complexity in large data bases using self-organizing maps*, Accounting Management & Information Technologies 8, 191-210.

Cai, Y. 1994. *The artificial neural network approach for hydrocarbon prediction by synthesizing multiple seismic information.* 56th Mtg. Eur. Assoc. Expl. Geophys., Extended Abstracts, , 94, Session:P153.

Chengdang, Z. 1993. *Application of Back-propagation Neural Networks and Simulated Annealing Technique to Well Log Interpretation.* Well Logging Technology, Vol. 17, No.4.

Deker, C.; Cersosimo, D.; Castagna, J. P.; and Eissa, M.A., 2001, *Geophysical reservoir characterization of Bermejo Field, Ecuador*, 71st Ann. Internat. Mtg: Soc. Of Expl. Geophys., pp. 1668-1669.

Dow R. J. y Sietsma J. 1991. *Creating Artificial Neural Networks that Generalize.* Neural Networks, vol. 4, no. 1, pp. 198-209.

Freeman, J. & Skapura, , D. 1991. *Neural Networks: Algorithms, Applications, and Programming Techniques.* Adison-Wesley.

Gallant, S. 1993. *Neural Network Learning & Experts Systems.* MIT Press, Cambridge, MA.

García Martínez, R. y Borrajo, D. 2000. *An Integrated Approach of Learning, Planning & Executing.* Journal of Intelligent & Robotic Systems. Vol. 29, Nber 1, Páginas 47-78. Kluwer Academic Press. 2000.

Gardner, G.H.F., Gardner, L.W., and Gregory, A.R., 1974, *Formation velocity and density-the diagnostic basics for stratigraphic traps*: Geophysics 39, 770-780.

Grosser, H., Britos, P. y García-Martínez, R. 2005. *Detecting Fraud in Mobile Telephony Using Neural Networks.* Lecture Notes in Artificial Intelligence 3533:613-615.

Haykin S. 1998. Neural Networks. *A Comprehensive Foundation.* Second Edition. MacMillan Publishing Company (2nd Edition).

Heggland, R., Meldahl, P., Bril, B. & de Groot, P. 1999a. *The chimney cube, an example of semi-automated detection of seismic objects by directive attributes neural networks: Part I;methodology*, Expanded Abstracts of the SEG 69th Annual Meeting, Houston, Oct. 31 – Nov. 5,

Heggland, R., Meldahl, P., Bril, B. & de Groot, P. 1999b. *The chimney cube, an example of semi-automated detection of seismic objects by directive attributes & neural networks: Part II; interpretation*, Expanded Abstracts of the SEG 69th Annual Meeting, Houston, Oct. 31 – Nov. 5.

Heggland, R., Meldahl, P., de Groot, P. & Aminzadeh, F.2000. *Chimneys in the Gulf of Mexico*, The American Oil & Gas Reporter, Feb. 2000.

Hertz J., A. Krogh y R. Palmer 1991. *Introduction to the Theory of Neural Computation.* Reading, MA: Addison-Wesley.

Holland, J. H., Holyoak, K. J., Nisbett, R. E., & Thagard, P. R. 1987. *Classifier systems, Q-morphisms, & induction.* In L. Davis (Ed.), Genetic algorithms & simulated aneling pp. 116-128.

Huang, Z. & Williamson, M. 1994. *Geological pattern recognition and modelling with a general regression neural network.* Can. J. Expl. Geophys., 30, no. 1, 60-68.

Zurada, J. 1995. *Introduction to Artificial Neural Systems.* West Publishing Company.

Johnston, D. 1993. *Seismic attribute calibration using neural networks.* 63rd Annual Internat. Mtg., Soc. Expl. Geophys., Expanded Abstracts, 93, 250-253.

Ping A. 1994. *The effect of random noise in lateral reservoir characterization using feed-forward neural networks.* Geological Survey of Canada. 1994

Rich E. y Knight, K. 1991. *Introduction to Artificial Networks.* Mac Graw-Hill. Publications.

Russell, B. 1988. *Introduction to Seismic Inversion Methods.* Society of Exploration Geophysicists.

Setiono R. & Liu. H. 1996. *Symbolic representation of neural networks.* IEEE Computer Magzine, pag. 71-77, 1996.

Sun, Q.; Eissa, M. A.; Castagna, J. P.; Cersosimo, D.; sun, S.; and Deker, C., 2001, *Porosity from artificial neural network inversion from Bermejo Field, Ecuador,* 71st Ann. Internat. Mtg: Soc. Of Expl. Geophys., pp. 734-737.

Stewart, R., Huddleston, P. and Tze Kong Kan. 1984. *Seismic versus sonic velocities: A vertical seismic profiling study*: Geophysics, 49,1153-1168.

Towell G. & Shavlik, J. 1994. *Knowledge-based artificial neural networks.* Artificial Intelligence, vol. 70, no. 1-2, pp. 119-165..

Treitel, S, Larry Lines, and Gary Ruckgaber *Geophysical Inversion and Applications*, 1993 142 pages.

Treitel, S & Essenreiter, R. 1995. *Predictive Deconvolution Revisited with Neural Nets*: 57th Mtg. Eur. Assoc. Expl Geophys. Extended Abstracts, 95, Session:P065.

Yao X. y Liu Y. 1998. *Toward Designing Artificial Neural Networks by Evolution.* Applied Mathematics & Computation, 91(1): 83-90

Wang, J. & Huang, Z. 1993. *Neural networks for robust recognition of seismic reflection patterns.* 63rd Annual Internat. Mtg., Soc. Expl. Geophys., Expanded Abstracts, , 93, 246-249.

Zhang, X., Li, Y., Hu, Q. & Feng, D. 1995a. *Early-stage reservoir analysis with SOMA: A neural network approach.* 65th Annual Internat. Mtg., Soc. Expl. Geophys., Expanded Abstracts, , 95, 138-141.

Zhang, X., Li, Y., Liu, F. & Wang, L. 1995b. *Estimating reservoir's lithological parameters from seismic data using neural network.* 65th Annual Internat. Mtg., Soc. Expl. Geophys., Expanded Abstracts, , 95, 606-608.

Improving the k-NN method: Rough Set in edit training set

Yailé Caballero[(1)], Rafael Bello[(2)], Delia Alvarez[(1)], Maria M. Garcia[(2)]
Yaimara Pizano[(3)]
[(1)]Department of Computer Science, Universidad of Camagüey, Cuba.
{yaile, dalvarez}@inf.reduc.edu.cu
[(2)]Department of Computer Science, Universidad Central de Las Villas, Cuba.
{rbellop, mmgarcia}@uclv.edu.cu
[(3)]Department of Computer Science, Universidad of Ciego de Avila, Cuba.

Abstract. Rough Set Theory (RST) is a technique for data analysis. In this study, we use RST to improve the performance of k-NN method. The RST is used to edit and reduce the training set. We propose two methods to edit training sets, which are based on the lower and upper approximations. Experimental results show a satisfactory performance of k-NN method using these techniques.

1 Introduction

A major goal of Machine learning is the classification of previously unseen examples. Beginning with a set of examples, the system learns how to predict the class of each one based on its features. Instance-based learning (IBL) is a machine learning method that classifies new examples by comparing them to those already seen and are in memory. This memory is a Training Set (TS) of preclassified examples, where each example (also called object, instance or case) is described by a vector of features or attribute values. A new problem is solved by finding the nearest stored example taking into account some similarity functions; the problem is then classified according to the class of its nearest neighbor. Nearest neighbor methods regained popularity after Kibler and Aha showed that the simplest of the nearest neighbor models could produce excellent results for a variety of domains. A series of improvements was introduced in the IB1 to IB5 [1]. IBL method is often faced with the problem of deciding how many exemplars to store, and what portion of the instance space it should cover.

An extension to the basic IBL paradigm consists in using the K nearest neighbors instead of just the nearest one; the class assigned is that of the majority of those K neighbors, taking into account the distance (or similarity) between the problem and each nearest neighbor. Instance-base learners are lazy in the sense that

Please use the following format when citing this chapter:

Caballero, Y., Bello, R., Alvarez, D., Garcia, M.M., Pizano, Y., 2006, in IFIP International Federation for Information Processing, Volume 218, Professional Practice in Artificial Intelligence, eds. J. Debenham, (Boston: Springer), pp. 21–30.

they perform little work when learning from the TS, but extend more effort classifying new problems.

The aspects that have the most interest in the k-NN method are the reduction of the classification error and the reduction of the computational cost. The k-NN method is very sensitive to the presence of incorrectly labelled examples or objects close to the decision's boundary; incorrect instances are liable to create a region around them where new examples will also be misclassified, also they can be very sensitive to irrelevant attributes; therefore IBL methods can improve their behavior by means of an accurate selection of attributes describing the instances [1,2,3,4].

On the other hand, the search for the nearest neighbor can be a very costly task, above all, in high dimension spaces. Two elements determine the computational cost of the k-NN method: the amount of features and the amount of objects. A major problem of instance-based learners is that classification time increases as more examples are added to training set (TS).

Alternative solutions to these problems have been to: (i) reduce the TS, (ii) improve the search method of the nearest neighbor, y (iii) achieve a selection process of the features or learning the relative importance of features. Rough Set Theory (RST) provides efficient tools for dealing with these alternative solutions.

2. Rough Sets Theory

Rough Sets theory was proposed by Z. Pawlak in 1982 [5]. The rough set philosophy is founded on the assumption that some information is associated with every object of the universe of discourse [6, 7]. A training set can be represented by a table where each row represents objects and each column represents an attribute. This table is called Information System; more formally, it is a pair S= (U, A), where U is a non-empty finite set of objects called the Universe and A is a non-empty finite set of attributes. A Decision System is any information system of the form SD=(U, $A \cup \{d\}$), where $d \notin A$ is the decision attribute. Classical definitions of lower and upper approximations were originally introduced with reference to an indiscernible relation which assumed to be an equivalence relation.

Let $B \subseteq A$ and $X \subseteq U$. B defines an equivalence relation and X is a concept. X can be approximated using only the information contained in B by constructing the B-lower and B-upper approximations of X, denoted by B*X and B*X respectively, where B*X={ x : [x]B $\subseteq$X } and B*X={ x : [x]B $\cap$ X$\neq\phi$ }, and [x]B denotes the class of x according to B-indiscernible relation. The objects in B*X are sure members of X, while the objects in B*X are possible members of X.

Rough set model has several advantages to data analysis. It is based on the original data only and does not need any external information; no assumptions about data are necessary; it is suitable for analyzing both quantitative and qualitative features, and the results of rough set model are easy to understand [8].

Different authors have given their opinion about using RST in data analysis [9, 10, 11, 12, 13, 14, 15].

Two methods for editing training set based on the lower approximation and upper approximation are presented in epigraph 3.2. Experimental results show a satisfactory performance of k-NN using these techniques.

3. Editing training set by using rough set concepts

3.1 About editing training sets

The selection of examples from a domain to include in a training set is a present problem in all of the computational models for learning from examples. This selection process can be carried out either by Edition or Reduction.

The Reduction techniques pursue as objective the elimination of patterns or prototypes for decreasing the size of the learning matrix. It is about decreasing the computational work and, at times, it is disposed or ready to pay with a little less precision of the system, but with more computational efficiency.

The Editing techniques are applied to eliminate the prototypes that induce an incorrect classification, even though it is certain that they produce elimination of prototypes, their fundamental objective is to obtain a training sample of better quality to have a better precision with the system.

Various techniques of reducing the training sets have been reported. Many of them appear in [16, 17, 18, 19] with the purpose of reducing the training sets based on the nearest neighbor theory. Six new methods called DROP 1-5 and DEL are reported in [19] which can be used to reduce the number of instances in the training sets.

Hart, in 1968, made one of the first attempts to reduce the size of the training set with his Condensed Nearest Neighbor Rule (CNN). The main goal of these algorithms is the reduction of the size of the stored set of training instances while trying to maintain (or even improve) generalization accuracy. This algorithm is especially sensitive to noise, because noisy instances will usually be misclassified by their neighbors, and thus will be retained [19].

Editing algorithms from the training sample are described in [20], which are focused on the detection and elimination of noisy or atypical patterns in order to improve the classification's exactitude. Some of these are ENN (Wilson, 1972), All k-NN (Tomek, 1976) and Generalized Editing Algorithm (Koplowitz and Brown, 1978). Another editing method is Multiedit Algorithm (Devijver and Kittler, 1980) [21].

Wilson in 1972 developed the Edited Nearest Neighbor (ENN). This technique consists in applying the k-NN ($k > 1$) classifier to estimate the class label of every prototype in the training set and discard those instances whose class label does not agree with the class associated to the majority of the k neighbors. The benefits – improvements of the generalization accuracy- of Wilson's algorithm have been supported by theoretical and empirical evaluations [20]. The Repeated ENN (RENN) applies the ENN algorithm repeatedly until all instances remaining have a majority of their neighbors with the same class, which continues to widen the gap between classes and smoothes the decision boundary.

Tomek in 1976 extended the ENN with his All k-NN method of editing. In his experiments, RENN produced higher accuracy than ENN, and the All k-NN method resulted in even higher accuracy yet. As with ENN, this method can leave internal points intact, thus limiting the amount of reduction that it can accomplish. These algorithms serve more as noise filters than serious reduction algorithms.

Koplowitz and Brown in 1978 obtained the Generalized Editing Algorithm. This is another modification of the Wilson's algorithm. Koplowitz and Brown were concerned with the possibility of too many prototypes being removed from the training set because of Wilson's editing procedure. This approach consists in removing some suspicious prototypes and changing the class labels of some other instances. Accordingly, it can be regarded as a technique for modifying the structure of the training sample (through re-labeling of some training instances) and not only for eliminating atypical instances.

In 1980 the Multiedit algorithm by Devijver and Kittler emerged. In each iteration of this algorithm, a random partition of the learning sample in N subsets is made. Then the objects from each subset are classified with the following subset applying the NN rule (the nearest neighbor rule). All the objects that were classified incorrectly from the learning sample in the previous step are eliminated and all the remaining objects are combined to constitute a new learning sample TS. If in the last I iterations no object has been eliminated from the learning sample, then end with the final learning sample TS. On the contrary, return to the initial step.

We have studied the performance of these algorithms when we use k-NN methods. The results are shown in table 1.

Aha in [1] presented some Instance-based Learning algorithms that use sample models, each concept is represented by sample set, each sample could be an abstraction of the concept or an individual instance of the concept.

Brighton and Mellish [22] introduced the batch edition method Iterative Case Filtering (ICF), this edition method is based on the reachable and coverage sets, which are based on the neighborhood and the set of associates of an object O. In [23] three edition methods were introduced: Depuration, k-NCN and iterative k-NCN. In [24] the NNEE (Neural Network Ensemble Editing) method was proposed. In [25] two edition schemes in order to reduce the runtimes of BSE without a significant reduction in the classification accuracy was proposed. In [26] a new method for selecting prototypes with Mixed Incomplete Data (MID) object description, based on an extension of the Nearest Neighbor rule was introduced.

3.2 Two methods for editing training set based on rough sets

There are two important concepts in Rough Sets Theory: Lower and Upper Approximation of decision systems. Lower approximation groups objects that certainly belong to its class, this guarantee that object inside lower approximation have no noise.

We have studied the application of rough sets for the edition of training sets. We propose two methods for editing training sets by using upper and lower approximations. First, we use the lower approximations of classes to create the edited training set.

The basic idea of employing rough sets for editing training sets is the following: in the training set we put the examples of the initial decision system that belong to the lower approximation of each class, that is, given an application's domain with m classes and the equivalence relation B, then,

$$TS = B^*(D1) \cap B^*(D2) \cap \ldots \cap B^*(Dm)$$

This is equivalent to saying that the training set will be the positive region of the decision system. In this manner, objects that are incorrectly labeled or very near to the decision's boundary can be eliminated from the training set which affect the quality of the inference/deduction. Studies on multiediting presented in [27] show that isolated objects included in other regions or near to the decision's boundary are frequently eliminated.

Edit1RS Algorithm:

Step1. Construct the set B, $B \subseteq A$. Preferably, B is a reduct from the decision system.

Step2. Form the sets $Xi \subseteq U$, such that all the elements of the universe (U) that have value di in the decision's attribute are in Xi.

Step3. For each set Xi, calculate its lower approximation $B_*(Xi)$.

Step4. Construct the edited training set as the union of all the sets $B_*(Xi)$.

In the second case, we use lower approximations and boundary region of classes to create the edited training set.

In the Edit1RS method only the elements which to the lower approximations are taken into account. Also, it is important to also take into consideration those elements that are in the boundary (BNB). The Generalized Editing Algorithm consists of removing some suspicious prototypes and changing the class labels of some other instances. Accordingly, it can be regarded as a technique for modifying the structure of the training sample (through re-labeling of some training instances) and not only for eliminating atypical instances [20]. The second algorithm is proposed taking into account these ideas.

Edit2RS Algorithm:

Step1. Construct the set B, $B \subseteq A$. Preferably, B is a reduct from the decision system.

Step2. Form the sets $Xi \subseteq U$, such that all the elements of the universe (U) that have value di in the decision's attribute are in Xi.

Step3. $S = \emptyset$

Step4. For each set Xi do:

Calculate their lower approximation ($B_*(Xi)$) and upper approximation ($B^*(Xi)$).

$S = S \cup B_*(Xi)$.

$Ti = B^*(Xi) - B_*(Xi)$.

Step5. Calculate the union of the sets Ti. $T = \bigcup Ti$ is obtained.

Step6. Apply the Generalized Editing method to each element in T and the result is the set T'.

Step7. S = S $\cup$ T'. The edited training set is obtained as the resultant set in S.

The computational complexity of our algorithms don't surpass O(ln^2), near to the ideal value of O(n^2), while in the rest of the algorithms (epigraph 2.1) it is of O(n^3).

The Edit1RS and Edit2RS algorithms based on the rough set theory are characterized in the following way:

Representation: Retain a subset of the original instances. In the case of the Edit2RS algorithm, this can change the class of some instances.

Direction of the search of the instances: The construction of the subset S from the training set E is achieved in batch form. In addition, the selection is achieved on a global vision of the training set not separated by decision classes.

Type of point of the space to retain: The Edit1RS algorithm retains the instances situated in the centre or interior of the classes. The Edit2RS algorithm retains these instances and others included in the boundary regions of the classes.

Volume of the reduction: The volume of the reduction depends on the amount of inconsistencies in the information system; there will always be a reduction in the training set, except if the information system is consistent.

Increment of speed: On decreasing the amount of examples the velocity of the next processing is increased.

Precision of the generalization: In the majority of cases, one of the algorithms or both of them increased significantly the efficiency of the k-NN method.

Tolerance to noise: The rough set theory offers a pattern oriented to model the uncertainty given by inconsistencies, for which it is effective in the presence of noise. In fact, the lower approximation eliminates the cases with noise.

Learning speed: The computational complexity of finding the lower approximation is O(ln2), according to [28] and [29], near to the ideal value of O(n2), and less than that of the calculation of the coverage (O(n3)), so 1 (amount of attributes considered in the equivalence relation) is in the majority of the cases significantly smaller than n (amount of examples).

Incremental growth: This is an incremental method so for each new instance that appears it is enough to determine if it belongs to some lower approximation of some class so that it can be added or not to the training set.

4 Experimental results

We have study the computational behavior of the algorithms when they are employed in the k-NN method. We have used decision systems constructed from the data bases that were found in: http://www.ics.uci.edu/~mlearn/MLRepository.html

The results that are shown in Table 1 and Table 2 allow you to compare the classification accuracy reached by the k-NN method using the original data bases, and the edited ones using various methods from the edition of training sets algorithms proposed by other authors and the two which are presented in section 3. We have considered two alternatives: (i) B uses all features, (ii) B is a reduct. A reduct is a minimal set of attributes from A that preserves the partitioning of universe (and hence the ability to perform classifications) [6].

Table 1. Classification accuracy using classic methods

Name of data base (CaseCount, FeatureCount)	Original data bases	ENN	All k-NN	Generalized Editing	MultiEdit
Ballons-a (20,4)	60.00	60.00	100	80.00	100
Iris (150,4)	94.66	100	100	98.65	100
Hayes-Roth (133,4)	23.48	70.37	66.66	22.10	100
Bupa (345,6)	67.82	88.74	88.11	84.98	100
E-Coli (336,7)	86.60	98.28	98.06	97.70	100
Heart (270,13)	82.22	97.30	98.40	96.10	100
Pima (768,8)	73.04	94.32	96.63	90.43	100
Breast- Cancer (683,9)	96.77	99.24	99.69	99.26	100
Yeast (1484,8)	59.02	90.02	93.76	90.00	99.73
Dermatology (358,34)	97.48	98.56	100	99.14	100
Lung-Cancer (27,56)	48.14	50.00	75.00	55.55	0.00
Average	71.93	86.08	92.39	83.08	90.88

Table 2. Classification accuracy using methods based on RST

Name of data base (CaseCount, FeatureCount)	Edit1RS		Edit2RS	
	B= Reduct	**B=All features**	**B= Reduct**	**B=All features**
Ballons-a (20,4)	100	100	100	80.00
Iris (150,4)	100	98.93	98.65	100
Hayes-Roth (133,4)	85.29	100	84.61	30.27
Bupa (345,6)	76.47	76.47	82.15	82.15
E-Coli (336,7)	91.89	61.53	95.70	96.49
Heart (270,13)	95.41	89.54	93.65	92.36
Pima (768,8)	80.00	80.00	90.36	90.36
Breast- Cancer (683,9)	98.01	98.27	97.65	97.35
Yeast (1484,8)	70.00	71.42	91.01	91.74
Dermatology (358,34)	93.46	98.78	95.01	98.26
Lung-Cancer (27,56)	77.77	48.14	72.22	48.14
Average	88.03	83.92	91.00	82.47
	90.00		91.56	

The two methods based on the Rough Set Theory show superior behavior to those results obtained without editing. The achieved results with Edit1RS and Edit2RS are similar to those achieved by the ENN, Generalized Editing method, Multiedit and All-KNN methods.

By comparing the two methods based on the Rough Set Theory the superior results obtained by the Edit2RS method are appreciated. By taking an average of the best results for each one of these methods (obtained with B = reduct or B = all the attributes) 90.00 % was obtained, while 91.56 % was obtained for Edit2RS. Results inferior to 71 % with the Edit1RS were superior to 91 % when the Edit2RS method was applied. In addition, our methods are very simple methods and are very easy of implementing.

The following graph show the classification accuracy with original data bases and the new methods.

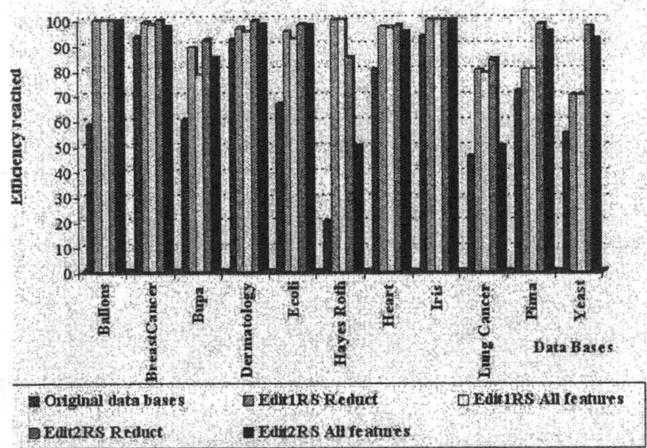

In order to verify efficiently the described results previously the statistical test of Crossed Validation was applied, for which each data set in 5 samples was divided, at every moment 4 of them were taken to train and the other to classify, so that each one of these sets was taken to classify in one of the 5 experiments of the same. A Student Test was applied to Cross Validation results and the p-value obtained was less than 0.05 for each one of the topics to demonstrate: i) The results of Edit2RS method were better in classification than Edit1RS one, and ii) Classification Accuracy percents for Edit1RS and Edit2RS methods were better by using a reduct than working with all the features. It's possible to state that there are significant differences between the results obtained by Edit1RS method and Edit2 RS one. The two methods based on the Rough Set Theory show superior behavior to those results obtained without editing. The achieved results with Edit1RS and Edit2RS are similar to those achieved by the ENN, Generalized Editing method, Multiedit and All-KNN methods.

5. Conclusions

The possibility of applying the elements of the Rough Set Theory for the analysis of data when the k-NN method is used was presented in this paper.

A study of the possibility of applying the elements of the Rough Set Theory in data analysis when the k-NN method is used was presented in this paper. Two methods for the edition of training sets are proposed. Experimental results show that using rough sets to construct training sets to improve the work of the k-NN method is feasible. Our methods obtained similar results to the methods with high performance and these obtained the best result in some case. Therefore, we think these new methods can be taking into account for editing training sets in k-NN method. The results obtained with the Edit1RS and Edith2RS methods were higher in the majority of cases when B is a reduct. Our methods are very simple methods and are very easy of implementing.

References

[1] Aha, D.W. Case-based Learning Algorithms. Proceedings of the DARPA Case-based Reasoning Workshop. Morgan Kaufmann Publishers. 1991.

[2] Domingos, P. Unifying instance-based and rule-based induction. International Joint Conference on Artificial Intelligence. 1995.

[3] Lopez, R.M. and Armengol, E.. Machine learning from examples: Inductive and Lazy methods.

[4] Barandela, R. et al.. The nearest neighbor rule and the reduction of the training sample size. Proceedings 9th Symposium on Pattern Recognition and Image Analysis, 1, 103-108, Castellon, España, 2001

[5] Pawlak, Z.. Rough sets. International Journal of Information & Computer Sciences 11, 341-356, 1982.

[6] Komorowski, J. Pawlak, Z. et al.. Rough Sets: A tutorial. In Pal, S.K. and Skowron, A. (Eds) Rough Fuzzy Hybridization: A new trend in decision-making. Springer, pp. 3-98. 1999.

[7] Polkowski, L.. Rough sets: Mathematical foundations. Physica-Verlag, p. 574. Berlin, Germany. 2002.

[8] Tay, F.E. and Shen, L.. Economic and financial prediction using rough set model. European Journal of Operational Research 141, pp. 641-659. 2002.

[9] Greco, S. Et al. Rough sets theory for multicriteria decision analysis. European Journal of Operational Research 129, pp. 1-47, 2001.

[10] Pal, S.K. and Skowron, A. (Eds).. Rough Fuzzy Hybridization: a new trend in decision-making. Springer-Verlag, 1999.

[11] Kohavi, R. and Frasca, B. Useful feature subsets and Rough set Reducts. Proceedings of the Third International Workshop on Rough Sets and Soft Computing. 1994.

[12] Maudal, O. Preprocessing data for neural network based classifiers: Rough sets vs Principal Component Analysis. Project report, Dept. of Artificial Intelligence, University of Edinburgh. 1996.

[13] Koczkodaj, W.W. et al.. Myths about Rough Set Theory. Comm. of the ACM, vol. 41, no. 11, nov. 1998.

[14] Zhong, N. et al.. Using Rough sets with heuristics for feature selection. Journal of Intelligent Information Systems, 16, 199-214. 2001.

[15] Pal, S.K. et al. Web mining in Soft Computing framework: Relevance, State of the art and Future Directions. IEEE Transactions on Neural Networks, 2002.

[16] Gates, G. W. The Reduced Nearest Neighbor Rule. IEEE Transactions on Information Theory, IT-18-3, pp. 431-433. 1972.

[17] Ritter, G. L. Woodruff, H. B. Lowry, S. R. Isenhour, T. L. An Algorithm for a Selective Nearest Neighbor Decision Rule. IEEE Transactions on Information Theory, 21-6, November, pp. 665-669. 1975.

[18] Lowe, David G. Similarity Metric Learning for a Variable-Kernel Classifier. Neural Computation., 7-1, pp. 72-85. 1995.

[19] Wilson, Randall. Martinez, Tony R. Reduction Techniques for Exemplar-Based Learning Algorithms. Machine Learning. Computer Science Department, Brigham Young University. USA 1998.

[20] Barandela, Ricardo; Gasca, Eduardo, Alejo, Roberto. Correcting the Training Data. Published in "Pattern Recognition and String Matching", D. Chen and X. Cheng (eds.), Kluwer, 2002.

[21] Devijver, P. and Kittler, J. Pattern Recognition: A Statistical Approach, Prentice Hall, 1982.

[22] Brighton, H. and Mellish, C. Advances in Instance Selection for Instance-Based Learning Algorithms. Data Mining and Knowledge Discovery, 6, pp. 53-172, 2002.

[23] Sánchez, J. S., Barandela, R., Marqués, A. I., Alejo, R., Badenas, J. Analysis of new techniques to obtain quality training sets. Pattern Recognition Letters, 24-7, pp. 1015-1022, 2003.

[24] Jiang Y., Zhou, Z.-H. Editing training data for kNN classifiers with neural network ensemble. In: Advances in Neural Networks, LNCS 3173, pp. 356-361, Springer-Verlag, 2004.

[25] Olvera-López, José A., Carrasco-Ochoa, J. Ariel and Martínez-Trinidad, José Fco. Sequential Search for Decremental Edition. Proceedings of the 6th International Conference on Intelligent Data Engineering and Automated Learning, IDEAL 2005. Brisbane, Australia, vol 3578, pp. 280-285, LNCS Springer-Verlag, 2005.

[26] García, M. and Shulcloper, J. Selecting Prototypes in Mixed Incomplete Data. Lectures Notes in computer Science (LNCS 3773), pp. 450-460. Springer, Verlag, Berlin Heidelberg. New York. ISSN 0302-9743 ISBN 978-3-540-29850.

[27] Cortijo, J.B. Techniques of approximation II: Non parametric approximation. Thesis. Department of Computer Science and Artificial Intelligence, Universidad de Granada, Spain. October 2001.

[28] Bell, D. and Guan, J. Computational methods for rough classification and discovery. Journal of ASIS 49, 5, pp. 403-414. 1998.

[29] Deogun, J.S. et al. Exploiting upper approximations in the rough set methodology. In Proceedings of First International Conference on Knowledge Discovery and Data Mining, Fayyad, U. Y Uthurusamy, (Eds.), Canada, pp. 69-74. 1995.

Membranes as Multi-agent Systems: an Application to Dialogue Modelling

Gemma Bel-Enguix and Dolores Jiménez López

Research Group on Mathematical Linguistics
Rovira i Virgili University
Pl. Imperial Tàrraco, 1, 43005 Tarragona, Spain
{gemma.bel,mariadolores.jimenez}@urv.net

Abstract. Human-computer interfaces require models of dialogue structure that capture the variability and unpredictability within dialogue. In this paper, taking as starting point P systems, and by extending it to the concept of dialogue P systems through linguistic P systems we introduce a multi-agent formal architecture for dialogue modelling. In our model, cellular membranes become contextual agents by the adjunction of cognitive domains. With this method, the passage from the real dialogue to the P systems model can be achieved in a quite intuitive and simple way.

1 Motivation

Computational work on discourse has focused both on extended texts and on dialogues. Work on the former is relevant to document analysis and retrieval applications, whereas research on the latter is important for human-computer interfaces. In fact, the development of machines that are able to sustain a conversation with a human being has long been a challenging goal. If we focus on dialogue modelling, we can distinguish two related research goals adopted by researchers on the field: 1) to develop a *theory of dialogue* and 2) to develop *algorithms* and procedures to support a computer's participation in a cooperative dialogue.

In this paper we introduce a *formal theory* of dialogue based in a model – P systems – already introduced in theoretical computer science, which should be easily implemented. Our aim is to introduce a theoretical model of conversation with the explicitness, formality and efficiency that are required for computer implementation.

The essential characteristic of the model is the use of a simple computational mechanism for the interaction between cellular membranes in order to generate a conversation structure. So, dialogue P systems can be placed in the line of those approaches to modelling conversation that use the so-called *dialogue grammars*, a useful computational tool to express simple regularities of dialogue behaviour.

P systems –introduced in [10]– are models of computation inspired by some basic features of biological membranes. They can be viewed as a new paradigm

---

Please use the following format when citing this chapter:

Bel-Enguix, G., López, D.J., 2006, in IFIP International Federation for Information Processing, Volume 218, Professional Practice in Artificial Intelligence, eds. J. Debenham, (Boston: Springer), pp. 31–40.

in the field of natural computing based on the functioning of membranes inside the cell.

Membranes provide a powerful framework for formalizing any kind of *interaction*, both among agents and among agents and the environment. An important idea in P systems is that generation is made by evolution, when the configuration of membranes undergoes some modifications, given by certain rules. Therefore, most of evolving systems can be formalized by means of membranes.

P systems have been already applied to linguistics in [2, 3] and other suggestions for different specific implementations have been given in [11].

The most important intuition for translating this natural computing model to natural languages is that membranes can be understood as *contexts* or more general environments, which may may be different words, persons, social groups, historical periods, languages. In this model agents can accept, reject, or produce changes in elements they have inside. At the same time, contexts/membranes and their rules evolve, that is, change, appear, vanish, etc. Therefore, membranes and elements of the system are constantly interacting.

In this paper, we suggest the a type of multi-agent P structures for dealing with dialogue modelling, since this is a topic where context and interaction among agents is essential to the design of effective and user-friendly computer dialogue systems.

In section 2, the definition of P systems is given, as well as an adaptation of the computational model to deal with linguistics, linguistic P Systems. Section 3 explains how, because of their flexibility, membranes can be used to model different parts of linguistics, being focalized in this paper for studying dialogue. In section 4 dialogue P Systems are introduced. In 5, we give some conclusions and lines of research for the future work.

2 P Systems and Linguistic P Systems

P systems, as a computational model based in biology, consist of multisets of objects which are placed in the compartments defined by the membrane structure –a hierarchical arrangement of membranes, all of them placed in a main membrane called the *skin membrane*– that delimits the system from its environment.

In general, P systems are a distributed parallel computational model based in the concept of *membrane structure*. Such structure is represented by a Venn diagram where all the sets, *membranes*, are inside a unique *skin membrane*. A membrane without any membrane inside is called *elementary membrane*. Every membrane delimits a *region*. *Objects*, placed in these regions, are able to evolve travelling to other membranes or being transformed in different objects.

Membranes are usually represented by the sign [ ], and they are labelled with a number between 1 and the number n of membranes in the system. For example, the structure in Figure 1 has the shape $[\,[\,]_2\ [\,]_3\ [\,[\,]_5\,[\,[\,]_8\,[\,]_9\,]_6\,[\,]_7\,]_4\,]_1$.

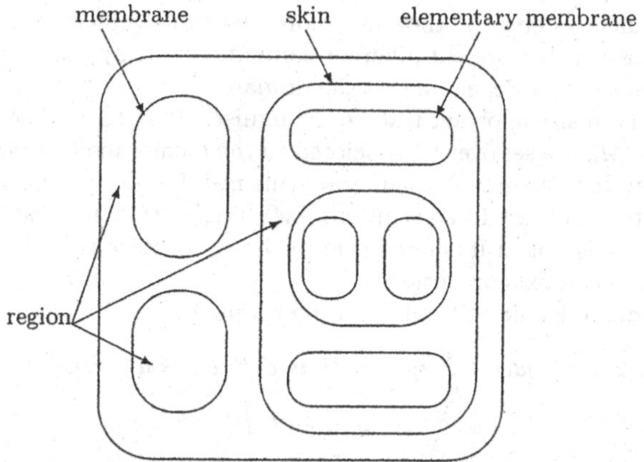

Fig. 1. A membrane structure.

Formal definitions and main issues related to the topic can be found in [10] and [11]. Nevertheless, we introduce the basic description of membranes, which can be useful to understand the relationship between general P systems and P systems for dialogue.

Definition 1 *A P system Π is defined as a construct*

$$\Pi = (V, \mu, w_1, ...w_n, (R_1, \rho_1), ..., (R_n, \rho_n), i_o),$$

where:

- *V is an alphabet; its elements are objects;*
- *μ is a membrane structure of degree n;*
- *w_i, $1 \leq i \leq n$, are strings from V^* representing multisets over V associated with the regions 1, 2,...n of μ;*
- *R_i, $1 \leq i \leq n$, are finite sets of evolution rules over V associated with the regions 1, 2,...n of μ; ρ is a partial order relation over R_i, $1 \leq i \leq n$, specifying a priority relation between rules of R_i.*
- *i_o is a number between 1 and n, which specifies the output membrane of Π.*

In membranes, rules of any type can be applied in any membrane, and the results can be sent to other membranes, increasing the computational power and efficiency of the model.

The adaptation of P systems to linguistics [2, 3] gave rise to linguistic P systems (LPS). Although the formalization is mainly the same, the aim of LPS is not to produce languages, but to model linguistic processes. The chief formal differences of LPS with regard to usual membrane systems are: a) they are not always parallel systems, b) they use more than one alphabet, c) membranes have domains which represent different contexts, in a way that membranes can accept objects or not depending on the domain.

Domains are an important feature of linguistic P systems. The domain D of a membrane M_n is a set over V associated to the membrane in every state of the computation. It is the set of semantemes this membrane accepts. The subscript $_i$ attached to an object in a membrane M_n means that it is not accepted by M_n because it is not in its domain. From here, we infer that domains can be understood as contexts or worlds.

From here, a definition of LPS can be given.

Definition 2 *A linguistic P system Π is defined as a 4-uple*

$$\Pi = \{\mu, V, I, R\},$$

where

- *μ is the membrane system of degree n,*
- *$V = \{V_1, \ldots, V_i\}$ is the set of alphabets associated to each membrane,*
- *$I = (\{u \ldots w\}, C, D, t)$ is the initial configuration of each membrane,*
- *$R = \{R_1, \ldots, R_n\}$ is the set of rules of every membrane of the system, including*
  - *evolutionary rules for alphabets*
  - *evolutionary rules for membranes*

To fully understand the working of such systems, several aspects have to be explained: a) relations between membranes, b) communication in μ, c) operations with membranes.

Concerning the point a), the way the membranes are related to the others is important in the moment they have to interact, and also in the configuration of the communication we are going to deal with later. There are mainly tree types of relations: *nesting*, *adjacency* and *command*.

Given two membranes M_1, M_2, it is said M_2 to be *nested* in M_1 when it is inside M_1. The outer membrane M_1 is called *parent membrane* and the inner membrane M_2 is called *nested membrane*. It is denoted $M_2 \subset M_1$: $[_1\ [_2\ ]_2\ ]_1$. *Degree of nesting* refers to the number of membranes between the nested one and the parent one. The degree of nesting is obtained by subtracting the depth of the parent membrane M_p to the depth of the nested membrane M_n. This is: $deg(M_n \subset M_p) = depth(M_n)\ -\ depth(M_p)$

Two membranes M_n, M_m are related by *sibling*, if they satisfy:

i. they have a common parent membrane, and

ii. they have the same depth.

Sibling is denoted $M_n \approx M_m$. Namely, in a membrane system denoted as $[_0\ [_1\ [_2\ ]_2\ ]_1\ [_3\ [_4\ ]_4\ ]_3\ ]_0$, $M_1 \approx M_3$ and $M_2 \approx M_4$.

Given two membranes M_n, M_m, M_n *commands* M_m iff:

i. they are not nested,

ii. both are nested in a membrane M_j,
iii.$deg(M_n \subset M_j) = 1$, $deg(M_m \subset M_j) > 1$

Command is denoted $M_n \lhd M_m$. Considering the existence of a system with the structure $[_1\ [_2\ ]_2\ ]_1\ [_3\ [_4\ ]_4\ ]_3$, $M_1 \lhd M_4$ and $M_3 \lhd M_2$.

In what concerns the communication between membrane in the system, if membranes are understood as social groups, conditions of marginality or integration may be modelled by means of the connection/non-connection between a concrete group and the others. If membranes refer to different agents in a dialogue, then it is easy to find agents which do not participate, wher eas some others keep the attention all the time.

These concepts can be approached by means of the introduction of communication channels between membranes. We establish that, between two membranes there is always a communication channel, that can be open $\odot$ or closed $\otimes$. Every membrane has the control over its communication channels – except the skin membrane, which is always connected.

For the communication to be possible between two given membranes M_n, M_m to be open, it is necessary for that channel to be open from M_n and M_m, what can be represented by $M_n \odot \odot M_m$. The other possibilities: $M_n \odot \otimes M_m$, $M_n \otimes \odot M_m$, $M_n \otimes \otimes M_m$, do not allow the exchange of information. It can be said, then, that the communication is bidirectional, and it is only possible if it is allowed from both sides.

When a membrane has every communication channel open, then it is said to be *fully connected.* It is represented by $\odot M_n$. When a membrane has every communication channel closed, then it is said to be *inhibited.* It is denoted by $\otimes M_n$. The states of the communication channels can be set and changed by specific rules during the computation.

Graphically, connection between two membranes is not represented, while inhibition is drawn with a double line for the membrane. If two membranes are not connected because one of them has closed that channel, it is represented by two parallel lines.

Concerning operations that can be applied in membranes during the computation, structure of P systems can undergo several variations. Some contexts can disappear or be extended during the progress of the conversation, others can merge, or be copied many times. The flexibility of LPS requires the formalization of some rules regulating different ways of interaction in the main components of P Systems, membranes. These operations are the ones defined in the sequel.

1. Dissolution. By means of deletion a membrane M_n is dissolved and its elements go to the immediately external membrane. The rule for deleting membrane M_n is written as: $[\ [\ v]_m]_n \Rightarrow [\ v]_n$.

2. Deletion. It is the operation by means of which a membrane M_n completely disappears with all its elements. The rule is $[\ [\ v]_n]_m \Rightarrow [\ ]_m$.

3. Merging. By merging, two adjacent membranes M_n, M_m join in just one by the rule: $[\ [u]_n\ [v]_m\ ] \Rightarrow [\ [uv]_j]$

4. Splitting By means of division, a membrane M_m is divided in two or more. Graphically, we write $[\ [uw]_m] \Rightarrow [\ [uv]_m\ [uv]_n]$.
5. Extraction. It is the operation by means of which a membrane nested in another one is extracted, being both related by sibling of degree 0 in the resulting configuration. It is denoted by $[\ [\ [u]_n\ ]_m\ ] \Rightarrow [\ [\ ]_m [u]_n\ ]$.
6. Insertion. It is the inverse operation of extraction. By thgis operation a membrane wich is adjacent to another one is nested in it with degree 0. It is denoted by $[\ [\ ]_m [u]_n\ ] \Rightarrow [\ [\ [u]_n\ ]_m\ ]$.

3 Different applications of LPS to linguistics

We think that the general definition of LMS that has been given introduces a quite flexible tool for modelling several linguistic aspects, especially the ones not directly related to syntax. To be adapted in order to suitably model these linguistic branches, only some aspects must be adjusted in the general description for them to be optimal for each field. The most important is the different interpretation of membranes that is allowed by the introduction of the notion of *domain*. But also the elements of the alphabets can be understood differently depending on the interpretation of the domains. We consider also the existence of turn-taking, which is on of the key points for modelling dialogue, and the different treatment of the output in each one of the systems.

Taking into account these variables, a table can be composed, which shows several parts of linguistics that can be approached by this method.

	Domains	Elements	TT	OM
Semantics	Contexts	Linguemes	No	μ
Lang. evolution	Languages	Lgc. units	No	μ
Sociolinguistics	Social groups	Lgc. units	No	μ
Dialogue	Competence	Speech Acts	Yes	CR
Anaphora resol.	Contexts	Anaphores	No	i_o

Table 1. Features of several applications on LMS in linguistics

From the results above, we are interested in the modelling of dialogue. Therefore, domains are interpreted as the personal background and competence of the agent, which includes concepts such as education, context, and knowledge of the world. The basic elements for generating the dialogue are speech acts [1, 14, 6] and a method for assigning the turn-taking has to be introduced. Finally, the output membrane for dialogue systems does not exist, and it is substituted by a Generation Register (CR)

In the sequel we deal with an example of representation of non task-oriented (NTO) dialogues by means of membranes.

4 Dialogue P Systems

Now, before going on with the introduction of the computing device, we have to introduce the main units in the system we want to define. Basic elements we deal with in here are *speech acts.* An speech act can be defined as a communicative event whose final meaning is not only related to syntax but also to the illocutionary strength of the speaker. Speech acts has been traditionally a central topic in pragmatics, now they have an increasing importance in the so-called dialogue games [5, 8], an attempt to start a formal study of pragmatic situations.

Combining both theories, several classifications of conversation act types have been given (cf. [15]). We just want to take into account a small list of acts including the most usual ones. The goal is to have a set of utterances to test the suitability of the model, since the final objective of this paper is not to discus about the taxonomy of acts in dialogue.

Therefore, adapting some general concepts to a *computational description*, we propose to distinguish the following types of acts in human communication: 1) *Query-yn* (yes, no), 2) *Query-w* (what), 3) *Answer-y* (yes), 4) *Answer-n* (no), 5) *Answer-w* (what), 6) *Agree,* 7) *Reject,* 8) *Prescription,* 9) *Explain,* 10) *Clarify,* 11) *Exclamation.* This list may be modified any moment depending on the convenience and accuracy of the theory.

Acts are usually gathered in topics during a conversation. For starting, closing, or changing a topic, some special expressions are usually used. They are *structural acts*, and should be added to the above list of sequences, obtaining: 12) *Open,* 13) *Close,* 14) *Changetopic.* Structural acts have some special features which make them different. *Open* is the first act, or at least the first instruction, in every dialogue or human interaction. However, *close* is not always present, in the same way that, many times, topics are not closed in conversations, and new ones arise without and ending for the previous. On the other hand, *changetopic* is a sequence of transition which cannot be followed by every agent.

Nevertheless, these concepts have to be adapted to the diversity of realistic situations, which may be quite unexpected. In a dialogue, not every agent has every type of speech act. Depending on the *competence* of each agent, some speech acts can be blocked. For instance, only an agent with certain power can use the act *prescription.* The distribution of speech acts among the agents will be very important in the development of the dialogue.

Definition of dialogue P systems (in short, DPS) is based in the general formalization of membrane systems introduced in Section 2, adding a special treatment for the turn-taking and a Generation Register (GR) for storing the output generated by the system.

Definition 3 *A dialog P system is a 5-uple,*

$$\Pi = (\mu, V, I, T, R),$$

where:

- *μ is the membrane system;*
- *$V = \{V_1, \ldots, V_i\}$ is the set of alphabets associated to types of speech acts;*
- *$I = (\{u \ldots w\}, C, D, t)$ is the initial configuration of each membrane, being:*
  - $\cdot$ *$\{u \ldots w\}$ the set of acts over V^*;*
  - $\cdot$ *D, the domain of the membrane;*
  - $\cdot$ *C, the communication state of the membrane;*
  - $\cdot$ *t is any element of T.*
- *T is the turn-taking set;*
- *$R = \{R_1, \ldots, R_n\}$ is the set of rules of every membrane of the system, where the order in which rules are given is also a preference for using them.*

Several concepts should be explained for clarifying the description and working of the system: a) configuration of alphabets, b) shape of the rules, c) domains, d) the turn-taking protocol T, e) halting criteria, and f) configuration of the output.

Configuration of Alphabets. Basic elements of DPS are speech acts. These speech acts are gathered in several types, following the classification given above. Every one of these types is an ordered set of elements which can be used just one time, according to the precedence.

We define a set of alphabets $V = \{\omega, \#, \kappa', \kappa, \alpha^y, \alpha^n, \alpha, \gamma, \varphi, \tau, \varepsilon, \lambda, \xi\}$, where every element is a set of speech acts, as follows: $\omega = \{o_1, o_2, ..o_n\}$, speech acts of type *open*; $\# = \{\#_1, \#_2, ..\#_n\}$, speech acts of type *close*; $\kappa' = \{q'_1, q'_2, ..q'_n\}$, speech acts of type *query-yn*; $\kappa = \{q_1, q_2, ..q_n\}$, speech acts of type *query-w*; $\alpha^y = \{a^y_1, a^y_2, ..a^y_n\}$, speech acts of type *answer-y*; $\alpha^n = \{a^n_1, a^n_2, ..a^n_n\}$, speech acts of type *answer-n*; $\alpha = \{a_1, a_2, ..a_n\}$, speech acts of type *answer-w*; $\gamma = \{g_1, g_2, ..g_n\}$, speech acts of type *agree*; $\varphi = \{f_1, f_2, ..f_n\}$, speech acts of type *reject*; $\pi = \{p_1, p_2, ..p_n\}$, speech acts of type *prescription*; $\varepsilon = \{e_1, e_2, ..e_n\}$, speech acts of type *explain*; $\lambda = \{l_1, l_2, ..l_n\}$, speech acts of type *clarify*; $\xi = \{x_1, x_2, ..x_n\}$, speech acts of type *exclamation*.

Shape of the rules Rules are understood as the way the membranes-agents exchange elements and interact each other. Every rule in the system has at the left side the indication of the turn-taking. At the right side it has, a) the generation in reply to the explicit invitation to talk (turn-taking element), and b) the agent whom the speech act is addressed to, if it exists.

The turn-taking allows applying just one rule.

Domains In DPS, *domain* of a membrane is related to the competence of an agent in a dialogue, this is, what the agent knows and can say. It is defined as the set of speech acts that every membrane is able to utter. It can include entire sets of acts defined for the system or just single acts coming from some set. Of course, just speech acts defined in V, this is, existing in the possible world described by μ, can be used. $DM_n = \{u, .., w \in V\}$.

Turn-Taking Protocol For dialogues we are dealing with, turn-taking must be free, this is, it is not given as a sequence, but as a set of active elements, at the beginning of the computation. Every turn is distributed by the agent that is talking. When somebody asks, explains, or clarifies something, in a dialogue, he/she does it to somebody among the others. Then, we establish that the addresser in each turn can choose next speaker. It does it by means of the *turn-taking rule* included at the end of each rule of the system. This is denoted by means of a letter depending of the speech act uttered in such rule.

Therefore, the following turn-taking symbols related to every speech act are considered : O (open), # (close,) Q' (Query-yn), Q (Query-w), A^y (Answer-y), A^n (Answer-n), A (Answer-w), G (Agree), F (Reject), P (Prescription), E (Explain), L (Clarify), X (Exclamation), H (Changetopic).

We include H for *changetopic* among these symbols, which is not related to any set of speech acts, because any type (except answer) can be a good reply to it. If no indication of turn is given in a rule, the turn goes to every membrane able to reply, this is, every membrane containing a rule with the required symbol in the left. If there are several membranes able to act, then the turn is indicated by the number of the membrane, which also establishes an order of precedence in the computation, this is $M_1 < M_2 < M_3 < .. < M_n$.

Halting Criteria We establish that the system stops if one of the following conditions is fulfilled: a) No rule can be applied in any membrane, b) just one membrane remains in the system, c) no more acts are available.

Configuration of the Output For DPS there are not output membranes. For the *configuration of the output*, we define the Generation Register (GR). The generation register gives account of the changes in the configuration of the system in every step. To look at the GR is the way to know what the final result of the system is.

5 Final Remarks

In this paper a new approach for a formal modelling of human communication in the framework of pragmatics using P systems has been introduced and several basic issues related to a membranes approach to conversation have been developed in order to test the suitability of the model.

We think that to apply P systems to linguistic topics has several advantages, among which we stress the flexibility of the model. Considering membranes as agents, and domains as a personal background and linguistic competence, the application to dialogue is almost natural, and simple from the formal point of view. Many variations can be introduced to the basic model presented in this paper in order to account for different features of conversation, and this can be a good research area for the future.

Nevertheless, since this is just an initial approximation to the possibility of describing conversation by means of membrane systems, many important aspects remain to be approached: formalization of task-oriented and institutional conversations, non-free turn-taking, interactions among ag ents, introduction of different conversation act types or modelling of parallel phenomena.

Finally, although the model is defined for formally describing human communication, we think that it can be applied to the generation of conversations in the framework of human-computer or computer-computer interface.

References

1. Austin, J.L. (1962), *How to Do Things With Words*, New York, Oxford University Press.
2. Bel Enguix, G. (2003), Preliminaries about Some Possible Applications of P Systems in Linguistics, in Păun, Gh., Rozenberg, G., Salomaa, A. & Zandron, C., *Membrane Computing*, Springer, Berlin.
3. Bel Enguix, G. & Jiménez López, M.D. (2005), Linguistic Membrane Systems and Applications, in Ciobanu, G., Păun, Gh. & Pérez Jiménez, M.J. (eds.), *Applications of Membrane Computing*, Springer, Berlin, pp. 347-388.
4. Bunt, Harry C. (1990), *DIT-Dynamic Interpretation in Text and Dialogue*, ITK Research Report, no. 15, Tilburg University, The Netherlands.
5. Carlson, L. (1983), *Dialogue games*, Dordretch, Reidel.
6. Grice, H.P. (1975), Logic and Conversation, in Cole, P. & Morgan, J. (eds.) *Syntax and Semantics 3: Speech Acts*, New York: Academic Press.
7. Jiménez-López, M.D. (2002), Formal Languages for Conversation Analysis, in García Español, A. (ed.), *Estudios Hispánicos y Románicos*, Universitat Rovira i Virgili, Tarragona.
8. Kwotko, J.C., Isard, S.D. & Doherty G.M. (1993), Conversational Games Within Dialogue, *Technical Report HCRC/RP-31*, HCRC Publications University of Edinburgh.
9. Morris, C. (1938), Foundations of the Theory of Signs, in Carnap, R. et al (eds.), *International Encyclopaedia of Unified Science*, 2:1, Chicago, The University of Chicago Press.
10. Păun, Gh. (2000), Computing with Membranes, *Journal of Computer and System Sciences*, 61, pp. 108-143.
11. Păun, Gh. (2002), *Membrane Computing. An Introduction*, Springer, Berlin.
12. Reed C.A., Long D.P. (1997), Collaboration, Cooperation and Dialogue Classification, in Jokinen, K. (ed) *Working Notes of the IJCAI97 Workshop on Collaboration, Cooperation and Conflict in Dialogue Systems*, Nagoya, pp. 73-78.
13. Sacks, H., Schegloff, E.A., & Jefferson, G. (1974), A Simplest Systematics for the Organization of Turn-Taking for Conversation, *Language*, 50, 4, pp. 696-735.
14. Searle, J. (1969), *Speech Acts: An Essay in the Philosophy of Language*, Cambridge University Press.
15. Traum, D.R. *Speech Acts for Dialogue Agents*, in Wooldride, M. & A. Rao (eds.), "Foundations of Rational Agency", Kluwer, Dordrecht, 1999, 169-201.

Agent Planning, Models, Virtual Haptic Computing, and Visual Ontology

Cyrus F Nourani
Academia USA California
Cardiff by The Sea, California
http://beam.to/af2im
cyrusfn@alum.mit.edu
Projectm2@lycos.com

Abstract. The paper is a basis for multiagent visual computing with the Morph Gentzen logic. A basis to VR computing, computational illusion, and virtual ontology is presented. The IM_BID model is introduced for planning, spatial computing, and visual ontology. Visual intelligent objects are applied with virtual intelligent trees to carry on visual planning. New KR techniques are presented with generic diagrams and appllied to define computable models. The IM Morph Gentzen Logic for computing for multimedia are new projects with important computing applications. The basic principles are a mathematical logic where a Gentzen or natural deduction systems is defined by taking arbitrary structures and multimedia objects coded by diagram functions.The techniques can be applied to arbitrary structures definable by infinitary languages. Multimedia objects are viewed as syntactic objects defined by functions, to which the deductive system is applied.

1. Introduction

Agent computing models are introduced with an intelligent multimedia dimension. An overview to a practical agent computing model based on beliefs, intentions, and desire is presented and possible augmentation to intelligent multimedia is explored. Genesereth-Nilsson [17] presents agent architectures as follows. Dynamics and situation compatibility in introduced as a structural way to compute and compare epistemic states. Worlds, epistemics, and cognition for androids are introduced with precise statements. The foundations are applied to present a brief on Computational Illusion, affective computing, and Virtual Reality. KR for AI Worlds, and Computable Worlds are presented with diagrams [7]. A preview to computational epistemology and concept descriptions is introduced. Deduction models and perceptual computing is presented with a new perspective. Intelligent multimedia interfaces are an important component to the practical

Please use the following format when citing this chapter:

Nourani, C.F., 2006, in IFIP International Federation for Information Processing, Volume 218, Professional Practice in Artificial Intelligence, eds. J. Debenham, (Boston: Springer), pp. 41–50.

computational aspects. Visual context and objects are presented with multiagent intelligent multimedia. Visual context abstraction and meta-contextual reasoning is introduced as a new field. Multiagent visual multi-board planning is introduced as a basis to intelligent multimedia with applications to spatial computing.

2. The Agent Models and Desire

Let us start with the popular agent computing model the Beliefs, Desire, and Intentions, henceforth abbreviated as the BID model (Brazier-Truer et.al.[1,6]. BID is a generic agent computing model specified within the declarative compositional modeling framework for multi-agent systems, DESIRE. The model, a refinement of a generic agent model, explicitly specifies motivational attitudes and the static and dynamic relations between motivational attitudes. Desires, goals, intentions, commitments, plans, and their relations are modeled. Different notions of strong and weak agency are presented at (Wooldridge and Jennings, 1995) [3]. (Velde and Perram, 1996) [10] distinguished big and small agents. To apply agent computing with intelligent multimedia some specific roles and models have to be presented for agents. The BID model has emerged for a "rational agent": a rational agent described using cognitive notions such as beliefs, desires and intentions. Beliefs, intentions, and commitments play a crucial role in determining how rational agents will act. Beliefs, capabilities, choices, and commitments are the parameters making component agents specific. The above are applied to model and to specify mental attitudes (Shoham, 1991-1993) [46], Rao and Georgeff, 1991[20], Cohen and Levesque, 1990, Dunin-Keplicz and Verbrugge, 1996 . A generic BID agent model in the multiagent framework DESIRE is presented towards a specific agent model. The main emphasis is on static and dynamic relations between mental attitudes, which are of importance for cooperative agents. DESIRE is the framework for design, and the specification of interacting reasoning components is a framework for modeling, specifying and implementing multi-agent systems, see (Brazier, Dunin-Keplicz, Jennings, and Treur, 1995, 1996; Dunin-Keplicz and Treur, 1995). Within the framework, complex processes are designed as compositional architectures consisting of interacting task-based hierarchically structured components. The interaction between components, and between components and the external world is explicitly specified. Components can be primitive reasoning components using a knowledge base, but may also be subsystems which are capable of performing tasks using methods as diverse as decision theory, neural networks, and genetic algorithms. As the framework inherently supports interaction between components, multi-agent systems are naturally specified in DESIRE by modeling agents as components that can be implemented applying author's 1993-1999.

2.1 Mental Attitudes

Agents are assumed to have the four properties required for the weak notion of agency described in (Wooldridge and Jennings, 1995). Thus, agents must maintain interaction with their environment, for example observing and performing actions in the world: reactivity; be able to take the initiative: pro-activeness; be able to perform social actions like communication, social ability; operate without the direct intervention of other (possibly human) agents: autonomy. Four main categories of mental attitudes are studied in the AI literature: informational, motivational, social and emotional attitudes. The focus is on motivational attitudes, although other aspects are marginally considered. In (Shoham and Cousins, 1994) [43], motivational attitudes are partitioned into the following categories: goal, want, desire, preference, wish, choice, intention, commitment, and plan. Individual agents are assumed to have intentions and commitments both with respect to goals and with respect to plans. A generic classification of an agent's attitudes is defined as follows: Informational attitudes: Knowledge; Beliefs.

1. Motivational attitudes: Desires; Intentions- Intended goals and Intended plans.
2. Commitments: Committed goals and Committed plans

In planning, see section 6, the weakest motivational attitude might be desire: reflecting yearning, wish and want. An agent may harbor desires which are impossible to achieve. Desires may be ordered according to preferences and, as modeled in this paper, they are the only motivational attitudes subject to inconsistency. At some point an agent must just settle on a limited number of intended goals, i.e., chosen desires.

2.2 Specifying BID Agents

The BID-architectures upon which specifications for compositional multi-agent systems are based are the result of analysis of the tasks performed by individual agents and groups of agents. Task (de)compositions include specifications of interaction between subtasks at each level within a task (de)composition, making it possible to explicitly model tasks which entail interaction between agents. The formal compositional framework for modeling multi-agent tasks DESIRE is introduced here. The following aspects are modeled and specified: (1) A task (de)composition,(2) information exchange, (3) sequencing of (sub)tasks, (4) subtask delegation, (5) knowledge structures. Information required/produced by a (sub)task is defined by input and output signatures of a component. The signatures used to name the information are defined in a predicate logic with a hierarchically ordered sort structure (order-sorted predicate logic). Units of information are represented by the ground atoms defined in the signature. The role information plays within reasoning is indicated by the level of an atom within a signature: different (meta) levels may be distinguished. In a two-level situation the lowest level is termed object-level information, and the second level meta-level information. Some specifics and a mathematical basis to such models with agent signatures might be obtained from (Nourani 1996a) [44] where the notion had been introduced since 1994. Meta-level information contains information about object-level information and reasoning processes; for example, for which atoms the values are still unknown (epistemic information). The generic model and specifications of an agent described above, can be refined to a generic model of a rational BID-agent capable of explicit reasoning about its beliefs, desires, goals and commitments.

3.Epistemitcs

3.1 Worlds and A Robot's Touch

Starting with the issues raised by Heidegger in 1935-36, and notion of "What is a thing" as put forth in (Heidegger 63). The author's was presented with such challenges to computing applications with philosophical epistemics, while visiting INRIA, Paris around 1992. His reaction was to start with "first principles", not touching such difficult areas of philosophy and phenomenology, and only present views to what they could imply for the metamathematics of AI. However, since the author's techniques were intended for AI computations and reasoning, rather than knowledge representation from observations, as it is the case in (Didday 90), Heidegger's definitions had to be taken further. The common point of interest is symbolic knowledge representation. However, the research directions are two essentially orthogonal, but not contradicting, views to knowledge representation.

3.2 Computational Illusion and Virtual Reality

Let us call “der Vielleicht Vorhandenen” objects that are only ‘Perhaps Computable,’ and therefore might be a computational illusion. That is the robot’s senses are not always real. The important problem is to be able to define worlds minimally to have computable representations with mathematical logic thus the ability to make definitive statements. Heidegger's Die Frage nach dem Ding will prove to be a blessing in disguise. Could it have computing applications to things without. Heidegger had defined three sorts of things. 1- Things in the sense of being "within reach", des Vorhandenen. 2. Things which "unify" things of the first kind, or are reflections on, resolution and actions. 3. Things of kind 1 or 2 and also any kind of things which are not nothing. To define logic applicable to planning for robots reaching for objects, the der Vielliecht Vorhandenen computational linguistics game is defined. To start, let us explore Heidegger's views of the "des Vorhandenen", having to do with what object is within "reach" in a real sense. In AI and computing applications notion of des Vorhandnen is not absolute. As an AI world develops the objects that have names in the world are at times des Vorhandnen and as defined by a principle of Parsimony only des Vorhandnen in an infinitary sense of logic (Nourani 1984,91) [32]. The logical representation for reaching the object might be infinitary only. The phenomenological problem from the robot's standpoint is to acquire a decidable descriptive computation [30] for the problem domain. Thus what is intended to be reached can stay always out of reach in a practical sense, unless it is at least what I call der Vielliecht Vorhandenen . The computing issues are the artificial intelligence computation and representation of real objects. That is, we can make use of symbolic computation to be able to "get at" a real object. At times, however, only infinite computations could define real world objects. For example, there is a symbolic computation for an infinite ordinal, by an infinite sequence of successor operations on 0. Furthermore, the present notion of der Vielliecht Vorhandenen is not intend to be the sense in which a robot cannot reach a particular object. The intent is that the language could have names for which the corresponding thing is not obvious in the AI world and there is incomplete information until at some point the world is defined enough that there is a thing corresponding to a name, or that at least there is a thing by comprehension, which only then becomes des Vorhandnen as the AI world is further defined or rearranged. These issues are examined in the computational context in the sections below. For example, the der Vielleicht Vorhandenen game has a winning strategy if the world descriptions by generic diagrams define the world enough to have a computation sequence to reach for an intended object. This implies there must be a decidable descriptive computation (Nourani 1994,96) for the world applied. The immediate linguistics example of these concepts from natural languages is a German child's language in which to "vor" and "handenen" are some corresponding things in the child's language world and mind, but "vorhandenen" is not a thing in that child's world and only becomes a thing as the linguistics world is further defined for the child.

3.3 Deduction Models and Perceptual Computing

Models uphold to a deductive closure of the axioms modeled and some rules of inference, depending on the theory. By the definition of a diagram they are a set of atomic and negated atomic sentences. Hence a diagram can be considered as a basis for defining model, provided we can by algebraic extension, define the truth value of arbitrary formulas instantiated with arbitrary terms. Thus all compound sentences build out of atomic sentences then could be assigned a truth value, handing over a model. It might be illuminating to compare the G-diagram techniques and computational epistemology to the (Konolige 1984) [24] starting with the consequential closure problem for artificial intelligence and the possible worlds. What Konolige starts with is the infeasibility premise for consequential closure, i.e. the assumption that an agent knows all logical consequences of his beliefs. The deductive model is defined for situations where belief derivation is logically incomplete. The area had been voiced since (Fodor 75) and (Moore 80). Konolige applies a model where beliefs are expressions in the agent's "mind" and the agent reasons about them by manipulating syntactic objects. When the process of belief derivation is logically incomplete, the deduction model does not have the property of the consequential closure. Konolige defines a saturated deduction model and claims a correspondence property: For every modal logic of belief based on Kripke possible world models, there exists a corresponding deduction model logic family with an equivalent saturated logic. The G-diagrams are defined for incomplete KR, modalities, and model set correspondence. What computational epistemology defines is a model theoretic technique whereby without the consequential closure property requirements on agents a model-theoretic completeness can be ascertained via nondeterministic diagrams. The author defined specific modal diagrams for computational linguistics models [27,29].

4.AffectiveComputing

(Picard 1999) [14] assertions indicate not all modules is a designed AI system might pay attention to emotions, or to have emotional components. Some modules are useful rigid tools, and it is fine to keep them that way. However, there are situations where the human-machine interaction could be improved by having machines naturally adapt to their users. Affective computing expands human-computer interaction by including emotional communication together with appropriate means of handling affective information. Neurological studies indicate that the role of emotion in human cognition is essential; emotions are not a luxury. Instead, emotions play a critical role in rational decision-making, in perception, in human interaction, and in human intelligence. These facts, combined with abilities computers are acquiring in expressing and recognizing affect, open new areas for research. The key issues in "affective computing," (Picard 1999a) [14] computing that relates to, arises from, or deliberately influences emotions. New models are suggested for computer recognition of human emotion, and both theoretical and practical applications are described for learning, human-computer interaction, perceptual information retrieval, creative arts and entertainment, human health, and machine intelligence. Scientists have discovered many surprising roles played by human emotion - especially in cognitive processes such as perception, decision making, memory judgment, and more. Human intelligence includes emotional intelligence, especially the ability to a accurately recognize and express affective information. Picard suggests that affective intelligence, the communication and management of affective information in human/computer interaction, is a key link that is missing in telepresence environments and other technologies that mediate human-human communication. (Picard-Cosier 1997) [25] discusses new research in affective intelligence, and how it can impact upon and enhance the communication process, allowing the delivery of the more natural interaction that is critical or a true telepresence.

5.Planning

The visual field is represented by visual objects connected with agents carrying information amongst objects about the field, and carried onto intelligent trees for computation. Intelligent trees compute the spatial field information with the diagram functions. The trees defined have function names corresponding to computing agents. Multiagent spatial vision techniques are introduced in (Nourani 1998) . The duality for our problem solving paradigm (Nourani 1991a,95a,95b) is generalized to be symmetric by the present paper to formulate Double Vision Computing. The basic technique is that of viewing the world as many possible worlds with agents at each world that compliment one another in problem solving by cooperating. An asymmetric view of the application of this computing paradigm as presented by the author and the basic techniques were proposed for various AI systems(Nourani1991a).

5.1TheIM_BIDModel

The co-operative problem solving paradigms have been applied ever since the AI methods put forth by Hays-Roth et.al. [14,35]. The muliagent multi-board techniques are due to the author (Nourani 1995a). The BID model has to be enhanced to be applicable to intelligent multimedia. Let us start with an example multi-board model where there multiagnt computations based on many boards, where the boards corresponds to either virtual possible worlds or to alternate visual views to the world, or to the knowledge and active databases. The board notion is a generalization of the Blackboard problem solving model (Hays-Roth 1985), (Nii 1986). The blackboard model consists of a global database called the blackboard and logically independent sources of knowledge called the knowledge sources. Agents can cooperate on a board with very specific engagement rules not to tangle the board nor the agents. The multiagent multi-board model, henceforth abbreviates as MB, is a virtual platform to an intelligent multimedia BID agent computing model. We are faced with designing a system consisting of the pair <IM-BID,MB>, where IM-BID is a multiagent multimedia computing paradigm where the agents are based on the BID model. The agents with motivational attitudes model is based on some of the assumptions described as follows. Agents are assumed to have the extra property of rationality: they must be able to generate goals and act rationally to achieve them, namely planning, replanting, and plan execution. Moreover, an agent's activities are described using mentalistic notions usually applied to humans. To start with the way the mentalistic attitudes are modulated is not attained by the BID model. It takes the structural IM-BID to start it. The preceding sections on visual context and epistemics have brought forth the difficulties in tackling the area with a simple agent computing model. The BID model does not imply that computer systems are believed to actually "have" beliefs and intentions, but that these notions are believed to be useful in modeling and specifying the behavior required to build effective multi-agent systems. The first BID assumption is that motivational attitudes, such as beliefs, desires, intentions and commitments are defined as reflective statements about the agent itself and about the agent in relation to other agents and the world. At BID the functional or logical relations between motivational attitudes and between motivational attitudes and informational attitudes are expressed as meta-knowledge, which may be used to perform meta-reasoning resulting in further conclusions about motivational attitudes. If we were to plan with BID with intelligent multimedia the logical relations might have to be amongst worlds forming the attitudes and event combinations. For example, in a simple instantiation of the BID model, beliefs can be inferred from meta-knowledge that any observed fact is a believed fact and that any fact communicated by a trustworthy agent is a believed fact. With IM_BID, the observed facts are believed facts only when a conjunction of certain worlds views and evens are in effect and physically logically visible to the windows in effect. Since planning with IM_BID is at times with the window visible agent groups, communicating, as two androids might, with facial gestures, for example (Picard 1998). In virtual or the "real-world" AI epistemics, we have to note what the positivists had told us some years ago: the apparent necessary facts might be only tautologies and might not amount to anything to the point at the specifics. Philosophers have been faced with challenges on the nature of absoulte and the Kantian epistemtics (Kant 1990) [25], (Nourani 1999a) [45] for years. It might all come to terms with empirical facts and possible worlds when it comes to real applications. A second BID assumption is that information is classified according to its source: internal information, observation, communication, deduction, assumption making. Information is explicitly labeled with these sources. Both informational attitudes (such as beliefs) and motivational attitudes (such as desires) depend on these sources of information. Explicit representations of the dependencies between attitudes and their sources are used when update or revision is required. A third assumption is that the dynamics of the processes involved are explicitly modeled. A fourth assumption is that the model presented is generic, in the sense that the explicit meta-knowledge required to reason about motivational and informational attitudes has been left unspecified. A fifth assumption is that intentions and commitments are defined with respect to both goals and plans. An agent accepts commitments towards himself as well as towards others (social commitments). For example, a model might be defined where a agent determines which goals it intends to fulfill, and commits to a selected subset of these goals. Similarly, an agent can determine which plans it intends to perform, and commits to selected subset of these plans. There are two component: goal_determination and plan_determination.

5.3 VR Computing and Computational Illusion

The IM Morphed Computing Logic for computing for multimedia are new projects with important computing applications. The basic principles are a mathematical logic where a Gentzen[25] or natural deduction systems is defined by taking arbitrary structures and multimedia objects coded by diagram functions. Multimedia objects are viewed as syntactic objects defined by functions, to which the deductive system is applied. Thus we define a syntactic morphing to be a technique by which multimedia objects and hybrid pictures are homomorphically mapped via their defining functions to a new hybrid picture. The logical language has function names for hybrid pictures. The *MIM Morph Rule* - An object defined by the functional n-tuple <f1,...,fn> can be Morphed to an object defined by the functional n-tuple <h(f1),...,h(fn)>, provided h is a homomrphism of abstract agent signature structures [35]. The *MIM TransMorph Rules*- A set of rules whereby combining hybrid pictures p1,...,pn defines an Event {p1,p2,...,pn} with a consequent hybrid picture p. Thus the combination is an impetus event. A computational logic for intelligent languages is presented in brief with a soundness and completeness theorem in [28]. The preliminaries to VR computing logic are presented since Summer Logic Colloquium 1997, Prague.

Theorem 5.1 Soundness and Completeness- Morph Gentzen Logic is sound and complete. □

Proposition 5.1 Morph Gentzen and Intelligent languages provide a sound and complete logical basis toVR.□

A virtual tree, or virtual proof tree is a proof tree that is constructed with agent languages with free Skolem functions. In the present paper we also instantiate proof tree leaves with free Skolemized trees. Thus virtual trees are substituted for the leaves. In the present approach, as we shall further define, leaves could be virtual trees. By a virtual tree we intend a term made of constant symbols and Skolem functions terms A plan is a sequence of operations in the universe that could result in terms that instantiate the truth of the goal formulas in the universe. That is what goes on as far as the algebra of the model is concerned. It is a new view of planning prompted by our method of planning with GF-diagrams and free Skolemized trees. It is a model-theoretic view. The planning process at each stage can make use of diagrams by taking the free interpretation of the possible proof trees that correspond to each goal satisfiability. The techniques we have applied are to make use of the free Skolemized proof trees in representing plans in terms of generalized Skolem functions. In planning with G-diagrams that part of the plan that involves free Skolemized trees is carried along with the proof tree for a plan goal. Proofs can be abstracted by generalizing away from constants in the proof. Thus, such a generalized proof can be defined by a whole class of minimal diagrams. This process is usually realized via partial deduction, which can be regarded as the proof-theoretical way of abducing diagrams whose littorals are necessary conditions for the proof. By not requiring the proof-tree leaves to get instantiated with atomic formulas, we get a more general notion of a proof. The mathematical formalization that allows us to apply the method of free proof trees is further developed and applied to theorem proving. Existentially quantified diagrams carry a main deficit- the Skolemized formulas are not characterized. Hilbert's epsilon symbol may be applied to solve this problem. Now we present the notion of a predictive diagram and apply it to provide a model-theoretic characterization for PD and related proof trees. A predictive diagram for a theory T is a diagram D[M], where M is a model for T, and for any formula q in M, either the function f: q → {0,1} is defined, or there exists a formula p in D[M], such that T U {p} proves q; or that T proves q by minimal prediction. By viewing PD from predictive diagrams we could define models for PD from predictive diagrams- thus a model theoretic formulation for PD emerges. We then define Hilbert models to handle the proof-model problems further on. The idea is that if the free proof tree is constructed then the plan has a model in which the goals are satisfied. The model is the initial model of the AI world for which the free Skolemized trees were constructed. Thus we had stated the Free Proof Tree Sound Computing Theorem.

Theorem 5.2 For the virtual proof trees defined for a goal formula from the G-diagram there is a canonical model satisfying the goal formulas. It is the canonical model definable from the G-diagram.

Proof <overview> In planning with generic diagrams plan trees involving free Skolemized trees is carried along with the proof tree for a plan goal. The idea is that if the free proof tree is constructed then the plan has a model in which the goals are satisfied. Since the proof trees are either proving plan goals for formulas defined on the G-diagram, or are computing with Skolem functions defining the GF-diagram, the model defined by the G-diagram applies. The model is standard canonical to the proof.□

Theorem 5.3 The Hilbert's epsilon technique implies there is a virtual tree model M for the set of formulas such that we can take an existentially quantified formula w[X] and have it instantiated by a Skolem function which can answer the satisfiability question for the model.

Proof Follows from the definitions. □

6. Conclusions

A basis to haptic computing and visual ontology is presented applying multiagent computing, morph Gentzen logic, and the IM_BID model. Specific paradigms are introduced and mathematical conclusions are reached on the computational properties, visual ontology, and haptic computing pragmatics. Implications are that the techniques will allow us to mathematically structure the processes and achieve specific deductive goals.

References

1. Brazier, F.M.T. , Dunin-Keplicz, B., Jennings, N.R. and Treur, J. (1997) DESIRE: modelling multi-agent systems in a compositional formal framework, International Journal of Cooperative Information Systems, M. Huhns, M. Singh, (Eds.), special issue on Formal Methods in Cooperative Information Systems, vol. 1.

2. Nourani,C.F.1996b, "Autonomous Multiagent Double Vision SpaceCrafts," AA99- Agent AutonomyTrack,Seattle,WA,.May1999.

3. Wooldridge, M. and Jennings, N.R. (1995). Agent theories, architectures, and languages: a survey. In: M. Wooldridge and N.R. Jennings, Intelligent Agents. (1993) 51- 92.

4.Woods, W. 1975, What is in a link?, In Representation and Understanding, Bobrow, D.G. and Collins, A (eds.) Academic Press, New York, 1975.

5. Williams, M. 1994, "Explanation and Theory Base Transmutations," *Proceedings 11th European* Conferenceon AI, Amsterdam, John Wiley and Sons Ltd. 346-350.

6. Dunin-Keplicz, B. and Treur, J. (1995). Compositional formal specification of multi-agent systems. In: M. Wooldridge and N.R. Jennings, Intelligent Agents, Lecture Notes in Artificial Intelligence, Vol. 890, Springer Verlag, Berlin, pp. 102-117.

7. Nourani, C.F. 1991, Planning and Plausible Reasoning in Artificial Intelligence, Diagrams, Planning, and Reasoning, Proc. Scandinavian Conference on Artificial Intelligence, Denmark, May 1991, IOS Press.

8. Cooper et.al 1996, Cooper, R., J. Fox, J. Farrington, T. Shallice, A Systematic Methodology For Cognitive Modeling AI-85, 1996, 3-44.

9. Nourani, C.F.,1999, Intelligent Multimedia- New Techniques and Paradigms, With Applications to Motion Pictures July 14, 1997.Creating Art and Motion Pictures with Intelligent Multimedia, 1997, Published as a chapter in the Intelligent Multimedia Textbook the author wrote. Intelligent Multimedia New Computing Techniques, Design Paradigms, and Applications, August 1999, Treelesspress, Berkeley. New . Preliminary edition. New edition available from http://www.lulu.com/CrisFN

10. Velde, W. van der and J.W. Perram J.W. (Eds.) (1996). Agents Breaking Away,Proc. 7th European Workshop on Modelling Autonomous Agents in a Multi-Agent World, MAAMAW'96, Lecture Notes in AI, vol. 1038, Springer Verlag.

11. Sphon, W. 1988, Ordinal Conditional Functions: A dynamic Theory of Epistemic States, In Harper W.L. and Skyrms, B. (eds.) Causation, in decision, belief change, and statistics, Klawer Academic Publishers, 0105-134, 1988.
12. Didday, E. 1990, Knowledge Representation and Symbolic Data Analysis, NATO AIS series Vol F61, edited by M Schader and W. Gaul, Springer-Verlag, Berlin.
13.AI 80, AI- Special Issue On Nomonotonic Logic, vol. 13, 1980.
14. Picard, R. W. 1999a, Affective Computing for HCI, *Proceedings of HCI*, Munich, Germany, August 1999.
15. Nourani, C.F. 2002, "Virtual Tree Computing, Meta-Contextual Logic, and VR," ASL Spring 2002, Seattle WA, March, BSL Vol 8. No. 3, ISSN 1079-8986.
16. Ford, K.M, C. Glymour, and P.J. Hayes 1995, Android Epistemmology, AAA/MIT Press. Formal specification of Multi-Agent Systems: a real-world case. In: V. Lesser
17. Genesereth, M.R. and N.J. Nilsson 1987, *Logical Foundations of Artificial Intelligence*,Morgan-Kaufmann,1987.
18. Nourani,C.F., 1999a Idealism, Illusion and Discovery, The International Conference on Mathematical Logic, Novosibirsk, Russia, August1999.
19. Heidegger, M. 1962, Die Frage nach dem Ding, Max Niemeyer Verlag, Tubingen.
20.Rao, A.S. and Georgeff, M.P. (1991). Modeling rational agents within a BID-architecture. In: R. Fikes and E. Sandewall (eds.), Proceedings of the Second Conference on Knowledge Representation and Reasoning, Morgan Kaufman, pp.473-484.
21.Nourani, C.F. 1995c, "Free Proof Trees and Model-theoretic Planning," *Proceedings Automated Reasoning AISB*, Sheffield, England, April 1995.
22. Kinny, D., Georgeff, M.P., Rao, A.S. (1996). A Methodology and Technique for Systems of BID Agents. In: W. van der Velde, J.W. Perram (Eds.), Agents Breaking Away, Proc. 7th European Workshop on Modelling Autonomous Agents in a Multi-Agent World, MAAMAW'96, Lecture Notes in AI, vol. 1038, Springer Verlag,
23. Koehler 1996- Koehler, J., Planning From Second Principles, AI 87,
24. Konolige, K. 1984, Belief and Incompleteness," Stanford CSLI-84-4, Ventura Hall, March 1984.
25. Nourani, C.F. and Th. Hoppe 1994,"GF-Diagrams for Models and Free Proof Trees," *Proceedingz Berlin Logic Colloquium,* Uniersitat Potsdam, May 1994.
25. Picard, R.W. and G. Cosier 1997, Affective Intelligence - The Missing Link,BT Technology J. Vol 14 No 4, 56-71, October.
26. Nourani, C.F. 1984, "Equational Intensity, Initial Models, and Reasoning in AI: A conceptual Overview," Proc. Sixth European AI Conference, Pisa, Italy, North-Holland.
27. Nourani, C.F. 1998d, "Syntax Trees, Intensional Models, and Modal Diagrams For Natural Language Models," Revised July 1997, Proceedings Uppsala Logic Colloquium, August1998, Uppsala University, Sweden.
28. Hays-Roth, B.(1985) Blackbaord Architecture for control, Journal of AI 26:251-321.
29. Nourani,C.F. 1994a, "Towards Computational Epistemology-A Forward,"," 1994. Preliminary brief at the *Summer Logic Colloquium*, Claire-Mont Ferrand, France. July 1994, Clermont-Ferrand, France.
30. Nourani,C.F 1996b, "Descriptive Computing, February 1996," Summer Logic Colloquium, July 1996, San Sebastian, Spain. Recorded at AMS,April 1997, Memphis.
31. Nourani, C.F. 1996a, " Slalom Tree Computing- A Computing Theory For Artificial Intelligence, "June 1994 (Revised December 1994), A.I. Communication Volume 9, Number 4, December 1996, IOS Press,Amsterdam.

Improving Interoperability Among Learning Objects Using FIPA Agent Communication Framework

Ricardo Azambuja Silveira[1], Eduardo Rodrigues Gomes[2], Rosa Vicari[2]
1 Universidade Federal de Santa Catarina, Campus Universitário, s/nº - Caixa Postal 476 Florian'opolis – SC, Brazil, silveira@inf.ufsc.br
2 Universidade Federal do Rio Grande do Sul, Av. Bento Gonçalves, 9500 Bloco IV Porto Alegre - RS –Brazil, {ergomes; rosa}@inf.ufrgs.br.

Abstract. The reusability of learning material is based on three main features: modularity, discoverability and interoperability. Several researchers on Intelligent Learning Environments have proposed the use of architectures based on agent societies. Learning systems based on Multi-Agent architectures support the development of more interactive and adaptable systems and the Learning Objects approach gives reusability. We proposed an approach where learning objects are built based on agent architectures. This paper discusses how the Intelligent Learning Objects approach can be used to improve the interoperability between learning objects and pedagogical agents.

1 Introduction

This paper addresses the improvement of interoperability among Learning Objects in agent-based Learning Environments by integrating Learning Objects technology and the Multi-Agent Systems approach. A Learning Object, according to Downes (2001, 2002), Mohan & Brooks (2003), and Sosteric & Hesemeier (2002), is a piece of learning content that can be used several times in different courses or in different situations. According to Downes (2001), the expense of developing learning materials for e-learning can be large, but as the content of related courses tend to be similar, the cost of developing the learning material can be shared. The learning object approach promises to reduce significantly the time and the cost required to develop e-learning courses. The design of learning environments using reusable learning objects improves quickness, flexibility and economy.

A learning object must be modular, discoverable and interoperable, in order to be reused (Friesen, 2001). To achieve these features and improve the efficiency, efficacy and reusability of learning objects, many people have dedicated a great effort. The main focus has been on the definition of standardization. Organizations

Please use the following format when citing this chapter:

Silveria, R.A., Gomes, E.R., Vicari, R., 2006, in IFIP International Federation for Information Processing, Volume 218, Professional Practice in Artificial Intelligence, eds. J. Debenham, (Boston: Springer), pp. 51–60.

such as IMS Global Learning Consortium (2004), IEEE (2004), ARIADNE (2004), and CanCore (2004), have contributed significantly by defining indexing standards called metadata (data about data). Metadata contain information to explain what the learning object is about, how to search, access, and identify it and how to retrieve educational content according to a specific demand.

Mohan & Brooks (2003) point out the limitations of current learning objects. According to them, an instructional designer must carefully examine each learning object to find the right object. This job may be quite time consuming and the learning object metadata are not very useful to support this task.

On the other hand, the state of the art in Intelligent Tutoring Systems (ITS) and Intelligent Learning Environments (ILE) points to the use of Agent Society-Based Architectures. Multiagent Systems (MAS) have proved to be appropriate for designing tutoring systems because learning is dealt with as a cooperative task (Johnson & Shaw, 1997). Using the MAS approach in designing ITS and ILE can result in faster, more versatile and low cost systems. The agents composing such systems use to be called Pedagogical Agents (Johnson & Shaw, 1997).

In Silveira et al (2005), we proposed the development of learning objects based on agent architectures: the Intelligent Learning Objects (ILO) approach. The use of agent-based architectures gives to the learning objects, the same features as presented above for agent-based learning environments.

2 Intelligent learning objects

An Intelligent Learning Objects (ILO) is a kind of agent able to promote learning experiences to students as the same way as learning objects can do. For this reason, an ILO can also be seen as a learning object built through the agent paradigm. The technological basis of this approach is composed by a combination between technologies developed for Learning Objects and Multiagent Systems.

There are many benefits of integrating learning objects and agents: An Intelligent Agent is a piece of software that works in a continuous and autonomous way in a particular environment, generally inhabited by other agents, and able to interfere in that environment, in a flexible and intelligent way, not requiring human intervention or guidance (Bradshaw, 1997). An agent is able to communicate with others by message exchange using a high-level communication language called Agent Communication Language (ACL), which is based on Logic concepts.

We have started from the learning object model called SCORM (ADL, 2004). SCORM performs the communication by calling methods (functions) and passing parameters, according to the Object Oriented Programming paradigm. An ILO uses ACL for communication among learning objects, hence the learning environments can perform a more powerful communication. ACL gives a more powerful semantic in communication using a formal protocol and a formal Content Language (CL) based on some logic formalism to express the messages content. By using ACL, it is possible to communicate not only variable values, but also facts, rules, mental states and more. The result is that communication by ACL and CL is potentially much better than the calling methods like in the object oriented approach.

The potential learning ability of intelligent agents. gives to the ILOs the ability to acquire new knowledge and perform different behaviors during its existence, as according to its own experience. Thus, by interaction with students and other ILOs, an ILO is able to evolve. It is not a static piece like current learning objects.

Agents can have coordination and cooperation mechanisms that help the agents` society to achieve its goals. Such agent features can be very useful due to the a self-organizing ILO society where it can promote richer learning experiences. The coordination and cooperation mechanisms enable complex behaviors and interactions among ILOs and, as a consequence, more powerful learning experiences.

Other agent features that promote interaction among learning objects are autonomy, pro-activity, sociability and benevolence. The autonomy of ILO gives it the capability to act based on its own behavior and knowledge with no external intervention. The pro-activity feature assures that the ILO must act in order to satisfy its own objectives. The sociability and benevolence features address the capability of social and cooperative behavior.

As a learning object, an Intelligent Learning Objects must be reusable. The *reusability* is given as a result of three features: interoperability, discoverability and modularity (Friesen, 2001). In Learning Objects approach, the use of metadata to describe the pedagogical content of the learning object gives discoverability. To enable this feature in ILO, we adopted the IEEE *1484.12.1 Standard for Learning Object Metadata* (LTSC, 2004). The *modularity* of learning objects can be reached with a good pedagogical project. So, the design of the pedagogical task of an ILO must be made according to the expertise of some object matter specialists and pedagogical experts. Some interoperability can be reached by the use of well-known standards. For this reason, we adopted two learning object standards: a) the IEEE *1484.12.1 Standard for Learning Object Metadata* (LTSC, 2004); and, b) *IEEE 1484.11.1 Standard for Learning Technology – Data Model for Content Object Communication.* The 1484.11.1 standard is defined for communication of learning objects with *Learning Management Systems* (LMS). We use this standard in interactions among ILOs. In order to assure interoperability among agents we have adopted the FIPA (2002) reference model and FIPA-ACL; as the language to be used for communication. We used these technologies to define a communication framework for ILOs. The ILOs must use this framework in order to communicate with each other.

The *discoverability* is the ability to be discovered in terms of its tasks and the services it provides. In addition to some services provided by the FIPA architecture, our communication framework contains a set of dialogues that ILOs should use. Besides those technological issues, one important requirement for an ILO is that it must have an educational purpose. Thus, an ILO must be created and applied in order to carry out some specific tasks to create significant learning experiences by interacting with the student. For this reasons, the project of an ILO needs a contents expert, an educational expert and a computing expert.

3 The ILO Multi-Agent Architecture

The agent society presented by Silveira et al (2005) encompasses three types of agents: *LMS agents* and *Intelligent Learning Objects agent* and *ILOR Agent.*

Intelligent Learning Objects are agents responsible for playing the role of learning objects. Its responsibility is to generate learning experiences to the students in the same sense of learning objects. *LMS Agents* are abstractions of Learning Management Systems. It is responsible for dealing with the administrative and pedagogical tasks involving a learning environment as a whole. It provides a way for students to access ILOs, and get information concerning the studentsto the LMS, *ILOR Agents* are abstractions of Learning Objects Repositories systems. It is responsible to store data about he ILOs to permit a user or an agent to find them. Figure 1 illustrates the proposed agent society. First, students interact with the LMS Agent in order to have learning experiences.

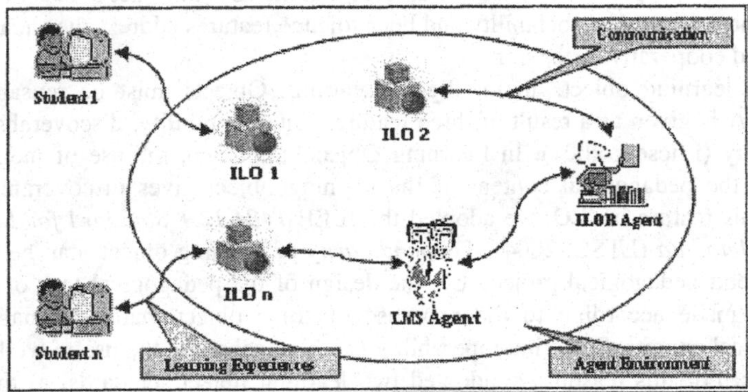

Fig. 1. Proposed agent society

The LMS Agent searches (with the aid of the ILOR Agent) the appropriate ILO and invoke it. The ILO is then responsible for generating learning experiences to the students. In this task it can communicate with the LMS agent and with other ILO agents in order to promote richer learning experiences. All the communication is performed by messages exchange in FIPA-ACL. The agent environment that these agents inhabit is a FIPA complaint environment. It provides all the necessary mechanisms for message interchanging among the agents.

3.1 Agent Communication structure

One of the main concerns of this research is the modeling of the communication processes among the agents. Through a well-defined communication framework it is possible to improve interoperability because it enables different types of agents to share information.

We defined a communication framework based on FIPA reference model (FIPA, 2002). FIPA uses the idea of communication as the exchange of declarative statements. In this kind of communication, agents receive, reply and send requests for services and information transported by messages. There are five main concepts: Agent Communication Languages (ACL), Content Languages (CL), Agent Interaction Protocols (AIP), Conversations and ontologies. An ACL is responsible for defining how the contents of a message have to be interpreted. A CL is a declarative knowledge representation language to encode the message's content. An AIP is a typical communication pattern with an associated semantic to be used by the agents. A Conversation occurs when an agent instantiates an AIP in order to communicate with other agents. Finally, an Ontology defines the terminology used to denote domain-specific concepts in the message's content. In this section we show the communication structure that must be used to build Intelligent Learning Objects.

3.2 Interaction protocol

The FIPA reference model presents a set of interaction protocols. In this work we use the FIPA-Request protocol (FIPA, 2002), which is the FIPA protocol that should be used for agents who want to do requests for services provided by other agents.

The FIPA-Request protocol begins with a *request* message denoting that the sender agent asks the receiver agent to perform the task defined in the content of the message. The content of the message is an *action* describing the task that the receiver agent is supposed to do. An action is an abstraction of a real concept of an action that an agent can execute. Its semantic is defined in an ontology. For example, the action *send-metadata,* defined in our ontology, can be used by an agent to ask the metadata about an ILO. If the receiver agent agrees to perform the requested task, the final message will be an *inform* containing a *predicate*. A predicate says something about the state of the world and can be true or false. In this work we used three predicates defined by FIPA:

a) *result*, which means that the result of the action pointed in the first argument is contained within the second argument;
b) *done*, which means that the action in its first argument is done and no result was returned; and
c) *set*, which introduces a set of concepts or predicates.

3.3 The ontology for intelligent learning objects

For the FIPA reference model, ontology is a set of domain-specific concepts within the messages contents. A typical FIPA ontology is defined by using predicates, actions and concepts (FIPA, 2002). Although simple, this definition is very pragmatic and satisfies all the requirements of the agent communication processes defined in this work.

This section shows the actions and concepts which compose the ontology used in this framework. As we used FIPA-SL0 (a sub-set of FIPA-SL) to encode the messages' content, this section also shows how these items shall be represented using FIPA-SL0. We are using **bold** to describe terminal symbols and *italic* to describe non-terminal symbols. Symbols defined in the ontology itself are enclosed by "<" and ">"

In addition to the following ontology, the agents must know the ontology defined in the document SC0000023 (FIPA, 2002), which defines the FIPA Agent Management Specification.

Concepts

a) Concept (**metadata :content** *string*): This concept asserts that there is a data model which contains metadata information about the educational content of the intelligent learning object. This information is contained in the **:content** parameter, and must be compliant with the *IEEE 1484.12.1 Standard for Learning Object Metadata* and must be coded using the *IEEE 1484.12.3 Standard for Learning Technology – Extensible Markup Language (XML) Schema Definition Language Binding for Learning Object Metadata.*

b) Concept (**dataModel :content** *string*): This concept asserts that there is a data model which contains information about the interaction between a student and an ILO. This information is contained in the **:content** parameter, must be compliant with the *IEEE 1484.11.1 Standard for Learning Technology – Data Model for Content Object Communication.*

c) Concept (**learner :name** *string* **:id** *string* **:data-model** *string*): This concept asserts that there is a student with the name defined in **:name**, which has an unique identifier contained in **:id**. The information about the interaction between this student and a ILO is contained in **:data-model**. This information must be compliant with the *IEEE 1484.11.1 Standard for Learning Technology – Data Model for Content Object Communication.*

d) Concept (**ilo :agent-id** *string* **:metadata** *string* **:location** *string*): This concept asserts that there is the ILO which metadata information is defined in **: metadata**. If this agent is operating in the agent society in a certain moment, the :agent-id parameter has its unique identifier. In the other case, :location has a reference for the location where the agent is found (for example, the agent's java class). The :metadata parameter must be compliant with the *IEEE 1484.12.1 Standard for Learning Object Metadata* and must be encoded with the *IEEE 1484.12.3 Standard for Learning Technology – Extensible Markup Language (XML) Schema Definition Language Binding for Learning Object Metadata.*

Actions

a) Action (**send-metadata**): Must be used when an agent needs the metadata information of ILO. This action does not have parameters

b) Action (**send-learner**): Must be used when an agent needs information about the student. This action does not have parameters.

c) Action (**search-ilo :metadata** <*metadata*>): Must be used when an agent needs to have the ILOR sending information about ILOs that satisfy the criteria defined in the **:metadata** parameter. This parameter must contain the minimum set of features that the ILO must have to be part of the result set of the action.

d) Action (**get-learner-lms :learner** *string* **:ilo** *string*): Must be used when an agent needs to have the LMS sending information about the student **:learner** related to the ILO **:ilo**. The parameters :learner and :ilo are unique identifiers for the student and the ILO, respectively.

e) Action **(put-learner-lms :learner** *<learner>* **:ilo** *<ilo>***):** This action must be used when an agent needs to have the LMS storing the information about a student **:learner** related to the ilo **:ilo**. The parameters :learner and :ilo contain the information about the student and the ILO.

f) Action **(put-learner-ilo :learner** *<learner>***):** This action must be used when an agent needs to have the ILO evaluating the information about a student **:learner.** The parameter :learner contain the information about the student.

g) Action **(activate :ilo** *<ilo>***):** Must be used when the ILO needs to have its status changed to activated in the ILOR's list of activated ILOs.

h) Action **(deactivate :ilo** *<ilo>***):** Must be used when the ILO needs to have its status changed to deactivated in the ILOR's list of activated ILOs.

3.4 Dialogues

Using the FIPA-Request protocol, we defined a set of conversations protocols that the agents must be able to perform. In this session we show some of them.

Registering in DF

The DF (Directory Facilitator) Agent is part of the FIPA Agent Reference Model. It works as a directory facilitator where agents can register the services they can provide to the other agents. The document SC0000023 (FIPA, 2004) specifies how this process must be made.

Requesting metadata information from an ILO

To request the metadata information of an ILO, agents must use the dialogue **get-metadata**. This dialogue is initiated by a request message containing the action **send-metadata** sent to the ILO. If the ILO agreed to execute the task when it is completed with success, the final message contains a **metadata** concept containing the ILO's metadata information. Table 1 shows the phases of this dialogue according to the FIPA-Request protocol.

Table 1. Phases of the get-metadata dialogue according to the FIPA-Request protocol.

Phase	Sender	Receiver	Performative	Content
1	Agent	ILO	**Request**	(**action** *<AID>* *<send-metadata>*)
2	ILO	Agent	**Agree**	(<phase 1 content>
	ILO	Agent	**Not-**	(<phase 1 content>
	ILO	Agent	**Refuse**	(<phase 1 content> <reasons>)
3	ILO	Agent	**Inform**	(**result** <phase 1
	ILO	Agent	**Failure**	(<phase 1 content> <reasons>)

Requesting learner information from an ILO

To request the information about the learner which the ILO is interacting with, agents must use the dialogue **get-learner**. This dialogue is initiated by a request message containing the action **send-learner** sent to the ILO. If the ILO agrees to execute the task and carries it out successfully, the final message contains a **leaner** concept containing the learner's information. Table 2 presents the phases of this dialogue according to the FIPA-Request protocol.

Table 2. Phases of the get-learner dialogue according to the FIPA-Request protocol.

Phase	Sender	Receiver	Performative	Content
1	Agent	ILO	**Request**	(**action** *<AID>* *<send-learner>*)
2	ILO	Agent	**Agree**	(<phase 1
	ILO	Agent	**Not-**	(<phase 1
	ILO	Agent	**Refuse**	(<phase 1 content> <reasons>)
3	ILO	Agent	**Inform**	(**result** <phase 1
	ILO	Agent	**Failure**	(<phase 1 content> <reasons>)

Requesting learner's information from an LMS Agent

The dialogue **get-learner-lms** must be used to request information about the interactions of a given student to the LMS agent. This dialogue is initiated by a request message, sent to a LMS Agent, containing the action **get-learner-lms.** This action contains the learner's identifier and the ILO's identifier. If the sender agent wants to obtain student/ILO information, the :ilo parameter must be filled. In the other case, the LMS Agent will send information about the learner and all the ILOS. The final message contains a set of **dataModel** concepts containing the requested information. Table 4 presents the phases of this dialogue according to the FIPA-Request protocol.

Table 3. Phases of the get-learner-lms dialogue according FIPA-Request Protocol.

Phase	Sender	Receiver	Performative	Content
1	Agent	LMS	**Request**	(**action** *<AID>* *<get-learner-lms>*)
2	LMS	Agent	**Agree**	(<phase 1 content>)
	LMS	Agent	**not-understood**	(<phase 1 content>)
	LMS	Agent	**Refuse**	(<phase 1 content> <reasons>)
3	LMS	Agent	**Inform**	(**result** <phase 1
	LMS	Agent	**Failure**	(<phase 1 content> <reasons>)
	ILO	Agent	**Failure**	(<phase 1 content> <reasons>)

3.3 Dynamic of the ILO society

The proposed agents in this work have three different states: not-initialized, activated e finalized.

In the first state, the agent is not instantiated or is not registered in the platform. When the agent is instantiated it must register itself in the DF and in the AMS using the dialogues defined by FIPA in the document SC0000023 (FIPA, 2002) and the schema for registering in those entities defined in this work. If the agent is an ILO, it must change its status within the ILOR Agent using the dialogue **modify-status** and the action **activate**. After this, the agent will be in the activated state. Then it is able to execute the tasks for what it has been defined for.

To get to the finalized state, the agent must deregister itself in the DF and AMS. To do so it must use the dialogues defined by FIPA in the document SC0000023 (FIPA, 2004) for this purpose. If the agent is an ILO, before deregistering in the DF and AMS, the agent must change its status within the ILOR Agent using the dialogue **modify-status** and the action **deactivate**. As soon as the agent gets the finalized state, it goes to the not-initialized state.

4 Conclusions

This paper presented the communication structure proposed for the ILO approach and how it can be used to improve interoperability among learning objects and pedagogical agents. At this point, our conclusion is in the way that we need to stop thinking of learning objects as chunks of instructional content and to start thinking of them as small, self-reliant computer programs. This means more than giving a learning object some sort of functionality, more than writing Java calculators or interactive animations. When we think of a learning object we need to think of it as a small computer program that is aware of and can interact with its environment. The agent approach can enable these features. Intelligent Learning Objects are able to improve the adaptability, interoperability and interactivity of learning environments built with these kinds of components by the interaction among the learning objects and between learning objects and other agents in a more robust conception of communication rather than a single method invocation as the object-oriented paradigm use to be.

5 References

Advanced Distributed Learning (ADL). (2004). *Sharable Content Object Reference Model (SCORM ®) 2004 Overview*. retrieved July 7, 2005 from www.adlnet.org.

ARIADNE (2004). *Alliance of remote instructional authoring & distribution networks for Europe* Retrieved July 7, 2005 http://ariadne.unil.ch.

Bradshaw, J. M. (1997). An introduction to software agents In: Bradshaw, J. M. Ed. *Software Agents*. Massachusetts: MIT Press, 1997.

CanCore (2004). Canadian Core About. Retrieved July 7, 2005 from http://www.cancore.ca/about.html.

Downes, S. (2001). Learning objects: resources for distance education worldwide. in *International Review of Research in Open and Distance Learning,* 2(1). 2001

Downes , S. (2002). *Smart Learning Objects.*

EMORPHIA (2005). *FIPA-OS - FIPA - Open Source.* retrieved September 19, 2005 from http://fipa-os.sourceforge.net/index.htm.

FIPA: The foundation for Intelligent Physical Agents (2002). *Specifications.* retrieved July 7, 2005 from http://www.fipa.org.

Friesen, Norm (2001). What are Educational Objects? Interactive Learning Environments, 3 (9).

IEEE Learning Technology Standards Committee (2004). *Specifications.* retrieved July 7, 2005 from http://ltsc.ieee.org.

IMS Global Learning Consortium. (2004). *Current specifications.* retrieved July 7, 2005 from http://www.imsglobal.org /specifications.cfm.

Mohan, P.and Brooks, C. (2003). Engineering a Future for Web-based Learning Objects. *Proceedings of International Conference on Web Engineering,* Oviedo, Asturias, Spain.

Silveira, R. A., Gomes, E. R, Vicari, R. M. (2005). Inteligent Learning Objects: An Agent-Based Approach of Learning Objects. In Weert, Tom Van, Tatnall, Arthur (Eds.) *Information and Communication Technologies and Real-Life Learning.*Boston Springer, 1103 - 110.

Wooldridge, M.; Jennings, N. R.; Kinny, D (1999). A methodology for agent-oriented analysis and design. In: Proceedings of International Conference on Autonomous Agent AAMAS, v.3. 1999.

Acknowledgment

This project is granted by Brazilian agencies: CNPq, CAPES and FAPERGS.

An Agent-Oriented Programming Language for Computing in Context

Renata Vieira[1], Álvaro F. Moreira[2], Rafael H. Bordini[3], and Jomi Hübner[4]

[1] Universidade do Vale do Rio dos Sinos
renata@exatas.unisinos.br

[2] Universidade Federal do Rio Grande do Sul
afmoreira@inf.ufrgs.br

[3] University of Durham
R.Bordini@durham.ac.uk

[4] Universidade Regional de Blumenau
jomi@inf.furb.br

Abstract. Context aware intelligent agents are key components in the development of pervasive systems. In this paper, we present an extension of a BDI programming language to support ontological reasoning and ontology-based speech act communication. These extensions were guided by the new requirements brought about by such emerging computing styles. These new features are essential for the development multi-agent systems with context awareness, given that ontologies have been widely pointed out as an appropriate way to model contexts.

1 Introduction

Context aware intelligent agents will be requeried if the vision of pervasive computing is to become real. Ontologies and ontology languages are becoming very popular as a way to model contexts, since they allow for the necessary reasoning to deal with the dynamic nature of this new computing style that is emerging. In other words, ontologies allow for different systems to come to a common understanding of the semantics of domains and services, and thus for the reuse of concepts in different contexts. In this complex new computing scenario, agent technologies, such as languages used to specify and implement them, have been left somewhat behind. In this paper, we present how we are extending an agent-oriented programming language for implementing agents that can operate in such environments. The AgentSpeak(L) programming language was introduced by Rao in [17]. The language was quite influential in the definition of other agent-oriented programming languages. AgentSpeak(L) is particularly interesting, in comparison to other agent-oriented languages, in that it retains the most important aspects of the BDI-based reactive planning systems on which it was based. Its relation to BDI logics [18] has been thoroughly studied [3] and a working

Please use the following format when citing this chapter:

Vieira, R., Moreira, Á.F., Bordini, R.H., Hübner, J., 2006, in IFIP International Federation for Information Processing, Volume 218, Professional Practice in Artificial Intelligence, eds. J. Debenham, (Boston: Springer), pp. 61–70.

interpreter for the language has been developed based on its formal operational semantics [15]. For AgentSpeak(L) to be useful in practice, various extensions to it have been proposed; from now on we refer to AgentSpeak(L) or any of its extensions generally as AgentSpeak. In particular, the formal semantics of an extended version of the language that allows for speech act-based communication, given in [16] has been used for the implementation of the *open source* interpreter ***Jason*** [1] [2]. Through speech act-based communication, an agent can share its internal state (beliefs, desires, intentions) with other agents, as well as it can influence other agents' states.

Despite the considerable improvement that has been achieved since the paradigm was first thought out [20], agent-oriented programming languages are still in their early stages of development and have clear shortfalls as far as their use in the software industry is concerned. One such shortfall of AgentSpeak has to do with the unrealistic simplicity of the way in which belief bases are implemented. A belief base that is simply an unstructured collection of ground predicates is just not good enough if we consider that mobile services and the semantic web make use of ontologies for representing knowledge (through more elaborate languages such as OWL, the Ontology Web Language). Due in part to this lack of structure, reasoning in AgentSpeak is limited to the unification mechanism applied to explicit knowledge. Another shortfall of AgentSpeak, that reduces its applicability for the development of semantic web multi-agent systems, is the absence of mechanisms to indicate the ontologies that have to be considered by agents in their reasoning. This shortfall imposes the assumption (that we had to adopt in [16], for instance) that all communicating AgentSpeak agents in a multi-agent application have a common understanding about terms that are used in the content of exchanged messages. This assumption is clearly unrealistic for semantic web applications as they typically require the integration of multiple ontologies about different domains.

The main contribution of this paper is to present an agent-oriented programming language which overcomes these limitations by bringing together: speech act-based inter-agent communication, improved descriptive and reasoning capabilities, and support for multiple ontology selection. The literature is abundant in proposals for speech-act-based communication and ontologies for the semantic web; we refer to [9, 23], just to mention a couple of examples.Pervasive, context-rich systems are being designed on the basis of the same apparatus [5]. Speech act theory is deeply related to BDI notions used in agent architectures, and in turn intelligent agents are also one of the key components in the pervasing computing vision. However, the design of such agents for such scenarios will require appropriate languages. To the best of our knowledge this is the first work aiming at integrating these technologies into a BDI agent-oriented programming language.

The paper is organized as follows: Section 2 gives a brief overview of the AgentSpeak language. Section 3 brings together ontologies and speech-act based communication in the AgentSpeak programming language. In the final section we draw some conclusions and discuss future work.

[1] `http://jason.sourceforge.net`

2 An Overview of AgentSpeak

The AgentSpeak programming language is an extension of logic programming for the BDI agent architecture, and provides an elegant framework for programming BDI agents. The BDI architecture is the predominant approach to the implementation of "intelligent" or "rational" agents [24].

$$
\begin{array}{lll}
ag & ::= bs \quad ps & \\
bs & ::= at_1 \ldots at_n & (n \geq 0) \\
at & ::= P(t_1, \ldots t_n) & (n \geq 0) \\
ps & ::= p_1 \ldots p_n & (n \geq 1) \\
p & ::= te : ct \leftarrow h & \\
te & ::= +at \mid -at \mid +g \mid -g & \\
ct & ::= at \mid \neg at \mid ct \wedge ct \mid \top & \\
h & ::= a \mid g \mid u \mid h; h & \\
g & ::= !at \mid \; ?at & \\
u & ::= +at \mid -at &
\end{array}
$$

Fig. 1. Syntax of AgentSpeak.

Figure 1 has the abstract syntax of AgentSpeak. An AgentSpeak agent is created by the specification of a set *bs* of base beliefs and a set *ps* of plans. In the original definition of the language an *initial set of beliefs* is just a collection of ground first order predicates. A plan is formed by a *triggering event* (denoting the purpose for that plan), followed by a conjunction of belief literals representing a *context*. The context must be a logical consequence of that agent's current beliefs for the plan to be *applicable*. The remainder of the plan is a sequence of basic actions or (sub)goals that the agent has to achieve (or test) when the plan, if applicable, is chosen for execution.

AgentSpeak distinguishes two types of goals: *achievement goals* and *test goals*. Achievement and test goals are predicates (as for beliefs) prefixed with operators '!' and '?' respectively. Achievement goals state that the agent wants to achieve a state of the world where the associated predicate is true. (In practice, these initiate the execution of *subplans*.) A *test goal* returns a unification for the associated predicate with one of the agent's beliefs; they fail otherwise. A *triggering event* defines which events may initiate the execution of a plan. An *event* can be internal, when a subgoal needs to be achieved, or external, when generated from belief updates as a result of perceiving the environment. There are two types of triggering events: those related to the *addition* ('+') and *deletion* ('-') of mental attitudes (beliefs or goals).

Plans refer to the *basic actions* (represented by the metavariable a in the grammar above) that an agent is able to perform on its environment. Such actions are also defined as first-order predicates, but with special predicate symbols (called action symbols) used to distinguish them from other predicates.

Consider a scenario where a tourist is walking around London's West End, planning his evening. The tourist's personal assistant can check for locally available plays

```
+concert(A,V,T) : likes(A)
   ← !book_tickets(A,V,T)

+!book_tickets(A,V,T) : ¬busy(T)
   ← call(V);
     ...;
     !choose_seats(A,V)
```

Fig. 2. Examples of AgentSpeak plans.

and concerts according to the user's preferences. Figure 2 shows some examples of AgentSpeak plans for this scenario. They tell us that, when a concert or play A is announced at venue V and T(so that, from the perception of the context, a belief concert(A,V,T) is *added*), then if this agent in fact likes artist A, then it will have the new goal of booking tickets for that concert. The second plan tells us that whenever this agent adopts the goal of booking tickets for A's performance at V, if it is the case that the agent is not busy at T, according to his agenda, then it can execute a plan consisting of performing the basic action call(V) (assuming that it is an atomic action that the agent can perform) followed by a certain protocol for booking tickets (indicated by '...'), which in this case ends with the execution of a plan for choosing the seats for such performance at that particular venue.

3 AgentSpeak with Speech-Act Based Communication and Ontological Reasoning

3.1 Speech Act-Based Communication

As BDI theory is based on the philosophical literature on practical reasoning [4], agent communication in multi-agent systems is inspired by philosophical studies on the speech act theory, in particular the work by Austin [1] and Searle [19]. Speech act theory is based on the conception of language as action [1, 19]. In natural language, one has an illocutionary force associated to a utterance (or locutionary act) such as "the door is open" and another to a utterance "open the door". The former intends belief revision, whereas the latter intends a change in the plans of the hearer. When the theory is adapted to agent communication the illocutionary force is made explicit, to facilitate the computational processing of the communication act.

The Knowledge Query and Manipulation Language (KQML) [12] was the first practical communication language that included high level speech-act based communications. KQML "performatives" refer to illocutionary forces and they make explicit the agent intentions with a message being sent. The FIPA standard[2] for agent communication is conceptually similar to KQML, the differences being only in the sets of available performatives and a few other details.

[2] http://www.fipa.org

An operational semantics for AgentSpeak extended with speech-act based communication was given in [16]. That semantics tells exactly how the computational representation of Beliefs-Desires-Intentions of an agent are changed when it receives a message. It has also formed the basis for the implementation of AgentSpeak interpreters such the ***Jason*** [2].

Speech act based communication fits well with BDI agent oriented programming languages, such as AgentSpeak, since the semantics of both is given in terms of the agents mental states such as beliefs, desires and intentions. For this same reason, speech act based communication is an ideal approach for communication among agents in the web, in particular in applications where agents have to reasong about each other in order to negotiate and cooperate.

3.2 Ontologies and Ontological Reasoning

Developing applications that make full use of machine-readable knowledge sources as promised by the Semantic Web vision is attracting much of current research interest. More than that, the Semantic Web technology is also being used as the basis for other important trends in Computer Science such as Grid Computing [8] and Ubiquitous Computing [5]. Among the key components of the Semantic Web are *domain ontologies* [21]. They are responsible for the specification of the domain knowledge, and as they can be expressed logically, they can be the basis for sound reasoning in the specified domain. Several ontologies are being proposed for the development of specific applications [6, 14, 7, 22]. Description logics are at the core of widely known ontology languages, such as the Ontology Web Language (OWL) [13]. An extension of AgentSpeak with underlying automatic reasoning over ontologies expressed in such languages can have a major impact on the development of agents and multi-agent systems that can operate in a Semantic Web context. Although applications for the Semantic Web are already being developed, often based on the Agents paradigm, most such development is being done on a completely *ad hoc* fashion as far as agent-oriented programming is concerned.

In the Semantic Web framework, agents are responsible for making use of the available knowledge, autonomously interacting with other agents, so as to act on the user's best interest. Effective communication among these agents requires *(i)* a common understanding about the meaning of terms used in the content of messages, and *(ii)* communication abilities that can allow agents to know about each other in order to negotiate and cooperate. Agents achieve these requirements by sharing domain ontologies and by using speech-act based performatives in their communication. In the next two subsections we discuss the implications of extending the agent-oriented programming language AgentSpeak with these two features.

3.3 Ontologies and AgentSpeak

We start by presenting in Figure 3 the syntax of AgentSpeak with support for ontological reasoning. An agent consists of the specification Ont of the ontologies used by the agent, a set *bs* of belies, and a set *ps* of plans.

$$
\begin{array}{lll}
ag & ::= Ont \quad bs \quad ps & \\
 & & \\
Ont & ::= context\_ontology(url_1, \ldots url_n) & \\
 & & \\
bs & ::= at_1 \ldots at_n & (n \geq 0) \\
at & ::= C(t) \mid R(t_1, t_2) & \\
 & \mid C(t)[s_1, \ldots, s_n; url] & (n \geq 0) \\
 & \mid R(t_1, t_2)[s_1, \ldots, s_n; url] & (n \geq 0) \\
s & ::= \texttt{percept} \mid \texttt{self} \mid id & \\
 & & \\
ps & ::= p_1 \ldots p_n & (n \geq 1) \\
p & ::= te : ct \leftarrow h & \\
te & ::= +at \mid -at \mid +g \mid -g & \\
ct & ::= at \mid \neg at \mid ct \wedge ct \mid \top & \\
h & ::= a \mid g \mid u \mid h; h & \\
g & ::= !at \mid ?at & \\
u & ::= +at \mid -at &
\end{array}
$$

Fig. 3. Syntax of AgentSpeak with ontologies.

The specification of the ontologies is given by $context\_ontology([url_1, \ldots url_n])$, a special purpose predicate where each url_i is the URL of an ontology, usually described in the ontology language OWL. Each ontology consists of a set of class and property descriptions, and axioms establishing equivalence and subsumption relationships between classes (unary predicates) and properties (binary predicates). The belief base *bs* describes the state of an application domain by asserting that certain individuals are instances of certain classes and that certain individuals are related by a property. Each element of the belief base can be annotated with its source, which can be either a term identifying which was the agent in the society (*id*) that previously sent the information in a message, `self` to denote internal beliefs, or `percept` to indicate that the belief was acquired through perception of the environment. Beliefs can also be annotated with the *url* of the ontology where their associated classes and properties are defined. AgentSpeak plans are essentially the same as presented in Section 2

We now proceed to discuss the impact that ontological reasoning has on plan selection and querying in AgentSpeak programs. In $context\_ontology(url_1, \ldots url_n)$, the ontologies are written in some ontology language such as OWL, for simplicity though, the small extracts of ontologies we provide in this paper are expressed in a fragment of description logic instead of OWL.

Plan Selection A plan is considered relevant in relation to a triggering event if it has been written specifically to deal with that event or if it is a plan with a more general relevance that can be suitable for the triggering event. As an example let us consider the case of checking for plans that are relevant for a particular event and consider that the agent has at its disposal the following ontology:

$$atendee \equiv person \sqcap resgistered \sqcap \neg presenter$$
$$presenter \equiv speaker \sqcup paperAuthor \ldots$$

Suppose that a sensor in a smart meeting room somehow has detected in the environment the arrival of the speaker $john$. This causes the addition of the external event whose signaling term is $+speaker(john)$ to the set of events. Suppose also that $speaker \sqsubseteq presenter$ can be inferred from the ontologies specified in by the $context\_ontology(url_1, \ldots url_n)$. Under these circumstances, a plan with triggering event `+presenter(X)` is also considered relevant for dealing with the event. Observe that using subsumption instead of unification as the mechanism for searching for relevant plans potentially results in a larger set of plans. A plan is applicable if it is relevant and its context *ct* can be inferred from the ontologies and from the belief base. A plan's context is a conjunction of literals[3] $l_1, l_2, \ldots$. We can say that $Ont, bs \models l_1 \wedge \ldots \wedge l_n$ if, and only if, $Ont, bs \models l_i$ for $i = 1 \ldots n$.

Again, due to the fact that the ontologies and the belief base are structured and that reasoning is based on subsumption as well as instantiation, the resulting set of applicable plans might be larger. Suppose that plans with triggering events `+presenter(X)` and `+speaker(X)` were both considered relevant and applicable. The *least general* plan among those in the set of applicable plans should be selected plan. Here, the selected plan should be the one with triggering event `+speaker` as probably this plan has been written to deal more particularly with the case of invited speakers arriving in the room, rather then the more general plan which can be used for other types of presenters as well. On the other hand, if the particular plan for invited speaker is not applicable (e.g., because it involves alerting the session chair of the arrival of the celebrity speaker but the chair is not present), instead of the agent not acting at all for lack of applicable plans, the more general plan for speakers can then be tried, the relevance being determined by the underlying ontology instead.

Querying The evaluation of a test goal $?C(t)$ consists in testing if the formula $C(t)$ is a logical consequence of the agent's ontologies and the belief base. The crucial difference is that now the reasoning capabilities include subsumption instead of unification only which allows agents to infer knowledge that is implicit in the ontologies.

As an example suppose that the agent belief base does not refer to instances of $atendee$, but instead it has the facts $speaker(john)$ and $paperAuthor(mary)$. A test goal like $?atendee(X)$ succeeds in this case producing substitutions that map X to $john$ and $mary$.

Consistency of the Belief Base The belief base of an agent contains class assertions $C(t)$ and property assertions $R(t_1, \ldots t_n)$. The representation of such information should, of course, be consistent with the ontologies in $context\_ontology(url_1 \ldots url_k)$. Suppose for instance that by the ontologies it can be inferred that the concepts $chair$ and $bestPaperWinner$ are disjoint. Clearly if the belief base has that $chair(mary)$, the assertion $bestPaperWinner(mary)$ is not to be added to it, otherwise the belief base will become inconsistent.

[3] Note that in the context of the Semantic Web, open world is often assumed, so negation here is "strong negation", in the usual sense in logic programming.

Observe that the belief base of the agent can be updated by the addition of $chair(mary)[id; url]$, without the need for checking consistency as far as url is not a url in the set of url's specified in $context\_ontology(url_1 \ldots url_k)$. A belief like this expresses that $chair(mary)$ has been communicated by a certain agent id and that, when reasoning about it, the ontology in url should be used.

3.4 Ontologies and Communication

As usual in practice, we assume that the implementation of the AgentSpeak interpreter provides, as part of the overall agent architecture, a mechanism for receiving and sending messages asynchronously; messages are stored in a mail box and one of them is processed by the agent at the beginning of a reasoning cycle. Messages are sent by the execution of the action `.send` in the body of plans. The format of messages is $\langle mid, id, Ilf, at, url \rangle$, where mid is a unique message identifier; id is the identity of the agent to which the message is addressed to; *Ilf* is the illocutionary force associated with the message, *at*, the message content, is an atomic belief, and *url* is the ontology that must be used when reasoning about the message content *at*. For the purpose of this paper the interesting performatives are those whose semantics can lead to belief base modification or that involve ontological reasoning. Four of these performative are briefly described below.

`tell:` s informs r that the sentence in the message (i.e., the message content) is true of s — that is, the sentence is in the knowledge base of s (i.e., s believes that the content of the message is true);
`ask-if:` s wants to know if the content of the message is true for r;
`ask-all:` s wants all of r's answers to a question;
`ask-how:` s wants all of r's plans for a triggering event;

A *Tell* message might be sent to an agent either as a reply or as an inform action. Either way, before being added to the recipient belief base, the message content is annotated with the sender id and with the ontologies specified in the message. The receiver of an ask_if message will respond to the request for information. The answer should be given in relation to the ontology specified in the ask message. Note that ask_if and ask_all differ basically in the kind of request made to the receiver. With the former, the receiver should just confirm whether the received predicate (in the message content) follows from its belief base and the specified ontology; with the latter, the agent replies with all the predicates in the knowledge base (specified ontology plus belief base) that match the formula in the content of the message. The answer for an ask_how message is a set of all plans that are relevant for a triggering event which constitutes the message content. Note that these relevant plans are collected based on the subsumption relation defined in the ontologies specified in the message.

Ontologies have been considered a fundamental element since the first proposal of communication frameworks such as KQML. The reference to an ontology is a way to make sure that messages are interpreted in a previously agreed context between sender and speaker. From the performatives discussed above we can note that another benefit of combining speech-act based communication with ontologies is that the results of message processing are more expressive, due mainly to the ontological reasoning based on the subsumption relations defined in ontologies.

4 Conclusions and Future Work

We have proposed an extension of the BDI agent-oriented programming language AgentSpeak that facilitates the development of agents that are able to communicate and reason about ontologies. These are important features for context aware agents. The AgentSpeak interpreter ***Jason*** [2] is currently being modified so that it can support the features discussed in this paper. ***Jason*** supports both closed and open-world assumption, and it is possible to run and debug the system in a distributed way over a network. Straightforward extensibility by user-defined internal actions, which are programmed in Java, is also available. To implement the AgentSpeak extension proposed here, ***Jason***'s inference engine needs to be extended to incorporate ontological reasoning, which of course can be done by existing software such as those presented in [10, 11]. We are currently considering the use of RACER [10] for extending ***Jason*** so that belief bases can also be written in OWL. The performatives tell, untell, achieve, and unachieve (amongst various others) have already been implemented. The practical usefulness of combining ontological reasoning and speech act based communication within an agent-oriented programming language for context computing seems quite clear, if we consider the increasing role of ontologies in the semantic web and pervasive computing. Although the semantic web and pervasive computing are still mostly visions for the future, with so much effort begin placed on this by the computer science community, these seem inescapable trends. As intelligent agents are central elements of both visions, languages with underlying ontological reasoning, as we proposed here, will be an important stepping stone towards consolidating those trends.

The language is suitable for the new scenario that pervasive computing applications are bringing about, agents are designed to act based on perceptions provided by the environments, such as the location of services and its availability. The services available may also be matched with specifications of users preferences and intentions.

Traditionally ontology-based systems are not multi-agent systems. The development of languages with support for ontological reasoning and multi-agent ontology based applications will require the use of techniques of ontology merging and ontology matching in order to allow heterogeneous agents to interoperate.

References

1. J. L. Austin. *How to Do Things with Words.* Oxford University Press, London, 1962.
2. R. H. Bordini, J. F. Hübner, and R. Vieira. ***Jason*** and the Golden Fleece of agent-oriented programming. In R. H. Bordini, M. Dastani, J. Dix, and A. El Fallah Seghrouchni, editors, *Multi-Agent Programming*, chapter 1. Springer, 2005.
3. R. H. Bordini and Á. F. Moreira. Proving BDI properties of agent-oriented programming languages: The asymmetry thesis principles in AgentSpeak(L). *Annals of Mathematics and*

Artificial Intelligence, 42(1–3):197–226, Sept. 2004. Special Issue on Computational Logic in Multi-Agent Systems.
4. M. E. Bratman. *Intentions, Plans and Practical Reason.* Harvard University Press, Cambridge, MA, 1987.
5. H. Chen, T. Finin, A. Joshi, F. Perich, D. Chakraborty, , and L. Kagal. Intelligent agents meet the semantic web in smart spaces. *IEEE Internet Computing*, 19(5):69–79, 2004.
6. H. Chen, F. Perich, T. Finin, and A. Joshi. SOUPA: Standard Ontology for Ubiquitous and Pervasive Applications. In *International Conference on Mobile and Ubiquitous Systems: Networking and Services*, Boston, MA, August 2004.
7. Y. Ding, D. Fensel, M. C. A. Klein, B. Omelayenko, and E. Schulten. The role of ontologies in ecommerce. In Staab and Studer [21], pages 593–616.
8. I. Foster and C. Kesselman, editors. *The Grid 2: Blueprint for a New Computing Infrastructure.* Morgan Kaufmann, second edition, 2003.
9. N. Gibbins, S. Harris, and N. Shadbolt. Agent-based semantic web services. *J. Web Sem.*, 1(2):141–154, 2004.
10. V. Haarslev and R. Moller. Description of the RACER system and its applications. In *Proceedings of the International Workshop in Description Logics 2001 (DL'01)*, 2001.
11. I. Horrocks. FaCT and iFaCT. In *Proceedings of the International Workshop on Description Logics (DL'99)*, pages 133–135, 1999.
12. Y. Labrou and T. Finin. A semantics approach for KQML—a general purpose communication language for software agents. In *Proceedings of the Third International Conference on Information and Knowledge Management (CIKM'94).* ACM Press, Nov. 1994.
13. D. L. McGuinness and F. van Harmelen, editors. *OWL Web Ontology Language overview. W3C Recommendation.* Avalilable at http://www.w3.org/TR/owl-features/, February 2004.
14. S. E. Middleton, D. D. Roure, and N. R. Shadbolt. Ontology-based recommender systems. In Staab and Studer [21], pages 577–498.
15. Á. F. Moreira and R. H. Bordini. An operational semantics for a BDI agent-oriented programming language. *Proceedings of the Workshop on Logics for Agent-Based Systems (LABS-02)*, pages 45–59, 2002.
16. Á. F. Moreira, R. Vieira, and R. H. Bordini. Extending the operational semantics of a BDI agent-oriented programming language for introducing speech-act based communication. In *Declarative Agent Languages and Technologies, Proceedings of the First International Workshop (DALT-03)*, LNAI, pages 135–154, Berlin, 2004. Springer-Verlag.
17. A. S. Rao. AgentSpeak(L): BDI agents speak out in a logical computable language. In *Proceedings of the Seventh Workshop on Modelling Autonomous Agents in a Multi-Agent World (MAAMAW'96), 22–25 January, Eindhoven, The Netherlands*, number 1038 in LNAI, pages 42–55, London, 1996. Springer-Verlag.
18. A. S. Rao and M. P. Georgeff. Decision procedures for BDI logics. *Journal of Logic and Computation*, 8(3):293–343, 1998.
19. J. R. Searle. *Speech Acts: An Essay in the Philosophy of Language.* Cambridge University Press, Cambridge, 1969.
20. Y. Shoham. Agent-oriented programming. *Artificial Intelligence*, 60:51–92, 1993.
21. S. Staab and R. Studer, editors. *Handbook on Ontologies.* International Handbooks on Information Systems. Springer, 2004.
22. R. Stevens, C. Wroe, P. W. Lord, and C. A. Goble. Ontologies in bioinformatics. In Staab and Studer [21], pages 635–658.
23. M. Uschold. Where are the semantics in the semantic web? *AI Magazine*, 24(3):25–36, 2003.
24. M. Wooldridge. *Reasoning about Rational Agents.* The MIT Press, Cambridge, MA, 2000.

A Little Respect (for the Role of Common Components in Heuristic Search)

Stephen Chen[1]

1 School of Analytic Studies and Information Technology, York University 4700 Keele Street, Toronto, Ontario M3J 1P3

sychen@yorku.ca

WWW home page: http://www.atkinson.yorku.ca/~sychen

Abstract. A search process implies an exploration of new, unvisited states. This quest to find something new tends to emphasize the processes of change. However, heuristic search is different from random search because features of previous solutions are preserved – even if the preservation of these features is a passive decision. A new parallel simulated annealing procedure is developed that makes some active decisions on which solution features should be preserved. The improved performance of this modified procedure helps demonstrate the beneficial role of common components in heuristic search.

1 Introduction

Heuristic search techniques can be analyzed by focusing on their "search operators" and their "control strategies". A search operator creates new solutions by making some (usually small) changes to existing solutions. All of the remaining aspects of a heuristic search technique can be included as part of its control strategy [15] – which search operator(s) to apply; which solutions to keep, change, or remove; and when to stop.

The role of the (local) search operator is to create a new candidate solution. Depending on the control strategy, (small) random changes may be sufficient. However, search operators should ideally perform two tasks in creating a new solution from the existing solution(s) – identify both the superior solution parts that are worth keeping and the weaker solution parts that should be changed. A search operator that performs these tasks and which produces better than random changes may be able to improve the performance of any control strategy/heuristic search technique that it is used with.

Examples of heuristic search techniques that normally use random search operators are hill climbing and simulated annealing [10]. In hill climbing, random changes are applied (e.g. two-opt swaps for the Travelling Salesman Problem) and

Please use the following format when citing this chapter:

Chen, S., 2006, in IFIP International Federation for Information Processing, Volume 218, Professional Practice in Artificial Intelligence, eds. J. Debenham, (Boston: Springer), pp. 71–80.

the control strategy accepts only improving changes. In simulated annealing, the control strategy accepts non-improving changes probabilistically based on the temperature which is adjusted according to a cooling schedule. Attempts to improve the performance of simulated annealing often focus on finding better cooling schedules [9].

Another heuristic search technique that emphasizes the features of the control strategy over the design of the search operator is tabu search [6]. In tabu search, the control strategy causes escapes from local optima by making certain operations tabu. However, this tabu list of restricted operators is not designed to improve the isolated performance of the search operators. Specifically, tabu search and simulated annealing can use the same search operators [8], so both of these heuristic search techniques are potential beneficiaries of improved search operators.

In the definitions of other heuristic search techniques like genetic algorithms [7], the search operators and the control strategy are both included. The primary search operator for genetic algorithms is crossover, and the three mechanisms of crossover are respect, transmission, and assortment [12]. Although assortment /recombination is seen as the "overt purpose" of crossover [14], respect/the preservation of common components is also an important feature [4]. In particular, this feature can be used to specify which solution parts should be kept – a useful complement to the focus that most search operators have on what to change.

In the meta-heuristic of memetic algorithms [13], it has previously been shown that respect/the preservation of common components can be a beneficial feature [5]. Since the local optima of a globally convex search space share many similar features [2][11], it is reasonable to restart the heuristic search technique in a neighbourhood near good local optima. However, the potential benefits of respect for single-parent search operators has not been analyzed in isolation.

To summarize, it is hypothesized that a search operator will be more effective if it actively performs both tasks of choosing what to keep and choosing what to change. Ideas for how to develop these operators will be taken from genetic algorithms in sections 2 and 3. These ideas will be transferred into simulated annealing in section 4. Experimental results will be developed and presented in sections 5 through 7. These results are discussed in section 8 before conclusions are drawn in section 9.

2 Background

The three primary features of a genetic algorithm (GA) are a population of solutions, fitness-based selection, and the crossover search operator [7]. In crossover, there are three mechanisms: "respect", "transmission", and "assortment" [12]. The principle of respect is that the common components of two parent solutions should be preserved in the offspring. Transmission states that all components in the final offspring should have come from one of the two parents, and assortment is the equivalent of recombination – parents with two non-competing traits should be able to produce an offspring with both features.

The two mechanisms that are unique to multi-parent operators are recombination and respect – it takes multiple parents to have/identify common and uncommon components that can be recombined or preserved. It is generally assumed that the advantage of crossover is its ability to assemble better offspring solutions by combining the superior solution parts of two parents [7][14]. However, attempts to transfer this advantage to other search operators and heuristic search techniques have led to mixed results and comments like "crossover can be compared to the very unpromising effort to recombine animals of different species" [16].

Focusing instead on the mechanism of respect, the Commonality Hypothesis [4] suggests that the advantage of the crossover search operator is its ability to leverage the knowledge accumulated in previous solutions and to use this knowledge as a foundation for further explorations. In particular, it has previously been shown that many combinatorial optimization problems have "globally convex" fitness landscapes that cause the best solutions to share many similarities [2][11]. By transferring respect to general search operators, it should be possible to allow other heuristic search techniques to more effectively explore globally convex fitness landscapes.

3 An Analysis of Respect and Recombination

Before adding respect to a search operator for simulated annealing, it is important to develop a functional model for how this mechanism generates benefits. To start, the performance of one-point, two-point, and uniform crossover are shown for the OneMax problem (where the fitness of a binary string solution is equal to its number of ones). The results presented in figure 1 are for 100 trials of a genetic algorithm with generational replacement where only solutions with a fitness higher than the average fitness of the entire population are allowed to mate.

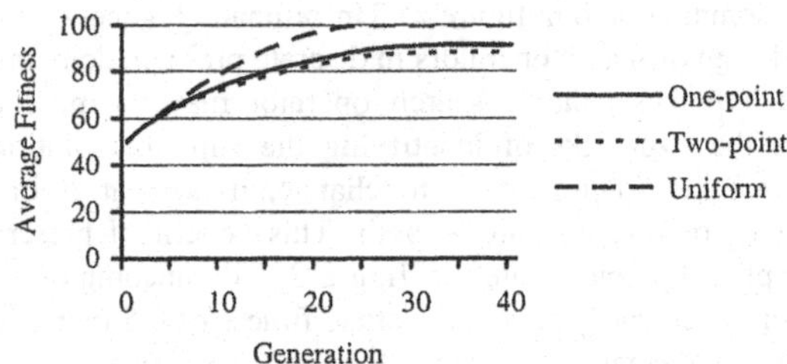

Fig. 1. Results for a 100 bit OneMax problem started from a random population of 100 solutions. 100 generations were used, but all trials converged within 40 generations. Average fitness refers to all solutions in the population and are averaged over 100 trials

One interpretation for the superior performance of uniform crossover is that its larger number of crossing sites allow greater opportunities for recombination.

However, it is shown in figure 2 that the uncommon components being recombined have a below average fitness compared to the solution as a whole and to the above average fitness of the common components preserved by all forms of crossover. In a binary solution space, an uncommon component is necessarily a 1 in one parent and a 0 in the other. Since these uncommon components will have an average fitness of 0.5 (for the OneMax problem), recombination is effectively random search in this instance.

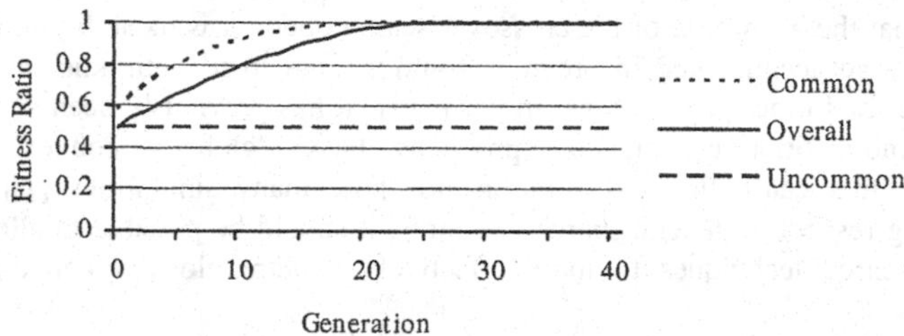

Fig. 2. Results for a 100 bit OneMax problem started from a random population of 100 solutions. 100 generations were used, but all trials converged within 40 generations. Average fitness refers to all solutions in the population and are averaged over 100 trials

An alternative interpretation for the superior performance of uniform crossover is that it is a more efficient search operator than one-point and two-point crossover. Although all three operators preserve common components, uniform crossover searches with the most "unbiasedness" [1]. Focusing on the common components, the concept of "genetic repair" [1] provides a worthy explanation for why the accumulation of common components can be a beneficial part of the search process – these common components (i.e. the population centroid) are fitter than the individual solutions (see the common ratio in figure 2). Unfortunately, genetic repair gives little guidance for the design of search operators in discrete problem domains.

Recalling the hypothesis that a search operator may be more effective if it actively performs the two tasks of identifying the superior solution parts worth keeping and the weaker solution parts to change, it is clear from figure 2 that preserving common components can do both. This benefit of preserving common components is explicitly demonstrated in figure 3. The uncommon components of two parent solutions necessarily have an average fitness of 0.5 (per component), and this will be below the average component fitness of two above-average parents (0.7 in figure 3). Therefore, the average fitness of the remaining common components must be even greater (0.83 in figure 3). The effectiveness of a search operator should benefit from preserving common components because a solution improvement is more likely when changes are applied to the less fit uncommon components.

```
Parent 1:      1 0 1 1 0 1 0 1 1 1
Parent 2:      1 1 0 1 0 1 1 1 0 1

Common:        1     1 0 1   1   1

Uncommon 1:      0 1       0   1
Uncommon 2:      1 0       1   0
```

Fig. 3. In the OneMax problem, an improvement occurs when a 0 is turned into a 1. A random change applied to either parent above leads to an improvement only 30% of the time. However, a "respectful" change that is applied to an uncommon component will lead to an improvement 50% of the time [4]

4 Simulated Annealing and Respect

The control strategy for simulated annealing (SA) is designed to allow probabilistic escapes from local optima. Assuming a minimization objective, the simulated annealing process can be visualized as a ball rolling downhill through a landscape of peaks and valleys. Depending on how much "energy" is in the ball, it has the ability to "bounce out" of local minima. When the temperature/energy approaches zero, the ball will come to rest in a final minimum – ideally the global minimum if the cooling schedule has been slow enough.

This control strategy does not specify how the "ball" will escape from local minima – it can climb any valley wall with equal probability. If local optima are randomly distributed throughout the search space, then this standard implementation of SA will be well suited. However, the local optima for many combinatorial optimization problems exhibit a "big valley" clustering – random local optima are more similar than random solutions, the similarities among local optima increase with their quality, and the global optimum is in the "centre" of the cluster of local optima [2][11].

The standard control strategy for simulated annealing is not as well suited for problems with "big valley" fitness landscapes. When escaping from local minima, simulated annealing makes no attempt to determine if it is climbing an "interior" wall (that is between the current solution and the global optimum) or an "exterior" wall (that is between the current solution and the perimeter of the big valley). (See figure 4.) Although the proof of convergence for simulated annealing does not require this insight, the practical (time-based) performance of an SA implementation may be affected.

Simulated annealing can be modified for big valley fitness landscapes by adding the mechanism of respect from genetic algorithms. Having features from both SA and GA, the new modified procedure is called SAGA. SAGA provides the multiple solutions required by respect to identify common components by using two parallel runs. (See figure 5.) Using an elitist SA approach where the best solution visited during each temperature cycle is used as the starting point for the next temperature cycle, common components are recorded from the best solution of each run.

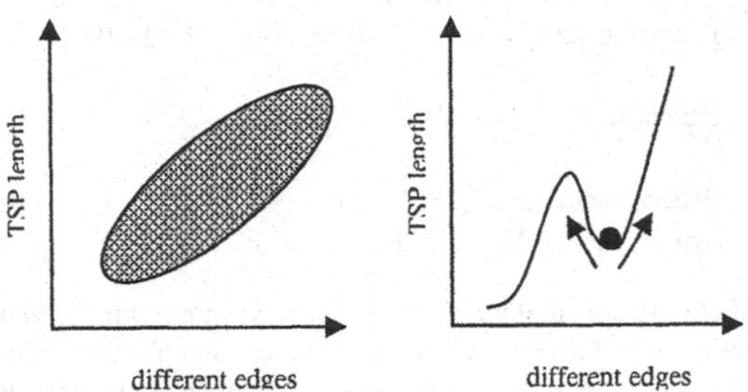

Fig. 4. In a typical distribution of two-opt minima for the TSP, the best solutions have more common edges [2]. When escaping from a local minimum, a change that produces additional different/uncommon edges may be moving away from the better solutions found at the centre of the big valley

The expectation that SAGA will perform better than a normal implementation of simulated annealing is based on the two previous observations. In figure 3, it can be seen that a change applied to an uncommon component is more likely to lead to an improvement. In figure 4a, it is shown that it is undesirable to have a large number of solution differences. By changing components that are already different, a respectful search operator is less likely to create additional solution differences that will lead the search process away from the centre of the big valley.

5 A Base SA Application for the TSP

To better isolate/emphasize the effects of the modified search operator, a relatively simple base SA application for the TSP (BaseSA) was used. BaseSA starts from a random solution, uses a geometric cooling schedule ($\mu = 0.9$) with $n = 500$ temperature cycles, applies two million two-opt swaps per cycle, and returns to the best found solution at the end of each temperature cycle. Since a fixed number of temperature cycles are used, the temperature is not decreased if the best solution does not improve during that cycle. To determine the initial temperature, a preliminary set of 50 two-opt swaps is used where only improving steps are accepted. At the end of this set, the initial temperature starts at the average length of the attempted backward steps divided by ln(0.5) (i.e. an average backward step has a 50% chance of being accepted).

```
   SAGA procedure
1  Begin
2    create initial random solution A
3    create initial random solution B
4    set initial temperature
5    For i = 1 to n
6      record common components of solutions A and B
7      For j = 1 to m
8        apply search operator to solution A
9        apply search operator to solution B
10     End
11     set solution A to best solution for A since line 6
12     set solution B to best solution for B since line 6
13     update temperature
14   End
15   return best of solution A or B
```

Fig. 5. Pseudocode for SAGA. The two parallel runs (A and B) use the same cooling schedule. Information on common components is shared on line 6 before each temperature cycle (lines 7-10). See sections 5 and 6 for the values of n and m

6 Developing SAGA for the TSP

SAGA has been developed for the TSP by using two parallel runs of BaseSA. Each instance of BaseSA uses all of the above parameters except that only m = 1,000,000 two-opt swaps are now used during each annealing stage. This modification ensures that SAGA uses the same overall number of two-opt swaps (and thus a similar amount of computational effort) as the benchmark implementation of BaseSA.

A two-opt swap changes two edges in a (single) solution. To implement the mechanism of respect so that common components can be preserved, SAGA records the common edges of the two parallel BaseSA runs at the beginning of each temperature cycle (see figure 5). The respectful two-opt operator will then select one uncommon edge and one random edge (which could be either common or uncommon). This preference to change uncommon components will help preserve common components which should help direct the overall search process towards the centre of the "big valley" of local minima.

The only parametric difference between SAGA and BaseSA is an additional parameter to specify how often to apply the respectful two-opt operator versus the standard two-opt operator. This parameter was chosen from the 11 probabilities shown in table 1 by conducting a set of tuning experiments on PCB442. Measuring the percent difference above the known optimal for the final solution in ten SAGA trials, it was determined that the respectful two-opt operator should be used 90% of the time (with random two-opt swaps being used for the remaining 10%). This parameter is used in all of the experiments presented in section 7.

The results of the above tuning experiments also indicate that the improvements in SAGA are not due strictly to the use of two parallel runs – a result that is more fully explored in [3]. With a 0% probability of using the respectful two-opt operator, SAGA is essentially two (smaller and less effective) independent runs of BaseSA. Compared to these two independent runs, the performance of SAGA tends to improve with the increased use respect. The key exception to this trend is for a probability of 100%. It appears that SAGA benefits from divergent changes just like traditional genetic algorithms benefit from mutation.

Table 1. Probability that the first-edge is specifically selected to be an uncommon edge. Values represent average percentage above optimal for 10 SAGA trials – n = 300 cycles, 60 million total two-opt swaps. Average performance of 10 BaseSA trials is provided for comparison

Probability	PCB442
0.0	4.21
0.1	3.60
0.2	3.92
0.3	3.68
0.4	3.76
0.5	3.49
0.6	3.01
0.7	3.17
0.8	3.08
0.9	**2.79**
1.0	3.40
BaseSA	3.79

7 Experiments

Using the above parameters, thirty trials of BaseSA and SAGA were each run on 5 test TSP instances (dsj1000, d1291, fl1400, fl1577, and pr2392). The results for the experiments are shown in table 2. The respectful two-opt operator in SAGA has led to consistent and significant improvements compared to the benchmark implementation of BaseSA.

It is important to note that only the relative results or differential performance should be considered from the above experiments. A rather simple control strategy was used in BaseSA to help isolate/emphasize the effects of the search operator. As a controlled parameter, any strengths or weaknesses in the basic operation of BaseSA should be reflected equally in the performance of both BaseSA and SAGA. Therefore, the superior performance of SAGA as compared to BaseSA is a clear demonstration of the benefits of respect.

Table 2. Average percentage above optimal for 30 trials of BaseSA and SAGA with one billion total two-opt swaps performed. One-tailed t-tests show that the chance of the SAGA results being the same as the BaseSA results is less than 0.01% for all five instances

Instance	BaseSA		SAGA	
	avg.	std. dev.	avg.	std. dev.
dsj1000	4.54	0.74	2.27	0.39
d1291	8.87	1.41	3.12	1.12
fl1400	3.07	1.04	2.00	0.88
fl1577	6.47	1.58	0.64	0.55
pr2392	9.24	1.37	6.53	0.56

8 Discussion

A heuristic search technique is defined by its search operator(s) and its control strategy. Some are defined almost exclusively by their control strategy (e.g. hill climbing, simulated annealing [10], and tabu search [6]). In these cases where there are relatively few restriction placed on the search operator, a new design model for search operators represents a broad opportunity to improve the performance of many implementations. The proposed design model suggests that the performance of a search operator (and of the heuristic search technique that uses it) can be improved if it preserves common components and focuses its changes on the uncommon components.

The role of common components has been examined under many situations (e.g. in crossover operators [12] and memetic algorithms [5][13]). However, all of these previous situations involve populations of solutions, and the effects of preserving common components have not always been considered as favourable (e.g. premature convergence in genetic algorithms). The new model for search operators appears to be unique in that it applies respect to a (nominally) single-parent operator.

It is interesting to note that the respectful search operator would not likely be accepted as a crossover operator since it does not use the mechanism of assortment/recombination. For example, imagine a two-parent operator where an offspring is created by making a random mutation to an uncommon component. The offspring would not be a recombination of the parent components and nothing would have "crossed over" between them, so the respectful search operator would not be a recombination/crossover operator. Since the crossover search operator is a defining feature of genetic algorithms [7][14], the new model for search operators may be more suitable to evolution strategies where it appears that nothing similar to the new respectful search operators has been used [1].

9 Conclusions

The difference between heuristic search and random search is that heuristic search exploits/preserves some information from previous solutions. The proposed model for respectful search operators suggests that in globally convex search spaces, these preserved components should be common components. A search operator that changes uncommon components can have a better than random chance of finding an improvement, and this increased effectiveness in the search operator may be able to improve the overall performance of a heuristic search technique.

References

1. Beyer, H.-G., Schwefel, H.-P.: Evolution Strategies: A comprehensive introduction. In Natural Computing, Vol. 1 (2002) 3-52
2. Boese, K.D.: Models for Iterative Global Optimization. Ph.D. diss., Computer Science Department, University of California at Los Angeles (1996)
3. Chen, S., Pitt, G.: The Coordination of Parallel Search with Common Components. In LNCS, Vol. 3533: Proceedings of the 18th International Conference on Industrial and Engineering Applications of Artificial Intelligence and Expert Systems. (2005)
4. Chen, S., Smith, S.F.: Introducing a New Advantage of Crossover: Commonality-Based Selection. In GECCO-99: Proceedings of the Genetic and Evolutionary Computation Conference. Morgan Kaufmann (1999)
5. Chen, S., Smith, S.F.: Putting the "Genetics" back into Genetic Algorithms (Reconsidering the Role of Crossover in Hybrid Operators). In Banzhaf, W., Reeves, C. (eds.): Foundations of Genetic Algorithms 5. Morgan Kaufmann (1999) 103-116
6. Glover, F.: Tabu search Part I. In Operations Research Society of America (ORSA) Journal on Computing, Vol. 1 (1989) 109-206
7. Holland, J.: Adaptation in Natural and Artificial Systems. The U. of Michigan Press (1975)
8. Hoos, H.H., Stützle, T.: Local Search Algorithms for SAT: An Empirical Evaluation. In Journal of Automated Reasoning, Vol. 24 (2000) 421 - 481
9. Johnson, D.S., McGeoch, L.A.: The Traveling Salesman Problem: A Case Study in Local Optimization. In Aarts, E.H.L., Lenstra, J.K. (eds.): Local Search in Combinatorial Optimization. John Wiley and Sons (1997) 215-310
10. Kirkpatrick, S., Gelatt Jr., C.D., Vecchi, M.P.: Optimization by Simulated Annealing. In Science, Vol. 220 (1983) 671-680
11. Mühlenbein, H.: Evolution in Time and Space – The Parallel Genetic Algorithm. In: Rawlins, G. (ed.): Foundations of Genetic Algorithms. Morgan Kaufmann (1991)
12. Radcliffe, N.J.: Forma Analysis and Random Respectful Recombination. In Proceedings of the Fourth International Conference on Genetic Algorithms. Morgan Kaufmann (1991)
13. Radcliffe, N.J., Surry, P.D. Formal memetic algorithms. In: Fogarty, T.C. (ed.): Evolutionary Computing: AISB Workshop. Springer-Verlag (1994)
14. Syswerda, G: Uniform Crossover in Genetic Algorithms. In Proceedings of the Third International Conference on Genetic Algorithms. Morgan Kaufmann (1989)
15. Talukdar, S.N., de Souza, P.: Scale Efficient Organizations. In Proceedings of 1992 IEEE International Conference on Systems, Man and Cybernetics (1992)
16. Wendt, O., König, W.: Cooperative Simulated Annealing: How much cooperation is enough? Technical Report, No. 1997-3, School of Information Systems and Information Economics at Frankfurt University (1997)

Recursive and Iterative Algorithms for N-ary Search Problems

Valery Sklyarov, Iouliia Skliarova
University of Aveiro, Department of Electronics and Telecommunications/IEETA, 3810-193 Aveiro, Portugal
skl@det.ua.pt, iouliia@det.ua.pt
WWW home page: http://www.ieeta.pt/~skl
http://www.ieeta.pt/~iouliia/

Abstract. The paper analyses and compares alternative iterative and recursive implementations of N-ary search algorithms in hardware (in field programmable gate arrays, in particular). The improvements over the previous results have been achieved with the aid of the proposed novel methods for the fast implementation of hierarchical algorithms. The methods possess the following distinctive features: 1) providing sub-algorithms with multiple entry points; 2) fast stack unwinding for exits from recursive sub-algorithms; 3) hierarchical returns based on two alternative approaches; 4) rational use of embedded memory blocks for the design of a hierarchical finite state machine.

1 Introduction

Adaptive control systems (ACS) are capable to change their functionality without modifying physical components. In general this can be achieved with the aid of reprogrammable devices such as field programmable gate arrays (FPGA). A method for the design of ACS on the basis of hierarchical finite state machines (HFSM) was proposed in [1] and it makes possible to realize modular and hierarchical specifications of control algorithms based on such alternative techniques as iterative and recursive implementations [2]. It was shown that recursive implementations are more advantageous in hardware in terms of the execution time although they might require slightly more FPGA resources. This paper suggests further advances in scope of hierarchical, in general, and recursive, in particular, specifications (as well as the relevant implementations) and presents new arguments in favor of the results [1,2].

There exists a technique [3] that enables recursion to be implemented in hardware through establishing a special control sequence provided by a hierarchical finite state machine. The paper shows that the efficiency of this technique can be significantly improved through the use of the following novel methods: 1) supporting

---

Please use the following format when citing this chapter:

Sklyarov, V., Skliarova, I., 2006, in IFIP International Federation for Information Processing, Volume 218, Professional Practice in Artificial Intelligence, eds. J. Debenham, (Boston: Springer), pp. 81–90.

multiple entry points to sub-algorithms that are called recursively; 2) employing a fast unwinding procedure for stacks used as an HFSM memory; 3) establishing flexible hierarchical returns; 4) the rational use of embedded memory blocks for the design of HFSM stacks.

The remainder of this paper is organized in four sections. Section 2 discusses N-ary search problems that can be solved using either iterative or recursive techniques. Section 3 characterizes known results for the specification and implementation of hierarchical algorithms and suggests four methods for their improvement. Section 4 describes the experiments. The conclusion is in Section 5.

2 N-ary Search Problems

Computational algorithms for many search problems are based on generation and exhaustive examination of all possible solutions until a solution with the desired quality is found. The primary decision to be taken in this approach is how to generate the candidate solutions effectively. A widely accepted answer to this question consists of constructing an N-ary search tree [4], which enables all possible solutions to be generated in a well-structured and efficient way. The root of the tree is considered to be the starting point that corresponds to the initial situation. The other nodes represent various situations that can be reached during the search for results. The arcs of the tree specify steps of the algorithm. At the beginning the tree is empty and it is incrementally constructed during the search process.

A distinctive feature of this approach is that at each node of the search tree a similar sequence of algorithmic steps has to be executed. Thus, either iterative or recursive procedures can be applied [2]. The only thing that is different from node to node is input data. This means that the entire problem reduces to the execution of a large number of repeated operations over a sequentially modified set of data.

Of course, exhaustive checking all possible solutions cannot be used for the majority of practical problems because it requires a very long execution time. That is why it is necessary to apply some optimization techniques that reduce the number of situations that need to be considered. In order to speed up getting the results various tree-pruning techniques can be applied.-

The other known method of improving the effectiveness of the search is a reduction [5], which permits the current situation to be replaced with some new simpler situation without sacrificing any feasible solution. However, reduction is not possible for all existing situations. In this case another method is used that relies on the divide-and-conquer strategy [4]. This applies to critical situations that have to be divided into N several simpler situations such that each of them has to be examined. The objective is to find the minimum number N.

Thus, an N-ary search problem can be solved by executing the following steps:

1. Applying reduction rules.
2. Verifying intermediate results, which permits to execute one of the following three sub-steps:
    2.1. Pruning the current branch of the algorithms and backtracking to the nearest branching point;
    2.2. Storing the current solution in case if this solution is the best;
    2.3. Sequential executing the points 3 and 4.

3. Applying selection rules (dividing the problem into sub-problems and selecting one of them).
4. Executing either the point 4.1 (for iterative algorithm) or the point 4.2 (for recursive algorithm).
   4.1. Executing the next iteration (see points 1-4) over the sub-problem.
   4.2. Recursive invocation of the same algorithm (see points 1-4) over the sub-problem.

Thus, either an iterative (see points 1-3, 4.1) or a recursive (see points 1-3, 4.2) algorithm can be executed and it is important to know which one is better.

Let us consider another example. Fig. 1 depicts a system, which receives messages from an external source. The messages have to be buffered and processed sequentially according to their priority. Each incoming message changes the sequence, because it has to be inserted in a proper position.

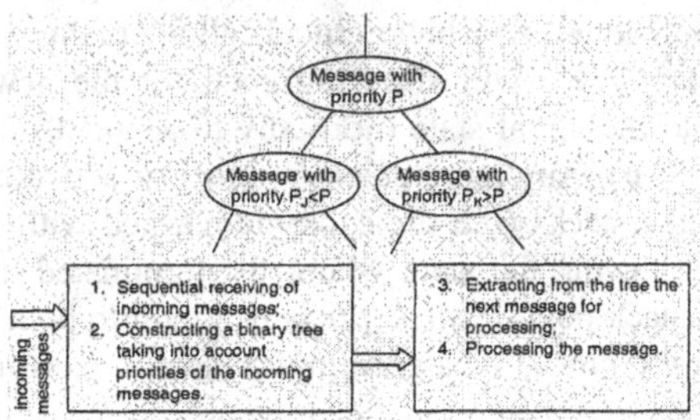

Fig. 1. Example of an adaptive embedded system

Let us assume that the following strategy is applied. All incoming messages are accommodated on a binary tree (N=2) whose nodes contain three fields that are: a pointer to the left child node, a pointer to the right child node, and the message identification, which is used to activate the respective processing procedure. The nodes are maintained so that at any node, the left sub-tree contains only messages that are less priority-driven (i.e. the messages that have smaller priority) than the message at the node, and the right sub-tree contains only messages that are more priority-driven. It is known that such a tree can be constructed and used for sorting various types of data [6] and for our particular example we can sort messages according to their priority. In order to build the tree for a given set of messages, we have to find the appropriate place for each incoming node in the current tree. In order to sort the messages, we can apply a special technique [6] using forward and backward propagation steps that are exactly the same for each node.

In case of modular specification the algorithm can easily be modified to change the sequence of processing. For example, messages with priorities less than some given value can be ignored; priorities can be flexibly changed dependently on some other external conditions, etc. Such changes do not require redesigning the complete algorithm and just a module responsible for task 2 in Fig. 1 has to be altered.

It is very important to note that hierarchical algorithms, in general, and recursive algorithms, in particular, can be very efficiently used for solving such problems and it was shown and proven in [2].

3 Specification and Implementation of Hierarchical Algorithms

3.1 Known Results

It is known [3] that hierarchical algorithms can be constructed from modules with the aid of the language called hierarchical graph-schemes (HGS). Recursion is provided through invocations of the same module. An HFSM permits execution of HGSs [3] and contains two stacks (see Fig. 2), one for states (*FSM_stack*) and the other for modules (*M_stack*). The stacks are managed by a *combinational circuit* (CC) that is responsible for new module invocations and state transitions in any active module that is designated by outputs of the *M_stack*. Since each particular module has a unique code, the same HFSM states can be repeated in different modules. Fig. 2 demonstrates how the HFSM executes an algorithm. Any non-hierarchical transition is performed through a change of a code only on the top register of the *FSM_stack* (see the example marked with •). Any hierarchical call alters the states of both stacks in such a way that the *M_stack* will store the code for the new module and the *FSM_stack* will be set to the initial state (normally to a_0=0…0) of the module (see the example marked with ■). Any hierarchical return just activates a pop operation without any change in the stacks (see the example marked with ♦). As a result, a transition to the state following the state where the terminated module was called will be performed. The stack pointer *stack_ptr* is common to both stacks. If the *End* node is reached when *stack_ptr*=0, the algorithm terminates execution.

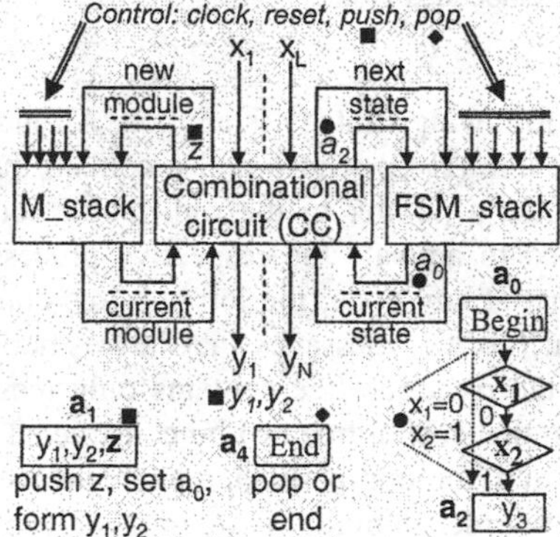

Fig. 2. Functionality of a hierarchical FSM

3.2 Novel Methods

Section 1 lists the proposed innovative facilities for HGSs and HFSMs. This subsection provides detailed explanations of these facilities augmented by examples that are illustrated through synthesizable **V**ery **H**igh Speed Integrated Circuits **H**ardware **D**escription **L**anguage (VHDL) specifications.

3.2.1. Providing Multiple Entry Points to Sub-algorithms

Fig. 3 demonstrates a fragment of a recursive sorting algorithm discussed in [2]. The two stacks used in a HFSM (such as depicted in Fig. 2) can be described in VHDL as follows (subscripts, such as 0 in a_0, are not allowed in VHDL but they have been used to provide consistency between VHDL codes and the relevant figures and textual descriptions):

```
process(clock,reset)                              (1)
begin
   if reset = '1' then
       -- setting to an initial state and initializing
       -- if reset is active
    elsif rising_edge(clock) then
        if hierarchical_call = '1' then
          if -- test for possible errors
          else
              sp <= sp + 1;
              FSM_stack(sp+1) <= a0;           -- ref1
              FSM_stack(sp)  <= NS;
              M_stack(sp+1)  <= NM;
          end if;
        elsif hierarchical_return = '1' then
          sp <= sp - 1;                          -- ref2
        else      FSM_stack(sp) <= NS;
        end if;
   end if;
end process;
```

Here any module invocation/termination is indicated through a signal *hierarchical_call/hierarchical_return*; *sp* is a common stack pointer; *NS/NM* is a new state/module, a_0 is an initial state of each module. Indicators *ref1*, *ref2* will be used for future references.

The combinational circuit (CC) in Fig. 2 has the following skeletal code (template):

```
process (current_module,current_state,inputs)    (2)
begin
   case M_stack(sp) is
      when z1 =>
          case FSM_stack(sp) is
             -- state transitions in the module z1
             -- generating outputs for the module z1
          end case;
       -- repeating for all modules, which might exist
   end case;
end process;
```

As we can see from Fig. 3 any hierarchical module invocation, such as that is done in the node a_2, activates the same algorithm once again, starting from the node *Begin* (a_0). Skipping the node a_0 removes one clock cycle from any hierarchical call. However in this case the algorithm in Fig. 3 must have multiple entry points and a particular entry point will be chosen by the group of rhomboidal nodes enclosed in an ellipse. This possibility is provided by the additional tests performed in the nodes with hierarchical calls (such as a_2 and a_3 in Fig. 3). The following fragment demonstrates how these tests can be coded in VHDL for the state a_2.

```
when a2 => -- generating outputs and the signal
        -- hierarchical_call
    NM<=z1;
    if x3='1' then  NM_FS <= a1;  -- this is because
    -- x1 cannot be equal to 1 after the state a2
    elsif x2 ='0' then NM_FS <= a5;
    elsif x4 ='0' then NM_FS <= a2;
    else NM_FS <= a3;
    end if;
```

Here *NM_FS* is the first state of the next module. The line *ref1* in (1) has to be changed as follows:

```
FSM_stack(sp+1) <= NM_FS;
```

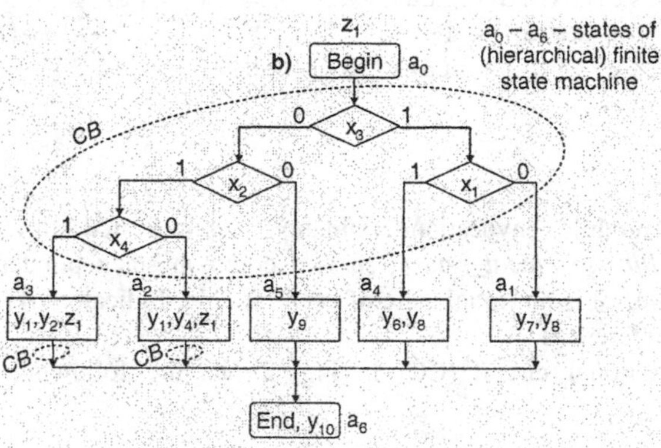

Fig. 3. HGS with multiple entry points provided through inserting the control block (CB) in the nodes with hierarchical calls

3.2.2. Fast Stack Unwinding

Since there is just the node *End* after a_2 and a_3, hierarchical activation of any one of the nodes a_1, a_4, a_5 (see Fig. 3) leads to termination of the algorithm. To implement this termination in [2] the lines in (1)

```
if hierarchical_return = '1' then
        sp <= sp - 1;
```

are executed repeatedly until the pointer *sp* receives the value assigned at the beginning of the algorithm (see the line `if reset = '1'` in (1) for our example). In the general case, this value is assigned during the first call of the respective module (such as that depicted in Fig. 3) followed by subsequent recursive invocations of the module. Repeated execution of the line `sp <= sp - 1;` requires multiple additional clock cycles. To eliminate these redundant clock cycles the proposed method of fast stack unwinding is employed. The line *ref2* in (1) is changed as follows:

```
sp <= sp - unwinding;
```

where the signal *unwinding* is calculated as

```
unwinding <= sp - saved_sp + 1;
```

and `saved_sp <= sp` at the first invocation of the module. Thus, redundant clock cycles for hierarchical returns will be avoided.

3.2.3. Execution of Hierarchical Returns

Hierarchical calls in [2] are carried out as follows:

```
if hierarchical_call = '1' then
        -- error handling
    sp <= sp + 1;
    FSM_stack(sp+1) <= a0;
    FSM_stack(sp) <= NS; -- ***
    M_stack(sp+1) <= NM;
```

The line indicated by asterisks sets the code of the next state during a hierarchical call. As a result, after a hierarchical return the top register of the *FSM_stack* contains the code of the proper HFSM state (i.e. no additional clock cycle is required). Since the next state is determined before the invocation of a module (such as z_1), the latter cannot affect the state transition, i.e. any possible change of the conditions x_1-x_4 in z_1 cannot alter the previously defined next state. For our example this does not create a problem. However, for many practical applications it is a problem and it must be resolved. The following code gives one possible solution:

```
if rising_edge(clock) then
       if hierarchical_call = '1' then
           -- error handling
               sp <= sp + 1;
               FSM_stack(sp+1) <= NM_FS;
               M_stack(sp+1) <= NM;
```

After a hierarchical return from *NM*, the code above sets *FSM_stack* to the state where the hierarchical call of *NM* was executed. This enables us to provide correct transitions to the next state because all logic conditions that might be changed in the called module *NM* have already received the proper values. However, this gives rise to another problem; namely it is necessary to avoid repeating invocation of the same module *NM* and iterant output signals. The following code overcomes the problem:

```
if rising_edge(clock) then                          (3)
      if hierarchical_call = '1' then
          -- error handling
              sp <= sp + 1;
              FSM_stack(sp+1) <= NM_FS;
              M_stack(sp+1) <= NM;
      elsif hierarchical_return = '1' then
          sp <= sp - 1;
          return_flag <= '1';
      else       FSM_stack(sp) <= NS;
                    return_flag <= '0';
      end if;
```

The signal *return_flag* permits module invocation and output operations to be activated during a hierarchical call and to be avoided during a hierarchical return. Indeed, the *return_flag* is equal to 1 only in a clock cycle when the signal *sp* is decremented (see the code (3) above). As soon as the currently active module is being terminated, the control flow will be returned to the point from which this module was called. Thus, the top of the *M_stack* will contain the code of the calling module and the top of the *FSM_stack* will store the code of the calling state. The *return_flag* enables us to eliminate the second call of the same module (and the second activation of the relevant output signals). This is achieved with the aid of the following lines that have to be inserted in the code (2):

```
when state_with_module_call => NS <=
                    -- testing the conditions and
                    -- computation of the next state
   if return_flag = '0' then
     hierarchical_call <= '1';
     -- specifying outputs
     NM <= -- assigning the next module
       else
          hierarchical_call <= '0';
          outputs <= (others => '0');
   end if;
```

Finally, the proposed technique permits logic conditions to be tested after terminating the called module, which might alter these conditions.

3.2.4. Using Embedded Memory Blocks

Synthesis of HFSMs from the specifications considered above has shown that stack memories (see Fig. 2) are very resource consuming. However, for implementing the functionality (1) embedded memory blocks can be used (such as that are available for FPGAs [1]). It should be noted that the majority of recent microelectronic devices offered on the market either include embedded memory blocks (such as FPGAs with block RAMs) or allow these blocks to be used.

4. Implementation Details and the Results of Experiments

Alternative iterative and recursive implementations for various problems were analyzed and compared in [2]. Two types of recursive calls were examined, namely for cyclic and binary (N-ary) search algorithms. The relevant comparative data were analyzed through modeling in software and synthesis and implementation in hardware from system-level (Handel-C) and RTL (VHDL) specifications. One of the results was the following: using recursive algorithms in hardware for problems of N-ary search seems to be more advantageous comparably with iterative implementations.

This paper suggests methods for further improvements of the results [2], which makes possible to demonstrate new advantages of recursive algorithms over iterative algorithms. The first column of Table 1 lists HFSMs for the problems P_1, P_3 and P_4 considered in [2] and for each of them shows the results of different implementations, where N_s is the number of the occupied FPGA slices and N_{clock} is the number of the required clock cycles. Note that the maximum allowed clock frequency, obtained with the aid of implementation tools, is practically the same for all columns related to the same problem.

Table 1. The results of experiments with HFSMs

Problem from [2]	N_s/N_{clock}			
	Implementation [3]	Block RAM	Distributed RAM	Multiple entries for [3]
P_1	192/72	50/72	53/72	189/59
P_3	68/62	17/62	19/62	67/51
P_4	49/11	15/11	16/11	47/9

Analysis of Table 1 demonstrates significant advantages of the proposed methods. Note that block and distributed RAM can also be used for synthesis from HGSs with multiple entry points. This gives nearly the same number of slices as for the columns *Block RAM* and *Distributed RAM*. Thus, combining different methods proposed in this paper permits to achieve the best results.

Table 2 lists the same examples P_1, P_3, P_4 that have been considered in [2] and shows (comparing with [2]) the percentage reduction in either hardware resources (FPGA slices) for the columns marked with N_s, or the number of clock cycles for the columns marked with N_{clock}. All the conditions for providing experiments are the same as in [2]. The synthesis and implementation of circuits from specification in VHDL were done in Xilinx ISE 8.1 for xc2s400e-6ft256 FPGA (Spartan-IIE family of Xilinx) available on the prototyping board TE-XC2Se [7]. Note once again that advantages of all columns (i.e. *Block RAM*, *Distributed RAM* and *Multiple entries*) can be combined. For example, considering for the problem P_1 HGSs with multiple entry points and using block RAMs for the implementation of HFSM enable us to decrease resources in 24% and reduce the number of cycles in 18%. Hence, in addition to comparison performed in [2], the results of this paper present further advantages which can be gained for modular algorithms in general, and recursive algorithms in particular over non-modular iterative implementations.

Table 2. Experiments with examples from [2]

Problem from [2]	N_s/N_{clock} (%)		
	Block RAM	Distributed RAM	Multiple entries
P_1	24/0	24/0	0/18
P_3	12/0	12/0	0/5
P_4	7/0	7/0	0/4

5 Conclusion

In this paper alternative recursive and iterative implementations of algorithms for N-ary search problems have been analyzed. Such algorithms are frequently used for describing functionality of adaptive control systems. From the results of [2] we can conclude that recursive implementations are more advantageous in hardware in terms of the execution time although they might require slightly more FPGA resources. The paper suggests four methods for further improvements in the specification, synthesis and hardware implementation of hierarchical, in general, and recursive, in particular, algorithms. To clarify their use in practical projects many useful fragments of synthesizable VHDL code are presented. The experiments described in the paper have proven significant advantages of the proposed methods comparing with other known results.

References

[1] V. Sklyarov, Models, Methods and Tools for Synthesis and FPGA-based Implementation of Advanced Control Systems, Proceedings of ICOM'05, Kuala Lumpur, Malaysia, 2005, pp. 1122-1129

[2] V. Sklyarov, I. Skliarova, and B. Pimentel, FPGA-based implementation and comparison of recursive and iterative algorithms, Proceeding of FPL'2005, Tampere, Finland, 2005, pp. 235-240.

[3] V. Sklyarov, Hierarchical Finite-State Machines and Their Use for Digital Control, *IEEE Transactions on VLSI Systems*, vol. 7, no 2, pp. 222-228, 1999.

[4] I. Skliarova and A.B. Ferrari, The Design and Implementation of a Reconfigurable Processor for Problems of Combinatorial Computation, *Journal of Systems Architecture*, Special Issue on Reconfigurable Systems, vol. 49, nos. 4-6, 2003, pp. 211-226.

[5] A.D. Zakrevski, *Logical Synthesis of Cascade Networks* (Moscow: Science, 1981).

[6] B.W. Kernighan and D.M. Ritchie, *The C Programming Language* (Prentice Hall, 1988).

[7] Spartan-IIE Development Platform, Available at: www.trenz-electronic.de.

PROCESS OF ONTOLOGY CONSTRUCTION FOR THE DEVELOPMENT OF AN INTELLIGENT SYSTEM FOR THE ORGANIZATION AND RETRIEVAL OF KNOWLEDGE IN BIODIVERSITY – SISBIO

Filipe Corrêa da Costa[1]; Hugo Cesar Hoeschl[1], Aires José Rover[1], Tânia Cristina D'Agostini Bueno [2]

[1] Research Institute on e-Gov, Juridical Intelligence and Systems – IJURIS, [2] WBSA Intelligent Systems S.A

{filipe, hudo, tania}@ijuris.org; aires.rover@gmail.com

http://www.ijuris.org

ABSTRACT: This work describes the ontology construction process for the development of an Intelligent System for the Organization and Retrieval of Knowledge in Biodiversity – SISBIO. The system aims at the production of strategic information for the biofuel chain Two main methodologies are used for the construction of the ontologies: knowledge engineering and ontology engineering. The first one consists of extracting and organizing the biofuel specialists′ knowledge, and ontology engineering is used to represent the knowledge through indicative expressions and its relations, developing a semantic network of relationships.

KEY WORDS: Ontologies, Knowledge Engineering, Ontology engineering, Bio-fuel

1. INTRODUCTION

The matter of energy has always been extremely important in the history of humanity. From craft production to the strong industrialization process, along with transportation and other uses, energy is an essential element for the development of the great powers of the world and is a limiting factor for the developing countries. For Sawin, "everything that we consume or use – our homes, their content, our cars and the highways on which we drive, our clothes and the food that we eat – require energy to be produced and packaged, delivered to the stores or homes, operated and then discarded" [1].

Market expansion caused by the strong industrialization process, the huge population growth and concentration, the military disputes, the forecasts of

Please use the following format when citing this chapter:

da Costa, F.C., Hoeschl, H.C., Rover, A.J., D'Agostini Bueno, T.C., 2006, in IFIP International Federation for Information Processing, Volume 218, Professional Practice in Artificial Intelligence, eds. J. Debenham, (Boston: Springer), pp. 91–100.

future lack of natural resources and globalisation, lead to an excessive consume of energy, elevating its value considerably. These factors, increased by the predominant use of fossil fuels, cause severe economic, social and environmental problems, i.e. the greenhouse effect and climate changes.

In this context, the production of biofuel became an effective way to improve the diversification of the energetic matrix, contributing for the preservation of the environment and the economic and social development. For this, it is necessary to establish mechanisms of support to the production and commercialisation of biofuel. It will only be possible through the production of strategic information that will help in variables such as the optimisation of resources, integration of public and private institutions and rural producers. This information must be reliable, and studies must be made to guarantee the juridical, environmental, social, technical and commercial viability and a knowledge management process becomes necessary.

The use of correct information is one of the best ways to manage natural resources in a sustainable way, and is an important instrument in the decision-making processes. In a globalised world characterised by the excess of digital documents, information technology is rapidly evolving and is providing applications for many knowledge domains. In Brazil, although there are many scientific studies and some financing mechanisms, there is no structure able to provide reliable information and integrate the many agents that take part in the biofuel chain. Biofuels have differentiated productive chains and very specific characteristics. In the chain of biodiesel, for example, we must take into consideration factors related to agriculture, storage, characterization and quality control, co-production and, finally, commercialization and distribution themselves. Another example, is the natural gas chain, that goes through the stages of exploration, exploitation, production, processing, transportation, storage and distribution.

For the visualization and conception of SISBIO model- Intelligent System for the Organization and Knowledge Retrieval in Biodiversity, bio-business was defined in the area of biofuel as the development of fuel from natural renewable resources, bringing about economic, social and environmental benefits at a local, regional and global level. In order to be characterized as a bio-business, this product must have some type of relationship with some sector (biofuel), an element (raw material) and an asset (biodiesel or solar energy).

In this sense, the present work intends to demonstrate that it is possible, through the development of an intelligent system for the organization and retrieval of knowledge in biofuel, to ally the concepts of socio-economic development and environment preservation, through the foment of biofuel along its chain.

SISBIO has its linguistic development based on ontologies, providing a more efficient and precise retrieval of relevant information.

The term ontology, often used in philosophy, is used here as a knowledge representation structure that aims at the sharing of knowledge from a domain between people and systems. In this sense, ontologies are used to bring a common understanding of a certain domain through the relation between words or indicative expressions that represent a context. They are used in the construction of Knowledge Based Systems (KBS).

The construction of ontologies enables a better performance of the system, mainly in the precision and contextualization of the search results. Comparing to key-work search, a system that uses ontologies has a great advantage, mainly when longer texts are inserted in the search field. Using ontologies, we can affirm that the longer the text, the better the results are and in the case of SISBIO, it is possible to enter texts up to 15.000 words. This performance is achieved because when knowledge is represented based on ontologies, the system is able to search using the context of the entry text and not only key-words and logic expressions.

The area of application of this work is the construction of an ontologies network for the development of SISBIO, enabling the identification of potential business related to the biofuel chain.

The conceptual development of SISBIO is described in the second section. The methodologies and techniques applied in the construction of the ontologies are presented in section 3, and some conclusions are discussed in section 4.

2. INTELLIGENT SYSTEM FOR THE ORGANIZATION AND RETRIEVAL OF KNOWLEDGE IN BIODIVERSITY – SISBIO

SISBIO software –Intelligent System for the Organization and Retrieval of Knowledge in Biodiversity, provides institutions, rural producers and investors an immediate access to relevant information for the decision making process. The system is able to generate dynamic reports and extract hidden knowledge from a database. It uses a methodology that enables the organization of information stored in structured and non-structured bases, generating extremely relevant knowledge for governmental institutions, rural producers and investors. Apart from producing, integrating and processing a big amount of relevant information, it also creates a relationship network among the agents that constitute a bio-business.

SISBIO is a system developed to organize knowledge and produce strategic information for the monitoring and decision-making processes. It is based on Artificial Intelligence, Knowledge Engineering and Ontology techniques, which enables the integration of structured databases – i.e. a table with graphs – with results from the processing of non-structured data, such as reports, dissertations, and theses among others.

It was developed to take care of the informational and organizational needs of the knowledge of the biofuel chain agents, besides stimulating the relationship between them. Its structure can be coordinated by an agricultural cooperative, organization of enterprise entities, such as the National Confederation of Industries - CNI, or even, something that would be more strategic, to be coordinated by some ministry of the federal government.

With the development and implementation of SISBIO, it will be possible to foment public and private investments for the sustainable use of the natural resources. This model based on knowledge will assist in the creation of an only database, fed by diverse sources, turning information more agile and transparent, stimulating the development of bio-business.

To reach its goal, the system must be prepared to monitor some kinds of information, such as: the national and international financing sources, subjects related to the production and price of biofuel and carbon credits negotiated in stock markets around the world, among other pieces of relevant information.

SISBIO presents the modules of collection, storage, analysis and relationship, apart from the ontologies and informative notes publisher.

The collecting module is responsible for the monitoring of open digital sources. Intelligent agents of collection are created, who monitor specific digital targets. The automatic agents of collect the pre-defined information of each source information indicated by the specialists of the domain and stores them in the knowledge base of the system.

The storing module is responsible for the organization of the knowledge based on the semantic ontologies and their relations. Each new document enclosed in the system, either by the observers, or Informative Notes, is automatically indexed and stored in the same structure. This module prepares the information to be retrieved and analyzed in the analysis modules.

The analysis module is responsible for the textual and graphic search through matching between the case presented and the documents stored in the knowledge base. Besides documents of the base, the informative notes are retrieved, which are documents inserted manually generally containing strategic analyses and information.

The relationship module is the environment that allows the identification of chances of bio-business through the registry of technological innovations and research in development, agricultural producers besides investors and owners of agriculturable lands. The module is fed by the insertion of data of the agents that compose the biofuel chain, each one with their own peculiarities.

The ontology editor is the environment for the creation and registry of the ontologies and their relations through the identification of relevant expressions and those that represent the knowledge domain. It is part of the ontology engineering that will be described in item 3.2.

The informative note environment is prepared to insert documents in the knowledge base produced by analysts and specialists of the domain, generally containing relevant and strategic information for the generation of bio-business.

3. METHODOLOGIES AND TECHNOLOGIES APPLIED IN THE CONSTRUCTION OF SISBIO

SISBIO has its linguistic development based on ontologies. Two main methodologies are used for the construction of ontologies: knowledge engineering and ontology engineering. The first one consists of extracting and organizing the knowledge of the specialists in biofuel, and ontology engineering is used to represent the knowledge through indicative expressions and its relations, developing a semantic network of relationships.

3.1 Knowledge Engineering

Knowledge engineering is a methodology for the development of knowledge based systems. It is a fundamental step for the development of the model. This process is considered multidisciplinary by nature and includes some kinds of research that are difficult to classify in a delimited approach [2].

This process is responsible for the analysis of the knowledge domains that are used for the retrieval of information stored in the knowledge base used by SISBIO. Its also responsible for the requirement analysis, studies related to the biofuel chain, identification of information sources and definition of the interface.

The development stage of SISBIO initiates with the stage of Knowledge Engineering, responsible for the analysis of requirements, studies related to biofuel chain, identification of the informational sources, and definition of the fields of the interface. It is organized in the Knowledge Engineering suite. The suite consists of an independent computational structure for the extraction, organization and representation of the knowledge extracted in the phase of Knowledge Engineering, beyond the construction and edition of ontologies performed in the coming phase of Engineering of ontologies. The Knowledge Engineering Suite was developed to act together with Dynamically Contextualized Knowledge Representation- DCKR. Among the main tools, we can highlight the frequency extractor and the semantic extractor and the ontology editor.

An important step is the selection of information sources that will be used by the system. For SISBIO, the sources are institutions that provide information about biofuel, research organizations and public databases. The informational sources are proceeding from the organisms that possess information about the biobusiness chain and research institutions, beyond public databases such as, the Brazilian Institute of Geography and Statistics - IBGE, Mines and Energy Ministry among others. It is through the analysis of documents found in these sources that the indices are defined, those that will be the base for the extraction of information. Those indices are defined to facilitate the process of retrieval of documents related to the consultation made by the user. This definition must be performed according to the relevance found in the content of the documents.

After that, the fields of the interface are defined that will be made available to the final user. This definition must undergo an analysis of criteria that involves the navigability, usability and ergonomics, based in norm ISO 9.241, and is described as "the capacity of a product to be used for specific users to achieve a specific goal with effectiveness, efficiency, and satisfaction in a specific context of use" [3].

As a multidisciplinary effort, knowledge engineering demands the participation of actors with different characteristics, as shown in figure 1:

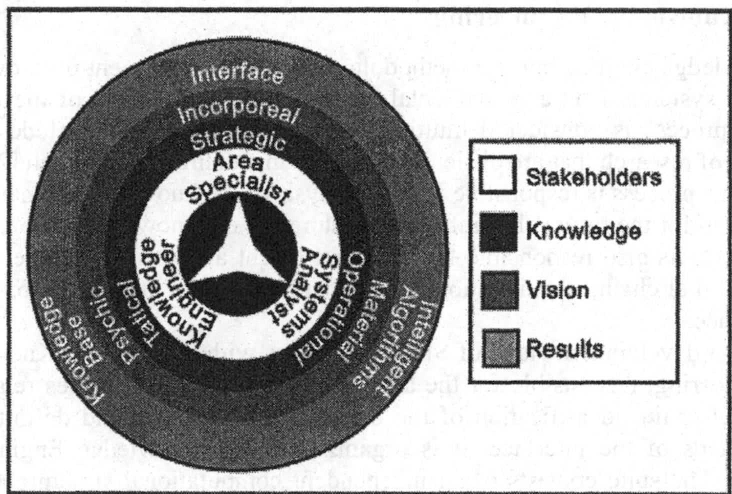

Figure 2: Knowledge Engeneering Actors

As it can be seen in the white area of the figure, there are three essential actors. The domain specialist is responsible for the organization and definition of the relevancy of the knowledge to be represented in the system knowledge base. Knowledge engineering is responsible for the extraction and representation of the knowledge of the specialist. Finally, the systems analyst is responsible for the definition of the tool adequate for the implementation of the requirements defined in this process.

3.2 Ontology Engineering

Ontology Engineering is a knowledge representation methodology that aims at the improvement of document retrieval performance. This representation is based on indicative expressions and the relations between them.

The use of ontologies enables the sharing of knowledge among people and the software, defining a common understanding about a defined knowledge domain. According to Studer et al. "an ontology is a formal, explicit specification of a shared conceptualization…Basically, the role of ontologies in the knowledge engineering process is to facilitate the construction of a domain model. Ontology provides a vocabulary of terms and relations with which a domain can be modeled" [4].

Systems that use ontology for document retrieval are less prone to risks of ambiguity of words or terms in the input text. These systems are able to "understand" the context of the search, returning better search results. Also, a special characteristic of SISBIO, the presentation of graphs based on ontologies, allows the user to interpret the results of the search in a temporal dimension.

The main steps in ontology engineering is the analysis of documents, domain visualization exercises, conceptual maps construction and inclusion of the ontologies in the system, using three tools called frequency extractor, semantic extractor and ontologies editor.

The frequency extractor is a tool used for the analysis of a set of documents, providing information about the frequency and distribution of words. This analysis also provides a statistical visualization, context analysis, and allows the verification of predominant subjects in the documents and the terminology used by the specialists of the domain.

The semantic extractor uses the knowledge base constructed with the ontologies editor and validates it comparing it to the content of the documents that were studied, allowing the reorganization of the textual knowledge map. It also allows the verification of the contexts related to the domain being considered. As a consequence of this analysis, it is possible to validate the vocabulary inserted in the ontologies editor and constructed through the frequency extractor.

The indicative expressions and its relations are added to the ontologies editor, creating a relationship tree considering the conceptual similarity of the terms and its relations and weights. It allows the storage of an associative structure of the knowledge of a domain. This kind of organization allows the dynamic attribution of weights to words or indicative expressions, related to the context of the search. It becomes a dynamic knowledge map.

It is after the first steps of the ontology engineering, the analysis of the documents, the definition of information sources and the interface, that the domains of the biofuel chain are defined, which will be addressed by the system. These domains represent the main variables that indicate the need of production of relevant information inside a knowledge area.

The next step is the elaboration of the lists of indicative expressions and the relations among them. The indicative expressions are extracted by the specialists in biofuel and the knowledge engineers in the previous steps of the knowledge engineering. From these expressions, the vocabulary is expanded by means of technical and usual relations and by the validation done with the semantic extractor. Through the vocabulary constructed by the ontology engineering are found expressions analogous to the ones defined in the norm, as well as many other terms found in documents in a usual way. As a consequence, the relationship tree constructed from the ontologies editor "defines the linguistic, semantic and axiological similarity of conditions that allows the determination of local similarities between the values of an index" [BUENO, 2005].

In SISBIO, there were around 95 indicative expressions considered important, which generated around 415 new expressions after the expansion of the list of expressions with synonyms, related terms, "type of" and "part of". The following table exemplifies some of the main expressions.

List of indicative Expressions
Growth of agricultural potential
Sugar cane intercrop
growth of Biodiesel production
Program for the encouragement to alternative sources of electricity
Emissions exchange market

Table 1. List of indicative expressions

The classification of the ontologies is made through its relations and may be:

"Synonym" relation:

This relation exists between two terms or expressions that present the same meaning inside the same domain. Ex. Biofuel is a synonym of clean fuel.

"Related terms" relation:

The related terms relation occurs when the terms or expressions represent a strong relation, but do not have exactly the same meaning and do not have any other relation. Ex: "Exploitation taxes" is related to royalties.

Relation "Type of":

The type of relation is based on the classification between class and subclass. Ex. Biodiesel is a type of biofuel.

Relation "Part of":

This type of relation refers to the matter of hierarchies or organizational levels. Ex. Alternative energy is part of PROINFA.

Figure 2 represents the ontology editor interface, based on the classification above.

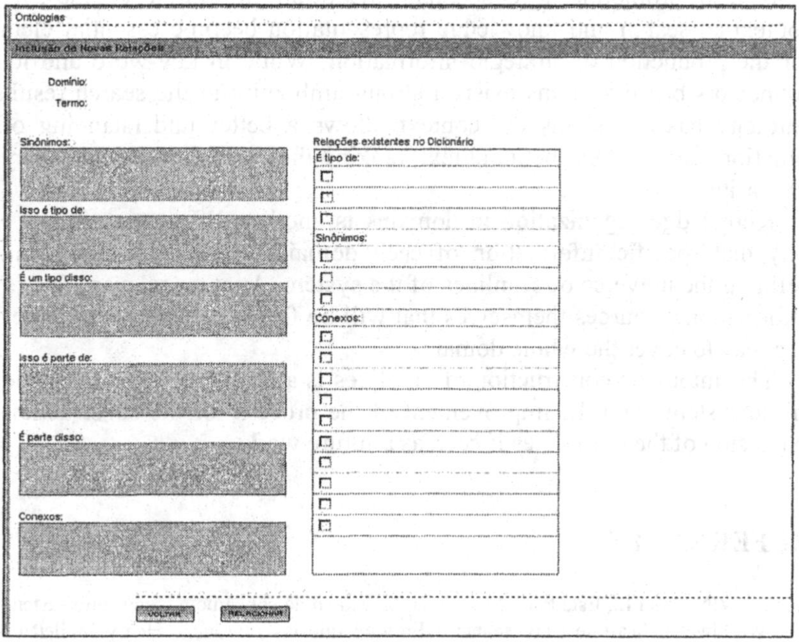

Figura 2 – Ontologies Editor
Fonte: Bueno, 2005

The ontology construction methodology consists of the following steps: 1. To produce an inventory of the whole domain, i.e. to catalogue all digital information sources that will be used as the database of the system; 2. to apply the frequency extractor in this database; 3. To make a comparison between the results of the extractors and the needs of the specialists; 4. To construct (with the aid of the specialist) a controlled vocabulary that represents the domain; 5. To apply the semantic extractor to the database, using the vocabulary; 6. To valuate the result based on the frequency of the indicative expressions found and define a list of words; 7. To construct ontologies to be used in the system based on this controlled vocabulary; 8. To define synonyms, homonyms and hyperonyms based on doctrines and the legislation [BUENO 2005].

4. CONCLUSION

The use of ontologies in informational systems based on knowledge is demonstrating a strong differential in terms of efficiency of the search results. The organization of knowledge through the construction of a expressions network allows the system to have documents as results organized by context and similarity degree in relation to the input document. It is also promoting a conceptual evolution in search engines, where contextual search and knowledge representation become essential elements for the production of strategic information. While in key-word and logical connectors based systems exists a strong ambiguity in the search results, in ontology based systems the context allows a better understanding of the situation presented by the input text, ranking the documents by relevancy and similarity.

Knowledge organization in domains is another differential, in the same way that specific information of each domain adopts particular contexts, defining the universe of scanlines of the system. Another relevant fact is that informational sources themselves that will be feeding the system are defined in a way to cover the whole domain.

The automatic construction of ontolgies is a challenge to be implemented in the system. And the improvement of the process for the construction and expansion of the ontologies is seen as a future work.

REFERENCES

1. SAWIN, Janet L.; Estado do Mundo, 2004: estado do consumo e o consumo sustentável / Worldwatch Institute ; apresentação Enrique Iglesias ; tradução Henry Mallett e Célia Mallett. - Salvador, BA : Uma Ed., 2004

2. BUENO T. C. D et al. Knowledge Engineering Suite: a Tool to Create Ontologies for Automatic Knowledge Representation in Knowledge-based Systems. in: The 2nd International Workshop on Natural Language Understanding And Cognitive Science (NLUCS-2005) in ICEIS - 7th international conference. 7TH International Conference on Enterprise Information Systems, 2005, Miami. Proceedings of Seventh International Conference On Enterprise Information Systems. 2005.

3. DIAS, Claudia Augusto. Métodos de avaliação de usabilidade no contexto de portais corporativos: um estudo de caso do Sanado Federal. 2001. 225 p. Tese (Doutorado) – Faculdade de Estudos Sociais Aplicados, Universidade de Brasília, Brasília/DF.

4. STUDER, R. et al., Situation and Perspective of Knowledge Engineering. In: J. Cuena, et al. (eds.), Knowledge Engineering and Agent Technology. IOS Press, Amsterdam, 2000.

Service interdependencies: insight into use cases for service composition

Witold Abramowicz, Agata Filipowska, Monika Kaczmarek, Tomasz Kaczmarek, Marek Kowalkiewicz, Wojciech Rutkowski, Karol Wieloch, Dominik Zyskowski

Department of Management Information Systems, the Poznan University of Economics, Poznan, Poland
{w.abramowicz, a.filipowska, m.kaczmarek, t.kaczmarek, m.kowalkiewicz, w.rutkowski, k.wieloch, d.zyskowski} @kie.ae.poznan.pl

Abstract. The paper analyses several most appealing use cases for Semantic Web services and their composition. They are considered from the perspective of service types, QoS parameters, semantic description and user preferences. We introduce different levels of service composition and discuss implications of the above.

Keywords: Web services, information services, service composition, use cases

1 Introduction

With the emergence of the idea of Semantic Web and Semantic Web Services a lot of different scenarios and use cases appeared, that were supposed to illustrate and justify their application in the real life. The primary purpose of introducing semantics into the world of Web services (WS) was to enable semantic-based discovery and composition. WS composition comes into play when a client request cannot be satisfied by one available service, but by an adequate combination of existing services. The autonomous agents should be able to discover services that would suit their goals, invoke them and execute series of tasks that required to this day human involvement. However, most of the scenarios defined to illustrate this vision fail a very basic test, namely applicability. This is not only a result of problems with semantics, interoperability or lack of features that numerous WS-standards try to address, but also many use cases for Semantic Web Services fail to take into account some general properties of services. This is particularly visible in scenarios where automatic service composition is considered.

Our motivation in this article is to clarify limitations of service composition, taking into account use cases already discussed in the literature. We rely on our experiences in several research projects that deal with semantic-enabled Web services. We also propose meta-requirements for use cases that include service composition at various levels. Additionally, we show interdependencies between different service types. The main focus of the paper is to present distinctions between Web services and real-world services, and show how these two worlds mix and interplay.

Please use the following format when citing this chapter:

Abramowicz, W., Filipowska, A., Kaczmarek, M., Kaczmarek, T., Kowalkiewicz, M., Rutkowski, W., Wieloch, K., Zyskowski, D., 2006, in IFIP International Federation for Information Processing, Volume 218, Professional Practice in Artificial Intelligence, eds. J. Debenham, (Boston: Springer), pp. 101–110.

The paper is structured as follows. First the related work is briefly discussed. In the following section a number of use cases used in the research projects and some practical examples of service exploitation are presented. Next, the service types that influence service compositions are given. Finally, the conclusions and future directions of research are discussed.

2 Related work

Service composition may be defined as building more powerful and feature-rich functionality from simpler elements. Each simple element (a service) must have discrete, independent capabilities of its own, but can also be added to (composed with) other elements to create more complex solutions [9]. Service composition has a lot to offer. It has triggered a considerable number of research efforts and is currently one of the most hyped and addressed issues in the Service Oriented Computing and Service Oriented Architecture as the Web services standards have largely been designed to be composable. The interoperability was the key requirement, and interoperability triggers composability. Moreover, the web is a particularly interesting domain for service composition for several reasons. Firstly, increasing numbers of interesting services are moving online and the web is fast transforming from a collection of static pages to a provider of numerous useful services. Another reason is that Web services conform to the standard HTTP protocol which makes it (relatively) easier to integrate them into a common framework. Third, because the web has many independent service providers providing related services, there is an inherent need for composing complementary services provided by independent providers to achieve the end-user's needs. [12]

Of course the ultimate challenge is not only service composition but automatic service composition performed by autonomous agents. Additionally, automatic composition has a large potential in the workflow area (see [5]) as it enables dynamic reconfiguration of workflow, which is hardly achievable if workflows are defined and managed manually. Milanovic and Malek [4] propose four requirements that must be satisfied by service composition mechanism: connectivity, nonfunctional quality-of-service (QoS) properties, correctness, and scalability. Connectivity guarantees that WS can be composed in terms of input and output messages. Nonfunctional QoS properties denote parameters like timeliness, security and dependability. Correctness assures that composed service's properties are verified and the composition framework must scale appropriately.

In order to illustrate the applicability of the Web services technology and Semantic Web services composition a lot of different use cases were invented. They are analyzed at different angels. There are many works and initiatives that look at the use cases from the perspective of what requirements to Web services, Web services' architecture and languages used to describe them, may be identified (see e.g. http://www.daml.org/services/use-cases.html for a choice of use cases). There is a tremendous ongoing research effort in several EU-funded projects that deal with semantics for Web services (e.g. DIP, Knowledge Web, InfraWebs, SEKT, SWWS, ASG and Esperonto). Some of these projects aim at applying Semantic Web Services to real-world scenarios. They deal with subjects such as semantic description of service capability, choreography, quality parameters, service discovery, invocation and composition. The main problem of such projects is to apply the results of scientific efforts in the real life. To handle this issue properly, special actions are undertaken. For example, in the ASG project [2] one work component is responsible for the preparation and further exploitation of use-cases. From the other side, there is another work component focused entirely on service composition matters. Their task is to define requirements to used services, prepare mechanisms capable of composing and creating all needed ontologies. However, to our best knowledge, there are no research initiatives looking at the use cases from the side as we present in this article.

3 Use cases discussion

In this section several of the scenarios that are considered when applying Semantic Web Services are discussed. The aim of this survey is to prepare ground for further analysis of common features of these use cases and comparison of different service types that take part in the scenarios. The scenarios were split into two groups. The first one includes scenarios that are tailored for using semantic descriptions or composing services and are the basis for various Web Services development projects (subsection A-F), like e.g. WSMO [14], ASG [2], USE-ME.GOV [16]. The second group consists of existing and running applications of WS in particular business areas.

A. Travel booking

The most popular use case for Web services deals with traveling [7]. In this scenario travel agent offers to book complete vacation packages. Airlines, hotels are providing Web services to query their offerings and perform reservations. This use case assumes that consistent ontology is used within the entire process. The other issue is services reliability and trustworthiness of parties engaged. Another travel based scenarios comes from WSMO group [14]. From the end-user point of view both scenarios give interfaces to external information systems. Both scenarios are based on a service (called Virtual Travel Agency and travel-agent service respectively) that behaves like some kind of integration platform with a fixed workflow.

B. Tourist attraction booking

The scenario presents a location based mobile service - the Attraction Booking Service (end service). It is part of a larger service platform in the ASG project, providing all kinds of tourist services for a mobile end user. In this scenario an end service customer (e.g. a tourist visiting a foreign city) wants to book a cultural event. Hence, the goal of the Attraction Booking Service is to provide the customer with information about attractions in the nearest surroundings of the current location. Additionally, the customer is able to perform certain actions based on this information (retrieve details, book, pay, get route description). First, the distributed platform that manages the services, and on the basis of the user request composes a flow of service specifications that can fulfill the goal. However, there is not only one service that implements the service specification – e.g. implementation of AttractionInformation service may be offered by three different service providers. So, the most suitable service implementation to be contracted by negotiation to each service specification is selected. At the very end the composed service is executed [2].

C. Buddy scenario

Buddy scenario assumes that the user owns a mobile device. The scenario is based on keeping contacts with your buddies. It allows to get the availability status and location of the buddies, and to set up a group communication, based on instant messenger, SMS or voice. The scenario typically consists of service components, which are configured dynamically (e.g. configuration of your buddy list, getting information about activities, identification of friends in the vicinity and group communication). The development of the service has to be dynamic, based on service components from different providers. For example, we want to check who of our friends is in the vicinity. In order to fulfill our need, the platform integrating the services must take advantage of three services: finding phone number, finding localization and drawing a map on the screen of mobile device. There is a set of services in each category and the platform must dynamically select the best services to be executed in the workflow taking into account QoS criteria and other user criteria [2].

D. Healthcare services

This is a scenario taken from a medical domain. Imagine that we would like to visit dermatologist. There are several health services provided by medical centers that offer us as a result the appointment at a dermatologist chosen. What differentiates them is a price of a service, quality of specialist and medical center, date of possible appointment. The service that will be chosen depends on user preferences (i.e. urgency, price, distance to medical center, etc.) [16].

E. Dynamic supply chain

The dynamic supply chain scenario [10] assumes the existence of QoS ontologies and of an engine capable of dynamic orchestration. The motivation of this use case is simple – the retailer wants to choose the best suppliers based on its business logic and the suppliers want to maximize their profit as well as increase their business with the retailer. A key feature of the scenario is the use of quality of service (QoS) as an essential criterion for dynamic selection of services that are later dynamically composed. The scenario assumes multiple interactions between the platform (as a proxy) and the user (retailer). The result of the interactions is a placed order.

F. Complaints handling by local authority

This is an example of e- or m-government solution. Most of the administrative processes are predefined by law or internal regulations of the institution e.g. when authority receives an inquiry or a request from citizen it is obliged to send response within a predefined time. Moreover also the processes in institutions are defined, so when citizen sends a complaint, it is redirected to a certain department, dealt with and then sender is notified about the action that was undertaken. It is envisioned that citizens could send complaints to the local authority with their mobile devices, and be notified of the status of the complaint and solution for it [16].

G. Bookstore on the Web

The bookstore scenario [3] motivates the need for semantic annotation in protocol definition languages. It is shown that WSDL does not describe some important aspects of web services such as implications and effects of an operation. Interested parties are the bookseller, the customer and Semantic Web services middleware vendors. On the bookstore side, Semantic Web services allow for the definition of more sophisticated behavior. On the customer side, the interest lies in easier understanding of the service's behavior and of how to leverage them. Similar order-purchase-like scenario is presented in [13]. For a B2B domain there is a scenario [11] whose actors are companies and organizations that would like to exchange messages that will trigger their business processes.

H. Amazon

The Amazon.com web application is compound in nature. It consists of several services: www service (which in turn comprises of search service, product catalog online etc.), transaction handling service, package delivery service. Some of the complexity of this service is exposed through Web service interface. This includes information services e.g. getting detailed information about particular item or list of items as a response to a query and shopping cart interface that allows for placing orders through Amazon. WSMO group (www.wsmo.org) has developed Amazon E-commerce Service use case which describes the service in the WSMO language. The functionality includes various kinds of searches and setting up shopping cart. Purchasing is not possible in this scenario, as well as through native service [15].

I. eBay

eBay's Web services allow for executing almost every operation accessible on the website (listing items, searching, receiving notifications), although they do not support bidding yet (as opposed to other regional auction services, e.g. www.allegro.pl). In the year 2004 the eBay Platform handled over 1 billion Web service requests per month [8].

J. Google

Last but not least is the example of simple Web service which is Google API. It allows querying the Google retrieval engine, and obtaining results in XML format. This is another example of successful application of Web services as an interface to the already existing information services.

The common point of all the services described in this section is the added value to the end user – the ability to query offerings, perform reservations, transmit documents and made payments etc. Moreover, some of the scenarios consider services that are performed in the real world, like health services, supply of materials, traveling or even book delivery. Finally, as one may see not only the semantics are important for successful composition of Web services but the other crucial criterion is the quality of service aspect. In the consequence, taking these three aspects into account, we may distinguish two types of Web services presented in the next section that have a crucial impact on the composition process.

4 Service types

The use cases presented above can be analyzed from the perspective of the type of services' results. The services in all the scenarios follow at least a simple interaction pattern: query – response. The queries are used to retrieve an offer of a particular kind (books, transportation routes, tickets, healthcare, industrial suppliers). The expected result is a list of interesting items (information result). The other type of interaction is to send a message with the goal to trigger some further workflow. The results in such a case are twofold. The first is an immediate confirmation sent to the user (order confirmation). The second is an actual, real-world (possibly postponed) service, e.g. the book delivered to the user, the reserved place on the plane the user is just entering, etc (real-world result). As there are two kinds of result of services we distinguish two kinds of services – real-word and information services. Real-world service is a service (properly defined piece of work) offered by some provider (through traditional channels like face-to-face communication and hand-to-hand delivery) in the real world. Information service is such a service that its sole relevant result is a piece of information and the result can be transmitted to the customer through any possible communication channel.

Note that in order to utilize a service in some information system the service must be wrapped-up with a machine-processable interface. Such an interface is a Web service according to the W3C, which states that it is a software system designed to support interoperable machine-to-machine interaction over a network. It has an interface that is described in a machine-processable format such as WSDL.

The above division (to real-world and information services) together with the notion of Web service as an interface allows us to describe services in terms of tangibility of their results by any information system. In case of information system the user is only interested in the result that can be captured by some Internet communication protocol. In case of a real-world service the user besides the feedback information is interested in results that cannot be controlled. This intangibility is an effect of the lack of full integration between service provider's system and systems of its environment as well as machines' inability to control physical results of provided services.

The use cases presented in the third section mix different notions of service. On one hand they are all information services. Actually some of the use cases utilize WWW browsers, some provides API, and some provides dedicated solutions. On the other hand the core of some of the use cases is to book or order something. Wrapping information service is quite simple, because information service may be seen as a computational function with simple input and output. Wrapping real-world service is more complex. We think that the goals for designing scenarios discussed above miss this distinction, which is the reason for the fact, that only simple, well known services like Amazon, Google, auctions actually works. Moreover only few of their capabilities are accessible through API (not GUI). Not taking into account differences in meaning of Web service is the reason, why it is hard to find good use cases that deal with real-world services, and yet requires Web services, and reach semantics and semantic-based composition.

5 The impact of service types on composition

Taking into account the types of service distinguished in the previous section, the conclusion appears that the service composition is not as monolithic as it would seem. If we take into account different service types and their semantic description accordingly, we obtain different levels of composition. The following levels of composition may be distinguished:

- Full composition – it appears in the scenarios that consider large set of substitutive services. When the user goal is formulated, then the process specification, taking into account desired inputs, outputs, preconditions and effects, needs to be defined. Then adequate services implementations are bound to the process specification.
- Limited composition – in this case the process definition is fixed in terms of types of services (service specifications), however different services (implementations from different providers) may be attached / negotiated to become a part of the composition. Those negotiated services may be already contracted or internal to the company, or they may be external. In the latter case, the composition usually requires SLA's and negotiation of contract.
- No composition – the process is fixed, the providers of services on each step of process are known.

Each of the composition levels mentioned above is available to both real-world services and information services (possibly wrapped into Web services). Yet due to characteristics of real-world services it is very hard to mix them with information services within one process. If we try to do so we would have to consider such effects of real-world services that are not accessible to information services. Moreover, composition is also dubious due to the approach to semantic service description. Real-world services may have semantic description which is just symbolic representation of what they perform. However information services (like ticket booking service) must be described as information delivering or changing service (in this example – enabling some other service), having only minor impact on the real world.

Mixing information and real-world services in one composed process is also challenging for its execution. It is only possible to monitor execution of real-world services (the platform that executed the whole process gets notifications when the service is finished), while for information services wrapped in WS it is actually possible to execute them remotely. Moreover, it is rather easy to handle the composition of information services, because an output of one service is an input of the next service. Real-world, complex services that really effect in the creation of real objects do not provide simple data types that can be processed electronically.

A few more limitations that may be applied to the service composition will be discussed in the following subsections.

5.1 The role of Quality of Service in service composition

Service composition is definitely limited by the quality of service considerations. It is important to note, that service composition is usually quality-driven, while its goal is to achieve certain functionality. However, when talking about quality of service issues two aspects need to be taken into account. On one hand the quality of Web service implementation (the interface) and on the other hand the quality of the resulting service, made available through the use of Web service. In the consequence, the quality concept should be divided into two groups – Quality of Execution (QoE) and Quality of Result (QoR) [1].

QoE parameters characterize services in general. They usually include execution time, execution cost (not to mistake with different prices appearing around the service), latency, response time etc. QoR in turn describes the output of the service – it is hard (or even impossible) to enumerate all the parameters for measuring quality of arbitrary output, however it always includes price. The example for this distinction may be ticket booking service (wrapped with WS). Its QoE parameters would measure how long did it take to book a ticket and what was the cost of using this particular service. However the price of the ticket is QoR for this service, together with place for which the ticket is booked, time, etc. Quality of Execution is rather domain-independent whereas QoR concept is domain specific. However, in some cases the differentiation between QoE and QoR is rather subjective. It depends strongly on the users' point of view, their previous experiences as well as goals and expectations.

Taking this all into account, the quality of service is not easy to be defined and measured. For those scenarios that include binding concrete services to their specifications (limited composition or second step of full composition), services are only distinguishable via their QoS. As QoS is only partially measurable it leads to problems in satisfying user preferences. Additionally, from the user perspective, problems with QoR have deep impact on possible queries that can be asked against service repositories. For example users can ask for cheapest services but not for services that would get them cheapest tickets because that would require executing the services even before they are chosen.

5.2 Requirements for service composition from the perspective of semantic service description and goals formulation

The indepth analysis of the use cases implies that different types of services (real-world, information) will have different semantic description. Does this influence composition capability (in terms of mixing both types or even within single type)?

It seems that the deepest challenges lie in the case of full composition. There the services are not known in advance because the user does not specify which service he or she would like to use. He or she only specifies the desired goal, giving its semantic description. This may be viewed as specifying service capabilities in terms of preconditions and effects. Four illustrative examples of such goals (corresponding to the scenarios discussed) would be:

- I want to have a certain book,
- I have a free evening and I want to get out spending it on something interesting,
- I'm in New York today (15th of January) and on March 12th I need to be in Hong Kong on the conference,
- I have ill sister and I want her to get better.

It seems like these questions would fit for bookstore, attraction booking, travel or healthcare use cases. However those scenarios require specifying the service composition on some general level first - preferably from certain available service categories. Those categories should include services that deliver books, make arrangements for evenings, transport or heal. While all what is described in the scenarios are information services: that inform about books (and allow ordering them), find attractions or book tickets. It is hard to match user goals expressed this way with such service descriptions.

Furthermore, it seems that the composition may be achieved only after knowing the outcomes of certain services. It is possible to bind some services to the process only if the results of previous services are known. For example: if my process includes paying for a ticket, the payment methods available for ticket booking service determine which transaction handling service I should use.

Users of platforms that act as middleware between service providers and customers need to query for service to be discovered and executed. This is often referred to as specifying user's goal. Several types of user queries are conceivable:

- Give me all available services that can do... – this is a general question about certain category of services. If they are not directly discoverable through semantic descriptions then full composition is required.
- I do not know what to do with my free evening... - another question that requires full composition.
- I want to go to the cinema on the movie titled... Which one do you propose? – here the user specifies some of the results of services that he or she would like to obtain. This is the case for limited composition - only some categories of services need to be considered, the process is fixed and all is necessary is finding the service that books tickets and then plays the right movie.
- I want to book a ticket for cinema... – in this case there is no need for composition. The process is fixed and the user specifies (indirectly) which service (from which provider) he would like to use.

The level of the above questions determines how the services should be described. For the first one any description is sufficient (even textual), however it is tremendously challenging even with fullest semantic description to conduct automatic service composition against such queries. The sheer number of variations of processes may be prohibitive, not to mention that the user will have to choose which one he or she prefers. With regard to the QoS and other parameters – user does not provide any values of parameters (possibly only some QoS parameters – like execution time of the whole composed service or its price; for example: evening for 100 USD)

For the second – the description should include information which cinemas a given service is able to book (+ values of other runtime parameters) – here the characteristic thing is that the user provides some of the input values with his or her goal description (here – the name of the movie). The problem here is how to check which of the service is able to handle the request prior to invoking it!

For the third, a concrete service may be successfully discovered and invoked. If there are many services available the user may choose one of them based on QoS parameters, his or her preferences or any external information.

6. Conclusions

Introducing several levels of service composition we discussed how the type of a service, its QoS parameters and semantic description influence the feasibility of composition. From the discussion of several use cases we clearly see that currently only simple information services are applicable, possibly with fixed workflows and limited composition. We observe that Web service composition use cases often miss the distinction between real-world services and information service. The reason for this is the misconception that Web services that serve as front-end for real-world services and may be described as if they would be the real services. Google and eBay examples show that Web services make sense in business environment where they really make business processes more efficient or simplify them.

Moreover, it is inherent for (real-world) services that they are partially undefined and become defined on the time of their execution (which also determines the price). Therefore for complex services it is very hard to automate the process of composition and even to deliver proper description. It is something that should be remembered.

References

1. W. Abramowicz et al., "A Survey of QoS Computation for Web Service Profiling , ISCA 18th International Conference on Computer Applications in Industry and Engineering, 2005
2. J. Noll et al., "ASG based scenarios in Telecommunications, Telematics and enhanced Enterprise IT", Deliverable on http://asg-platform.org , 2004
3. B. Benatallah, F. Casati, F. Toumani, "Conversation Protocol of the book purchase service", 2003
4. N. Milanovic, M. Malek, "Current Solutions for Web Service Composition", Internet Computing Vol. 8, No. 6(6), pp. 51-59, 2004
5. M. Gajewski, M. Momotko, "Dynamic Failure Recovery of Generated Workflows", 16th International Workshop on Database and Expert Systems Applications (DEXA'05) pp. 982-986, 2005
6. G. Piccinelli, Service Provision and Composition in Virtual Business Communities (HPL-1999-84), Technical report, Hewlett-Packard, 1999
7. H. Haas, Web service use case: Travel reservation, 2002
8. W. Iverson, "Web Services in Action: Integrating with the eBay Marketplace", retrieved 10th January 2005, http://developer.ebay.com/join/whitepapers/webservicesinaction, 2004
9. P. Lipton, "Composition and Management of Web Services", SOA Web Services Journal., 2004
10. K. Verma, A. Sheth, J. Miller, R. Aggarwal, "Dynamic QoS based Supply Chain", retrieved 10th January 2005, http://www.daml.org/services/use-cases, 2004
11. C. Bussler, M. Zaremba, "Semantic Web-enabled Business Protocol Standards", retrieved 10th January 2005, http://www.daml.org/services/use-cases, 2003
12. S. R. Ponnekanti, A. Fox, "SWORD: A Developer Toolkit for Web Service Composition", in the Eleventh World Wide Web Conference (WWW2002), 2002
13. H. He, H. Haas, D. Orchard, "Web Services Architecture Usage Scenarios", retrieved 10th January 2005, http://www.daml.org/services/use-cases, 2004
14. M. Stollberg, R. Lara, "WSMO Use Case <<Virtual Travel Agency>>", retrieved 10th January 2005, http://www.wsmo.org, 2004
15. J. Kopecky, D. Roman, J. Scicluna, "WSMO Use Case: Amazon E-commerce Service", retrieved 10th January 2005, http://www.wsmo.org, 2005
16. D. Tilsner, W. Abramowicz, M. Wiśniewski, P. Moore,G. Peinel, USE-ME.GOV (USability-drivEn open platform for MobilE GOVernment), The Proceedings of the First European Conference on Mobile Government, 2005, University Sussex, Brighton UK, ISBN 9763341-0-0Baldonado, M., Chang, C.-C.K., Gravano, L., Paepcke, A.: The Stanford Digital Library Metadata Architecture. Int. J. Digit. Libr. 1 (1997) 108–121

Combining Contexts and Ontologies: A Case Study

Mariela Rico[1], Ma. Laura Caliusco[2], Omar Chiotti[3], and Ma. Rosa Galli[3]
1 CIDISI-UTN-FRSF, Lavaysse 610, 3000, Santa Fe, Argentina,
mrico@frsf.utn.edu.ar
2 CIDISI-UTN-FRSF,CONICET,Lavaysse 610, 3000, Santa Fe, Argentina,
mcaliusc@frsf.utn.edu.ar
3 INGAR-CONICET-UTN, Avellaneda 3657, 3000, Santa Fe, Argentina
{chiotti,mrgalli}@ceride.gov.ar

Abstract. In the last years different proposals that integrate ontologies and contexts, taking advantages from their abilities for achieving information semantic interoperability, have arisen. Each of them has considered the problematic from different perspectives. Particularly, through an actual case study this paper shows which are the problems related to support information semantic interoperability between different parties involved in a collaborative business relation over the Internet. Furthermore, this paper analyzes those problems from previous proposals perspective and highlights the weaknesses and strengths of them.

1 Introduction

Due to the necessity of creating explicit models of the semantic associated to information with different objectives, such as knowledge management, information interoperability and so on; two different approaches have separately arisen: ontologies and contexts. On the one hand, ontologies represent an explicit specification of conceptualization shared within a domain [1]. On the other hand, a context could be defined in a general way as an environment within a fact is considered. This environment is characterized by a set of axioms and true facts [2].

Ontologies and contexts have both strengths and weaknesses. On the one hand, shared ontologies define a common understanding of specific terms, and thus make it possible interoperable systems on a semantic level. On the weak side, ontologies can be used only as long as consensus about their content is reached. On the other hand, contexts encode not shared interpretation schemas of individuals and they are easy to define and to maintain because they can be constructed with a limited consensus with the other parties. On the weak side, since contexts are local to parties,

Please use the following format when citing this chapter:

Rico, M., Caliusco, M.L., Chiotti, O., Galli, M.R., 2006, in IFIP International Federation for Information Processing, Volume 218, Professional Practice in Artificial Intelligence, eds. J. Debenham, (Boston: Springer), pp. 111–120.

communication can be achieved only by constructing explicit mappings among the elements of the contexts of the involved parties [3].

Therefore, considering that the strengths of ontologies are the weaknesses of contexts and vice versa, and therefore that they can be seen as complementary approaches, a new research area arises which integrate both concepts to achieve semantic interoperability of information. The most relevant works that integrate contexts and ontologies have been developed in the following areas: Semantic Web [3], information system interoperability [4, 5], document classification [6, 7], and context-aware applications [8, 9]. These works consider the problem from different perspectives and we think that some of these perspectives have to be integrated into one in order to efficiently describe semantics to achieve information interoperability.

The aim of this paper is to analyze how ontologies and contexts could be related in order to support semantic interoperability of information interchanged between parties involved in a collaborative business relation. To achieve this objective, first, we present a case study in which through examples we analyzed different ways of ontologies and contexts combination. Then, some related works are analyzed and compared with the results of the case study. Finally, our conclusions and future works are presented.

2 Case Study: Partner–To–Partner Collaborative Model

The integration problem of a supply chain via Internet is a typical problem of information interoperability, where the business documents must be interpreted by the information systems of different trading partners. This involves the collaboration in one or more stages of the business process, from production planning to sale stage.

A collaborative production planning model defines a collaborative business process divided into three subprocesses; each of them implies a different collaborative business process [10]. These subprocesses are:

- Consensus at level of Production Aggregated Planning (PAP), which objective is that enterprises reach a consensus about a material provision plan at PAP level. Here, trading partners agree about which products they will collaborate (at the product family level), in which periods of time (horizon is between 6 and 18 months) and approximate quantities of them.
- Consensus at level of Production Master Program (PMP), with which enterprises have to arrive to a consensus about a material provision scheduling at PMP level. At this level, products are defined at highest detail level required by the manufacturer enterprise. Also, periods of time and quantities are specified at a higher level of detail. The customer specifies required material quantity and due date. The supplier defines the date and the size of provision orders, considering what has been agreed in the frame agreement. This is "probable" information.
- Consensus at level of Provision Orders Program (POP), which objective is that trading partners reach a consensus about the definition of a provision orders scheduling. At this level, "sure" information is handled. Periods of time indicate an accurate day in which products will be available to be dispatched. A provision and a production order schedule for both trading partners are defined.

A collaborative relation management implies coordinating: private processes that are executed by an enterprise; and collaborative processes that are jointly executed by trading partners. The latest are defined as abstract ones; and to implement it, each trading partner has to define a business interface process (IP). This IP is responsible for the role that a partner plays in a collaborative process, and the invocation and execution of those private processes required for carrying it out. Furthermore, to interchange information Electronic Business Documents (EBDs) are sent as a part of messages exchanged between trading partners. EBDs are standardized data structures that replace traditional business documents; they support the exchange of information required to execute collaborative processes, like order forecasting [2].

Fig. 1 shows a collaborative relation between a brewery (supplier) and one of its clients (retailer). When the IP receives an EBD, it has to translate the information contained in the document to the private processes according to the semantic of corresponding enterprise domains. Then, when the IP has to send an EBD, it has to populate the EBD with the information generated by the corresponding enterprise domains according to the collaborative process semantics. So, to achieve information system interoperability, the IP has to solve a number of conflictive situations at the semantic level that are analyzed in the rest of the paper.

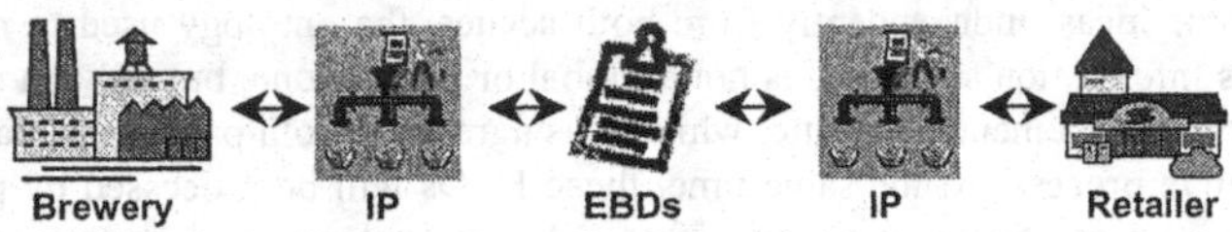

Fig. 1. A collaborative relation between a brewery (supplier) and one of its clients

Supposing a collaborative relation like that above showed, some of the EBDs used in each collaborative subprocess could have the following structures:

Table 1. EBD's structure to interchange in the PAP subprocess

Horizon: *[months]*		
Period	Product	Quantity
[months]	*[Local, Strong, NKH, DUF]*	*[liters]*

Table 2. EBD's structure to interchange in the PMP subprocess

Horizon *[weeks]*										
Period	Product				Quantity	Price		SuggestedPrice		Payment Way
	Type	Trademark	Packaging			Coinage	Amount	Coinage	Amount	
			Size	Type						
[week]	*[Local, Strong, NKH, DUF]*	*[EFS, HCS, NKH, DUF]*	*[cm³]*	*[can, bottle]*	*[units of pack]*	*[$, U$S]*	*[float]*	*[$, U$S]*	*[float]*	*[string]*

In the PMP, for each stage, the quantities are defined in units of pack and new information is incorporated such as price, suggested price and payment way. Generally, time horizon comprises two months, i.e. eight weeks.

Table 3. EBD's structure to interchange in the POP subprocess

Date	Product				Quantity	Price		SuggestedPrice		Payment Way
	Type	Trade mark	Packaging			Coinage	Amount	Coinage	Amount	
			Size	Type						
[day]	*[Local, Strong, NKH, DUF]*	*[EFS, HCS, NKH, DUF]*	*[cm^3]*	*[can, bottle]*	*[units of pack]*	*[\$, U\$S]*	*[float]*	*[\$, U\$S]*	*[float]*	*[string]*

In Table 3, Date column indicates an accurate day in which the products will be available to be dispatched. In a POP, are detailed the quantities, products, prices and payment ways that must be dispatched in the indicated date.

When two enterprises establish a collaborative relation, they have to solve semantic interoperability problems [11]. For that, trading partners must define a way to represent the interchanged information semantic. From this perspective, there are two possible scenes: to develop a single ontology which describes all the EBDs, or to develop an ontology for each EBD. Before analyzing these scenes, it is necessary to clarify some ideas: independently from both scenes, the ontology used to represent the EBDs information semantics is not a global or general one, but only an ontology that describes documents semantic, which was agreed by both partners as part of the collaborative process. At the same time, these EBDs will be processed by partners' private processes; and these may affect different enterprise departments, which usually belong to different domains. That is, at the same enterprise, the same afore mentioned problems of semantics interoperability exist. Then, it is clear that each enterprise has its own ontologies to describe the semantics of its systems and internal areas. These ontologies are different from those agreed with the trading partners.

In spite of afore mentioned, we will concentrate now in the problematic of achieving semantic interoperability at level of EBDs. Following, each of those scenes is analyzed considering possibilities of integrating contexts and ontologies.

2.1 Use of the Same Ontology to Describe the Interchanged Information

Observing the tables that represent the needed information, we can see that there are repeated data in all of them although with particular features. Therefore, it is possible to suppose the use of a single EBD that must be defined as at syntactic as at semantic level to achieve the information interoperability at content level [4]. That is, it is necessary to describe how the information is structured and the meaning of that.

Fig. 2 presents an ontology schematic representation which describes "part of" and "is a" relations between terms of the EBD's structure. This structure had been defined in a consensual way to be used in each stage of the process. In this figure it is considered that the value by default of the relation cardinality is 1. According to this figure, a Plan can be compound by a Horizon or none. By other side, a Plan is compound by one to n Products. Each Product has associated a Quantity to be solicited or supplied, and a Period in which the Product will be solicited or delivered. Finally, a Plan can indicate a Price for each Product, a sale Suggested Price of it, and the Payment Way. Furthermore, in Fig. 2 it is represented that Production Planning, Production Program, and Provision Program are a Plan.

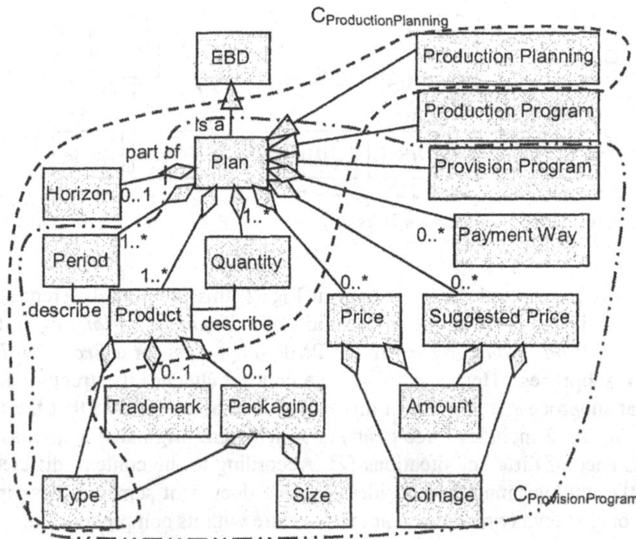

Fig. 2. Ontology of the consensual EBD

The scheme of Fig. 2 is the base to define a shared ontology between trading partners involved in a collaborative relation. That is, according to different ontology development methodologies [12, 13] one of the design stages is the conceptualization stage. This stage can be divided into two tasks that facilitate the definition of ontology: the task to represent the concepts by means of terms and its relations, and the axiomatization task (to add semantic restrictions and relations to the ontology). In this paper are only analyzed examples about the first task.

If the *Type* term of Fig. 2 is considered, this is associated to the *Packaging* and *Product* terms. Even though *Type* has the same semantics, since it describes the class or nature of the concepts which it is associated to, the possible values it may take are different. In the case of *Packaging, Type* can be *Can* or *Bottle*. On the other hand, for *Product, Type* can be *Local, Strong, DUF* or *NKH*. This presents an ambiguity problem that could be resolved replacing the term *Type* by *PackagingType* and *ProductType*. In this way, however, terms are unnecessarily added to the ontology, and this practice could lead to a size increase. A better solution would be to consider *Product* and *Packaging* as different contexts inside of which the term *Type* is interpreted (Fig. 3). In this example, the contexts are been generated with the purpose of resolving name ambiguities [14]. This is solved in other technologies with the namespace concept, which is a space (context) in which object names are unique.

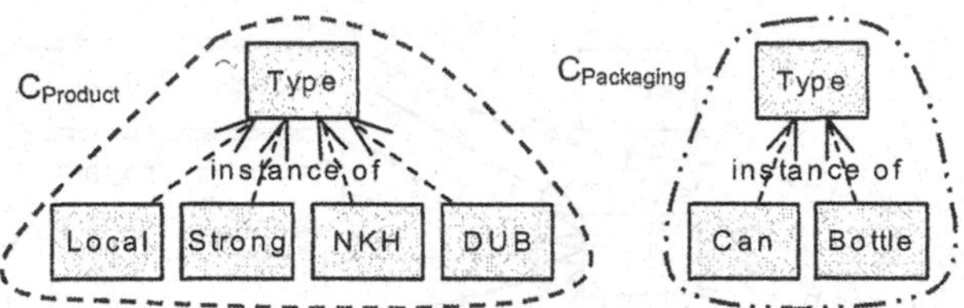

Fig. 3. Contexts that represent name spaces

Now, if it is analyzed the *Plan* term in Fig. 2, this presents different structures depending on if it represents the information of a *Production Planning* in the PAP subprocess, a *Production Program* in the PMP subprocess, or a *Provision Program* in the POP subprocess. Hence, in this case a concept changes its structure according to for what subprocess it is used. In this way, it can be considered that the ontology presented in Fig. 2 includes three contexts which were originated as a consequence of the existence of different situations [2]. According to the context, different terms of the EBD ontology must be considered to the document semantic description. In Fig. 2 are only shown two contexts not to interfere with its comprehension.

Then, as a conclusion of the discussed scene in this section, it can be said that an ontology can describe many contexts, and that a context can contain other contexts.

2.2 Use of Different Ontologies to Describe the Interchanged Information

In this scene it is supposed that different EBD's structures are used in the same collaborative subprocess. In this way, it would have several smaller ontologies to manage in each subprocess.

If the Production Aggregated Planning subprocess is considered as an example, this is divided into many stages [10]: Collaborative agreement, Aggregated planning, Acceptance / counterproposal, and Definitive acceptance.

In the Collaborative agreement stage, trading partners must agree on which products they will go to collaborate and, if they will go to work upon ranges of values, which are the ranges of quantities that the supplier partner is involved to deliver to the client partner. Table 4 shows the EBDs structures to be used to interchange this information.

Table 4. EBDs structures with a collaborative products list and the quantities ranges to supply

Date of agreement: *[date]*
Validity of agreement: *[months]*
Product
[Local, Strong, NKH, DUF]

Horizon: *[months]*			
Period	Product	Quantity	
		Minimal	Maximal
[months]	*[Local, Stronge, NKH, DUF]*	*[liters]*	*[liters]*

Fig. 4 shows the schematic representation of ontologies shared by the collaborative trading partners. Fig. 4a shows the ontology associated to the collaborative products list in so far as Fig. 4b shows the ontology associated to the ranges of quantities to supply.

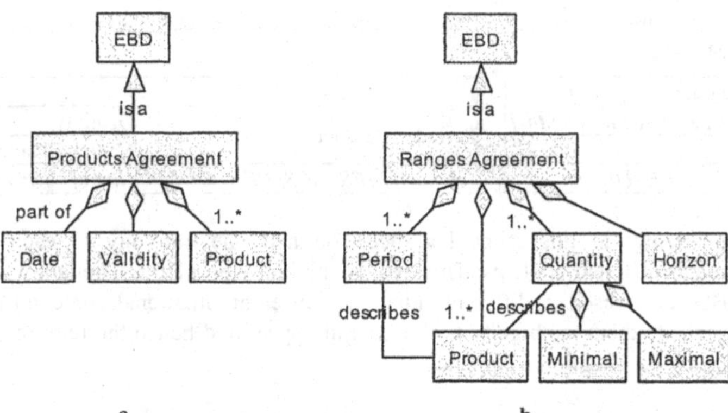

Fig. 4. Shared ontologies in the Collaborative agreement stage of PAP subprocess. a) Products agreement ontology b) Ranges agreement ontology

As well as in the previous scene each subprocess was treated as a different context, also we can think that in each subprocess each stage constitutes a context. That is, the PAP context could be formed by contexts: Collaborative agreement, Aggregated Planning, Acceptance / Counterproposal, and Definitive acceptance.

If it is considered the Collaborative agreement context, this is compound by two ontologies that describe the corresponding EBDs. Analyzing the terms of these ontologies, it is observed that *Product* appears in both of them with the same possible values (*Local*, *Strong*, *NKH*, and *DUF*) but different relations. Though, this not represents a problem since the term belongs to two different ontologies.

Up to here then, it is not evidenced the requirement to make explicit the context. Each partner of collaborative process would be capable to process both types of EBDs without ambiguities. Though, as well as the Production Aggregated Planning subprocess is divided in stages, also the other two subprocesses are [10]. In particular, the Production Master Program subprocess also has a stage named Collaborative agreement. Therefore, it could be used the same EBDs of the Collaborative agreement in the PAP subprocess. Table 5 shows the EBDs structures to be used to interchange information of this stage.

If Tables 4 and 5 are compared, it is observed that the difference between them locates in the possible values of *Product* column. *Product*, in the Collaborative agreement context of PAP, can takes the *Local*, *Strong*, *NKH*, or *DUF* values, whereas that in the Collaborative agreement context of PMP can corresponds to *EFS*, *HCS*, *NKH*, or *DUF*. That is, even though the terms of the structures are the same, the allowed values vary because those represent different concepts. In the Collaborative agreement context of PAP, the *Product* term represents the concept of aggregated product. In so far as in the Collaborative agreement context of PMP, the *Product* term represents the concept of disaggregated product. Hence, to be possible to the partner of the collaborative process to treat correctly the received EBD, he needs to know of which of the subprocess the EBD correspond, i.e., it is necessary to make explicit the context.

Table 5. EBDs structures with a collaborative products list and the quantities ranges to supply for the PMP subprocess

Date of agreement: *[date]*
Validity of agreement: *[months]*
Product
[EFS, HCS, NKH, DUF]

Horizon: *[months]*			
Period	Product	Quantity	
		Minimal	Maximal
[months]	*[EFS, HCS, NKH, DUF]*	*[liters]*	*[liters]*

Summarizing, in this scene had been defined one ontology to each EBD, considered as different contexts. This avoids ambiguity problems. Though, when the same EBDs are reused in different situations (different situational contexts) to that which originate them, ambiguity problems can appear and hence the requirement to make explicit the situational context.

3 Related Works

The objective of this section is to show how the ideas, presented in previous works in different knowledge disciplines, about contexts and ontologies combination are related with the results of the case study presented in the previous section.

The most relevant works that integrate contexts and ontologies have been developed during the last years in the following areas: Semantic Web [3], system information interoperability [4, 5], document classification [6, 7], and context-aware applications [8, 9].

The idea of using contexts to disambiguate terms (synonymous and homonymous) presented in Section 2.1, has been discussed by DeLeenheer and Moor [7]. However in this case, the authors state that the context represents the information source from which terms are extracted and they do not consider another term as a possible context generator. We have shown in the case study that a term can be a context generator as the case of Product and Packaging terms.

Furthermore, from Fig. 2 we can deduce that ontology concepts are the union of context sets. This idea is similar to that presented by Segev and Gal [6] in the document classification area, who proposes a formal mechanism with the objective of mapping contexts, which are views of a domain automatically extracted, to ontologies concepts. This mechanism is used by the authors for routing mails (from the context are extracted) within a government organization composed by departments each of them described by an ontology.

In addition, it is possible to observe from Fig. 2, that there is an intersection between contexts and an inclusion of contexts. Furthermore, context could change along time. This idea is similar to that considered by Gu et al. [9] in the context-aware applications, who present a context model based on an ontology in order to support diverse tasks within intelligent environments. This model supports the representation of semantic contexts by defining a high level ontology that capture the general context knowledge about the physical world within pervasive computing environments, and providing a set of domain specific ontologies that define the details of general concepts and their properties within each sub domain (context into other context).

As a conclusion from two previous paragraphs, the case study shows that it is possible to have union, intersection and inclusion of contexts, but none of the analyzed proposals manage all the possibilities.

In contrast, to achieve the semantic interoperability among heterogeneous information systems, Wache and Stuckenschmidt [5] propose the use of a shared terminology of properties used to define different concepts. This terminology has to be enough general to be used through different information sources (contexts) to be integrated but enough specific to make possible significant definitions. Then, the authors use this basic shared vocabulary to derived relations into a shared ontology.

Finally, Bouquet et al. [3] present the idea of contextual ontologies. The authors say that an ontology is contextualized when its contents are kept local, and therefore not shared with other ontologies, and mapped with the contents of other ontologies via explicit context mappings. This idea of contextual ontologies does not fit into the problematic of semantic interoperability between trading partners we are putting forward because we have seen in the case study that both concepts are related in other ways. However, in [3] is discussed the mapping between concepts, which is not considered in this paper.

4 Conclusions and Future Works

In this paper, through an actual case study, we have analyzed the problematic of integrating contexts and ontologies in order to support the interoperability of a collaborative business process over the Internet. We have presented two situations: one in which an ontology involves different contexts and another in which one context involves different ontologies. In both cases, we can observe that the document reutilization for information interchange drives the necessity to make the context explicit. Furthermore, we have seen that none of previous proposals solve all interoperability problems of a collaborative business process.

From the case study presented in Section 2 we can enumerate some advantages from contexts and ontologies combination:

- *To reduce the ontology size.* Working with a universe of reduced terms makes the tasks of information retrieval and interoperability more easy and efficient.
- *To show important details.* The context use allows the creation of concept groups which are important for a particular situation, hiding those concepts that are not relevant.
- *Information sources reutilization.* It is possible to have a unique data structure (tables or XML documents) associated to different contexts, in which the information within these structures be processed according to the context features where the information has to be integrated.

These advantages are not the only ones. Future research will focus on defining other case studies in order to discover other advantages. However, these advantages are significant enough to think about integrating ontologies and context to represent information semantic.

Furthermore, it is necessary to analyze the effort required to achieve the combination of contexts and ontologies. Also, we will study the problematic of mapping between private ontologies of trading partners and EBDs ontologies, considering involved contexts and their representations.

References

1. T.R. Grüber, Toward Principles for the Design of Ontologies Used for Knowledge Sharing, International Journal of Human-Computer Studies, Special Issue on Formal Ontology in Conceptual Analysis and Knowledge Representation, (1993).
2. M. L. Caliusco, A Semantic Definition Support of Electronic Business Documents in e–Colaboration (Universidad Tecnológica Nacional, F.R.S.F., 2005). ISBN 987–43–9158–8.
3. P. Bouquet, F. Giunchiglia, F. van Hamelen, L. Serafini, and H. Stuckenschmidt, Contextualizing Ontologies, Journal of Web Semantics, 1(4), 325–343 (2004).
4. A.P. Sheth, in: Interoperating Geographic Information Systems/ Changing Focus on Interoperability in Information Systems: from System, Syntax, Structure to Semantics, edited by M. Goodchild, M. Egenhofer, R. Fegeas, and C. Kottman (Kluwer Academic Publishers, Norwell, Massachussets, USA, 1999), pp. 5–30.
5. H. Wache, and H. Stuckenschmidt, in: Modeling and Using Context: Third International and Interdisciplinary Conference/ Practical Context Transformation for Information System Interoperability, edited by V. Akman, P. Bouquet, R. Thomason, and R.A. Young (Springer-Verlag GmbH, Dundee, UK, 2001), pp. 367–380.
6. A. Segev, and A. Gal, in: Contexts and Ontologies: Theory, Practice and Applications: Papers from the 2005 AAAI Workshop/ Putting Things in Context: a Topological Approach to Mapping Contexts and Ontologies, edited by P. Shvaiko, J. Euzenat, A. Leger, D.L. McGuinness, and H. Wache (AAAI Press, Menlo Park, California, 2005), pp. 9–16.
7. P. De Leenheer, and A. de Moor, in: Contexts and Ontologies: Theory, Practice and Applications: Papers from the 2005 AAAI Workshop/ Context-driven Disambiguation in Ontology Elicitation, edited by P. Shvaiko, J. Euzenat, A. Leger, D.L. McGuinness, and H. Wache (AAAI Press, Menlo Park, California, 2005), pp. 17–24.
8. H. Chen, T. Finin, and A. Joshi, An Ontology for Context-Aware Pervasive Computing Environments, The Knowledge Engineering Review, Special Issue on Ontologies for Distributed Systems, 18(03), 197–207, 2003.
9. T. Gu, X. Wang, H. Pung, and D. Zhang, in: Proceedings of Communication Networks and Distributed Systems Modeling and Simulation Conference/ An Ontology-based Context Model in Intelligent Environments (San Diego, California, USA, 2004).
10. P. Villarreal, M.L. Caliusco, M.R. Galli, E. Salomone, and O. Chiotti, in: Emerging Issues on Supply Chain Management/ Decentralized Process Management for Inter-Enterprise Collaboration, edited by B. Sahay (MacMillan India Limited, New Delhi, India, 2004).
11. M.L. Caliusco, M.R. Galli, and O. Chiotti, Ontology and XML–based Specifications for Collaborative B2B Relationships, CLEI Electronic Journal, Special Issue of Best Papers presented at JIISIC'2003, 7(1), Paper 5 (2004).
12. N. Noy, and D. McGuinness, Ontology Development 101: A Guide to Creating Your First Ontology, Stanford Knowledge Systems Laboratory, Technical Report KSL-01-05, and Stanford Medical Informatics, Technical Report SMI-2001-0880, March 2001.
13. A. Gómez-Pérez, M. Fernández, and A.J. de Vicente, in: Proceedings of the Workshop on Ontological Engineering/ Towards a Method to Conceptualize Domain Ontologies, edited by P. van der Vet (Budapest, Hungary, 1996), pp. 41–52.
14. M. Theodorakis, Contextualization: An Abstraction Mechanism for Information Modeling, PhD thesis, (Department of Computer Science, University of Crete, Greece, 2001).

The RR Project – A Framework for Relationship Network Viewing and Management

César Stradiotto[1], Everton Pacheco[1], Andre Bortolon[1], Hugo Hoeschl[2]
1 WBSA Sistemas Inteligentes SA, Parque Tecnológico Alfa, Centro de Tecnologia IlhaSoft , SC 401 Km 1 - Módulo 10 - Térreo B - João Paulo - 88030-000 - Florianópolis, SC – Brasil
{cesar,evertonpp,bortolon, hugo}@wbsa.com.br
WWW home page: http://www.wbsa.com.br
2 Instituto de Governo Eletrônico, Inteligência Jurídica e Sistemas – IJURIS, Rua Lauro Linhares, 728 – sala 105 – Trindade - 88036-0002 - Florianópolis – SC – Brasil
WWW home page: http://www.ijuris.org

Abstract. The Relationship Networks Project (RR - Redes de Relacionamento) is an innovative project, which intends to create a framework, which allows - through a fast data modeling - implementing interface elements that describe in a clearly visual way, in two-dimensional presentation, a relationship network among heterogeneous items. This environment also allows the machine to do operations over these relations, such as to find paths or sets, to help the implementation of AI algorithms, or data extraction by the final user. Through graph theory, with visual items, it is possible to find elements with specific characteristics and relationships between them, by the application of filters, refining searches inside an extreme large datasets, or showing differentiated connection maps. Two prototypes were created with this framework: A system which allows seeing telephonic calls sets and financial transactions, and a system for ontology viewing for a digital dictionary inside a semantic network. Another software, in prototypical phase, also for semantic network vision, is being constructed. This document will present the basic RR structure, showing and justifying the creation of the two referred software above.

Introduction

Recent studies have directed its focus statistical properties of networked systems, like Internet or social networks. By Girvan [1] researchers have concentrated particularly on some common properties to many types of networks: the small world property, distribution degrees following potential functions, network transitivity, and one more property: the community structure, where the net nodes are grouped closely, and between these groups, there are some weak connections.
Jumping from mathematics to biology and linguistics, Barabasi [2] says that researches on networked systems also include items such protein actuation over

Please use the following format when citing this chapter:

Stradiotto, C., Pacheco, E., Bortolon, A., Hoeschl, H., 2006, in IFIP International Federation for Information Processing, Volume 218, Professional Practice in Artificial Intelligence, eds. J. Debenham, (Boston: Springer), pp. 121–130.

Problems involving data relationship networks occurs with high frequency, needing media through which it can be possible the clear vision over these data. Together with that, data and relation types between them vary largely, depending on the problem scope.
In this way, software that could describe some type of data, inside a determined scope, could not fit for another type of problem, or it had to suffer some modifications to adequate to the new problem.
The Relationship Network Project (or in Portuguese: RR - Redes de Relacionamento) intends to allow the software project manager to implement in fast way a software that make two-dimensional demonstration of heterogeneous data, related by vertex and edges, including edition and analysis, and Artificial Intelligence tools.
In the following document it will be described two case studies involving the use of the same environment of RR project: 1) Vision and edition of telephone calls and money transferring, and 2) Vision of ontology dictionaries from a semantic network.

1 Environment Basic Structure

1.1 Structure

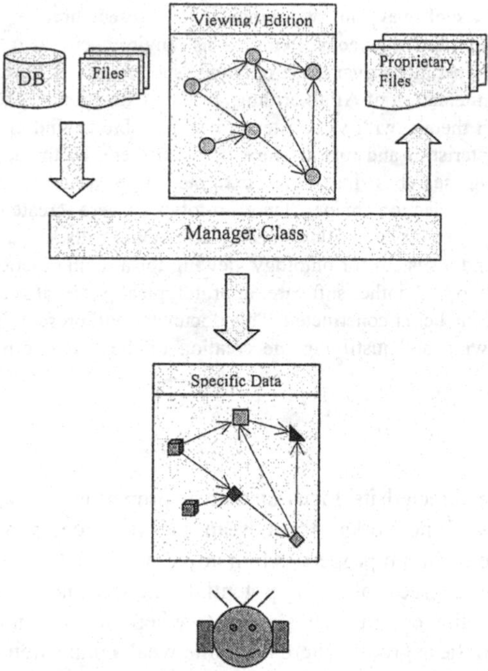

Fig. 1. Environment Basic Structure

The environment basic structure (Fig. 1) is composed by five modules: Management, Data Reading, Viewing / Edition, Specific Data, and Data Writing. Such structure allows maintaining the independent programming between these modules; in such a way that makes easy the implementation work to achieve the new entered data types.

Managing Module It's the module that contains the menus, which allows the user to execute the system main activities. Also contains rules that will be used by the Viewing / edition module, and filters, which can be applied to the working data.
In this module it's possible to choose the picture to represent the data from its type, or to execute filtering and require data reading or writing. Here are implemented also the Artificial Intelligence and Graph Theory algorithms, responsible by the automatic processing of the information about to be analyzed.

Data Reading Module Does the inclusion of data inside the system, be it originated on databases, electronic datasheet, proprietary files or formatted text. It does exist just to make compatible data from different natures, to be shown inside the viewing system as a linked network.

Viewing / Edition Module Responsible for showing the connected data to the final user, allowing its edition, navigation, and responsible for showing analysis results. This module is present inside any application for network data viewing developed over the RR environment.

Specific Data Module Contains the application specific data. And such application is built over the RR framework.

Data Writing Module Responsible for managing data persistence, in a proprietary format for the implemented application, or in a specific format, depending on the client's demand, allowing data compatibility with another framework or software.

1.2 Used technologies

The framework is done over Windows platform, with Borland C++ Builder IDE. The communication with databases is done via ODBC. Visual Data are stored in proprietary format.

2 Interface

The interfaced is based on MDI (Multiple Document Interface). So it allows many visual instances from many data groups (Fig. 2).

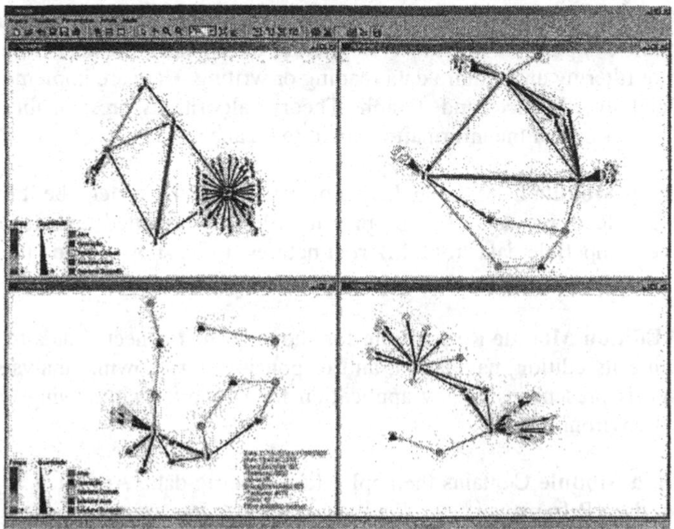

Fig. 2. MDI Application sample made with the RR framework.

3 Case Studies

3.1 Telephone calls and financial transactions networks management

Telephony case

Accordingly Siqueira [3] the numbers of telephone calls inside Brazil have raised 600% between 1994 and the beginning of 2002, starting from 103 million calls a day to 715 million. In that time the country had 70 million telephonic accesses, being 40 million made by common telephones, against 30 million cellular. Each of these generating a mean number of 10 calls a day. In the same time, the number of Internet users jumped from 200 thousand to 14 million users, including voice, data and image traffic services.

Dias [4] says that in November of 2003, the numbers of cellular telephones was 43 million, and the number of common telephones was estimated to be about 39,4 million units. A good number of these calls made a network of illegal or criminal acts, being necessary its tracking under judicial orders for investigation and analysis. In this group are included common telephones, cellular telephones with voice and textual calls, modem's with Internet access, fax, and email messages, among others.

Lobato [5] quotes the existence of 10 thousand judicial processes and queries involving fraudulent acts made by cellular and standing telephony in Brazil. These including public telephone cable deviation, cellular cloning, cold fiscal notes for stolen cellular telephone habilitation, and clandestine telephonic interception.

Financial Cases

Correspondingly the news agency IDG NOW [6] "Trojan attacks, virtual mechanisms that induce users to give personal information like passwords or bank data, raised 1184% in Brazil, between July and December last year... In the same time interval, the mean rate of attacks in another countries raised 293%."

Filho [7] affirms that money losses from Brazil to foreign countries through CC5 type cash accounts stands by US$ 40 billion, due to law features, which allows such money transferring by secret ways, and without the payment of corresponding taxes to Brazilian Central Bank.

Mcdowell [8] enumerate some damage suffered by governments and enterprises, due to money-washing processes. Some quoted damages are:

- Exposition of emergent markets, where money-washing groups invests their money on properties or companies, creating monopolies or breaking that countries / companies taking back the invested money, without any accordance. Such behavior also damages the invested company public image;

- Creation of apparent companies, which can practice prices lower than that practiced on the local market, breaking concurrent industries;

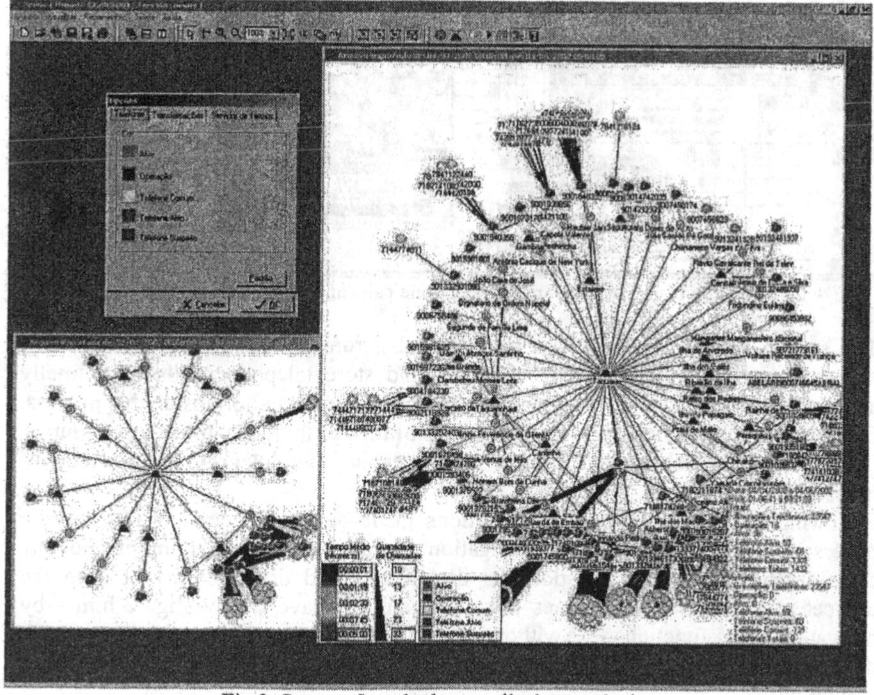

Fig.3. System for telephone calls data analysis.

Observing the necessity of a tool to help investigators that works on problems like the ones described above, the RR framework was created initially as a basic module for a software able to make analysis of telephonic calls datasets [9] (Fig.3), being a graphic tool that clearly shows the worked data, able to give relevant information, even when the data is first viewed. This tool has filtering resources, edition modes, storage and data recovery, telephonic calls pathfinder and report generation. After that, the system was evolved for load, analysis and persistence also of financial transaction data (Fig.4).

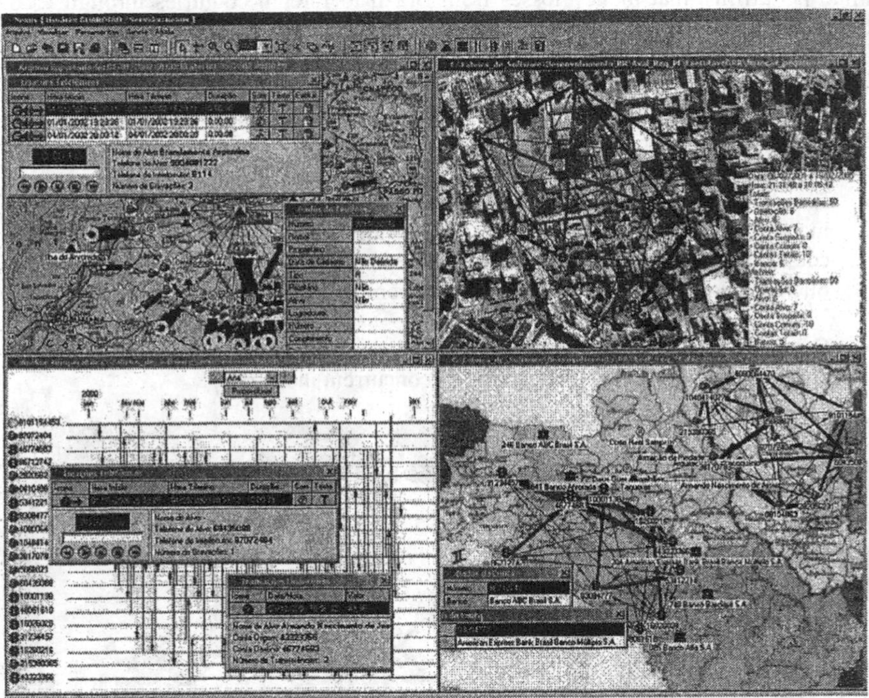

Fig. 4: Screen taken from the software for telephone calls and financial transactions analysis.

The system enables juridical area professionals, from police intelligence, security, and financial government organs, to track and store telephone calls by a totally automated and confidential way, without any human intervention inside this process. In this way the systems avoid totally the possibilities of fraud or human errors during the process of catching and storing calls, keeping the integrity and secrecy of investigative operations.

Following Mendroni [10] "... investigations made before prosecution acts may be necessarily secrets. If not, the investigation is frustrated by its beginning. For the same reason that a criminal does its illegal acts and does not reveal it to the competent authorities, these ones not only can, but have to investigate him - by obligation of its functions - ... without show its contents, until it can group enough data to made a convincement, and after all that, take the adequate decisions about that crime."

3.2 Vision of semantic networks

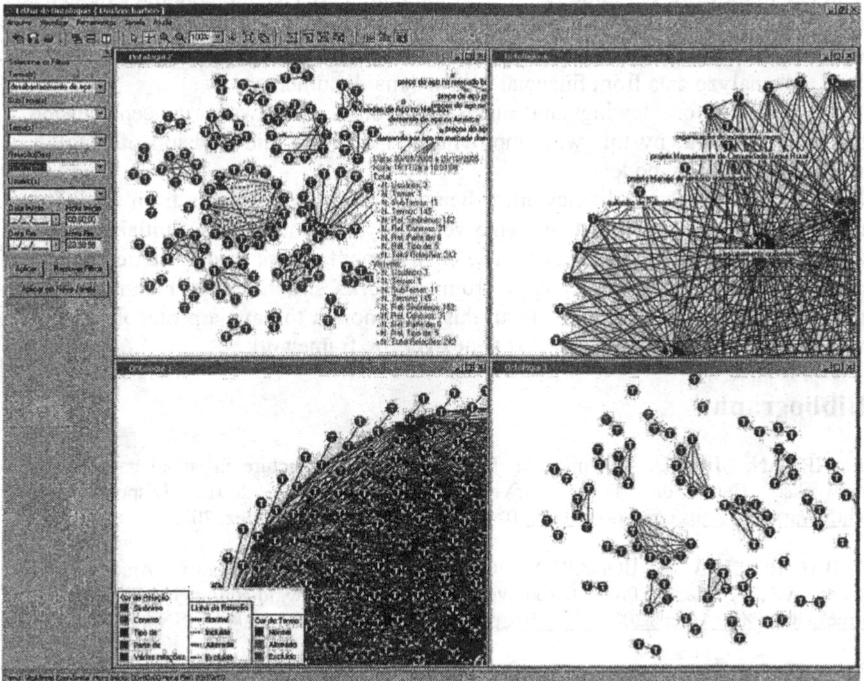

Fig. 5. Exemplo de ferramenta para visão de redes de ontologias.

The number of applications involving knowledge representation has increased more and more at last times, and many models used to implement these applications do these representations through semantic networks [14,15,16,17,18]. Such systems also need edition tools used by the responsible professional that takes care of these semantic nets.

Cawsey [19] affirms that a semantic network is a relationship network, where the nodes inside the graph represent concepts, and the edges represents binary relations between these concepts.

The RR framework goes inside there like a tool for viewing relationships, hierarchies and rules inside a semantic net production environment. A sample environment to produce ontologies is described on Bueno[20]. The first used prototype (Fig.5) was a case for edition of rules and relations for the ontology dictionary inside KMAI project [21]. The RR framework allows a clear visual disposal of the net, and inclusion of concepts and relations between them, all of these represented by vertex and edges.

4 Conclusions

The RR framework fits initially for software that serves as a telephonic call analysis tool, causing a sensible impact in the way these types of data were analyzed, showing recently its first results. After that, the software evolved for a tool that can load and analyze data from financial transactions documents.

It served also for viewing and analysis of relations between concepts inside a semantic network, by this way improving the creation and revision of ontologies inside a production model.

By the fact that the RR framework is being used inside problems from so different domains, such fact shows its extreme versatility. Although these initial results, its applicability doesn't finishes here. The environment shows itself generic enough to deal with data from diverse types, from networks structured over simple lists to multimedia inside the web. To do all this, it's enough to have a protocol to feed de visual net inside the software that is done over the framework.

Bibliography

1. GIRVAN, Michelle.; Newman, M. E. J. Community structure in social and biological networks. Base de Dados arXiv.org – 07 dec. 2001. Disponível em: <http://arxiv.org/abs/cond-mat/0112110> página 2. Acesso em: 12 dez. 2003

2. BARABÁSI, A. L.; BONABEAU, E. Scale-Free Networks. Scientific American, New York. v.1, 7 dec. 2001. Disponível em: <http://www.nd.edu/~networks/PDF/Scale-Free%20Sci%20Amer%20May03.pdf>. p52. Acesso em: 14 Jan. 2004 - ISSN 0036-8733.

3. SIQUEIRA, E. Brasil fala 600% mais que em 1994. 24 mar. 2002. O Estado de São Paulo. Disponível em: <http://txt.estado.com.br/colunistas/siqueira/2002/03/siqueira020324.html>. Acesso em: 12 dez. 2003

4. DIAS, J. A. Telefonia Atrairá Investidor Externo. Folha de São Paulo. 11 jan. 2004. Caderno Folha Dinheiro. Disponível em: <http://www1.folha.uol.com.br/fsp/dinheiro/fi1101200410.htm>. Acesso em: 12 jan. 2004.

5. LOBATO, E. Fraude Telefônica Fica Mais Sofisticada. 23 nov. 2003. Folha de São Paulo. Caderno Folha Cotidiano. Disponível em <http://www1.folha.uol.com.br/fsp/cotidian/ff2311200317.htm>. Acesso em: 30 nov. 2003.

6. IDGNOW .Cavalos de Tróia crescem 1184% em 2004. http://idgnow.uol.com.br/AdPortalv5/SegurancaInterna.aspx?GUID=4D152F5C-4EB6-4884-9AAE-E301FDFD74E$&ChannelID=21080105 IDG NOW \ SEGURANÇA \ NOTÍCIA Publicado em 2 fevereiro de 2005.

7. FILHO, A.G.P. As contas CC5 e as instituições financeiras internacionais. Portal de Contabilidade. 20 de janeiro de 2006. http://www.cosif.com.br/publica.asp?arquivo=20050407cc5ilegais Acessado em janeiro de 2006.

8. MCDOWELL, J, NOVIS, G. As Conseqüências da Lavagem de Dinheiro e dos Crimes Financeiros. Perspectivas Econômicas, Maio de 2001 http://usinfo.state.gov/journals/ites/0501/ijep/ie0502.htm Acessado em novembro de 2005.

9. STRADIOTTO, C. R. K.; BORTOLON, A.; HOESCHL, H. C.; MARAFON, M. J.. Ferramenta de Desenvolvimento de Software para Representação Visual de Redes de Relacionamento. In: CONGRESSO NACIONAL DE TECNOLOGIA DA INFORMAÇÃO E COMUNICAÇÃO, 2004. http://www.sucesu2005.com.br/palestras2004/24.html Acessado em Janeiro de 2006

10. MENDRONI, M. B. O Sigilo da Fase Pré-Processual. Revista Justitia, p1. São Paulo [2004] Disponível em: <http://www.mp.sp.gov.br/justitia/CRIMINAL/crime%2035.pdf>. Acesso em: jan. 2004.

11. BARRETO, A. S.; BUENO, T. C. D.; HOESCHL, H. C. Applying Case Based Reasoning to Knowledge Representation of Tributary Decisions. In: THE 9th INTERNATIONAL CONFERENCE ON ARTIFICIAL INTELLIGENCE AND LAW, 2003, Edimburgh. Proceedings... New York: Association for Computer Machinery (ACM) – p. 77. ISBN 1-58113-747-8.

12. BUENO, T. C. D. et al. Using RBC to Classify Judicial Petitions on e-Court. In: THE 9th INTERNATIONAL CONFERENCE ON ARTIFICIAL INTELLIGENCE AND LAW, 2003, Edimburgh. Proceedings... New York: Association for Computer Machinery (ACM) – p83. ISBN 1-58113-747-8.

13. COSTA, F.C.; BUENO, T.C.D.; RIBEIRO, E.B.Q. New Procedures for Environmental Licensing with Artificial Intelligence – CIPPLA. In: THE 9th INTERNATIONAL CONFERENCE ON ARTIFICIAL INTELLIGENCE AND LAW, 2003, Edimburgh. Proceedings... New York: Association for Computer Machinery (ACM) – p87. ISBN 1-58113-747-8.

14. HOESCHL. H.C. et al. Dynamically Contextualized Knowledge Representation of the United Nations Security Council Resolutions. In: THE 9th INTERNATIONAL CONFERENCE ON ARTIFICIAL INTELLIGENCE AND LAW, 2003, Edimburgh. Proceedings... New York: Association for Computer Machinery (ACM) – p. 95. ISBN 1-58113-747-8.

15. HOESCHL. H.C. et al. Knowledge-Based System Applied on the Previous Consent of Brazilian National Defense Council. In: THE 9th INTERNATIONAL CONFERENCE ON ARTIFICIAL INTELLIGENCE AND LAW, 2003, Edimburgh. Proceedings... New York: Association for Computer Machinery (ACM) – p. 97. ISBN 1-58113-747-8.

16. MATTOS, E.S. et al. A Knowledge Base for Automatic Capitulation in Expert System. In: THE 9th INTERNATIONAL CONFERENCE ON ARTIFICIAL INTELLIGENCE AND LAW, 2003, Edimburgh. Proceedings... New York: Association for Computer Machinery (ACM) – p. 99. ISBN 1-58113-747-8.

17. RDF. Resource Description Framework. Disponível em: <http://www.w3.org/RDF/>. Acesso em: jan. 2004.

18. XU, Z.; WU, J. A Survey Of Knowledge Base Grid For Traditional Chinese Medicine. In: THE FIFTH INTERNATIONAL CONFERENCE ON ENTERPRISE INFORMATION SYSTEM, v. 4. Software Agents and Internet Computer, 2003, Angers. Proceedings... Setúbal: Escola Superior de Tecnologia de Setubal. p. 136. ISBN: 972-98816-1-8. Disponível em: < http://www.iceis.org>. Acesso em: 19 jan. 2004.

19. CAWSEY, A. Semantic Nets. Disponível em: <http://www.cee.hw.ac.uk/~alison/ai3notes/subsection2_4_2_1.html>. Acesso em: jan. 2004.

20. BUENO T. C. D et al. Knowledge Engineering Suite: a Tool to Create Ontologies for Automatic Knowledge Representation in Knowledge-based Systems. in: The 2nd International Workshop on Natural Language Understanding And Cognitive Science (NLUCS-2005) in ICEIS - 7th international conference. Proceedings of 7th International Conference On Enterprise Information Systems. 2005.

21. RIBEIRO, M. S. KMAI: da RC2D à PCE. 2003. 190f. Dissertação (Mestrado em Engenharia de Produção) – Universidade Federal de Santa Catarina, Florianópolis, 2003.

Web Service-based Business Process Automation Using Matching Algorithms

Yanggon Kim[1] and Juhnyoung Lee[2]
1 Computer and Information Sciences,
Towson University, Towson, MD 21252, USA,
ykim@towson.edu
2 IBM T. J. Watson Research Center
Yorktown Heights, New York 10598, USA,
jyl@us.ibm.com

Abstract. In this paper, we focus on two problems of the Web service-based business process integration: the discovery of Web services based on the capabilities and properties of published services, and the composition of business processes based on the business requirements of submitted requests. We propose a solution to these problems, which comprises multiple matching algorithms, a micro-level matching algorithm and macro-level matching algorithms. The solution from the macro-level matching algorithms is optimal in terms of meeting a certain business objective, e.g., minimizing the cost or execution time, or maximizing the total utility value of business properties of interest. Furthermore, we show how existing Web service standards, UDDI and BPEL4WS, can be used and extended to specify the capabilities of services and the business requirements of requests, respectively.

1 Introduction

A *business process* refers to a process in which work is organized, coordinated, and focused to produce a valuable product or service. Business processes comprise both internal and external business partners and drive their collaboration to accomplish shared business goals by enabling highly fluid process networks. A *business process solution* consists of a model of the underlying business process (referred to as a *process model* or a *flow model*) and a set of (flow-independent) business logic modules. The abstractions of the elementary pieces of work in a flow model are called *activities*; the concrete realizations of these abstractions at process execution time are referred to as *activity implementations*. The prevalent technique for creating business process solutions follows a manual and tedious approach involving assimilation of varied process design and vendor specifications and writing vast amount of code that produces a tight inflexible coupling between processes. *Web*

Please use the following format when citing this chapter:

Kim, Y., Lee, J., 2006, in IFIP International Federation for Information Processing, Volume 218, Professional Practice in Artificial Intelligence, eds. J. Debenham, (Boston: Springer), pp. 131–140.

services provide a set of technologies for creating business process solutions in an efficient, standard way. The promise of Web services is to enable a distributed environment in which any number of applications, or application components, can interoperate seamlessly within an organization or between companies in a platform-neutral, language-neutral fashion. From the perspective of business process solutions, a Web service could represent an activity within a business process, or a composite business process comprising a number of steps [7]. A Building a business process solution by using Web services involves specifying the potential execution order of operations from a collection of Web services, the data shared among the Web services, which business partners are involved and how they are involved in the business process, and joint exception handling for collections of Web services. A basis for these specification tasks is the discovery, composition, and interoperation of Web services, which are primary pillars of automatic process integration and management solutions. In this paper, we focus on the following two problems of the Web service-based business process automation: the location of services based the capabilities of published services, and the composition of business processes based on the business requirements of submitted process requests. This paper discusses solutions to these problems, and, especially, focuses on the following aspects: the specification of the capabilities of services and the requirements of requests, and algorithms for matching published services and submitted process requests in terms of service capabilities and requested business requirements.

The rest of this paper is structured as follows: Section 2 summarizes the previous work on the problems of interest, discusses their limitations, and explains how the work presented in this paper addresses them. Section 3 addresses issues involved with the specification of business requirements in process request documents. Section 4 presents a matching algorithm for locating services based on service capabilities and properties. Section 5 presents matching algorithms that are deigned to satisfy the business requirements and provide optimal solutions in terms of meeting certain business objectives. In Section 6, conclusions are drawn and future work is outlined.

2 Related Work

Recently, there have been active studies related to the Web service-based process automation in both academia and industry. Industrial effort for the business process automation is centered around the Business Process Execution Language for Web Services (BPEL4WS), which is an XML-based workflow definition language that allows companies to describe business processes that can both consume and provide Web services [14]. Along with complementary specifications, WS-Coordination and WS-Transaction, BPEL4WS provides a basis for a business process automation framework, and is viewed to become the basis of a Web service standard for composition. With the BPEL4WS specification, vendors such as IBM provide workflow engines (e.g., BPWS4J [13]) on which business processes written in BPEL4WS can be executed. Running on Web application servers such as Apache Tomcat, the workflow engines support the coordinated invocation, from within the process, of Web services. There are some studies, mostly from academia, done for the specification of service capabilities and process requests by using semantic knowledge-based markup languages, notably, OWL-S(formerly known as DAML-S) [2].

For matching published services and submitted process requests in terms of service capabilities and requested business requirements, we propose a system multiple matching algorithms, a *micro-level matching algorithm*, which matches the capabilities and attributes of published services with activities in a process request, and *macro-level matching algorithms*, which are used to compose a business process by selecting one service for each activity among the candidate services selected by the micro-level algorithm. Some previous work envisioned the task of business process composition as an AI-inspired *planning* problem [3, 11]. They represent a Web service by a rule that expresses the service capable of producing a particular output, given a certain input. Then, a rule-based expert system is used to automatically determine whether a desired composite process can be realized using existing services, and construct a plan that instantiates the process.

3 Requirement Specification

In this section, we address issues involved with the specification of business requirements and objectives in process request documents. We discuss what information on business requirements and preferences need to be specified in process request documents and how the information may be used in the discovery of services and the composition of processes. We extend the BPEL4WS specification to accommodate this information in business process documents. Business process documents written in BPEL4WS mostly consist of the following parts, which are primary components of BPEL4WS [14]:

- Process definition,
- Partner definition,
- Container definition,
- Flow model, and
- Fault handling.

Fig. 1 shows an example of specifying several requirements for a business process, i.e., cost, time and quality of services. In Section 5, we will explain how this requirement information is used in selecting services for composing a business process with an algorithm for optimizing certain business objectives, or a multi-attribute decision analysis algorithm that maximizes the total utility value of selected service combinations.

```
<businessRequirements>
  <requirement name="processBudget"
         type="cost"
         value="30000.00"
         unit="USD"
         limit="maximum"
         weight="10" />
```

```
    <requirement name="processTime"
            type="time"
            value="365"
            unit="days"
            limit="maximum"
            weight="7" />
    <requirement name="processAvailability"
            type="quality"
            value="98.0"
            unit="%"
            limit="minimum"
            weight="5" />
</businessRequirements>
```

Fig. 1. Specification of business requirement

In addition to business requirements, users of business processes sometimes need to express their preferences in selecting Web services for implementing processes. An example is the preference regarding whom a company prefers (or does not prefer) partnering with in a business process depending on its existing business relationship with service providers.

4 Service Discovery with Micro-Level Matching

This algorithm returns a (pre-specified) number of services that sufficiently match with an activity in the request. It is based on the previous work in [3, 9] which allows service providers to advertise their services in OWL-S service profile markup, and match submitted requests again in OWL-S profile markup with appropriate services. Unlike this previous work, our work does not depend on OWL-S profile, but utilizes the specification of service capabilities and request requirements directly stored in UDDI records and BPEL4WS documents, respectively. This algorithm is referred to as a *micro-level matching algorithm*, because it mostly deals with a single atomic process of a request.

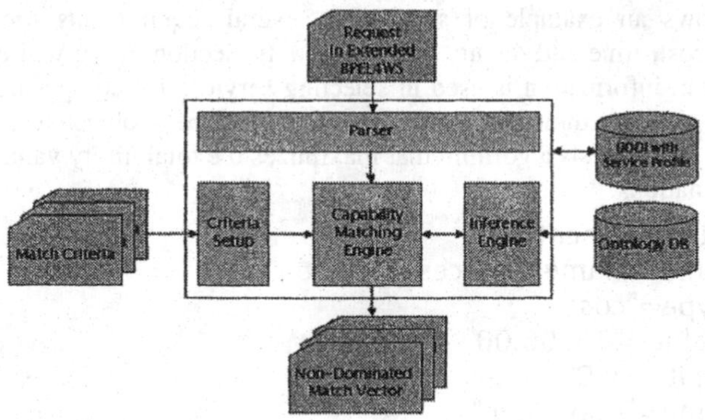

Fig. 2. The micro-level matching algorithm

Fig.2 depicts the architecture of the micro-level matching algorithm. The Parser module is capable of parsing an input BPEL4WS document and creates objects storing business requirements specified in the documents. The Inference Engine module parses and reasons with ontologies that provide the working model of entities and interactions in knowledge domains of interest, specified in the OWL language [5, 6]. The Capability Matching Engine is based on the semantic matching algorithms outlined in [3, 9]. While the matching algorithm presented in [9] is constrained to match only input and output messages of Web services, the algorithm proposed in [3] generalized the previous algorithm to match for any attribute of services and requests by parameterizing the match criteria such as quality, service categories as well as input and output messages. Figure 4 outlines the main control loop of the matching algorithm, which is based on the work in [3]. The *degree of match* is a measure of the semantic distance between the conceptual meanings of the service attributes [3, 9]. Each attribute has a lexical concept attached to it that is defined in the Ontology Database available to the Inference Engine. We use three different degrees of matches based on specialization relationship as defined in [9]. As given in the degreeOfMatch module of Fig.3 , the degrees of match are preferentially ordered based on the semantic distance that the degree represents: an EXACT match between concepts is preferred to a PLUG_IN match, and a PLUG_IN match is preferred over a SUBSUMES match [9].

```
matchAttribute(request, service, matchCriteria) {
  for each criteria in matchCriteria do {
    requestAttributes = request(attributeCriteria);
    serviceAttributes = service(attributeCriteria);
    for each requestAttribute in requestAttributes do {
      for each serviceAttribute in serviceAttributes do {
        degreeMatch = degreeOfMatch(requestAttribute,
                                    serviceAttribute);
        if (degreeMatch < matchLimit)
          return fail;
        if (degreeMatch < globalDegreeMatch)
          globalDegreeMatch = degreeMatch;
      }
    }
  }
  return success;
}
degreeOfMatch(requestAttribute, serviceAttribute) {
 if requestAttribute is SameClassAs serviceAttribute return EXACT;
 if serviceAttribute is SubClassOf requestAttribute return PLUG_IN;
 if requestAttribute is SubClassOf requestAttribute return SUBSUMES;
 else return FAIL;
}
```

Fig. 3 Capability matching algorithm

5 Macro-Level Matching

The micro-matching algorithm works with other matching algorithms, *macro-level matching algorithms*, which are used to compose a business process by selecting one service for each activity in the request. The output from the macro-level matching algorithms satisfies the business requirements of the submitted request, and provides optimal solutions in terms of meeting a certain objective, e.g., minimizing the cost or execution time, or maximizing a certain quality measure. In this paper, we model the macro-level matching problem as a variation of the *multiple-choice knapsack problem* [8], and design a configurable, generic optimization engine, which can be repeatedly run with variations of configuration criteria in search for a business process solution best fit the need. In addition, we alternatively model the macro-level matching problem as a *multi-attribute decision making problem*. This model is particularly useful when it is not sufficient to provide an optimal solution for a single measure, but requires maximizing the total utility value of multiple business measures of interest. Our algorithm is based on *multi-attribute decision analysis*, which computes the scores of the candidate service combinations by considering their attributes values and capabilities, ranks the candidates by score, and selects services among the top-rankers.

5.1 Multiple-Choice Knapsack Algorithm

Fig.4 displays the architecture of the macro-level matching algorithm. The input to the matching algorithm is a set of Non-Dominated Match Vectors, one vector for each atomic activity in the request, which were generated by the micro-level matching algorithm. The output of the optimization engine is a set of services selected from the input, one service from each Non-Dominated Match Vector. The match engine can be customized for different business objectives and constraints as specified in another input to the engine, the Configuration.

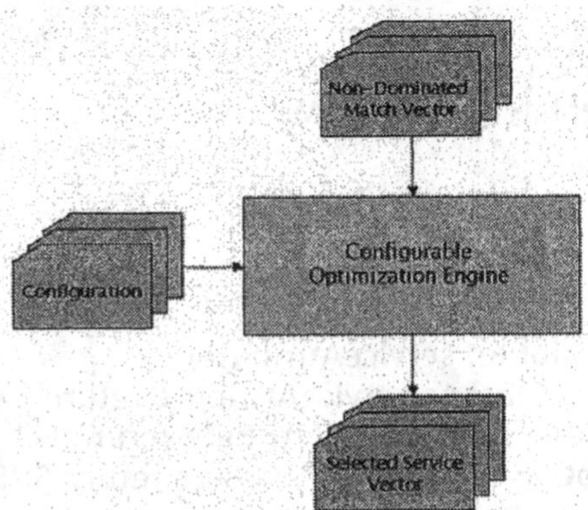

Fig.4. The macro-level matching algorithm

We model the macro-level matching problem as a variation of the *multiple-choice knapsack problem* [8]. The "multiple-choice" term in this problem designation refers to the requirement of selecting exactly one service from each candidate list, i.e., each Non-Dominated Match Vector. For a specific example, consider the following problem: We are given a set of m business activities in our business process request, $a_1, \ldots, a_m$ such that activity, a_i, contains n_i candidates of Web services from the micro-level matching step. The j-th candidate for activity a_i has cost c_{ij}, and execution time t_{ij}. Given the total execution time limit T for this business process, the goal of this macro-level matching algorithm is to compose an implementation plan for this business process by selecting one and only one Web service candidate from each candidate list such that the overall cost is minimized without exceeding our total execution time limit. If we use indicator variable x_{ij} to indicate whether the j-th service from the candidate list for activity a_i was selected, we can formalize the problem with the following equations:

$$\text{minimize} \qquad C = \sum_{i=1}^{m} \sum_{j=1}^{ni} c_{ij} x_{ij}$$

$$\text{subject to} \qquad \sum_{i=1}^{m} \sum_{j=1}^{ni} t_{ij} x_{ij} \leq T$$

$$\sum_{j=1}^{ni} x_{ij} = 1, i = 1, \ldots, m$$

$$x_{ij} \in \{0,1\}, \forall i, j.$$

The multiple-choice knapsack problem is known to be NP-hard [8]. It is possible to exactly solve the above problems using branch-and-bound algorithms, but because the worst-case running time of these algorithms is exponential in both the number of activities and the number of candidates on each list, branch-and-bound algorithms are often too slow to be useful. An alternative approach is to use dynamic programming techniques, and there are a number of algorithms known in this direction [8]. By using off-the-shelf software packages of optimization algorithms such as IBM's OSL [12], the given problem can be implemented in a straightforward manner. With this model in place, we can vary the problem with different objective functions and constraints. The variation of the problem can be implemented by using the Configuration component in Fig.4. For example, some processes may need to be optimized for execution time, while other measures such as cost will be treated as a constraint. In this case, the problem can be re-formulated as follows: We are given a set of m business activities, $a_1, \ldots, a_m$ such that activity, a_i, contains n_i candidates of Web services. The j-th candidate for activity a_i has cost c_{ij}, and execution time t_{ij}. Given the total cost budget C for this business process, the goal of this algorithm is to compose an implementation plan for this business process by selecting one and only one Web service candidate from each candidate list such that the overall execution time is minimized without exceeding our total execution time limit.

If we use indicator variable x_{ij} to indicate whether the j-th service from the candidate list for activity a_i was selected, we can formalize the problem with the following equations:

$$\text{minimize} \qquad T = \sum_{i=1}^{m} \sum_{j=1}^{ni} t_{ij} x_{ij}$$

subject to
$$\sum_{i=1}^{m}\sum_{j=1}^{ni} c_{ij}x_{ij} \le C$$

$$\sum_{j=1}^{ni} x_{ij} = 1, i = 1,\ldots,m$$

$$x_{ij} \in \{0,1\}, \forall i, j.$$

Yet another variation of this problem is an optimization on an interesting metric such as the degree of match described in the previous section. For example, the problem can be formulated as follows: We are given a set of m business activities, $a_1, \ldots, a_m$ such that activity, a_i, contains n_i candidates of Web services. The j-th candidate for activity a_i has combined degree of match d_{ij}, cost c_{ij}, and execution time t_{ij}. Given the total cost budget C and the total execution time limit T for this business process, the goal of this algorithm is to compose an implementation plan for this business process by selecting one and only one Web service candidate from each candidate list such that our overall degree of match is maximized without exceeding our total cost budget and the total execution time limit.

If we use indicator variable x_{ij} to indicate whether the j-th service from the candidate list for activity a_i was selected, we can formalize the problem with the following equations:

maximize
$$D = \sum_{i=1}^{m}\sum_{j=1}^{ni} d_{ij}x_{ij}$$

subject to
$$\sum_{i=1}^{m}\sum_{j=1}^{ni} c_{ij}x_{ij} \le C$$

$$\sum_{i=1}^{m}\sum_{j=1}^{ni} t_{ij}x_{ij} \le T$$

$$\sum_{j=1}^{ni} x_{ij} = 1, i = 1,\ldots,m$$

$$x_{ij} \in \{0,1\}, \forall i, j.$$

The degree of match of an activity can be more important than those of other activities. In such a case, the variant importance of degree of match of different activities can be reflected in the model by the assignment of weight w_i for each a_i. Then the objective model is slightly modified as follows:

maximize
$$D = \sum_{i=1}^{m} w_i \sum_{j=1}^{ni} d_{ij}x_{ij}$$

5.2 Multi-Attribute Decision Analysis

Another approach to solving the macro-level matching problem is a *multi-attribute decision analysis*. This method is particularly useful when it is not sufficient to provide an optimal solution for a single measure, but requires maximizing the total utility value computed by considering multiple business measures such as cost, execution time, degree of match, quality, category, and business entity relationship. The input to this algorithm is a set of n service combinations, s_1, ..., s_n such that service combination, s_i, contains m Web services, one service for each activity in the given business process. Also, each service combination has k business attributes, x_1, ..., x_k such that business attribute, x_j, is assigned a relative weight w_j (Remember the weight attribute of the <requirement> tag in Fig. 1.). Then this algorithm uses additive value function in order to compute the scores of the alternative service combinations. The system then ranks the alternative combinations by score, and selects the winning combinations among the top-rankers. The basic hypothesis of this multi-attribute decision analysis algorithm is that in any decision problem, there exists a real valued function U defined along the set of feasible alternatives, which the decision maker wishes to maximize. This function aggregates the criteria x_1, ..., x_k. Besides, individual (single-measure) utility functions $U_1(x_1)$, ..., $U_n(x_n)$ are assumed for the k different attributes. The utility function translates the value of an attribute into "utility units". The overall utility for an alternative is given by the sum of all weighted utilities of the attributes. For an outcome that has levels x_1, ..., x_k on the k attributes, the overall utility for an alternative i is given by

$$U(x_1, \ldots, x_k) = \sum_{i=1}^{k} w_i U(x_i)$$

The alternative with the largest overall utility is the most desirable under this rule. Each utility function $U(x_i)$ assigns values of 0 and 1 to the worst and best levels on that particular objective and

$$\sum_{i=1}^{k} w_i = 1, \; w_i > 0$$

Consequently, the additive utility function also assigns values of 0 and 1 to the worst and best conceivable outcomes, respectively. A basic precondition for the additive utility function is preferential independence of all attributes, which has been the topic of many debates on multi-attribute utility theory [1, 4].

6. CONCLUDING REMARKS

In this paper, we addressed two primary problems of the Web service-based business process automation: the location of services on the basis of the capabilities of published services, and the composition of business processes on the basis of the business requirements of submitted process requests. We proposed a solution, which comprises multiple matching algorithms, a micro-level matching algorithm and a macro-level matching algorithm. The first algorithm reasons with semantic information of services and returns services that sufficiently match with an activity in the request. The second algorithm solves a variation of the multiple-choice knapsack problem that models the macro-level matching problem for optimizing a business objective and fulfilling other business constraints. In addition, we proposed a multi-attribute decision analysis algorithm, which can be used with the optimization algorithm in a complementary fashion for a better process composition result. This algorithm is particularly useful when it requires maximizing the total utility value computed by taking multiple business measures into account. For securing information required for the execution of the matching algorithms, we explained how existing standards, UDDI and BPEL4WS, could be used and extended to specify service capabilities of services and business requirements, respectively.

7. REFERENCES

1. R. T. Clemen, Making Hard Decisions: an Introduction to Decision Analysis, Wadsworth Publishing Company, Belmont, CA, 1996.
2. DAML-S Coalition, "DAML-S: Web Service Description for the Semantic Web," Proceedings of the 1st International Semantic Web Conference, June 2002.
3. P. Doshi, R. Goodwin, R. Akkiraju, S. Roeder, "A Flexible Parameterized Semantic Matching Engine," IBM Research Report, 2002.
4. W. Edwards, "How to Use Multi-Attribute Utility Measurement for Social Decision Making," IEEE Transactions on Systems, Man, and Cybernetics SMC, vol. 7:326-340, 1977.
5. D. Fensel, I. Horrocks, F. van Harmelen, D. L. McGuinness, and P. F. Pate, "OIL: An Ontology Infrastructure for the Semantic Web," IEEE Intelligent Systems, Vol. 16, No. 2, 2001.
6. J. Hendler, and D. L. McGuinness, "DARPA Agent Markup Language," IEEE Intelligent Systems, Vol. 15, No. 6, 2001.
7. F. Leymann, D. Roller, and M. T. Schmidt, "Web Services and Business Process Management," IBM Systems Journal, Vol. 41, No. 2, 2002.
8. S. Martello, and P. Toth, Knapsack Problems, Chichester, New York, John Wiley & Sons, 1990.
9. M. Paolucci, T. Kawamura, T. R. Payne, and K. Sycara, "Semantic Matching of Web Services Capabilities," Proceedings of the 1st International Semantic Web Conference, June 2002.
10. M. Paolucci, T. Kawamura, T. R. Payne, and K. Sycara, "Importing the Semantic Web in UDDI," Workshop on Web Services, e-Business, and the Semantic Web: Foundations, Models, Architecture, Engineering and Applications, Toronto, Ontario, Canada, May 2002.
11. S. R. Ponnekanti, and A. Fox, "SWORD: A Developer Toolkit for Web Service Composition," Proceedings of the 11th World Wide Web Conference, Honolulu, Hawaii, May 7-11, 2002
12. IBM Optimization Solutions and Library, http://www-3.ibm.com/software/data/bi/osl/index.html.
13. "BPWS4J," IBM Corporation, http://alphaworks.ibm.com/tech/bpws4j, August 2002.
14. "Business Process Execution Language for Web Services, Version 1.0," BEA Systems, IBM Corporation, and Microsoft Corporation, Inc., http://www.ibm.com/developerworks/library/ws-bpel/, July 2002.

A Graphic Tool for Ontology Viewing Based on Graph Theory

César Stradiotto[1], Everton Pacheco[1], André Bortolon[1], Hugo Hoeschl[2]
1 WBSA Sistemas Inteligentes SA, Parque Tecnológico Alfa, Centro de Tecnologia IlhaSoft , SC 401 Km 1 - Módulo 10 - Térreo B - João Paulo - 88030-000 - Florianópolis, SC – Brasil
{cesar,evertonpp,bortolon, hugo}@wbsa.com.br
WWW home page: http://www.wbsa.com.br
2 Instituto de Governo Eletrônico, Inteligência Jurídica e Sistemas – IJURIS, Rua Lauro Linhares, 728 – sala 105 – Trindade - 88036-0002 - Florianópolis – SC – Brasil
WWW home page: http://www.ijuris.org

Abstract. The Knowledge Engineering Suite is an ontology production method, based on relationship networks, for knowledge representation inside specific contexts. The production of these ontologies has three basic steps, since catching the client data, knowledge base creation, and information retrieval and consult interfaces for the final users. During the knowledge base creation process, data verification is required, for nonconformity identification on the produced ontological network. Because it has a tabular interface, the verification step has some limitations about data vision, and consequently the tool usability, making the work for tracking errors or missing data uncomfortable, and susceptible to more errors. To make easier the vision of the created ontologies, in the real shape they are planned, it was implemented a software to viewing these new created ontologies, so the work for data error tracking became more efficient. Such software offers filtering and data selection resources too, to give a way to isolate common groups, when the Knowledge Engineer is looking for nonconformities. This software and its functions are described here.

Introduction

On its classical definition, ontology is a branch of metaphysics that deals with the "being", including there the natural theory and being types. (HOESCHL [1]). GRUBER *apud* BATEMAN [2,3], borrows the definition from philosophy for the ontologies: a systematic narrative of the existence, and define an ontology as an explicit specification of a conceptualization, having a set of representative terms linked by definitions. Such ontology definition is further detailed by DENNY [4], that observes two main approaches as a common core for virtually all ontologies: 1 - A vocabulary of terms that refer to the things of interest in a given domain; 2 - Some specification of meaning for the terms, [ideally] grounded in some form of logic.

Please use the following format when citing this chapter:

Stradiotto, C., Pacheco, E., Bortolon, A., Hoeschl, H., 2006, in IFIP International Federation for Information Processing, Volume 218, Professional Practice in Artificial Intelligence, eds. J. Debenham, (Boston: Springer), pp. 141–150.

According with DENNY [4], ontologies are arranged inside taxonomies of classes (called *concepts*) and subclasses, having its properties and restrictions. Finally, the union of ontology with a group of instances of its classes constitutes a *knowledge base*.

In DENNY [4,6] there is an excellent reference for ontologies and its corresponding tools, differentiated by application space, storage type, particularities, good and bad points about everyone of them.

1 The Data Structure Model for the Ontology Network

On the ontology model of BUENO [7], Fig. 1, a given ontology can be represented by a directed graph, taking its basic elements: vertices (the **terms**, or ontology concepts) connected by straight lines (called **relations**). An ontology containing terms and relations, is inside a group called sub-theme, which represents a specific subject, and, for last, many sub-themes can be inside a theme, that represents a generic subject. The domain is the last layer, that has inside itself many themes. Such model was constructed with the methodology described in HOESCHL [8].

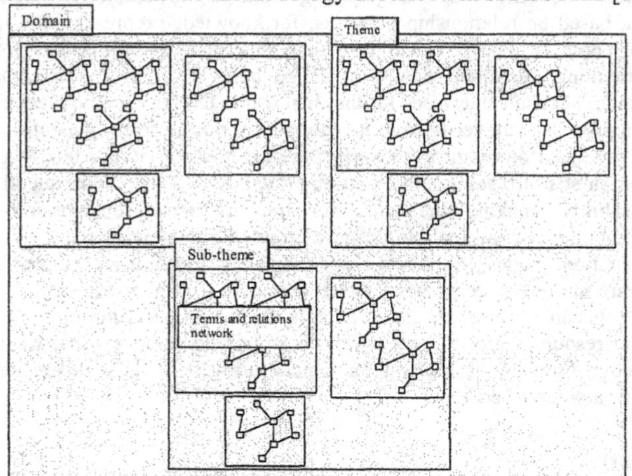

Fig. 1: Ontology structure for the knowledge base read by the software.

2 Knowledge Engineering Suite

Knowledge Engineering is a definition used to describe the global process of system development, based on knowledge. Typically it evolves a special form of interaction between the system builder, called Knowledge Engineer, and the professional specialist about the worked subject domain. Being by nature a multidisciplinary field, the knowledge engineering comprehends research types, which have a difficult classification, if this research is inside a limited approach (VALENTE [9]).

The Knowledge Engineering process main objective is to catch and incorporate the domain specialist fundamental knowledge, and its prognostics and control systems. This process includes information grouping, turning the knowledge engineer familiar to the subject domain, project analysis and a big effort. Beyond that, the cumulated knowledge may be codified, tested and refined (BUENO [10]).

The knowledge engineer extracts procedures, strategies and practical rules from the specialist professional, commonly used to the problems solutions, and constructs this knowledge inside an intelligent system. The final result is a software project, which solves specific problems like human specialists (BUENO [10]).

Aiming an information retrieval tool inside the enterprise knowledge bases, to allows a fast information recovery by its employees / users, BUENO [7] describes a method for ontology construction, denominated Knowledge Engineering Suite, composed basically of four basic steps (Fig. 2):

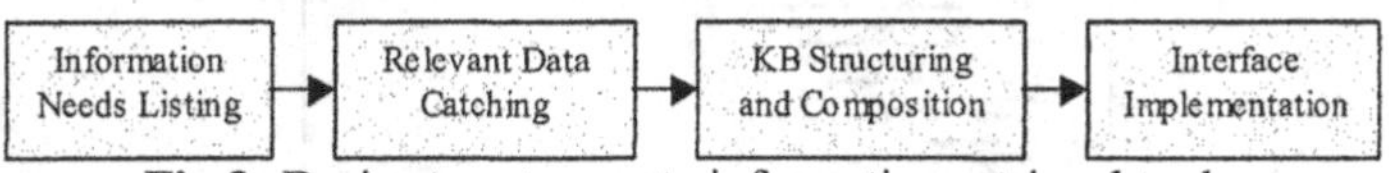

Fig.2: Basic steps to create information retrieval tools.

1. Listing the information needs, inside the client enterprises;
2. Catching the relevant data to the context of the information that may be represented;
3. Structuring and composition of the knowledge bases, which contains that data;
4. Implementation of the final user interfaces, with searching tools, which work over those knowledge bases.

The suite is characterized for grouping a set of professionals, tools and production procedures, which starts from capturing the implicit knowledge inside client enterprises, and results in the creation of information recovery resources to these same enterprises.

This production system is made by three types of professional: The system analyst, which takes care of the technical part of the implementation, the domain specialist, who knows the information needs inside his enterprise, and the knowledge engineer, which works over the knowledge base production over what the retrieval information system will work.

After the expected vocabulary survey is done, its concepts (also called "terms") and relations are included inside databases through collaborative tools, using navigable pages. This data inclusion is done at same time by many knowledge engineers, who evaluate what representative terms and relations have to make part of the edited ontology.

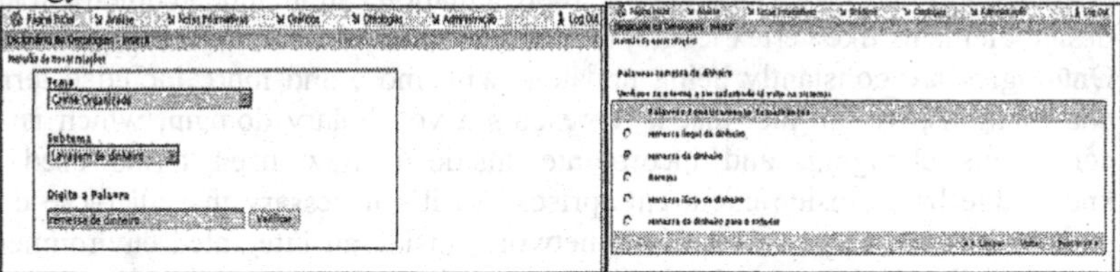

Fig. 3: Two pages of an interface for data inclusion inside an ontology.

During data edition, the navigation is made with steps. Each step is presented as a dynamic page, so the user loses the vision of the process as a whole. In Figure 3 there are two sample pages, used in data edition for only one ontology project.

After data inclusion, it is made its revision through keyword-based search engines, and terms and relations listing. Although being planed as relationship networks, such ontologies are still managed as table data (Fig. 4). The more the data is added on the knowledge base, more difficult, slower and stressing is its management, demanding greater attention from the knowledge engineer responsible for its production, and increasing the risks for inconsistencies and correction work, what represent a bottleneck over ontology production.

Fig. 4: Sample of a table formatted generated report about ontology terms e relations.

3 The Proposed Solution

Disposing from an already existent framework, for network viewing (STRADIOTTO [11]), and observing the lack of production continuity, and the limitation given by table format data vision, it was suggested an integrated graphic solution, which allowed the knowledge engineer to verify its production results in a network format, inside a tool that integrated all navigation and searching resources inside a single environment, and which reused all functionalities from that framework.

3.1 Relevant Ontology Properties

The creation of a software that allowed ontology data vision while it was being created, considered the following properties:

1. Ontologies are relationship networks, and have their simplest format as a directed graph made by its vertex (its concepts) connected by edges (the relations between vertex). Its graphic representation can include geometrical and design elements like vertex length, line width, colors and term symbol.
2. Ontologies are constantly being updated, with more and more included terms and relations, by the fact that it represents a vocabulary domain, which is on continuous changing, and incorporate inside it new used terms used in knowledge bases inside client enterprises. So it's necessary that all these data have to be seen as part of a whole network, inside an integrated environment, also including searching and data treatment tools.
3. Terms and relations have their internal data, which refers, respectively the concepts, and the relations between them.

3.2 Tool Requirements for Graphical and Integrated Data Presentation

Observed the Knowledge Engineering Suite needs, and the ontology properties seen above, the proposed integrated environment, which is created to solve the verification step, have to satisfy the following objectives:

1. Showing nodes and corresponding connections like an interlinked network with vertex and edges, with its properties represented as graphical identifiers, like formats, colors and drawing styles;
2. Loading ontology data according to user selected criteria;
3. Positioning clearly these data in the screen, manually or automatically, in cases where the user requires it;
4. Allowing whole or partial network vision, immediately, according to knowledge engineer chosen criteria;
5. Allowing user seeing internal information from the elements inside the graph;
6. Offering the user searching and data refinement resources;
7. Allowing user persisting network transformations, for ulterior consult;
8. Showing to the user an integrated environment with all verification tools needed to manage the new produced ontologies.

Satisfying these objectives, data control and verification problems can be solved, and knowledge engineer gain continuous production and efficiency on ontology production.

3.3 Project Considerations and Limits

The software implementation for network like ontology viewing had as premises:
1. The existent framework classes for network like data viewing were reused;
2. The software loads data from only one type of database format, with only one type of knowledge base structure;
3. This data loading is done considering the following initial pre-selection criteria: chosen theme and sub-theme, initial term and connected ones, initial and final date and time for data inclusion;
4. Terms are represented by icons or points, together with internal texts or not;
5. Relations are represented by edges, colored accordingly its type, with style accordingly to the storage situation on the knowledge base;
6. Data refinement can be done by the same criteria on item 7.3, including type of relation to be shown;
7. Due to the existence of another types of knowledge bases, the software will have generalized some items, which will compose a derived framework, made to ontology network management;
8. The new application is Multiple Document Interface type, which can show the load data through many integrated, but independent windows;
9. The application does not persist the edited network ontology, but only the final picture of the graphic result, serving only for visual purposes.

3.4 The Final Result and Working Model

The resulting software, its load and filter process and some of its main features are described as follows. In figure 6, left side, is shown the main screen, having four data group samples.

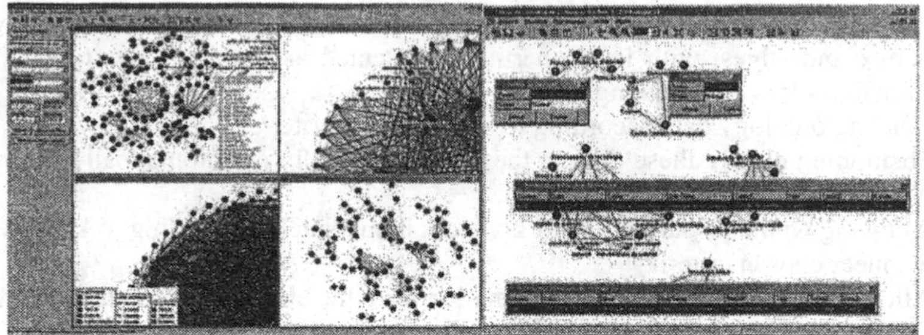

Fig. 5: Ontology viewer main screen, and at its right side many windows showing internal terms and relations properties.

The software has its data working made with 3 steps: 1 – Loading, 2 – Edition and filtering, 3 – Picture persistence

The available tools are the following:
Selective data loading - There are five non-exclusive criteria to chose, before loading knowledge base data: Theme, Sub-theme, Term and neighbors, Specific Relation, and Time Interval.
Internal data viewing (Fig. 5, right side) - Terms and relations internal properties can be seen through specific data windows.
Data edition (Fig. 6, left side) – According with its needs, user can dispose data manually, with manual operations over data groups, or over all loaded network.

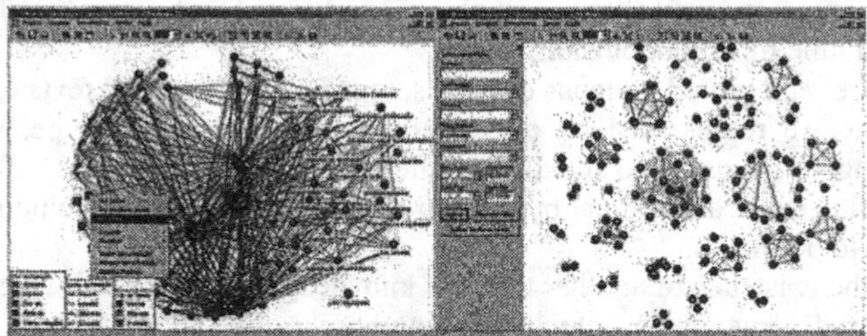

Fig. 6: Menu with operations over groups or isolated data. At its right side, a filter applied only over relations

Data drawing options - Edges show internal data referring to its represented relation, and to its state inside the knowledge base, so as the vertex with its internal parameters. The knowledge engineer can chose the way these data are shown on screen, changing parameters like color or style on edges or color on vertex.

Filtering (Fig. 6, right side): In the cases of ontology networks with a large amount of data, the filtering tool can help the user to visually select data by its internal properties, like edition time, by whole texts or wildcards like ? and * (MS-DOS) for vertex, or its corresponding theme or sub-themes, and relations by its type.

Network union (Fig. 7): if the user needs to verify if some terms are contained inside two different themes or sub-themes, he can use the network union tool. It corresponds to the fusion of two different sets of data. Identical data are not duplicated after the union operation.

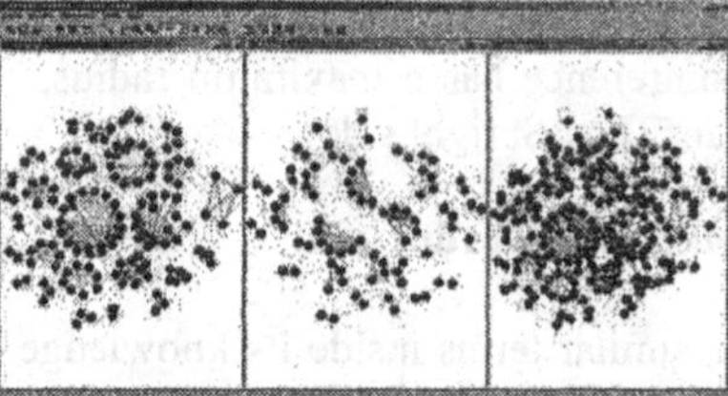

Fig. 7: Windows showing two initial networks, and the result after network union operation.

Persistence of visual disposition of data: For situations where it is needed report generation or ontology production generation, data visual disposing on planar space can be stored on bitmap or jpeg style pictures.

4 Complementary research approaches

Beyond accomplish the needs of data verification, the application was a research point about graph drawing and wildcard-based text search algorithms, and a research point for library modularity for code reuse.

4.1 Graph Drawing Algorithms for Ontology Network

It was proposed the research of two simple algorithms of vertex distribution on two-dimensional space. These were based on a circular distribution, due to its relatively easy implementation and fast drawing, with different principles:

N-Part Radial Disposal

This distribution makes a division of the total angle (2PI radians) in N parts, chosen by the project manager. Figure 8, left side, has a 10 step angular distribution. The distribution circle starts from the smallest radius (zero, on this case), and it's increased every time the angular counter completes N steps (in this case N = 10). Inside the network are three disconnected vertex, so they are drawn apart of the major vertex group.

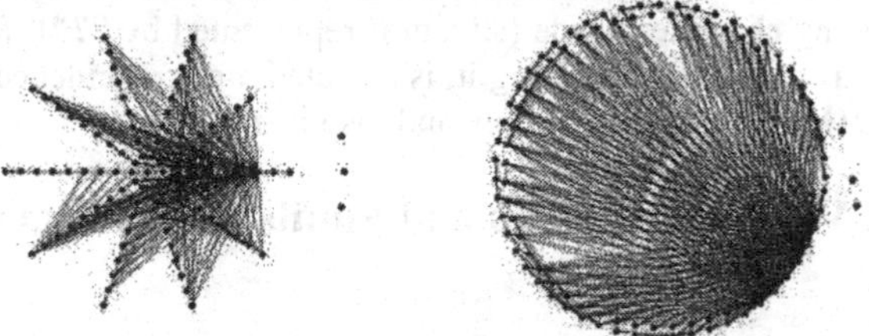

Fig. 8: 10-Part Radial Disposal, right side: Radial Disposal by CAL.

Radial Disposal by Constant Arc Length

In this model, the vertex are been accumulated over a circumference in such a way that a given vertex stays at a constant radial distance from its immediate neighbor.

This distance is measured by the arc length that remains between the two following vertex. As the vertex are positioned, there is an angle increment *I* that varies accordingly with the actual radius, from circumference which is actually being covered. The initial circumference has a maximum radius, and is being reduced as the vertex reach 2PI radians (Fig. 8, right side).

4.2 Textual Search through Wildcards

In any ontology network, similar terms inside its knowledge base occurs frequently, be it because the terms have identical stems, suffix, or because two terms have identical textual sequences. Aiming to make easy the search for groups of terms with textual similarities, the software has a filtering tool that works with wildcards: the symbol "*", that means any text with any length, or the symbol "?", meaning a single position inside the searched text, similarly to the file searching command **DEL** used in the Microsoft Disk Operating System (MS-DOS).
Figure 9 shows an initial data group, with two applied wildcard filters: **"terr*"**, for the result case shown at the left-bottom, and **"*o?a*"** for the right-bottom result case. Obviously, more complex cases can be tried.
On the left-bottom case (string **"terr*"**), the filter shows only the terms which starts with the string **"terr"** and finishes with any string: **terrorismo químico-biológico, terrorismo islâmico, terrorismo**, and **terrorismo radical**. The immediate neighbors of these selected terms are also shown.

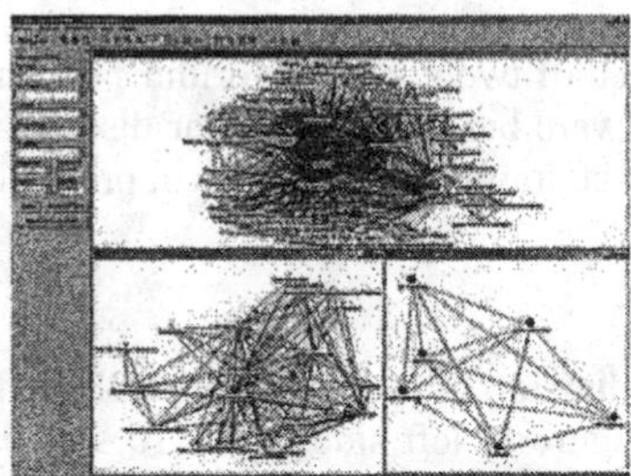

Fig. 9: Wildcard filtering: Made from the greatest data group. Left: filtering by the string **"*o?a*"**. Right: filtering by the string **"terr*"**.

On the right-bottom case, only terms which starts with any string followed by the letter **"o"**, with any character inside (situation represented by **"?"**), followed by the letter **"a"**, and has any string following it, is selected. For coincidence, only the term with the string **"Hezbollah"** was chosen, and also its neighbors.

5 Network Viewing Libraries and Similar Work on Ontology Viewing

At Internet there are some available *frameworks* or libraries for network viewing: GRAPHLET [12], BROWN [13], LINK [14], JGRAPHT [15], JGEF [16], JUNG, [17], or graphical interface application for ontology edition, like KAON [18], KAON2 [19], MR3 [20], ONTOTRACK [21] and PROTÉGÉ [22].

6 Conclusions

Comparing the suggested solution with the obtained results, there is a notable evolution about the ontology revision speed. With the application, the following objectives were reached:

1. The software shows the edited ontologies as a two-dimensional network;
2. The data load, network viewing, manipulation, and data search visual modules are all integrated inside the same environment;
3. The data-filtering module is based on multiple criteria: specific term, sub-themes and themes with wildcards, relation types, and time interval;
4. There are features for vertex selection, and viewing formats management for vertex and edges. So, interesting groups of data to knowledge engineers can be detached from another groups, turning easier the verification step on ontology production;
5. Users can manage colors and drawing styles of the described relations inside the knowledge base, and also vertex colors, accordingly its situation inside this same base;
6. The visual results can be persisted in raster pictures (jpeg or bitmap formats) for ulterior consultancy and reports.
7. The framework described on STRADIOTTO [11] had its classes reused, avoiding code repetition;
8. Terms and relations internal data can be identified almost immediately, due to information shown through colors and shaping on graphic mode;

Finally, knowledge engineers had a considerable time gaining due better usability with the new graphical interface, during ontology verification and report.

Although this advances, there are still some items to be approached on a near future:

1. The system doesn't do textual reports, but only pictures of the actual visual distribution of the ontological data;
2. The software works over only one database, inside only one data structure, needing further adaptations for cases where new database formats and structures are used;
3. It would be interesting allowing the software to write directly on the managed knowledge bases, being a complete knowledge management system. Actually it can only read data;
4. About data protection, the knowledge bases are protected with ciphered data. This type of protection demands creation or use of translation libraries, which are not implemented inside the actual system;

Bibliography

1. HOESCHL, H. C. ; BUENO, Tânia Cristina D' Agostini ; SANTOS, Cristina Souza ; MATTOS, Eduardo da Silva ; BORTOLON, Andre . The study of ontologies in the development of intelligent systems for the management of juridical knowledge. 34ª Jornadas Argentinas de Informática e Investigación Operativa, 2005, Rosario, 2005.

2.BATEMAN, J. John Bateman's Ontology Portal. http://www.fb10.uni-bremen.de/anglistik/langpro/webspace/jb/info-pages/ontology/ontology-root.htm - Acessed on december 2005.

3.GRUBER, T. . A translation approach to portable ontology specifications. Knowledge Acquisition 5:199-220; 1993

4.DENNY M. Ontology Building: A Survey of Editing Tools. November, 2002. XML.com http://www.xml.com/pub/a/2002/11/06/ontologies.html

5.USCHOLD, M. GRUNINGER, M. Ontologies and Semantics for Seamless Connectivity. SIGMOD Record, Vol. 33, No. 4, December 2004.

6.DENNY M. Ontology editor survey results. November, 2002. XML.com http://www.xml.com/2002/11/06/Ontology_Editor_Survey.html

7.BUENO T. C. D et al. Knowledge Engineering Suite: a Tool to Create Ontologies for Automatic Knowledge Representation in Knowledge-based Systems. in: The 2nd International Workshop on Natural Language Understanding And Cognitive Science (NLUCS-2005) in ICEIS - 7th international conference. Proceedings of 7th International Conference On Enterprise Information Systems. 2005.

8.HOESCHL, Hugo. C. BUENO, Tania. C. D., BARCIA, Ricardo. M., BORTOLON, Andre., MATTOS, Eduardo Da Silva. Olimpo: Contextual structured search you improve the representation council of UN security with information extraction methods In: ICAIL 2001 Proceedings. New York: ACM SIGART, 2001, p.217 – 218.

9.VALENTE, A. Legal Knowledge Engineering: A modeling approach. IOS Press: Amsterdam, 1995. p8.

10. BUENO, T. C. D. Engenharia das Mentes. (Tese de doutorado). Engenharia de Produção. Universidade Federal de Santa Catarina. 8 de setembro de 2004.

11. STRADIOTTO, C. R. K.; BORTOLON, A.; HOESCHL, H. C.; MARAFON, M. J.. Ferramenta de Desenvolvimento de Software para Representação Visual de Redes de Relacionamento. In: CONGRESSO NACIONAL DE TECNOLOGIA DA INFORMAÇÃO E COMUNICAÇÃO, 2004. http://www.sucesu2005.com.br/palestras2004/24.html . Acessado em Janeiro de 2006

12. GraphLet, A toolkit for graph editors and graph algorithms. http://www.infosun.fmi.uni-passau.de/Graphlet/. Acessado em dezembro de 2005.

13. Brown, J., Data Structure Project. http://www.helsinki.fi/~jbrown/tira/overview.html. Acessado em janeiro de 2006.

14. LINK -- Programming and Visualization Environment for Hypergraphs. http://www.cs.sunysb.edu/~algorith/implement/link/implement.shtml. December 2005

15. JGraphT. http://jgrapht.sourceforge.net/ Acessado em janeiro de 2006

16. JGEF. Java Graph Editing Framework. http://gef.tigris.org/ Accessed on december 2005

17. JUNG.Java Universal Network/Graph Framework. http://jung.sourceforge.net/ Accessed on January 2005

18. KAON. In: http://kaon.semanticweb.org Accessed on January 2006.

19. KAON2. In: http://kaon2.semanticweb.org/ Accessed on January 2006.

20. MR^3. Meta-Model Management based on RDFs Revision Reflection. In: http://panda.cs.inf.shizuoka.ac.jp/mmm/mr3// Accessed on January 2006.

21. ONTOTRACK. In: http://www.informatik.uni-ulm.de/ki/ontotrack/ Acesso em 17 de janeiro de 2006.

22. PROTÉGÉ. In: http://protege.stanford.edu/index.html Accessed on January 2006.

Using Competence Modeling to create Knowledge Engineering Team

Aline T. Nicolini[1] , Cristina S. Santos[2], Hugo Cesar Hoeschl, Dr.[3], Irineu Theiss, M.Sc.[4], Tânia C. D. Bueno, Dr.[5]
[1]Master Program in Engineering and Knowledge Management of the Federal University of Santa Catarina - alinen@ijuris.org
[2] Master Program in Engineering and Knowledge Management of the Federal University of Santa Catarina - cristina@ijuris.org
[3] Institute of Electronic Government, Juridical Intelligence and Systems and WBSA Sistemas Inteligentes S.A.
hugo.hoeschl@wbsa.com.br
[4] WBSA Sistemas Inteligentes S.A. – irineu.theiss@wbsa.com.br
[5] Institute of Electronic Government, Juridical Intelligence and Systems – tania@ijuris.org

Abstract. The present paper is about applying competence modeling for a knowledge engineer in the case of the company WBSA Sistemas Inteligentes S.A. The process was based on Lucia and Lepsinger model, by which competences are characterized through the identification of situations and behaviors considered relevant to the engineer performance. As one of the different techniques suggested by the model for collecting data, a number of individual interviews were undertaken and at the end it was defined and validated a set of eleven competence regarded as necessary for a satisfactory performance of a knowledge engineer.

Introduction

Knowledge-based systems (KBS) are computer programs that use explicitly represented knowledge to solve problems. Such systems handle knowledge and information by an intelligent manner and are used to solve problems that require a high volume of specialized knowledge [1].

To build a knowledge-based system implies to create a computational model with the objective of developing the capability of solving problems similar to the capability of a domain specialist [2].

In this context, the Knowledge Engineer plays an essential role since he will be the actor responsible for sharing with the specialists his procedures, strategies, and practical rules to solve problems and for building that knowledge into an intelligent system. When this process is correctly performed the result is a system that provides solutions similarly to a human specialist.

Please use the following format when citing this chapter:

Nicolini, A.T., Santos, C.S., Hoeschl, H.C., Theiss, I., Bueno, T.C.D., 2006, in IFIP International Federation for Information Processing, Volume 218, Professional Practice in Artificial Intelligence, eds. J. Debenham, (Boston: Springer), pp. 151–159.

The objective of this paper is to present the competence modeling process for the Knowledge Engineer, identifying the set of knowledge, skills, and attitudes required for a high performance of the engineer.

1 The Concept of Competence

Due to the diversity of knowledge domains where the concept of competence is applied, it is acceptable that there is no consensus about its definition. That is true even in the context of management.

According to Woodruffe [3], at the center of the debate about management a sensitive field is found where the term competence brings a different meaning when used by different people.

Ruzzarin, Amaral and Simionovisci [4] say that there is no doubt that the concept of competence is at the same time one of the concepts most commonly used and one of the most controversial one in the modern language of management.

Currie and Darby stated that the concept became popular due to Boyatzis, who defined competence as the characteristics of a person that can be observed and can be expressed in terms of motivation, skills, and aspects related to his image or role or the amount of knowledge.

Despite the historical importance of the concept presented by Boyatzis, it is considered too broad and its usage is limited to the field of organizational management. More objective definitions as the one presented by Parry [6] become more commonly used. Parry defines competence as a set of knowledge, skills, and attitudes that mostly affect a work, and keep a relation with the performance; they can be measured through some accepted tools and can be improved by training and development.

As per Cooper [7], the four criteria presented by Parry should be used when defining the profile of competence inherent to a function or a position. Given that any characteristic not included in those criteria should be excluded from the definition of a profile, from the set of factors defining a competence the author eliminates personality traces, capabilities, abilities and attitudes.

Contrary to the approach of Cooper, for Lucia and Lepsinger [8] characteristics as attitudes and capabilities are important for the success in some specific positions, although they having a more subjective character. Another relevant aspect is that even characteristics not so easily quantifiable can be measured and evaluated when translated into behaviors.

The approach based on behaviors was first developed by McClelland and shows wide acceptance by models used nowadays, because "it is only through their behaviors that human beings affect the context where they act" [9].

In line with this perspective, Lucia and Lepsinger suggest that the definition of a competence can be represented in a similar way to a pyramid, the pyramid of competences. As shown by Figure 1, at the top are the behaviors and the base, which provides support to the behaviors, is structured by the skills, knowledge, abilities, and personal characteristics.

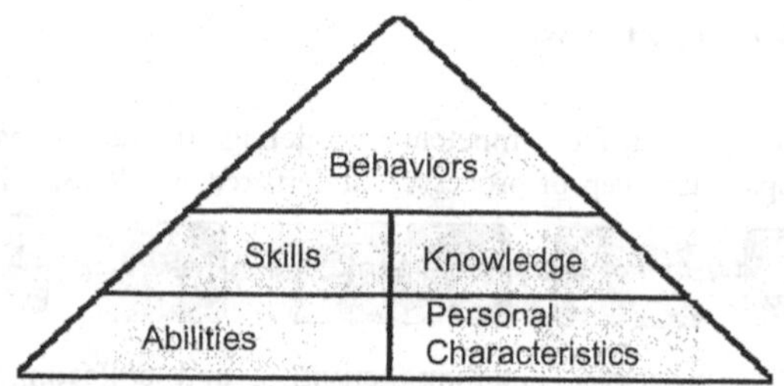

Fig. 1 – Pyramid of competences - Lucia and Lepsinger (1999)

This paper is based on the concept of competence presented by Lucia and Lepsinger. It is considered more adequate because it takes into account attitudes and other subjective, personal characteristics as part of competence.
Furthermore, the chosen model turns possible to measure and evaluate those components of competence due to the fact that it uses the approach based on behaviors to describe competences.
On the other hand, the concept proposed by the above mentioned authors keeps compatibility to the work of Parry and McClelland, which are regarded as important references in the field of management based on competences.

2 Competence Modeling

As stated above, the present paper keeps coherence with the concept of competence proposed by Lucia and Lepsinger. Three steps are considered when applying the model: planning, development, and finalizing and validating the model.

2.1 The case study

2.1.1 The Company

WBSA Sistemas Inteligentes S.A. was created in the context of the knowledge era. It is an Information Technology company in line with the worldwide *avant-garde* in terms of applying artificial intelligence techniques to information systems.
The origin of the company is strongly linked to university post-graduate programs, still maintaining academic and research partnership with them.
Years of research and development efforts undertaken by WBSA team consolidated the excellence of its intellectual capital, which is recognized worldwide through more than fifty papers already presented and edited by international conferences.
The company developed its expertise in providing solutions based on artificial intelligence techniques for knowledge management systems. In this regard WBSA is recognized by the Brazilian Software Companies Association (ABES) for having well-known specialization.
WBSA stated as its mission "to provide the best intelligence resources applied to the use of information".

2.1.2 The Working Process

With the aim of applying the competence modeling for the company, the first step was to prepare the map of processes undertaken by WBSA. It consists of

understanding the processes, detailing activities, and collecting information about inputs and outputs [10]. Figure 2 shows the company's workflow.

Fig. 2 – Processes in WBSA

2.1.3 The Position of Knowledge Engineer

The term Knowledge Engineering is used to describe the whole development process of knowledge-based systems. It is part of the process a special way of interaction between the system developer, called the knowledge engineer, and one or more specialists on the knowledge domain [11].
In the past, knowledge engineering was the process of transferring knowledge from the specialist into the system knowledge base. That approach normally caused failures because it is not possible for the specialist to translate into words all the knowledge involved in his task [12].
The objective of the knowledge engineering process is to capture the knowledge of a domain specialist, as well as his forecast and control procedures on the subject. This process involves becoming familiar with the domain, to collect information, to do analysis and evaluate the effort required by the project. Furthermore, the knowledge being accumulated has to be codified and tested; the scope of work has to be defined, establishing exactly what the user requires to be efficiently retrieved; the quantity and quality of documents have to be analyzed; and the construction of the vocabulary to support the retrieving process.

2.2 Applying the model

2.2.1 Planning

The definition of the objectives and scope of the project took as reference the analysis of the critical organizational process with the aim of establishing a competence model for a relevant position in the organization.
Given the importance of the role of the knowledge engineer for the success of the system implementation phase, the knowledge engineering process was elected as a critical process for the Company. And the position of knowledge engineer was chosen to apply the model.
Afterwards the expected result of the project was discussed and the different phases and activities were described.

2.2.2 Development

Data Gathering: was done through individual interviews with the three professionals working as knowledge engineers in the organization, following the questionnaire proposed by Lucia and Lepsinger.
Situations and behaviors observed along the interviews and used as reference for identifying knowledge, attitudes, and skills required for a knowledge engineer are shown on Tables 1, 2 and 3.
The three interviewers produced separate tables with their own observations, which were then evaluated to form a consensus about the internal competence model. Each one of the items included in the competence model (knowledge, skills, and attitudes) was clearly defined and the result is shown on the Tables.

2.2.3 Competence Modeling

Table 1. Knowledge required for a knowledge engineer

KNOWLEDGE	DEFINITION	INTERVIEW EVIDENCE
Business modeling	To know how to apply techniques for users interaction with the aim of understanding the problems of the organization and identifying potential improvements as part of the system requirements.	To define the needs and knowledge required by the client to improve his tasks
Requirements analysis (system modeling)	To know how to use techniques to establish the requirements for the system development	To work in the system development, in data and user's expectations gathering, and to pass it on to the development team
Organizational context analysis methodology	TO know how to use techniques and tools for understanding the organization context, process, personnel and technologies mapping	Organization context: mapping of processes, people, functions, and existing technologies to identify opportunities of implementing technology
Knowledge representation alternatives	In the context of Artificial Intelligence, to represent knowledge means to make it explicit in such a way that a system can understand and take decisions close to what a specialist would do	Knowledge organization / non-structured documents. To implement knowledge representation in the form of ontologies. To organize content in the form of ontologies
The use of ontologies editor and Word extractor	The ontologies editor and the extractor are tools developed to facilitate the process of extracting, organizing, and representing the knowledge involved in the process of developing an intelligent software	The use of technological tools: extractors and search engines
Framework and system functions	Understanding the product to be offered to the user is essential in the process of business prospects. Communication is facilitated when one knows the limits of the proposal, the implementation timeframe and the complexity of the system features	Understanding technology: not how to program, but to know how the system works and what is the role of ontology. Identifying interfaces that provide answers to the client needs. To understand the functions of the tool.
Basic informatics and searching tools	Office and searching tools are used to produce reports, proposals, manuals, presentations, and research about the client domain on the Internet	Searching the Internet (Google, clients sites, bibliography, Word, PowerPoint, Excel, Extractors)
Project management	Set of concepts, techniques, and tools required for project planning and control	Follows the development work related to the client expectations fulfillment
Interpersonal relationship	Set of techniques used to facilitate the	To interact with the client for

KNOWLEDGE	DEFINITION	INTERVIEW EVIDENCE
techniques	contact and communication with other people or groups	establishing empathy and knowledge exchange
Conflicts solving techniques	Techniques and methodologies required for negotiation and mediation	Ontologies delivered did not keep coherence with the subject. Absence of knowledge sharing
Interview methodology and document analysis	To know interview techniques and content extraction techniques	Interview and document analysis. TO extract the clients reasoning

Table 2. Skills of a knowledge engineer

SKILLS	DEFINITION	INTERVIEW EVIDENCE
Systemic vision	To see more than just specific and technical subjects, analyzing all the aspects involved in the system development	To interact with all and everything, in line with the company's strategy. Possibility of systemic vision
Facility of synthesis	Capacity of resuming and detecting the priorities for	To develop efficient knowledge transfer mechanisms. To identify tasks of the specialist that can be done with the tool. Resuming and defining concepts for the system
Facility for systemic thinking	To classify information and actions according to its importance and influence in the system planning	Support material production (manual, guide books, ontologies)
Leadership	Capacity of leading people or group of people to accept ideas and to work for a common objective	If the client does not understand the importance of his participation, it can be harm the system development
Organization	Capacity of organizing his own work, promptly solving problems or delegating what is urgent	Absence of process formalization can be the reason for a bad development process. To develop efficient mechanisms for knowledge transfer
Capacity to take decisions	To do the best choice of alternatives, analyzing the opportunity and viability of the decision	Increase in the perception of defining priorities
Team working	Capacity of interacting with the group to become influent and accept influence	To improve processes performed collectively. To work in synchronicity doing group meetings and disseminating knowledge
To work under pressure	To develop the work under urgency, maintaining emotional equilibrium and behavior	Due to short timing used only two persons to construct ontologies. Need of negotiating the term period
Capacity of moderation and negotiation	Capacity of maintaining good understanding, consensus, and action to pursue common objectives	Interface between the client and system developers. Not enough contact with the client and lack of scope of work
Influence	Capacity of influencing and leading people to attain a common objective	If the client does not understand the importance of his participation, it can be harm the system development. Contact with the client to obtain his agreement
Communication skills	To present ideas in a clear, objective and consistent way, respecting the audience and making sure the message was understood	To work in synchronicity doing group meetings and disseminating knowledge. Communication ability

Table 3. Attitudes of a knowledge engineer

ATTITUDES	DEFINITION	INTERVIEW EVIDENCE
Patience	Listen, listen, listen… keeping good humor	capacitation of specialists who will help to define the system
Curiosity /	Professional growth and development,	To identify clients needs and to define system

ATTITUDES	DEFINITION	INTERVIEW EVIDENCE
Researcher profile	with authonomy and seeking an adequate way of improving knowledge	functions. To obtain knowledge from the client
Proactivivity	To start working by his own and influencing the course of action	To work intuition / action
Sociability	Interact with different groups preserving its individuality, cooperating and exchanging experiences with the group.	Interact with everything and everybody.
Communicability	Take part actively in meetings, asking, informing and answering.	Assure a apt team for a continuous ontologies development work. Continuous sharing (basic premise)
Flexibility	Experiment, accept and adapt easily to new situations related to the work.	Interact and solve communication problems. Necessity of interaction with clients, developers and commercial department.
Creativity	Present new patterns, ideas and innovative solutions in the development of systems.	Identify specialist's tasks that the tool may perform. Construction of support material (manuals, reports, ontologies).
Diplomacy	Ability to present him/herself in a manner in which the relationships are kept in a higher degree of respect, pursuing associations and consensus in difficult situations.	Interact with the client to establish a empathy process and knowledge exchange. Make the developer understand what the client wishes and make the client understand the developer.
Responsibility	Assure that his/her action transmits confidence to the others, keeping them tranquil.	New discussions about the process and restarting. Convince the client is a challenge.
Determination	Keep focus to reach the defined goal, overwhelming eventual difficulties.	Feeling of satisfaction by the client and the Knowledge Engineer, giving the idea that the path chosen was the correct one.
Compromise	Show availability, assuring that the collective results will be reached.	Follow the development of the systems. The lack of compromising must be avoided.

2.3 Finalizing and validating the model

During this phase, the internal competence model was presented to a group of people working in the same environment, but not in the same position, with the aim of doing an analysis of the general model and identifying those competences regarded as essential for the performance of the knowledge engineer.
Since the knowledge engineer interacts with most of the other people working in the company, it was not difficult to form the focus group to discuss and validate the model.
As presented on Tables 1, 2, and 3 there were identified thirty-three competences, from which eleven is the number of knowledge abilities, eleven are skills, and eleven are attitudes.
With the output of the evaluation phase, a focus group discussion was conducted with the objective of refining the model. The result presented on Table 4 shows a list of competences regarded as being essential for a satisfactory performance of a knowledge engineer in the context of the company WBSA.

Table 4. Essential competences of a knowledge engineer

Knowledge	Skills	Attitudes
Ways of knowledge representation. The use of ontolies editor and extractor. Framework and system functions. Basic informatics and searching tools	Communication skills Team working Organization Systemic vision	Diplomacy Communicative Curiosity / Researcher profile Responsiveness

It was verified that, based in the studies about Competences Modelling, the best practice is to identify 5 to 9 competences for each function. That was the goal during this phase, but the conclusion was that, because of the complexity in performing the function, it became crucial to consider the set of competences listed in table 04.

Validate the model and determine the correlation of the competences with the best performances: As this model is being constructed to allow the training and development of the Knowledge Engineers, the application of this phase in the model (a 360° evaluation) was not necessary. The evaluation made in the precedent phase was enough to identify the competences that assure the good performance of the evaluated function.

Finalizing the model: Considering the complexity of the position being analysed, it is understood that the competences identified by the focal group are actually those that must be worked essentially in all Knowledge Engineers of the company. However, the other competences surveyed in the precedent phase (temporary model).

So, it is considered that the competences identified as essential must be searched for the position of Knowledge Engineering; the other may be worked by the company in its training processes and developments, aiming at the improvement and ideal performance of its collaborators.

Conclusions

The position of Knowledge Engineer is relatively new, beginning with the emerging of expert systems in the 80's. With the evolution of the knowledge based systems the position changed its characteristics considerably. So, the establishment of the competences was very interesting as it wasn't a position with consolidated characteristics as opposed to a traditional position.

This research established the competences necessary to the position of Knowledge Engineer in the company WBSA Sistemas Inteligentes SA using Lucia's and Lepsinger's model.

Following the model proposed by the above mentioned authors, the competence modelling may start from a list of competences previously established or from a new one, specifically for the position. In this work, because of the particularities of the position, the second option was adopted.

In the application of the model, some phases were not performed or were adapted, aiming a satisfactory development of the work.

The choice of the position was made taking as reference the mapping of processes and the concept of critical organizational processes.

In this sense, interviews where made with collaborators that occupy this position in the company, and a provisory model of competences was established and lately validated by a broader group. A relevant question diagnosed in the process was the difficulty in differentiate the abilities and attitudes related with the competences identified.

At the end of the process the twelve essential competences to the satisfactory performance by the Knowledge Engineer were established and defined. This list will be initially used in the training and development activities, and may be

lately expanded for the other activities of the process of human resources management.
Beyond the benefit related with the competences modelling, other positive aspect of the application of the model was the reflection exercise made during the interviews about the role of the Knowledge Engineer in the context of the company. This reflection was useful as the company had already worked in the formalization of its responsibilities.

References

1 REZENDE, Solange Oliveira. **Sistemas Inteligentes: fundamentos e aplicações**. Barueri, SP: Manole,2003.

2 STUDER, R. et al., **Situation and Perspective of Knowledge Engineering**. In: J. Cuena, et al. (eds.), Knowledge Engineering and Agent Technology. IOS Press, Amsterdam, 2000.

3 WOODRUFFE, C. **Competent by any other name.** Personnel Management, Vol. 23, No. 9, September 1991, pp. 30-33.

4 RUZZARIN, Ricardo. AMARAL, Augusto. SIMIONOVSCHI, Marcelo. **Gestão por competências: indo além da teoria**. Porto Alegre: Sebrae/RS, 2002.

5 CURRIE, Graeme. DARBY, Roger. **Competence-based management development: Rhetoric and reality.** Journal of European Industrial Training. Bradford: 1995. Vol.19, Num. 5; pp. 11-19.

6 PARRY, Scott B. **Just what is a competency? (And why should you care?).** Training. June 1998. Vol.35. Num. 6. pp. 58-61.

7 COOPER, K. C. **Efective competency modeling & reporting**. New York: Amacon, 2000.

8 LUCIA, A.D.; LEPSINGER, R. **The art and science of competency models**. San Francisco: Jossey-Bass, 1999.

9 BECKER, Brian E. HESELID, Mark A. ULRICH, Dave. **Gestão estratégica de pessoas com o scorecard: interligando pessoas, estratégia e performance**. Rio de Janeiro: Campus, 2001.

10 LGTI - Laboratório de Gestão Tecnologia e Inovação. Universidade Federal de Santa Catarina. Disponível em: http://www.lgti.ufsc.br/posgraduacao/. Acesso em: 20 de maio de 2005

11 BUENO, Tania. **Engenharia das Mentes**. Tese (Doutorado em Engenharia de Produção) – Universidade Federal de Santa Catarina, Florianópolis. 2005.

12 SCHREIBER, Guus; et al. **Knowledge Engineering and Management: The CommonKADS Methodology.** Londres: MIT Press, 2002.

13 SANTOS, Armando C. **O uso do método Delphi na criação de um modelo de competências.** Revista da Administração. Vol. 36, No. 02, pp. 25-32, abril/junho 2001.

14 SHIPPMANN, Jeffery S. ASH, Ronald A. CARR, Linda. HESKETH, Beryl. et al. **The pratice of competency modeling**. Personnel Psychology. Durham: Autumn 2000. Vol. 53, Num. 3; pp. 703-740.

Intelligent Systems Engineering with Reconfigurable Computing

Iouliia Skliarova
University of Aveiro, Department of Electronics and Telecommunications, IEETA, 3810-193 Aveiro, Portugal
iouliia@det.ua.pt,
WWW home page: http://www.ieeta.pt/~iouliia/

Abstract. Intelligent computing systems comprising microprocessor cores, memory and reconfigurable user-programmable logic represent a promising technology which is well-suited for applications such as digital signal and image processing, cryptography and encryption, etc. These applications employ frequently recursive algorithms which are particularly appropriate when the underlying problem is defined in recursive terms and it is difficult to reformulate it as an iterative procedure. It is known, however, that hardware description languages (such as VHDL) as well as system-level specification languages (such as Handel-C) that are usually employed for specifying the required functionality of reconfigurable systems do not provide a direct support for recursion. In this paper a method allowing recursive algorithms to be easily described in Handel-C and implemented in an FPGA (*field-programmable gate array*) is proposed. The recursive search algorithm for the knapsack problem is considered as an example.

1 Introduction

Intelligent computing systems (ICS) comprising microprocessor cores, memory and reconfigurable user-programmable logic (usually, *field-programmable gate arrays* - FPGA) represent a promising technology which is well-suited for applications that require direct bit manipulations and are appropriate to parallel implementations, such as digital signal and image processing, cryptography and encryption, etc. In such ICS, the reconfigurable part is periodically modified in response to dynamic application requirements. Creation and validation of scalable, distributed ICS architectures requires a closely coordinated hardware and software development effort in the areas of FPGA-based accelerators, runtime control libraries and algorithm mapping [1]. This paper focuses on the algorithm mapping.

In ICS, real-world problems are formulated over simplified mathematical models, such as graphs, matrices, sets, logic functions and equations, to name a few.

Please use the following format when citing this chapter:

Skliarova, I., 2006, in IFIP International Federation for Information Processing, Volume 218, Professional Practice in Artificial Intelligence, eds. J. Debenham, (Boston: Springer), pp. 161–170.

Then, by applying mathematical manipulations to the respective model, a solution to the original problem is obtained. The involved mathematical manipulations differ according to the ICS type, but frequently they recur to combinatorics and require the solution of different combinatorial problems. Typical examples of these problems are finding the shortest or longest path in a graph, graph-coloring, Boolean function optimization, set covering, set encoding, etc.

It happens that many of the combinatorial problems of interest belong to the classes *NP-hard* and *NP-complete*, which implies that the relevant algorithms have an exponential worst-case complexity, imposing consequently very high computational requirements on the underlying implementation platform. This fact precludes the solution of many practical problems with conventional microprocessors. This is because conventional microprocessors are programmed with instructions selected from a predefined set, which are combined to encode a given algorithm. The use of conventional microprocessors is justified for problems where their performance is adequate because the design cost is very low. Besides, any required change in the algorithm can easily be incorporated in the respective implementation. However, since the conventional microprocessors are not optimized for solving the combinatorial problems, the resulting performance is very scant.

As opposed to the previous approach, a hardware-based solution can be tailored to the requirements of a given algorithm guaranteeing in this way an optimal performance. However, a specialized hardware circuit is only capable of executing a task, for which it has been designed, whereas a conventional microprocessor might be reutilized for different tasks via a simple modification of instruction sequence. This software/hardware compromise obligates designers to trade off between performance and flexibility.

The development of dedicated hardware systems for specific problems and domains involves considerable cost and design time. The experience shows that the resulting benefits are often scant and even non-existent, because of the current rate of evolution of conventional processor technology, which enforces supplanting specialized and optimized computing structures by those that are less efficient for a given application domain. Besides, the proper heterogeneity of combinatorial problems discourages from developing specialized hardware accelerators.

The invention of high capacity field-programmable logic devices, such as FPGA, set up an alternative method of computing. An FPGA is composed of an array of programmable logic blocks interlinked by programmable routing resources and surrounded by programmable input/output blocks. The logic blocks include combinational and sequential elements allowing both logic functions and sequential circuits to be implemented. The routing resources are composed of predefined routing channels interconnected by programmable routing switches. A logic circuit is implemented in an FPGA by distributing logic among individual blocks and interconnecting them subsequently by programmable switches. Recent FPGA incorporate also various heterogeneous structures, such as dedicated memory blocks, embedded processor cores, multipliers, transceivers, etc., which allow for the implementation of systems-on-chip.

The FPGA enable attaining both the hardware performance and the flexibility of software, since they can be optimized for executing a specific algorithm and reutilized for other algorithms via a simple reprogramming of their internal structure. As a result, ICS's engines can be constructed that are optimized for a given application via *reprogramming* the functionality of basic FPGA logic blocks, i.e.

without introducing any changes on the "hardware" level. Implementations based on reconfigurable hardware permit the execution of the relevant algorithms to be optimized with the aid of such techniques as parallel processing, personalized functional units, optimized memory interface, etc.

The applications, for which FPGA-based reconfigurable systems have been constructed, cover diversified domains such as image processing, video processing, search engines in genetic databases, pattern recognition, neural networks, high-energy physics, etc. The best performance was achieved for such applications that exhibited a high level of parallelism, had large amounts of data to process, and used a non-standard format of information representation. The combinatorial problems possess all these characteristics and are therefore eminently suitable to FPGA-based implementations. Such implementations, tailored at combinatorial problems, would allow the exponential growth in the computation time to be delayed, thus enabling more complex problem instances to be solved.

Recently, several attempts have been made to employ FPGA for solving complex combinatorial problems. Many of such problems are well suited for parallel and pipelined processing. Therefore, FPGA-based implementations can potentially lead to drastic performance improvements over traditional microprocessors. For instance, significant speedups have been shown for difficult instances of the Boolean satisfiability [2] and covering [3] problems comparing to a software solution.

Three different specification methods have been employed for the description of the respective hardware problem solvers: a schematic entry, a hardware description language, and a general-purpose programming language. The schematic-based approach is probably not appropriate because instead of thinking in terms of algorithms and data structures it forces the designer to deal directly with the hardware components and their interconnections. Contrariwise, the *hardware description languages* - HDLs (such as VHDL and Verilog) are widely used for specification of combinatorial algorithms [4] since they typically include facilities for describing structure and functionality at a number of levels, from the more abstract algorithmic level down to the gate level. The general-purpose programming languages, such as C and C++, have also been employed, being the respective descriptions transformed (by specially developed software tools [5]) to an HDL, which was used for synthesis. The higher portability and the higher level of abstraction of language-based specifications have determined their popularity and widespread acceptance.

Recently, commercial tools that allow digital circuits to be synthesized from *system-level specification languages* (SLSLs) such as Handel-C [6] and SystemC [7] have appeared on the market. In this area, C and C++ with application-specific class libraries and with the addition of inherent parallelism are emerging as the dominant languages in which system descriptions are provided. This fact allows the designer to work at a very high level of abstraction, virtually without worrying about how the underlying computations are executed. Consequently, even computer engineers with a limited knowledge of the targeted FPGA architecture are capable of producing rapidly functional, algorithmically optimized designs.

Obviously, the higher level of abstraction leads to some performance degradation and not very efficient resource usage, as evidenced by a number of examples [8]. On the other hand SLSLs have many advantages such as portability, ease to learn (any one familiar with C/C++ will recognize nearly all features of SLSLs), ease of change and maintenance, and a very short development time. Therefore, we can expect that as the tools responsible for generating hardware (more specifically, either an EDIF – *electronic design interchange format* file or an HDL file) from system-level source code advance, the SLSLs may become the predominant hardware description methodology, in the same way as general-purpose high-level programming languages have already supplanted microprocessor assembly languages.

Although SLSLs are very similar to conventional programming languages there are a number of differences. In this paper we explore one of such differences, namely in the way in which recursive functions can be called. We consider Handel-C [6] as a language of study and the knapsack combinatorial problem [9] as an example.

2 Functions in Handel-C

It is known that functions in Handel-C may not be called recursively [10]. This can be explained by the fact that all logic needs to be expanded at compile time to generate hardware. Three ways have been proposed to deal with recursive functions [10]:

- Using recursive macro expressions or recursive macro procedures. It should be noted that the depth of recursion must be determinable at compile time, therefore limiting the applicability of this method to rather simple cases. As an example, consider the problem of counting the number of ones in a Boolean vector. This can be accomplished with the aid of a recursive macro expression as shown in the code below. It should be noted that this is not a true recursion since the macro *count_ones* will be expanded as necessary and executed in just one clock cycle.

Example of a recursive macro expression used for calculating the number of ones in a Boolean vector:

```
unsigned 6 one = 1;
macro expr count_ones (x) = select ( width(x) == 0, 0,
       count_ones(x\\1) + (x[0] == 1 ? one : 0) );
void main()
{
    unsigned 32 vector;
    unsigned 6 number;

    vector = 0x1234abdf;
    number = count_ones(vector);
}
```

- Creating multiple copies of a function, for instance through declaring an array of functions. As in the previous case the number of functions required must be known at compile time.
- Rewriting the function to create iterative code. This is relatively easy if the function is calling itself (direct recursion) and the recursive call is either the first or the last statement within the function definition [11]. The recursive macro expression considered above can be rewritten as an iterative Handel-C function as shown below. This code is not equivalent to the code presented above since it will require 32 clock cycles (i.e. the number of bits in a vector) to execute.

Example of an iterative function used for calculating the number of ones in a Boolean vector:

```
void main()
{
   unsigned 32 vector;
   unsigned 6 number, i;

   par
   {  vector = 0x1234abdf;
      number = 0;
      i = 0;
   }
   while (i != width(vector))
      par
      {  number += (0 @ vector[0]);
         vector >>= 1;
         i++;
      }
}
```

Generally, recursion should be avoided when there is an obvious solution by iteration. There are, however, many good applications of recursion, as section 3 will demonstrate. This fact justifies a need of implementation of recursive functions on essentially non-recursive hardware. This involves the explicit handling of a recursion stack, which often obscures the essence of a program to such an extent that it becomes more difficult to comprehend. In the subsequent sections we will demonstrate an easy way of handling the recursion stack in Handel-C.

3 The Knapsack Problem

We have selected the knapsack problem for our experiments because: 1) it represents a very large number of real-world problems; and 2) it provides very good teaching material. It is known that many engineering problems can be formulated as instances of the knapsack problem. Examples of such problems are public key encryption in cryptography, routing nets on FPGAs interconnected by a switch matrix [12], analysis of power distribution networks of a chip [13], etc. We consider the knapsack problem to be a good teaching material because the students are typically familiar with it from a course on data structures and algorithms and consequently we can use it in a 4th year reconfigurable computing course as an example for the design and implementation of hierarchical finite state machines (as described in section 4).

There are numerous versions of the knapsack problem as well as of the solution methods. We will consider a 0-1 problem and a branch-and-bound method. A 0-1 problem is a special instance of the bounded knapsack problem. In this case, there exist n objects, each with a weight $w_i \in Z^+$ and a volume $v_i \in Z^+$, i=0,…,n-1. The objective is to determine what objects should be placed in the knapsack so as to maximize the total weight of the knapsack without exceeding its total volume V. In other words, we have to find a binary vector $\mathbf{x} = [x_0, x_1, \ldots, x_{n-1}]$ that maximizes the objective function $\sum_{i=0}^{n-1} w_i x_i$ while satisfying the constraint $\sum_{i=0}^{n-1} v_i x_i \le V$.

A simple approach to solve the 0-1 knapsack problem is to consider in turn all 2^n possible solutions, calculating each time their volume and keeping track of both the largest weight found and the corresponding vector **x**. Since each x_i, i=0,…,n-1, can be either 0 or 1, all possible solutions can be generated by a backtracking algorithm traversing a binary search tree in a depth-first fashion. In the search tree the level i corresponds to variable x_i and the leaves represent all possible solutions. This exhaustive search algorithm has an exponential complexity $\Theta(n2^n)$ (because the algorithm generates 2^n binary vectors and takes time $\Theta(n)$ to check each solution) making it unacceptable for practical applications. The average case complexity of the algorithm may be improved by pruning the branches that lead to non-feasible solutions. This can easily be done by calculating the intermediate volume at each node of the search tree, which will include the volumes of the objects selected so far. If the current volume at some node exceeds the capacity constraint V the respective branch does not need to be explored further and can safely be pruned away since it will lead to non-feasible solutions.

The pseudo-code of the employed algorithm is presented below. A simple backtracking algorithm involves two recursive calls responsible for exploring both the left and the right sub-trees of each node. Since one of the recursive calls is the last statement in the algorithm it can be eliminated as illustrated in the code below.

Pseudo-code of the algorithm employed for solving the knapsack problem:

```
x = 0; //current solution
opt_x = 0; //optimal solution found so far
opt_W = 0; //weight of the optimal solution
cur_V = 0; //volume of the current solution
level = 0; //level in the search tree

Knapsack_1 (level, cur_V)
{
   begin:
      if (level == n)
      {
         if (Σ_{i=0}^{n-1} w_i x_i > opt_W )
         {
            opt_W = Σ_{i=0}^{n-1} w_i x_i;      opt_x = x;
         }
      }
      else
      {
         if ( (cur_V + v_level) ≤ V )
         {
            x_level = 1;
            Knapsack_1(level+1, cur_V + v_level);
         }

         x_level = 0;
         level++;
         goto begin;
         //instead of Knapsack_1(level+1, cur_V);
      }
}
```

4 Specification in Handel-C and Hardware Implementation of Recursive Algorithms

For hardware implementation, the selected recursive algorithm has firstly been described with the aid of *Hierarchical Graph-Schemes* (HGS) [14]. The resulting HGS composed of two modules z_0 and z_1 is shown in Fig. 1(a). The first module (z_0) is responsible for initialization of all the variables of the algorithm and is activated in the node *Begin* and terminated in the node *End* with the label a_1. The execution of the module z_0 is carried out in a sequential manner. Each rectangular node takes one clock cycle.

Any rectangular node may call any other module (including the currently active module). For instance, the node a_0 of z_0 invokes the module z_1. As a result, the module z_1 begins execution starting from the node *Begin* and the module z_0 suspends waiting for the module z_1 to finish. When the node *End* in the module z_1 is reached the control is transmitted to the calling module (in this case, z_0) and the execution flow is continued in the node a_1. The rhomboidal nodes are used to control the execution flow with the aid of conditions, which can evaluate to either *true* or *false*.

An algorithm described in HGS can be implemented in hardware with the aid of a *recursive hierarchical finite state machine* (RHFSM) [14]. Fig. 1(b) depicts a structure of a generic RHFSM that can be used for implementation of any recursive algorithm. The RHFSM includes two stacks (a stack of modules – *M_stack* and a stack of states – *FSM_stack*) and a combinational circuit (*CC*), which is responsible for state transitions within the currently active module (selected by the outputs of *M_stack*). There exists a direct correspondence between RHFSM states and node labels in Fig. 1(a) (it is allowed to repeat the same labels in different modules). In the designed circuit the *CC* is also employed for computing the solution of the knapsack problem.

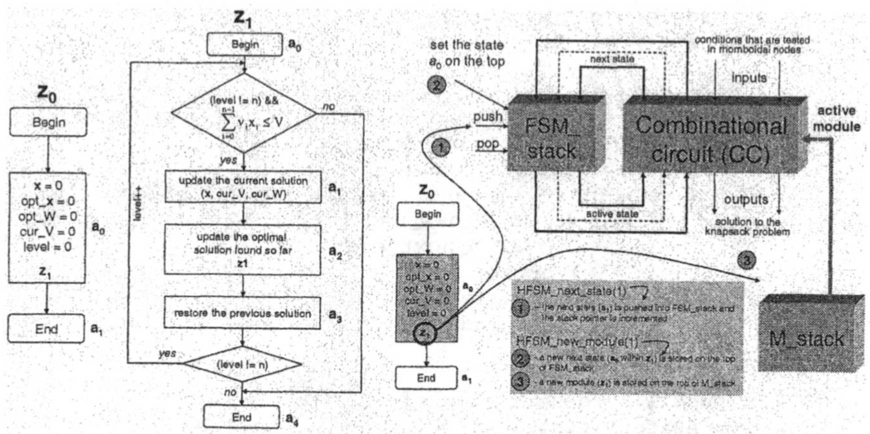

Fig. 1. **(a)** An HGS describing the recursive search algorithm employed for solving the knapsack problem; **(b)** Recursive hierarchical finite state machine with a Handel-C example of a new module invocation.

The code below demonstrates how to describe an RHFSM from Fig. 1 in Handel-C. The functions employed for the RHFSM management are presented in Fig. 2. Firstly, the RHFSM is reset and the node a_0 in the module z_0 is activated. This node calls the function *HFSM_next_state* in order to push the next state (a_1) into the *FSM_stack* (see Fig. 1(b)). In parallel, a new module z_1 is called with the aid of function *HFSM_new_module*. This function increments the stack pointer and stores at the top of stacks *M_stack* and *FSM_stack* a new module (z_1) and a node a_0, respectively.

The execution proceeds on module z_1 until *HFSM_end_module* function is called. This function decrements the stack pointer allowing the previously active module and the respective node within that module to be recovered.

The remaining functions are trivial and their implementation is shown in Fig. 2. Besides of state transitions, computations required by the algorithm from Fig. 1(a) are performed in each node. These computations are very simple and are not shown in the code below for the sake of simplicity.

Note that the presented code supports recursive calls. For such purposes, in the state a_2 of z_1, a new module z_1 is invoked. This causes the next state within the currently active module (a_3) to be pushed into the stack and the stack pointer to be incremented.

Handel-C function designed for solving the knapsack problem

```
void ExhaustiveSearch()
{  unsigned STATE_SIZE state;
   unsigned MODULE_SIZE module;
   unsigned 1 done;

   HFSM_reset();
   do
   {  par //initialize stacks
      {  module = get_module();
         state = get_state();   }

      switch(module)
      {
         case 0: //description of the module z0
           switch (state)
           { case 0: // state a0 - initialize variables
                par {   HFSM_new_module(1);
                        HFSM_next_state(1);
                    } break;
             case 1: //state a1
               HFSM_end_module();
           }   break;

         case 1: //description of the module z1
           switch (state)
           { case 0: // state a0
                if (/*condition*/) HFSM_next_state(1);
                else HFSM_end_module();
                break;
```

```
                case 1: //state a1 - update current solution
                  par {  //construct the current solution
                         HFSM_next_state(2);
                      }break;

                case 2: // state a2
                   par { // update the best solution
                          HFSM_new_module(1); //recursive call
                          HFSM_next_state(3);
                       } break;

                case 3: //state a3
                   par {  //restore the previous solution
                          if (/*condition*/) HFSM_next_state(0);
                          else HFSM_end_module();
                       } break;
            }
        } done = test_ends();
    } while(!done);
}
```

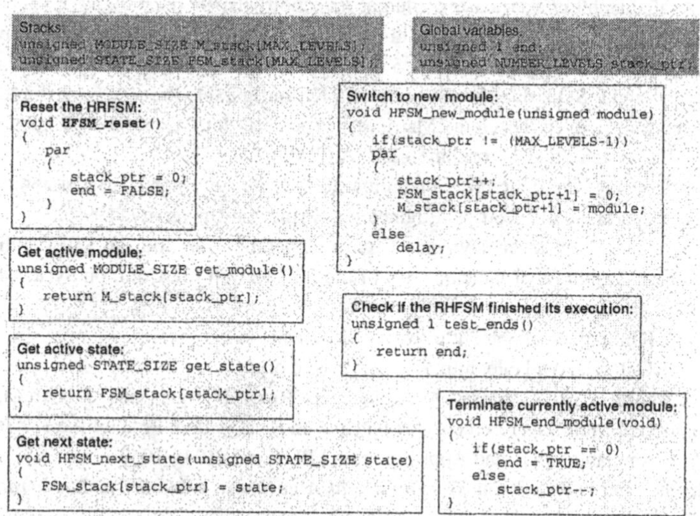

Fig. 2. Handel-C functions, which are responsible for resetting the RHFSM, controlling state transitions, performing hierarchical module calls and returns, etc.

The algorithm considered has been implemented and tested in an XC2S200 Spartan-II FPGA from Xilinx [15]. For experimental purposes the board RC100 [6] of Celoxica has been used. The stacks have been declared as Handel-C arrays of the required dimensions (determined by the maximum number of levels *n* in the search tree). It should be more efficient to implement the stacks (by declaring them as dual-port RAMs) in embedded memory blocks (available in Spartan-II family FPGAs). This is possible since at most two stack locations are accessed in a single clock cycle.

5 Conclusion

Reconfigurable hardware supplies very vast opportunities for implementing effective ICS engines targeted at accelerating computing processes. Since these processes involve often recursively formulated functions, an efficient hardware implementation of recursion is needed. In this paper a simple RHFSM-based method was described that allows recursion to be easily implemented in hardware. The proposed technique permits complex algorithms to be specified and realized on the basis of relatively simple circuits. The suggested design method has been applied for solving the knapsack problem by a backtracking algorithm. An RHFSM model is also very useful for specifying control algorithms in an HDL as shown in [14].

References

1. B. Schott, S. Crago, C. Chen, J. Czarnaski, M. French, I. Hom, T. Tho, and T. Valenti, Reconfigurable Architectures for System Level Applications of Adaptive Computing, [Online], Available: http://slaac.east.isi.edu/papers/schott_vlsi_99.pdf.
2. I. Skliarova and A.B Ferrari, Reconfigurable Hardware SAT Solvers: A Survey of Systems, *IEEE Trans. on Computers*, vol. 53, issue 11 (2004) 1449-1461.
3. V. Sklyarovand I. Skliarova, Architecture of a Reconfigurable Processor for Implementing Search Algorithms over Discrete Matrices, Proc. of Int. Conf. on Engineering of Reconfigurable Systems and Algorithms – ERSA (2003) 127-133.
4. P. Zhong, Using Configurable Computing to Accelerate Boolean Satisfiability, Ph.D. dissertation, Department of Electrical Engineering, Princeton University (1999).
5. O. Mencer and M. Platzner, Dynamic Circuit Generation for Boolean Satisfiability in an Object-Oriented Design Environment, Proc. of the 32nd Hawaii Int. Conf. on System Sciences (1999).
6. Handel-C, [Online], Available: http://www.celoxica.com/.
7. SystemC, [Online], Available: http://www.systemc.org/.
8. E.M. Ortigosa, P.M. Ortigosa, A. Cañas, E. Ros, R. Agís, and J. Ortega, FPGA Implementation of Multi-layer Perceptrons for Speech Recognition, Proc. of the 13th Int. Conf. on Field-Programmable Logic and Applications – FPL (2003) 1048-1052.
9. D.L. Kreher and D.R. Stinson, *Combinatorial Algorithms. Generation, Enumeration, and Search*, CRC Press (1999).
10. DK2, Handel-C Language Reference Manual, Celoxica Ltd (2003).
11. M. Wirth, *Algorithms and Data Structures*, Prentice-Hall, Inc. (1986).
12. A. Ejioui and N. Ranganathan, Routing on Field-Programmable Switch Matrices, *IEEE Trans. on Very Large Scale Integration (VLSI) Systems*, vol. 11, n. 2 (2003) 283-287.
13. M. Zhao, R.V. Panda, S.S. Sapatnekar, and D. Blaauw, Hierarchical Analysis of Power Distribution Networks, *IEEE Trans. on Computer-Aided Design of Integrated Circuits and Systems*, vol. 21, n. 2 (2002) 159–168.
14. V. Sklyarov, FPGA-based Implementation of Recursive Algorithms, *Microprocessors and Microsystems*, n. 28 (2004) 197-211.
15. Spartan-IIE FPGA Family, [Online], Available: http://www.xilinx.com.

Ontological Evaluation in the Knowledge Based System

Tania C. D. Bueno[2], Sonali Bedin[1], Fabricia Cancellier[2] and Hugo C. Hoeschl[1]

1 Instituto de Governo Eletrônico, Inteligência Jurídica e Sistemas – IJURIS, Rua Lauro Linhares, 728 – sala 105 – Trindade - 88036-0002 - Florianópolis – SC – Brasil {hugo, sonali}@ijuris.org, www home page: http://www.ijuris.org

2 WBSA Sistemas Inteligentes SA, Parque Tecnológico Alfa, Centro de Tecnologia IlhaSoft , SC 401 Km 1 - Módulo 10 - Térreo B - João Paulo - 88030-000 - Florianópolis, SC – Brasil {tania, fabricia}@wbsa.com.br www home page: http://www.wbsa.com.br

Abstract. In the last few years, several studies have emphasized the use of ontologies as an alternative to organization of the information. The notion of ontology has become popular in fields such as intelligent information integration, information retrieval on the Internet, and knowledge management. Different groups use different approaches to develop and verify de effectiveness of ontologies [1] [2] [3]. This diversity can be a factor that makes the formularization difficult of formal methodologies of evaluation. This paper intends to provide a way to identify the effectiveness of knowledge representation based on ontology that was developed through Knowledge Based System tools. The reason is that all processing and storage of gathered information and knowledge base organization is performed using this structure. Our evaluation is based on case studies of the KMAI system [4], involving real world ontology for the money laundry domain. Our results indicate that modification of ontology structure can effectively reveal faults, as long as they adversely affect the program state.

1 Introduction

Testing the application is an important stage of the system development process. These tests aim at the verification of all the functionalities of the tool, inferring that the results are the ones expected when the system was conceived. However, it is

Please use the following format when citing this chapter:

Bueno, T.C.D., Bedin, S., Cancellier, F., Hoeschl, H., 2006, in IFIP International Federation for Information Processing, Volume 218, Professional Practice in Artificial Intelligence, eds. J. Debenham, (Boston: Springer), pp. 171–180.

particularly difficult to engage in ontology evaluation where the entire system design assumes a high degree of interaction between the user and the system, and makes explicit allowance for clarification and retrieval. This is the case of KMAI - an intelligent knowledge management platform [5].

The only approach towards the formal evaluation of ontologies is OntoClean [6], as it analyses the intentional content of concepts. Although it is well documented in numerous publications, and its importance is widely acknowledged, it is still seldom used due to the high costs for applying OntoClean, especially on tagging concepts with the correct meta-properties. Open response tests, especially those making use of nonsense words, require an extensive training of the listeners. However, additionally to the word and phoneme scores, possible confusion between phonemes is obtained. This allows for diagnostic analysis. Redundant material (sentences, rhyme tests) suffers from ceiling effects (100% score at poor-to-fair conditions) while tests based on nonsense words may discriminate between good and excellent conditions.

In earlier works, we used a methodology called Mind Engineering [7] to identify and organize ontologies using a collaborative web tool called Knowledge Engineering Suite (see item 2.2). This tool is a module of KMAI system. Mind Engineering allows building a knowledge base, improving the construction of the ontology of the domain and the automatic representation of cases in knowledge-based systems, either in the juridical area or any other knowledge management domain [8]. Our methodology of testing is focused on the verification of the results expected from the system when using ontologies for the retrieval of the information and observes the principles of the methodology used in the ontology development. The tests are affected from the terms that are part of the domain ontologies created for a specific application.

Despite the fact that testing provides a proof of correctness for only those test cases that pass, it remains popular partly due to its low, incremental cost. Our evaluation is based on two case studies involving real world applications based on ontology. Our results indicate that specification based assertions can effectively reveal faults, as long as they adversely affect the state of the program.

Therefore, our paper is organized as follows: In section 2, we present KMAI System and Knowledge Engineering structure. In section 3, we describe the participation of the ontological structure in KMAI System and aspects of ontology application. In turn, these aspects will be applied to our recall measures. In section 4, we introduce the ontology evaluation process. Section 5 develops recall measures for ontology in KMAI system. We end with a brief conclusion and future work.

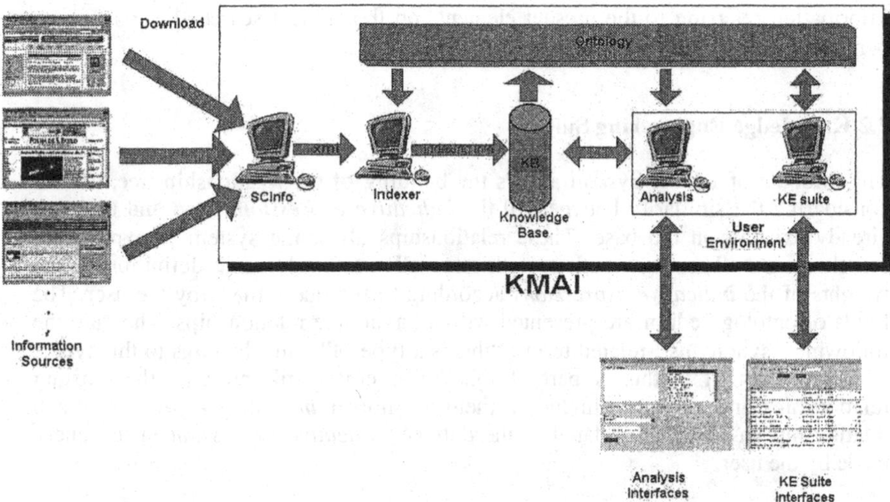

Fig. 1. The participation of the ontology structure in the KMAI System.

2 The KMAI System

The KMAI System embraces the whole cycle of strategic information production, from the collecting process to the retrieval by the user. Part of the visualization of the system is in figure 1. It begins in the election of the digital sources to be monitored (Knowledge Engineering), separating structured from non-structured data (about 90%) and submitting them to differentiated treatments. Data obtaining is made through Collecting Agents connected to collections, each one representing a source of information, which can be from specific websites to documents storage directories (textual documents, spreadsheets, e-mails and reports in general) digitally existent in the organization.

The vision of the storage structure is physical, containing the items collected in files organized by domains. The collections are converted for a common pattern that allows communication with structured databases. The chosen format was XML (Extensible Markup Language). Text Mining is devoted to extract concepts, statistics and important words of a group of documents to minimally structure them.

In that phase, three types of information are extracted: metadata (common document information, such as title and author), indexes (terms that describe the content of the document) and concepts (terms that describe the context of the document). These concepts are based on the ontologies defined in the Knowledge Engineering Suite (see item 2.2). Therefore, the cycle of information production is completely assisted in a digital and intelligent way.

The retrieval process is cyclical, as the user describes the subject to be searched on and the system shows the related information, organized by the degree of similarity with the subject described, enabling the increasing of more specific information referring to the present elements on the subject searched, for instance, periods of time or informational sources.

2.2 Knowledge Engineering Suite

This Module of KMAI System allows the building of the relationship tree, always considering the similarity between all the *indicative expressions* filed and the ones already existing on the base. These relationships allow the system to expand the search context. The organization of the tree allows the dynamic definition of the weights of the *indicative expressions* according to the query made by the user. The fields of ontology editor are presented with all available relationships. They are the following: -synonyms; -related terms; "this is a type of"; "this belongs to this type"; "this is a part of"; "this is part of this". The editor still presents the existing relationships and allows to including them to another *indicative expression*. Each relationship has a weight related to the defined *indicative expression* in the query made by the user.

3 The Process of Ontology Construction

The ontologies structure is the heart of the KMAI System. The reason for it is that all processing and storage of gathered information and knowledge base organization is performed using this structure. It also plays an important role in the quality of the results presented to the user.

The participation of the ontology structure in System KMAI occurs in three moments (see figure 1). At the first moment, the system extracts information from different previously selected sources. Each one of these documents is indexed based on the ontologies defined by the specialists and knowledge engineers during the knowledge engineering process. It means that the system will mark the documents with all indicative expressions found in the text, storing them in an organized way in the knowledge base. Thus, it is possible to make a pre-classification of the cases in the base according to what was defined in the knowledge organization promoted by the ontologies.

In a second stage, ontologies are important in the analysis interface available to the user. The process begins at the moment in which the user types the input text for the search. It is at this point that the indicative expressions defined by the user that coincide with the ones presented in the ontology are identified. These expressions identified in the entry case determine the stream of relations that will be used by the system. It means that there is a dynamic relation between the way the user enters the indicative expression in the analysis interface and the way the relations in the Knowledge Engineering Suite are defined for this expression.

The first versions of the Knowledge Engineering Suite worked with key expressions, an approach that resulted in some rigidity in the ontology organization. The weight of the information that was typed by the user in the search text was not considered. For this new approach, the importance of the indicative expressions to be considered is defined by the user. The system gives priority to the expressions and search for the corresponding derivations for each case, according to the knowledge base. A priori, there is no hierarchy in the organization of ontologies in the knowledge base. The weight of relations will be based only on what is required by the search, where the context intended by the user is defined.

The third moment when the ontology takes part is in the Knowledge Engineering Suite, available in the system and integrated in its architecture. Through the Knowledge Engineering Suite, the user is able to update the knowledge base with new expressions. At each new update in the ontology, the system re-indexes all the texts stored in the knowledge base, so that users may use this new ontology organization to search for documents previously indexed. It allows the verification of old documents that are related to a context that is important at the present moment. This way, it is possible to define a dateline about a subject, locating its start point.

It is important to highlight that this structure of contextualized ontologies allows automatic information indexing by the system and a knowledge acquisition that gives more qualitative answers in the retrieval process.

4 Ontology Evaluation

In KMAI System, the *indicative expressions* are organized in sub-domains, the following of relevance in the domain. The retrieval process is based on similarity between the number of terms, ontology and relationships presented in the text. These relationships are based on relevancy of the connection (synonyms – 0,99; related terms – 0,75; "this is a type of"- 0,30; "this belongs to this type"- 0,30; "this is a part of"- 0,30; "this is part of this"- 0,30), see item 2.2.

In this perspective, the recall tests identifies if the ontology relationships improve the quality of the results in the KMAI System. Thus, the ontology is inserted in the analysis for evaluation in two ways: textually, in the analyzer search, where the document is presented orderly based on the similarity of the ontology and ontology relationships, or yet in the form of graphs that allow the evaluation of the quantity of the documents where that ontology and its relationships appear.

The process of test and evaluation of the ontologies define the effectiveness of relationships considering the amount of documents retrieved.

The first test is performed by the Knowledge Engineer during the ontology construction phase. First of all, the relations of synonyms are created, for instance: "money laundering" is synonymous with "dirty money" and "laundering operations". After that, the search function of the system is performed to verify the number of documents found and then the engineer starts to create "type of" and "part of" relations (e. g., combating money laundering, Offshore Financial Centers, Global Programme Against Money Laundering). To check if the relation falls within the context, a small increase in the number of documents retrieved has to be observed. Otherwise, if the number of documents retrieved is higher than 70% of the documents retrieved through the synonyms, then the relation will be considered not adequate; in the aforementioned example, "Offshore Financial Centers" is an expression too wide for the term "money laundering". The last relations to be inserted are the related terms (e.g. crime against the financial system, ideal financial heaven, organized crime) with weight 0.75. In this case, if the relation brings a search result above 150% of the documents retrieved by the first step, the term should be considered as inadequate for that set of relationships. In the example given, the expression "organized crime" presented a search result higher than 150% and the engineer should create a separate relation for that *indicative expression* with synonymous and other relations, if the term is considered important for the domain he is working on.

Thus, after the definition of the search domain, the process is developed in some stages, such as the following description. As an example, we will call the *indicative expression* A and B in the description of the process: a. Previous analysis of the A terms; b. Analysis of B terms; c. Elaboration of the relation of the terms A and B; d. Representation of error.

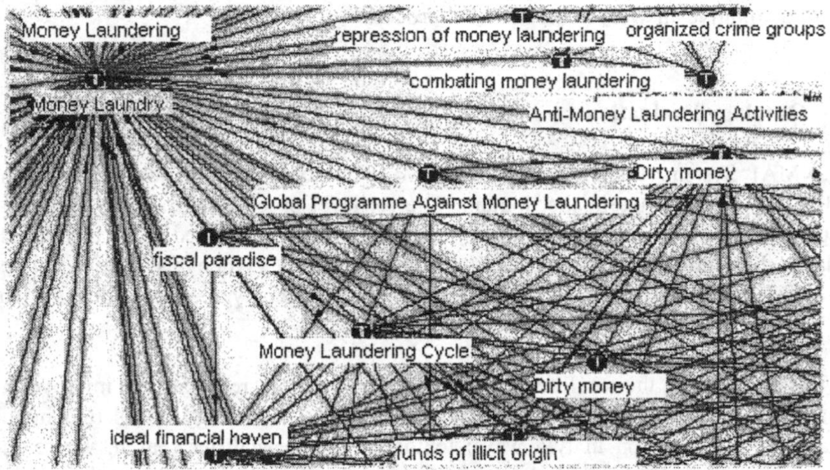

Fig. 2. Part of Money Laundry Ontology.

4.1 Previous analysis of the A terms

Initially, a previous analysis must be performed of the "indicative expressions" pertinent to this domain, aiming at verifying if they are relevant and if the retrieval represents a considerable number of news.

It is important to remark that, previously, the system must contain registered sources and knowledge base news of a minimum period of thirty days. These key-terms can be part of the ontology target of the analysis, and does not affect the expected final results.

The analysis of the representation of these words will be made initially in the first page of retrieval of the system, where there will be news in which these words are contemplated.

4.2 Analysis of B terms

In this stage, the same analysis previously accomplished will contemplate other words, chosen randomly or because they are part of the ontologies, as previously said. Also the aim here is also the retrieval of news, but using a set of news, from the first test.

4.3 Elaboration of the relation of the terms A and B

After the individual evaluation of the terms A and B, with the registry of the results got, it takes the construction of the relation. This construction is accomplished by the association of term B as synonymous of term A, inserting both as an ontology in the system. From this insertion, automatically the relation of synonymy will be created, which is one of the types of semantic relations found in the system. This relation for synonymy will imply simultaneously the retrieval of the news pertaining to terms A and B, in one same analysis.

At this stage of the test, a result is expected such as the retrieval of the same news that was part of the individual analyses, considering that key-terms A and B were inserted as synonyms. It is important to point out that here, the test with ontology formed of a few terms will result in an evaluation with bigger indices of trustworthiness, achieving 100%, considering that the evaluation of a lesser number of retrieved news becomes faster.

From the insertion of the "indicative expression" it is already possible to infer that, if an ontology is not well constructed will result in the retrieval with low indices of precision or, in many cases, a completely inefficient retrieval, compromising the performance of the system.

Taking domain SOCCER as an example, which is the object of this test and considering the insertion of the indicative expression "The King of Soccer", the term is verified by the system in the domain, after the insertion of the term and normalizes the grammatical accent. Thus, for the domain SOCCER, "Pelé" will be related as synonymous the term "The King of Soccer", with or without grammatical accent. But, "pele" in Portuguese means "skin". In this case, when the analysis of the system retrieves news about skin, or dermatology, or allergies, however, and something about Pelé, the football player, it is considered that the error presented is not of the system, but an error of the ontology construction. When the ontology was not constructed in the correct form to represent the expected knowledge, we proceed to the elimination of the "indicative expression" and initiate the construction of new "indicative expression" and its relationships, for a new stage of tests.

4.4 Representation of error

The following stage of tests is related to the representation of error, considering that the ontology is correctly constructed, already identified and the errors of relationship are corrected. The test consists of the construction of the relationship of the ontology constructed to a term that does not represent any relation with the ontology.
For example, we take the indicative expression "money laundry (lavagem de dinheiro)" (see fig. 2), this expression is related to money laundry ontology in KMAI system. In this way, the system recovered 4,516 documents, in the period of two years, from one source (*Agência Brasil).*

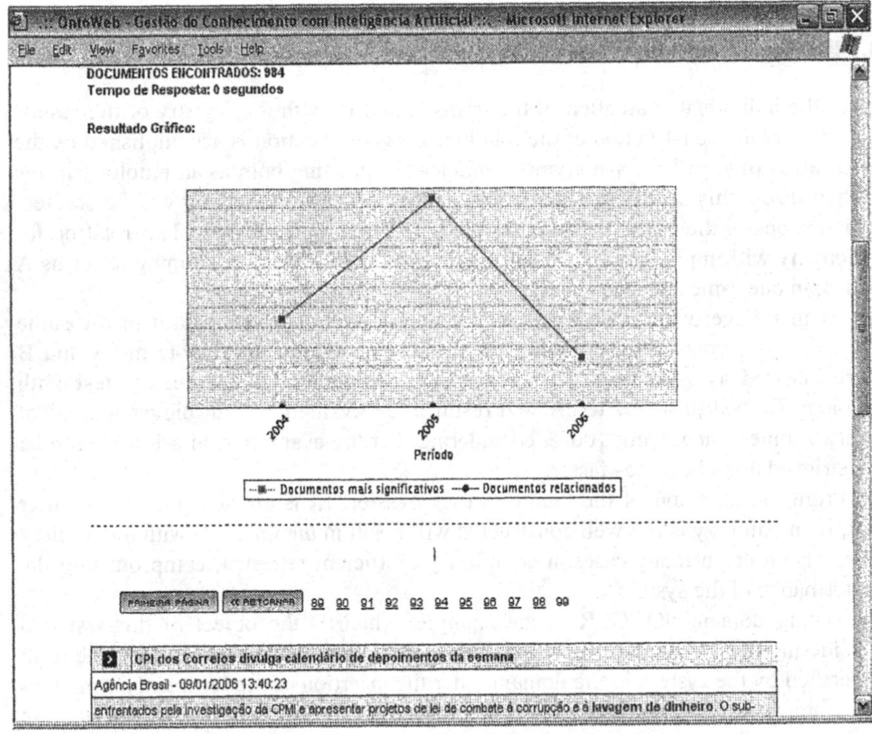

Fig. 3. The Result of Money Laundry ontology in the KMAI System.

It was observed that documents with a low degree of similarity were retrieved due to the terms "bank secrecy" and "kidnapping". When testing the term "bank secrecy" the result was within the context of money laundering; however, other terms like "kidnapping" were totally out of the subject. The term "bank secrecy" retrieved 984 documents, for the same two-year period, and the documents with a low degree of similarity contained the term "money laundering" (see Figure 3). When testing the term "kidnapping", 1,422 documents were retrieved, with the most similar not referring to the "money laundering" crime; only the fifth, the sixth and the seventh documents connected "kidnapping" to "money laundering".

As another example, we define the term "soccer play", synonymous with the term "Fabricia" (see item 2.2). After that, the user will precede the search on soccer and will retrieve, in bigger similarity, a notice as a result that consists of information on "Fabricia". However, they do not have a real relation with soccer, or soccer game. The system makes automatically this relation of synonyms and presents, the relations of "soccer" and the relations of "Fabricia" as results. The retrieval, considering this relation, will demonstrate if the system is working correctly. Another possible verification is related to the results, or either, the verification of the results got to see if they are the results expected.

It is possible to point out when the evaluation of the result is made, that an external factor call problem of the oracle can make it difficult and affect the analysis. The problem of the oracle is related to the absence of documentation and knowledge of the domain object of the test. In the case the responsible for the test does not know the domain and it were not part of the team that constructed the ontologies, he does not have any conditions to evaluate the result. Additionally, the absence of documentation that bases the knowledge of the domain can affect in the results and in many cases deprive the system of characteristics related to its initial conception. The team responsible for the construction of the net of ontologies, also responsible for the tests suggests considering that the knowledge of the domain is basic for the analysis of the results.

5 Results

The procedure adopted to do the recall test in KMAI was made to invite some users who are experts in the domain, but work in different areas, to make some questions. Experts in the money laundry domain were chosen because knowledge engineers that don't work with them couldn't identify the retrieved texts that belong to the domain with precision. For each question, a complete ontology was elaborated. Then, the query was formulated with the "indicative expression" that is part of the domain ontology. Each user made their own evaluation according to their specific knowledge about the domain.

Since KMAI measures the similarity with all documents and, due to conceptual premises, any document that has a similarity superior to 50% would be returned and the recall test has a particular aspect. Only the set of documents that contains the most similar ones were considered to calculate the recall. For instance, the 4,516 documents returned by the query "money laundry" are all pertinent to the context, because all documents have more than 50% of similarity. However, to verify the relevance of each *indicative expression* that composes the money laundry ontology we use the process described in item 4.4 and observe that when the expression was changed, a significant variation in the graph appears, superior to the number of the existing documents about the subject in the knowledge base. With this, it was possible to identify the less significant expressions and the most ambiguous ones.

6 Future Work

We need instead to develop a specification from the available documentation. The specification must then be validated as correct by domain experts. Once a formal specification has been obtained or created, the next task is to convert it into assertions. To facilitate this task, it is better to write the specification using a formal language and structure that matches the one of the programme.

References

1. Duineveld, A. J. et al, 1999. WonderTools? A comparative study of ontological engineering tools. Twelfth Workshop on Knowledge Acquisition, Modeling and Management.Voyager Inn, Banff, Alberta, Canada.
2. Eriksson, H. et al, 1999. Automatic Generation of Ontology Editors. Twelfth Workshop on Knowledge Acquisition, Modeling and Management.Voyager Inn, Banff, Alberta, Canada.
3. Benjamins, V.R., 1998. The ontological engineering initiative (KA)2, Formal Ontology in Information systems. IOS Press, Amsterdam.
4. KMAI System. Available at: http://www.kmai.com.br Access on: 02 janeiro 2006.
5. Ribeiro, Marcelo Stopanovski. KMAI, da RC²D à PCE. Gestão do conhecimento com inteligência artificial, da representação do conhecimento contextualizado dinamicamente à pesquisa contextual estruturada. [2004]. Dissertação (Mestrado em Engenharia de Produção) – Universidade Federal de Santa Catarina, Florianópolis, 2003.
6. Völker, Joahnna, Vrande i , Denny and Sure, York. Automatic Evaluatioversn of Ontologies (AEON). Lecture Notes in Computer Science. Springer-Verlag GmbH. Vol. 3729/2005. Pag. 716 – 731.
7. Bueno, Tania C. D. et al, 2005. Knowledge Engineering Suite: A Tool to Create Ontologies for Automatic Knowledge Representation in Knowledge-Based Systems. Lecture Notes in Computer Science. Springer-Verlag GmbH. Volume 3591/2005. Page: 249.
8. Hoeschl, Hugo. C. et al, 2003. Structured Contextual Search For The Un Security Council. Proceedings of the fifth International Conference On Enterprise Information Systems. Anger, France, v.2. p.100 – 107.6. Bueno, Tânia C. D. et al, 1999. JurisConsulto: Retrieval in Jurisprudencial Text Bases using Juridical Terminology. Proceedings of the Seventh International Conference On Artificial Intelligence And Law. ACM, New York.
9. Faatz, Andreas, Steinmetz, Ralf. Ontology Enrichment Evaluation. Lecture Notes in Computer Science. Springer-Verlag. Vol. 3257/2004. Pag. 497 – 498.

A Model for Concepts Extraction and Context Identification in Knowledge Based Systems

Andre Bortolon, Hugo Cesar Hoeschl, Christianne C.S.R. Coelho, Tania Cristina D'Agostini Bueno
IJURIS – E-Gov, Juridical Intelligence and Systems Institute
Lauro Linhares, St. 728. 105. Trindade. 88036-002
Florianopolis, SC, Brazil
bortolon@ijuris.org, metajur@digesto.net, ccsrcoelho@aol.com, tania@ijuris.org
Home Page: http://www.ijuris.org

Abstract. Information Retrieval Systems normally deal with keyword-based technologies. Although those systems reach satisfactory results, they aren't able to answer more complex queries done by users, especially those directly in natural language. To do that, there are the Knowledge-Based Systems, which use ontologies to represent the knowledge embedded in texts. Currently, the construction of ontologies is based on the participation of three components: the knowledge engineer, the domain specialist, and the system analyst. This work demands time due to the various studies that should be made do determine which elements must participate of the knowledge base and how these elements are interrelated. In this way, using computational systems that, at least, accelerate this work is fundamental to create systems to the market. A model, that allows a computer directly represents the knowledge, just needing a minimal human intervention, or even no one, enlarges the range of domains a system can maintain, becoming it more efficient and user-friendly.

Keywords: Artificial Intelligence, Information Retrieval, Knowledge-Based Systems.

1 Introduction

The huge amount of documents on Internet has become a challenge to everyone that tries to find any information on any subject. [1] developed a method that allows us to estimate the size of Internet in 8.25 billions of pages on June 2003. The same work says the most known search engine, Google, has indexed only 37% of those

Please use the following format when citing this chapter:

Bortolon, A., Hoeschl, H., Coelho, C.C.S.R., D'Agostini Bueno, C., 2006, in IFIP International Federation for Information Processing, Volume 218, Professional Practice in Artificial Intelligence, eds. J. Debenham, (Boston: Springer), pp. 181–190.

pages. In 2005, [2] says Google has more than 8 billion pages indexed. Assuming that Google has maintained the rate of indexed documents on the size of Internet, it is not exaggerated to affirm that Internet has around 21.6 billion of documents. These documents deal with a wide variety of subjects, giving different, or even opposite, points of view on them.

In general, Information Retrieval (IR) systems work with indexes to represent the documents. These indexes can be built with or without a controlled vocabulary. Controlled vocabularies are lists of all important words in a specific domain. However, to build a controlled vocabulary is an expensive task, demanding much time and people. Besides, the absence of a domain specialist can produce low quality vocabularies, lowering the system's performance.

Ontologies are used to extend the controlled vocabularies, allowing knowledge engineers to relate terms among them. But, considering the Internet, it is almost impossible to build ontologies that represent all domains, besides all the time that is necessary to execute the representation.

The objective of this work is to develop a computer model to automatic extraction of terms from a random set of text documents, aiming at finding concepts and identifying the context that the document belongs. Or, at least, to provide information to a domain specialist and/or a knowledge engineer to build an ontology on one or more domains, simultaneously. In this case, the time spent in the construction of the ontology can be highly reduced.

This paper presents the preliminary results of the work. Its studies aren't completed yet, needing more detailed research to finish it.

Section 2 shows the technologies that base the model, section 3 shows the proposed model, and section 4 presents the conclusions obtained up to now and future works.

2 Involved Technologies

2.1 Information Retrieval

Information Retrieval (IR) [3, 4] is the traditionally applied technique to retrieve textual documents to a specific problem. However, unlike its name suggests, IR do not retrieve the information in the sense it delivers the facts that satisfy some necessary information. According to [3], "An information retrieval system does not inform (that is, change the knowledge of) the user on the subject of his inquiry. It merely informs on the existence (or non-existence) and whereabouts of documents relating to his request."

To represent the documents, IR systems can work with either a logical or a complete representation. The former uses a keyword list, which is previously built by a human. The latter uses all words from the document. But, both have problems. The first one needs well-trained specialists to represent adequately the domain that the document belongs. The lack of keywords ends by degrading the performance, since the system cannot answer some queries, even they are related to the domain. The second representation maintains all the words, which can retrieve documents that are not related to the context. So, it is necessary to find more refined techniques to represent the documents aiming at contextualized searches.

2.2 Knowledge Engineering

According to [5], Knowledge Engineering (KE) is the process of construction of a knowledge base. In a simplified way, a knowledge base can be understood as a set of representations of facts on the world.

The construction of a knowledge base is done through a process called knowledge acquisition, where the knowledge engineers work together with domain specialists on the study and gathering of rules and concepts that are relevant to that domain. In the knowledge representation, a domain is some part of the world on which it is desired to express some knowledge. Normally, the knowledge engineer is not a domain specialist. He/she just needs one to support the study of knowledge acquisition.

There are many processes of knowledge engineering. Here, it is focused on the process used in Dynamically Contextualized Knowledge Representation (DCKR) methodology [6]. This process is well described in [7]. This work focuses on the problems that a knowledge engineering team has to create a knowledge base if both KE team and the domain specialists are not synchronized and shows a methodology to obtain this synchronization.

Briefly, the process can be described as a sequence of steps [7]. First one is to divide the domain in subdomains, as much as necessary. After that, knowledge engineers elaborate a conceptual map of the subdomain that will be worked on. Then, they identify the domain's usual vocabulary, visualize the results and identify the relevance of these results to the domain. The last step is to insert the terms and relations in the system. [7] says, "Although the Intelligent Systems has been demonstrated their importance and maturity, their use still has some challenges for their wide dissemination and implantation. The knowledge acquisition stage still is manual and subjective."

One alternative to accelerate the time is to build an automatic system that can extract the terms of the documents and relate them. So, the KE team would only have to examine the results of the system and approve or decline them.

2.3 UNL

The Universal Networking Language (UNL) [8] can be defined as a digital metalanguage for the description, storage and dissemination of information independently of machine or natural language. It has been developed by United Nations University (UNU) since 90s and, later, distributed to various research centers around the world. UNL works in the same way as an interlingua, that is, all the natural languages can be converted to UNL and UNL can be converted in any natural language.

UNL works with the premise that the most important information in a sentence is the concept in it. This concept is represented through Universal Words (UW) and Relations. Both UWs and Relations are universal, that is, all languages can represent them. So, the sentence "the dog runs" is represented by the UNL sentence:

agt(run(icl>do).@entry, dog(icl>animal).@def),

where "run(icl>do)" and "dog(icl>animal)" are UWs that represent the concepts "run" and "dog", respectively, and "agt" represents the relation between those UWs, indicating the second concept is the agent of the first one.

UNL's structure is based on three basic elements:

Universal Words: are the UNL vocabulary, representing a concept related to a word. Divided in two parts: headword, corresponding the concept; and, constraint list, representing the interpretation of the UW, that is, in which domain the UW is inserted. All the UWs are unified in a Knowledge Base. This Knowledge Base is hierarchical, allowing a better classification of the words.

Relations: relate two Universal Words through their syntactic behavior. They intent to describe the objectivity of the sentence. Examples: "agent", "object", "and".

Attributes: on the contrary of relations, the Attributes describe the subjectivity of the sentence. They show what is been said from the speaker's point of view.

Beside these mechanisms, UNL has some tools that are responsible for the translation process. The most important are the Enconverter and the Deconverter. The former is responsible for translation the natural language to UNL. The latter does the inverse.

Due to its organization, UNL has a great potential to represent element that can be used in both Information Retrieval and Knowledge Based Systems.

3 A Model to Automatic Extraction of Terms and Contexts

The model described here intends to identify terms automatically and join these terms trying to determine contexts. To do this task, the model follows these steps:

1) Separation of text in sentences;
2) Separation of sentences in tokens;
3) Classification of tokens;
4) Mapping the tokens;
5) Building of the relationship tree;
6) Calculation of relationship's weights;
7) Calculation of relationship's proximity value.

3.1 Separation of text in sentences

In first step, all the sentences are separated to facilitate next steps. According to Brazilian grammar, described in [9], a sentence "is any linguistic enunciation that has complete sense. It can have one or more words, with or without a verb." Examples: "Hi." "Attention!" "The house is yellow."

So, it is necessary to find all punctuation marks that indicate the end of a sentence: periods (.), exclamation points (!), and question marks (?). In some cases, colons (:) and semi-colons (;) can finish sentences, but they are not considered in this model. Finding all those punctuation marks, it is available a list of sentences.

For instance, considering the text: "The Palestinian president, Yasser Arafat, died in Paris. His body will first be carried to Cairo, Egypt, to the funeral reverences. The burial will be in Hamalah, Cisjordania." It should be divided in three sentences: (1) The Palestinian ...Paris; (2) His body ... reverences; and (3) The burial ... Cisjordania.

The next six steps are applied sentence by sentence, since the process is very similar to syntactic analysis.

3.2 Separation of sentences in tokens

Separation in tokens is a common process in IR indexing and Natural Language Processing systems. Here, it is used in same way.

3.3 Classification of tokens

Each token is classified in four categories:

Number: every sequence of number characters, with or without separators. Ex.: "87", "1.439,26[1]";

Dates: every sequence of number characters with date separators (both "-" and "/"). Ex.: "25/04/2006";

Punctuation marks: all Brazilian Portuguese punctuation marks. Ex.: periods (.), commas (,), parentheses (());

Words: every sequence that cannot be classified in the previous ones. So, it is possible to classify all elements that appear in the text.

3.4 Mapping the tokens

Fourth step is to map each token to one of the ten morphological categories from Brazilian Portuguese grammar, such as: Nouns, Adjectives, Articles, Pronouns, Verbs, Numerals, Adverbs, Preposition, Conjunctions, and Interjections. This map is done comparing each token with a dictionary.

If a token has more than one entry in the dictionary, all the entries become candidates. For instance, the word "meio[2]" can belong to four different categories: Numeral, Noun, Adjective, and Adverb. To solve this problem, it is necessary to verify the words that are related to the ambiguous word in the sentence, establishing a context. This process is executed in the next step.

Other problem that appears in the mapping process is when the token doesn't have an entry in the dictionary. This situation occurs due to four main reasons. The first is the proper nouns. Normally, names of people, places, etc. don't appear in

[1] Brazilian number format.

[2] In English, "half".

dictionaries. There are special dictionaries to deal with people names, places, and so on, but they cannot be complete, specially related to people, since parents are very creative people when naming their children. Considering an elegant and well-done texts, proper nouns start with a capital letter. So, this can be considered as a rule to identify them in the texts.

The second reason for tokens without entries is those that correspond to words with morphologic inflections, such as, plural, verbs (in Portuguese, all persons have a specific inflection), and gender (there are different suffixes to masculine and feminine). Two approaches can be used to solve the problem: insert all inflections of the word in the dictionary, indicating the correspondence with the main word; or, build a set of rules to replace suffixes and find the main form of the word.

Tokens that correspond to words incorrectly spelled or with typing errors are the third reason. The most common causes for typing errors are:

Missing character: a missing character in any part of the word. Ex.: "snd" instead of "send";

Extra character: an extra character in any part of the word. Ex.: "sensd" instead of "send";

Wrong character: a wrong character typed. Ex.: "semd" instead of "send";

Changed character: two characters typed inversely. Ex.: "sned" instead of "send";

Absence of accent marks: the word doesn't have the accent marks. Ex.: "coleção" is typed as "colecao". This error is very common in search engine queries. Although, in regular documents, its occurrence is low.

The most common way to solve this problem is using an algorithm that generates all the words that should be the actual word, considering all the possible errors. But, this approach is questionable, since a simple five-letter word has 295 possible words (except absence of accent marks) as candidates. Other technique uses heuristics to find the most common errors (for instance, the absence of one "s" in words with "ss"). One other technique is to use probabilistic rules to determine the most similar entries to the given token.

The last reason is the tokens that aren't a word, so no entry can be related to them. For instance "abcde". In these cases, the word is mapped to a noun.

The option of mapping all the unknown tokens as nouns comes from the fact that it is almost impossible to have a complete dictionary of proper nouns. So, if a token isn't an incorrect or inflected word, very probably it is a proper noun. The documents used as a test base confirm it, since they don't have words without any meaning in their body.

Therefore, the result of the third step is a list of tokens and their corresponded grammatical category. For instance, the sentence "Peter broke the window with a rock." has the following list[3]:

Peter={(Peter; noun)}

broke={(brake; verb), (broke; adjective)}

[3] The English categories for the words come from [10]. The examples are illustrative. The model has just been tested in Brazilian Portuguese.

the={(the; article), (the; adverb), (the; preposition)}
window={(window; noun)}
with={(with; preposition)}
a={(a; noun), (a; article), (a; preposition), (a; verb)}
rock={(rock; verb), (rock; noun)}

3.5 Building of the relationship tree

The relationship between words is a process that can be done through syntactic analysis. Among all the current available technologies, the chosen one is UNL, because it can perform both syntactic and semantic analysis. But, UNL rules for Portuguese aren't completely ready, yet. So, the solution was build a structure based in UNL, but with simpler representation and mechanism.

To build this structure, a study was performed to find which are the elements in language that can be put together to form terms. It was analyzed 1,042 terms of the KMAI System's ([11]) ontology. As expected, 100% of terms have a noun as part. These nouns were mainly related to other nouns and adjectives. More than 90% of terms with more than two words have a preposition relation the two other words. The conclusion was prepositions could be used as the element of relation between two words. The words that don't have a preposition between them are related with a underscore (_).

This simpler structure was improved using the UNL attributes that indicates number, time, concept (definite or indefinite nouns and negation), and a special one necessary to Portuguese, gender.

Therefore, the relation's structure is described as:

relation(word1.attributes, word2.attributes),

where *relation* is the preposition between the words or the character "_", *word1* and *word2* are the words and *attributes* are the attributes of each word. For instance, the previous sentence "Peter broke the window with a rock.", becomes[4]:

_(Peter, brake.@past)
_(brake.@past, window.@def)
with(window.@def, rock.@indef)

3.6 Calculation of relationship's weights

To determine which relationships correspond to terms, it is necessary to calculate some weights to the relations. In this model, it is used the same weights that are used in regular IR systems, such as, term frequency (tf) and inverse document frequency (idf). Since the weights are based in the relations, they become relation frequency (rf) and relation's inverse document frequency (ridf). They are calculated by the same formula:

[4] Again, the example is illustrative. The model has just been tested in Brazilian Portuguese.

$$rf_i = \frac{n_i}{\sum_k n_k}$$

where n_i is the number of times the relation appears in the document and n_k is the number of relations of the document.

$$idf_i = \log_2\left(\frac{N}{n_i}\right)$$

where N is the number of documents and n_i is the number of documents with the relation.

3.7 Calculation of relationship's proximity value

The last step is to establish a proximity value between the relations, aiming at the creation of contexts. To do this, it is used a model based in the statistic co-occurrence of words, described in [4]. There, the similarity coefficients between two terms are based on coincidences in the term associations in the documents from the collection. The documents are represented by a matrix based in the vector-space model, where the rows are the documents' individual vectors and the columns identify the associations of terms and documents. In the model described in the paper, relations between two words are represented in the columns rather than terms. So, the matrix becomes as shown in Table 1.

Table 1. Matrix of association of terms

	R_1	R_2	...	R_k	...	R_m
D_1	rf_{11}	rf_{12}	...	rf_{1k}	...	rf_{1m}
...	...	...	...	...	...	...
D_n	rf_{n1}	rf_{n2}	...	rf_{nk}	...	rf_{nm}

The similarity between two relations can be calculated by the formula:

$$sim(REL_k, REL_l) = \frac{\sum_{i=1}^{n} rf_{ik} \cdot rf_{il}}{\sum_{i=1}^{n} rf_{ik}^2 + \sum_{i=1}^{n} rf_{il}^2 - \sum_{i=1}^{n} rf_{ik} \cdot rf_{il}}$$

where rf_{ik} indicates the frequency that relation i appears in document k and n is the number of documents in the base.

The similarity value indicates the probability that the two relations have to be related each other, since it indicates how many times one relation appeared and other also did. Doing the calculus for many relations can create cohesion between the relations, generating groups of relations that might be contexts.

Considering the matrix showed in Table 2:

Table 2. Example Matrix

	(1)	(2)	(3)	(5)	(6)	(10)
D_1	1	1	1	1	1	1
D_2	0	1	1	0	0	0
D_3	0	1	1	0	0	0
D_4	0	0	1	0	0	1
D_5	0	0	0	0	1	0

The similarities between the relations are disposed in Table 3.

Table 3. Similarities between relations

	(1)	(2)	(3)	(5)	(6)	(10)
(1)	X	0.33	0.25	1	0.5	0.5
(2)	0.33	X	0.75	0.33	0.25	0.25
(3)	0.25	0.75	X	0.25	0.2	0.5
(5)	1	0.33	0.25	X	0.5	0.5
(6)	0.5	0.25	0.2	0.5	X	0.33
(10)	0.5	0.25	0.5	0.5	0.33	X

To really find a context, it is necessary to put a minimum threshold to initiate the grouping. Tests have been done trying to determine this value, but no result was obtained yet. Basically, the test is to get one context and select a number of documents on it. So, extract the relations and calculate the similarity between that. Also, it is necessary to find other relations that should be considered in other contexts. After that, get other context related to the first and calculate the frequency of the relations from the first one appears and compare the values. Last, get a third context that does not have any relation with the first and do the same process. So, we can get some average from the three values and test in a generic set of documents.

4 Conclusions

Since the research is not finished yet, there are not so many results achieved up to now. But, the reducing of time to build a initial set of terms to analyze and build an ontology has already been evidenced. The main reason for it is that the simple structure of the model create documents that allow a fast recognizing of related words, creating a lot of candidate terms. Usage of weights also highlight the terms that happens with more frequency and which are normally related.

The model is also ready to be used in a Information Retrieval System, improving the representation and the results to the users.

Also, the model can be used in any IR system that uses UNL to structure the documents in the base, since the representation is strongly based in UNL.

References

[1] SOARES, António; BARROSO, João; BULAS-CRUZ, José. Estimativa da PIW através de Motores de Pesquisa de Grande Escala. In: Conferência IADIS Ibero-Americana WWW/Internet 2004. Madrid, 2004.

[2] ARNOLD, Stephen A. The Google Legacy. Chapter 3. Infonortics. 2005. Available at: http://www.infonortics.com/publications/google/technology.pdf.

[3] VAN RIJSBERGEN, C. J. Information Retrieval. Second Edition. Butterworths. London, 1979.

[4] SALTON, C.; MCGILL, M. Introduction to Modern Information Retrieval. McGraw-Hill, New York, 1983.

[5] RUSSELL, Stuart; NORVIG, Peter. Artificial Intelligence: A Modern Approach. Prentice-Hall. New Jersey, 1995.

[6] HOESCHL, H. C. Sistema Olimpo: tecnologia da informação jurídica para o Conselho de Segurança da ONU. Tese de Doutorado (Engenharia de Produção). Universidade Federal de Santa Catarina. Florianópolis, 2001.

[7] BUENO, Tânia Cristina D' Agostini; Engenharia da Mente: Uma Metodologia de Representação do Conhecimento para a Construção de Ontologias em Sistemas Baseados em Conhecimento. Tese de Doutorado (Engenharia de Produção). Universidade Federal de Santa Catarina. Florianópolis, 2005.

[8] UCHIDA, Hiroshi; ZHU, Meiying; DELLA SENTA, Tarcisio; The UNL, A Gift for a Millennium. UNU Institute of Advanced Studies. Tokyo, 1999.

[9] FARACO, Carlos Emílio; MOURA, Francisco Marto de; Língua e Literatura. 23ª Edição. Ática. São Paulo, 1995. v. 3.

[10] Merriam-Webster Online Dictionary. http://www.m-w.com. Accessed at: 26/04/2006.

[11] KMAI. Knowledge Management with Artificial Intelligence. Software. http://www.kmai.com.br.

Proposal of Fuzzy Object Oriented Model in Extended JAVA

Wilmer Pereira
Grupo de Investigación en Inteligencia Artificial y Robótica (GIIAR)
Escuela de Ingeniería Informática, Universidad Católica Andrés Bello
Caracas, Venezuela, wpereira@ucab.edu.ve

Abstract. The knowledge imperfections should be considered when modeling complex problems. A solution is to develop a model that reduces the complexity and another option is to represent the imperfections: uncertainty, vagueness and incompleteness in the knowledge base. This paper proposes to extend the classical object oriented architecture in order to allow modeling of problems with intrinsic imperfections. The aim is to use the JAVA object oriented architecture to carry out this objective. In consequence, it is necessary to define the semantics for this extension of JAVA and it will be called Fuzzy JAVA. The NCR `FuzzyJ` library allows represent the vagueness (fuzziness) and uncertainty in class attributes. JAVA extended allows to model fuzzy inheritance.

1 Introduction

In computer science, one of the most popular formalism to model problems, is the object oriented model by their generality and versatility. As the complexity of the problems always increases, it is important to use this methodology in order to make easy the problem representation. However, in many cases, the complexity comes from: the uncertainty, the fuzziness or the incompleteness [10]. Thus, it is desirable to consider theories and methodological tools that represent these knowledge imperfections inside the object oriented model. This would allow the user to specify problems when the knowledge has intrinsic imperfections. In [11] appeared a version of an object oriented model to represent these imperfections using fuzzy sets and possibilistic logic. This proposal was called *Fuzzy Object Oriented Model*. This approach was developed initially for monovalued and multivalued attributes [12]. This paper details a proposal to extend JAVA, considering the knowledge imperfections in: attributes with fuzzy values, fuzzy inheritance and fuzzy or uncertain membership of the objects to the classes.

Please use the following format when citing this chapter:

Pereira, W., 2006, in IFIP International Federation for Information Processing, Volume 218, Professional Practice in Artificial Intelligence, eds. J. Debenham, (Boston: Springer), pp. 191–200.

Precedent papers have revised theses ideas. In [1] is presented an object oriented model of visual data based on graph. It allows to model fuzzy attributes and fuzzy membership from objects to their class. In both cases, it is necessary to use linguistic labels and degrees of uncertainty. With regard to the fuzzy membership of the subclass to the superclass, this paper does not consider it necessary in order to model problems. On the other hand, in [15] is defined the generalized fuzzy sets for fuzzy attributes and fuzzy membership from the objects to class. It defines two degree of uncertainty depending on the attribute membership to his class. There are also two values for the object membership to its class. Here, like in the previous paper, it does not consider the fuzzy inheritance. As for [6], it is defined the membership function for the fuzzy relation: object-class and superclass-subclass. The article has a lot of formulas with not too theoretical support but a good intuition and common sense of the authors. Also in [5] membership functions are specified, characterizing the difference between typical ranges and permissible ranges. The properties between the supports and the kernel of possibility distribution, define the inclusion of superclass-subclass and the membership function from an object to its class. This last article relates quantitative and qualitative aspects that the designer uses to model knowledge base. Our paper defines a semantic for a fuzzy object oriented model on JAVA that we will call *Fuzzy JAVA*. We consult ideas of previous works and we propose new ideas to extend JAVA language structure.

2 Preliminaries

2.1 Fuzzy Sets

These sets are an extension of regular sets because they allow express membership degree of the elements of the universe [7]. These degrees are represented using of a *membership function* whose range is the real interval [0,1]. The membership function of a fuzzy set F is denoted with the symbol μ_F such that: $\mu_F : U \rightarrow [0,1]$. This characteristic function usually has trapezium form and it is defined by a 4-tuple of the universe (a,b,c,d).

In logical terms, a trapezium represents a *fuzzy predicate* where the boolean value stem from membership function of the fuzzy set. In this way, for example the fuzzy predicate `youth` is defined on the universe of ages {0 ..125} with the membership function μ_{youth}=(0,0,25,50). The associated trapezium is:

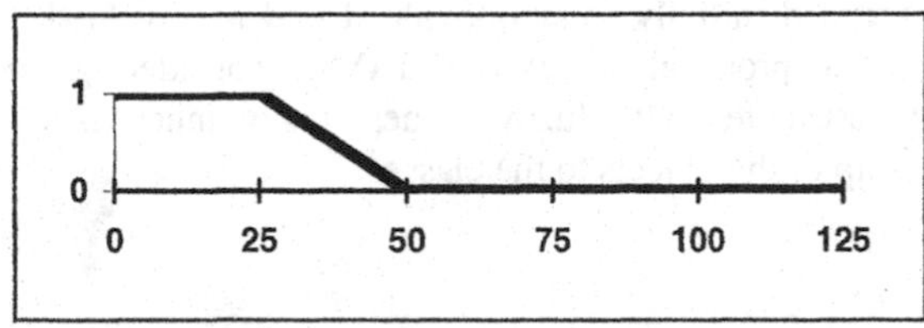

Fig. 1. A fuzzy predicate `youth`

2.2 Possibility Distribution and Possibility Theory

A *possibility distribution* is a function of an universe U to the real interval [0,1], just as membership function of the fuzzy sets. A possibility distribution π depend on a fuzzy set F: $\pi(x = a) = \mu_F(a)$. With these possibility distributions it is possible to obtain two measures called *possibility* (Π) and *necessity* (N), whose determine the degree of certainty or trust of a statement [4]. This is a less rigorous way to represent the uncertainty than probability theory. The possibility measure is a function whose domain is part of the universe in the interval [0,1], Π:P(U) → [0,1] such that:

$$\forall A,B \in \mathrm{P}(U)\big(\Pi(A \cup B) = max(\Pi(A),\Pi(B))\big) \quad (1)$$

$$\forall A \in \mathrm{P}(U)\big(max(\Pi(A),\Pi(\bar{A})) = 1\big) \quad (2)$$

It is important to remark that if A and its complement set are totally possible, it represent a situation of total ignorance. This is an advantage of the possibility theory on the probability theory, which does not allow represent ignorance on probabilities. The necessity measure is the dual concept of possibility measure that is also defined on the parts of U in the real interval [0,1]. The necessity and possibility measure are weaker than probabilities values because they do not impose conditions on the event probability and its event complement. Besides the sum of the possibility or necessity measures do not have to add 1. Consequently, these measures are better adapted to model of subjective uncertainty according to the appreciations of a designer.

With regard to the operations on fuzzy sets, the intersection is defined like a combination of sets possibilities measures by means of a triangular norm T.

$$\mu_{F \cap G}(x) = T\big(\mu_F(x), \mu_G(x)\big) \quad (3)$$

A triangular norm is a binary operator on the real interval [0,1] that is associative, commutative, monotonic, for which 1 is the neutral element. Usually, the intersection uses the biggest triangular norms that is the minimum (MIN). On the contrary, the union of two fuzzy uses a triangular conorm S.

$$\mu_{F \cup G}(x) = S\big(\mu_F(x), \mu_G(x)\big) \quad (4)$$

A triangular conorm has duals properties with regard to triangular norm and the union use the maximum (MAX). The properties of the union and the intersection depend on the measure triangular pair.

Finally another operator used in this paper, is the *α-cut*. This operator links fuzzy sets with traditional sets. This traditional set contains all the elements whose membership to the fuzzy set is bigger than a minimum level of tolerance. The α-cut of a fuzzy set F is denoted by F_α

$$F_\alpha = \{x \in U \,/\, \mu_F(x) \geq \alpha\} \quad (5)$$

2.3 NRC Fuzzy Library for JAVA

This JAVA library defines and manipulates fuzzy concepts in order to obtain fuzzy reasonings [9]. This tool was created by the NRC (National Research Council of Canada). `FuzzyJ` is focused fundamentally in the fuzzy concepts, by means of the creation and manipulation of membership functions. The most important classes in this library or API are:

<u>`FuzzyVariable` class</u>: An object of this class specifies the universe that will be used to manipulate a fuzzy concept, for example temperature, pressure, etc. To create an instance of this class is necessary to indicate as parameters: a name, the superior and inferior limit of the universe and the variable units. For example:

```
FuzzyVariable temp = new FuzzyVariable("temperature", 0, 100, "C");
```

<u>`FuzzySet` class</u>: The objects of this class allow define possibility functions. To create an instance of this class, is necessary to indicate as parameters an array of `x` values, an array of `y` values (which define the `FuzzySet`) and also the cardinality of the arrays. For example:

```
double xvalues [] = {0.1, 0.3, 0.4, 0.5, 0.8};
double yvalues [] = {0.0, 1.0, 0.65, 1.0, 0.0};
FuzzySet example = new FuzzySet(xvalues, yvalues, 5);
```

Then, it is necessary to add possibility functions on a predetermined universe. The method `addTerm` of the class `FuzzyVariable`, receives as parameters a name and the possibility function.

```
temp.addTerm("Cold", new TrapezoidFuzzySet(0.0,0.0,5.0,15.0));
```

<u>`FuzzyValue` class</u>: An object of this class is used to define a group of values `x` and `y`. These values determine the form of a possibility function. There is not a specific concept associated to this function. The `FuzzyValue` associates a `FuzzySet` to a `FuzzyVariable`, that is to say, it associates the possibility function to a universe. The `FuzzyValue` generally, but not always, provides a linguistic expression that gives a comprehensible meaning to the `FuzzySet`.

3 Fuzzy Object Oriented Model

This paper presents a study of a possible fuzzy semantics for: the attributes of objects, the fuzzy inheritance and the fuzzy membership of objects to classes.

3.1 Fuzzy Attributes

There are several ways to associate a fuzzy characteristic to an attribute. There are two classical dimensions on attributes values: the vagueness (fuzziness) with possibility distribution and the uncertainty with possibilistic value. In [12] besides the attributes was presented as monovalued and multivalued but in this paper is presented only fuzzy monovalued attributes.

A monovalued attribute takes a value which defines its state. For example, a class `person` can contain as attributes: `IDNumber`, `Age`, `Height`, `Address`, `EducationDegree`, `TelephoneNumber`, `PreferedColors`, `FirstLanguage` and `SecondLanguage`. Each individual `person`, for example, `Nathalie` is an object, that is to say, an instance of `person` class. The object `Nathalie` will have specific values for each one of these attributes. For example, the attribute `Age = 8` or `TelephoneNumber = 2426290`. Methods carry out operations on person objects changing their state. For example, `ChangeAddress`, `NewDegree`, etc. In the classical objects oriented model is assumed that all the attributes take a precise value. However we will consider imperfections like fuzziness and uncertainty.

With respect to fuzziness, an attribute can take a linguistic label associated to a possibilistic distribution, in other words, a vague or fuzzy value [12]. In this case, a `person` object can have assigned the linguistic label `youth`. This defines a possibility distribution whose domain is the possible ages and the range is on [0,1], μ_{youth} : `[1,125]` → `[0,1]` (see Figure 1). So if the age of `Nathalie` object is `youth`, then the possibility distribution associated to the attribute `Age` of the object `Nathalie` is:

```
{1/1,1/2,...,1/25,0.95/26,0.9/27,...,0.1/48,0.05/49,0/50,...,0/125}
```

In NCR `FuzzyJ` it is represented in this way:

```
FuzzyValue age = null; …
FuzzyVariable uddAge = new FuzzyVariable("Age", 0.0, 100.0, "years");
uddAge.addTerm("Youth", new RightLinearFuzzySet(40.0, 60.0));
nathalie.age = new FuzzyValue(uddAge, "youth");
```

With respect to uncertainty, let us suppose a monovalued attribute with a precise value but who defines it (designer), assigns it a degree of uncertainty, which can turns like a possibility measure. For example, let us suppose the object `Wilmer` that has the value of attribute `SecondLanguage` in English with a degree of uncertainty or possibility of 0.6. The representation in JAVA is:

```
(unc Uncertainty) Attribute = Value;
```

where *`Attribute`* is a variable of a primitive type or an object `String`, *`Value`* is an element of the attribute type and *`Uncertainty`* is a real value, `double` type, belonging to [0,1] interval (possibility measure). The default possibility value is 1.

For example: `(unc 0.6) wilmer.SecondLanguage = English;`

To recover the uncertainty of an attribute, it is made calling the method:

```
unc(Attribute)
```

Finally when fuzziness and uncertainty are considered, a monovalued attribute can be defined like a λ-trapezium [2]. For example let us suppose an object `Nathalie` with its `Height` attribute whose value is the linguistic label: "`more or less 1m10`". The designer adds 0.3 possible of uncertainty to this affirmation. In other terms the designer wants to model: "*it is 0.3 possible that the height of Nathalie is of more or less 1m10*". The trapezium that represents `more or less 1m10` is:

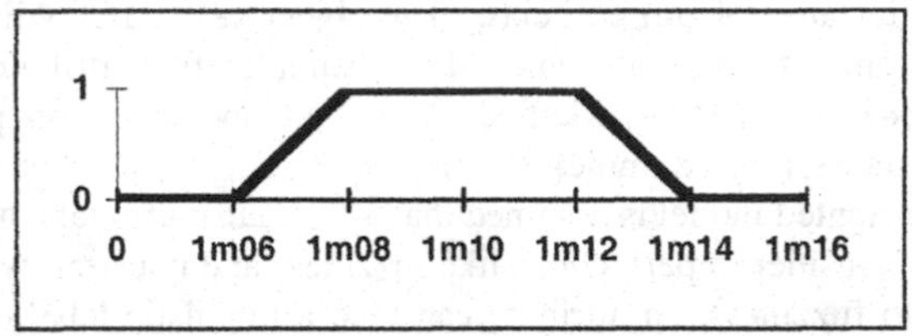

Fig. 2: Trapezium of the fuzzy label more or less 1m10

The possibility of 0.3 on the attribute `height` of the object `Nathalie` introduces a λ-support on the λ-trapezium. When the possibility measure is 1, it represents total uncertainty.

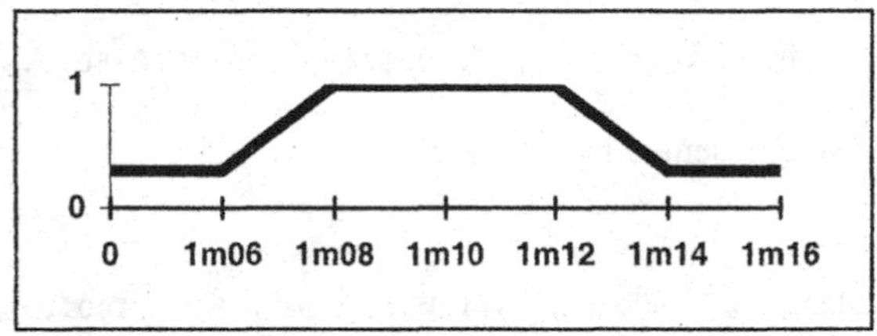

Fig. 3: λ-trapezium of the fuzzy label more or less 1m10

To model this expression implies to assign to an attribute a fuzzy value and a degree of uncertainty. In this way an object `FuzzyValue` should be created, with the possibility measure:

```
(iunc Uncertainty) Variable FuzzyValue = Value;
```

It is important to remark that, in this case, `iunc` is used instead of `unc`. The cause is that default value for `unc`, only for a precise attribute, is 1. While the default value for `iunc`, always on an imprecise or fuzzy attribute, is 0. This is evident for the way to calculate the λ-trapezium. An example in `FuzzyJ` of this mixture of imperfections in the knowledge (fuzziness + uncertainty) is:

```
FuzzyValue height = null;
```

```
FuzzyVariable uddHeight=new FuzzyVariable("height", 0.0, 230.0, "cm");
uddEstatura.addTerm("moreorless110",new
    TrapezoidFuzzySet(106.0,108.0,112.0,114.0));
(iunc 0.3) height = new FuzzyValue(uddHeight, "moreorless110");
```

3.2 Fuzzy Inheritance

In the classical object oriented model, a class inherits all properties of its superclass, as much methods as attributes (except for overwrite rules). In the fuzzy object oriented model, it can be uncertain the application of the properties of a superclass toward the subclass. The cause is, the designer can create a class that inherits of another with a certain level of uncertainty. This will be expressed:

```
class subclass extends superclass (imem membership) {…}
```

For example: `class coniferous extends tree (imem 0.78) {…}`

In the multiple inheritance, like in the simple inheritance, it is possible the fuzzy membership a class to their superclass. In other words, a subclass can have a degree of partial inclusion toward different superclass. Since in classic JAVA does not exist the multiple inheritance, the way to represent it in fuzzy JAVA it is by means of the interfaces:

```
class subclass implements interfaz (imem membership) {,interfaz (imem
membership)} {…}
```

For example: `class roundedsquare implements circle (imem 0.8), square (imem 0.6) {…}`

As much for the simple inheritance as for the multiple inheritance, when membership is not specified from a class to its superclass, this it will be assumed that the degree of inclusion of the superclass in the subclass is 1. For examples more specific, see [13].

3.3 Fuzzy Membership of an Object to their Class

In fuzzy object oriented model, an object can have a degree of membership to its class. This degree can be specified when the object is declared or it can be calculated automatically. The explicit definition of object possibility measure on the class, is expressed to the moment to create the object.

```
NomClass NomObject = new NomClass(Parameters) (omem membership);
```

For example: `Dinosaur dino = new Dinosaur () (omem 0.5);`

With regard to the level of membership calculated automatically from the object to the class, an example of multiple inheritance is presented to illustrate better this concepts. Let us suppose a hierarchy of dinosaurs where is obvious the fuzzy character of the classification for the difficulty of identify without ambiguity the evidences. The specialists in dinosaurs only have incomplete fossils to determine the characteristics of a dinosaur and to classify it in the well-known hierarchy until that moment. In this hierarchy of dinosaurs classes the relationship or inheritance is fuzzy, the attributes are not necessary and the membership of each dinosaur to the classification is uncertain.

It is clear that the uncertainty expands for the classification due to the fuzzy and imprecise character of the objects, the inheritance and the attributes. Next the necessary calculations are presented (relative to the norm and triangular conorm) to calculate like it extends the uncertainty and the fuzziness.

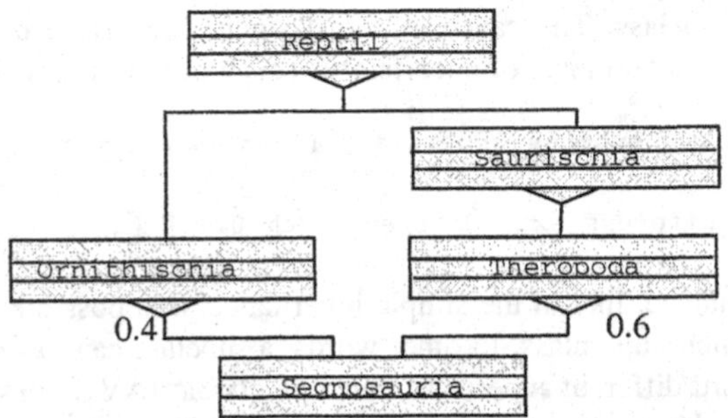

Fig. 4: A fuzzy portion of the hierarchical classification of the dinosaurs

Let us suppose a particular object of the `Segnosauria` class and it will be called `sigy`. Since the anthropologist has not enough documentation on the segnosaurios, `sigy` is believed with a measure of possibility of 0.5:

```
Segnosauria sigy = new Segnosauria () (omem 0.5);
```

Now which the measure of `sigy` possibility is with regard to the superclass `Ornithischia` and `Theropoda`?. It is reasonable that the possibility measure of the object with regard to an immediate superclass is the norm triangular "minimum" (formula 3). In this case the minimum would be between the possibility measure of the object and the possibility measure of the inheritance relationship. The calculations are carried out lineally, as it ascends in the hierarchy toward the superior levels. This way, `sigy` will have as measures of possibility 0.4 with regard to the superclass `Ornithischia` and 0.5 towards the superclass `Theropoda`. When an inheritance relationship does not have an explicit value, it has as possibility measure 1. Therefore, with regard to the superclass `Saurischia`, `sigy` has a possibility measure of 0.5 because the norm triangular minimum, that is to say, min{1, 0.5}.

Now let us see that it happens to `sigy` with regard to the `Reptilian` superclass. There are two "path" in the inheritance hierarchy that converge the superclass, Which the `sigy` possibility degree is in this case? Here it is reasonable to calculate the possibility measure like the conorm triangular "maximum" for the values that converge in the superclass (formula 4). In this case `sigy` has as possibility degree 0.5 to because it is the maximum of the possibilities degrees that converge in the `reptilian` superclass, max{0.4, 0.5}. Recapitulating, the measures of `sigy` possibility are: 0.4 for the `ornithischia` class, 0.5 for the `theropoda` class, 0.5 for the `saurischia` class and 0.5 for the `reptilian` class

In conclusion, when the object moves lineally in the hierarchy of fuzzy inheritance, the calculation is carried out like a conjunction, that is to say, by means of the bigger than the triangular norms: the minimum. On the other hand, when the object is in an intersection, the calculation is made like a disjunction, that is to say, with the smaller than the triangular conorms: the maximum.

3.4 Selective Inheritance of Methods and Attributes

In classical object oriented model, it is clear that the objects of a class have all the properties from the class to which it belong. However, in the fuzzy object oriented model, because the membership of an object to its class can be uncertain, the applicability of the properties of the class to the object also is uncertain. For this reason, it is defined thresholds like a minimum level of tolerance that the programmer assigns in time of compilation. This allows determine when the objects of the class can use method or attributes, taking into account the level of membership from these to the class. This is represented with α-cut. By default the methods that do not have threshold will only be able to be applied by objects with membership degree 1. This way it is avoided to apply methods that would be insecure for certain objects. The form of assigning a threshold to a method is the following one:

```
(thr threshold) TypeReturn NomMethod (Parameters) {…}
```

For example, the class `Adult` has the methods `puberty` that returns a boolean and `MarriedYears` returns an integer, each one with thresholds 0.3 and 0.7 respectively:

```
(thr 0.3) boolean puberty () {return (age <18);}
(thr 0.7) int MarriedYears(int years) {return (2004 - years);}
```

The object `María` of the class `Adult` is believed with a membership degree of 0.4. On this object one will be able to apply the method `puberty` because it possesses a smaller threshold to the membership degree of `María`, but one will not be able to apply `MarriedYears` because the threshold of the method is higher than the membership degree of the object. In form similar to the methods, an attribute of a class is applicable to an object according to its membership degree. The attributes threshold is defined by the programmer in time of compilation. The form of assigning a threshold to an attribute is:

```
(thr Threshold) Type Attribute;
```

4 Conclusions

The present work defines the semantics of a fuzzy object oriented model using JAVA object oriented model. Tough the API `FuzzyJ` adds fuzzy concepts in applications, it is not comparable with this our approach because we modify the own object oriented model of JAVA. This API only represents and manipulates fuzzy information using a traditional object oriented model.

At this moment we have a prototype for fuzzy JAVA only translates in JAVA classic for the monovalued and multivalued attributes [3]. The following step is to define the grammar that allows us to have an automatic translator from fuzzy JAVA to JAVA classic.

5 Bibliography

[1] G. Bordogna, D. Lucarella and G. Pasi., A Fuzzy Object Oriented Data Model, *III IEEE Int. Conference on Fuzzy Systems,* 1994.

[2] J. C. Buisson, H Farreny and H. Prade, Dealing with Imprecisión and Uncertainty in Expert System DIABETO-III, *Innov. Tech. Biol. Med.,* Vol. 8, N. 2, 1987.

[3] J. Costa and M. Mijares, Análisis Diseño e Implementación de un Modelo Orientado a Objetos Difuso (OOD), Tesis de Grado de la Escuela de Ingeniería Informática, UCAB, 2004

[4] D. Dubois and H. Prade, Théorie des Possibilités: Applications a la Représentation des Connaissances en Informatique, *Editorial Masson,* 1988.

[5] D. Dubois, H. Prade and J-P. Rossazza, Vagueness, Typicality, and Uncertainty in Class Hierarchies *International Journal of Intelligente Systems,* Vol. 6, 1991.

[6] R. George, B.P. Buckles and F.E.Petry, Modelling Class Hierarchies in the Fuzzy Object-Oriented Data Model, *Fuzzy Sets and Systems,* Vol. 60, 1993.

[7] J.P. Haton et al, Raisonnement en Intelligence Artificielle, *InterEditions,* Paris, 1991.

[9] R. Orchard, NCR FuzzyJ Toolkit for the Java Platform; User's Guide, (`http://ai.iit.nrc.ca/IR_public/fuzzy/fuzzyJToolkit2.html`) *National Research Council Canada,* 2003.

[10] W. Pereira, Une Logique Modale pour le Raisonnement dans l'Incertain, *Tesis de Doctorado, Universidad de Rennes I,* Francia, 1992.

[11] W. Pereira and L. Tineo, Modelo Orientado a Objetos Difuso, *L Convención Anual ASOVAC,* Universidad Simón Bolívar, Noviembre/2000, Caracas, Venezuela.

[12] W. Pereira, Atributos Monovaluados y Multivaluados sobre un Modelo Orientado a Objetos Difuso, *1^{eras} Jornadas de Investigación de la UCAB,* 27-28 Noviembre 2001, Caracas, Venezuela.

[13] W. Pereira, Imprecisión e Incertidumbre en un Modelo Orientado a Objetos Difuso, *Trabajo de Ascenso,* UCAB, 2002, Caracas, Venezuela.

[14] A. Thayse et al, Approche Logique de l'Intelligence Artficielle, Volume I y II, *Dunod Informatique,* Paris, 1989.

[15] N. Van Gyseghem, R. De Caluwe and R. Vandenberghe, UFO: Uncertainty and Fuzziness in Object-oriented model, *II IEEE Int. Conference on Fuzzy Systems,* San Francisco, 1993.

Adopting Knowledge Discovery in Databases for Customer Relationship Management in Egyptian Public Banks

A. Khedr and J. N. Kok
Leiden University, Leiden Institute of Advanced Computer Science
P.O. Box 9512, 2300 RA Leiden, The Netherlands
Email: khedr@liacs.nl

Abstract. We propose a framework for studying the effect of KDD on CRM in the Egyptian banking sector. We believe that the KDD process and applications may perform a significant role in Egyptian banks to improve CRM, in particular for customer retention. Our believe is supported by the results of the field survey at the largest Egyptian bank.
Keywords. Adopting new technology, Knowledge Discovery in Databases (KDD), Customer Relationship Management (CRM), and banking sector.

1 Introduction

Innovative technology is defined as any new developmental technology in organizations [1]. It can involve creating or reengineering products or services to meet the new market demand, introducing new technologies to improve productivity, developing or applying new marketing techniques to expand the sales opportunities, and incorporate the new forms of management systems and techniques to improve the operational efficiency [2].

As a result of the continuous increase of the business needs, the amount of data in database systems is growing fast. Since the cost of data storage is decreasing continuously, users tend to store all available information in the databases, to retain information that might be useful in the future, even if it is not of a direct value [3].

In the banking sector, the increasing competition, the deregulation, and the adoption of new technologies, have contributed to the growth of customer's power. Customers may switch the banks on a whim. To win the new customers and retain the existing ones, banks may adopt the Knowledge Discovery in Databases (KDD) for analyzing the customers' behaviors and the needs. In the banking sector of Western Europe and the United States, KDD has been widely adopted.

In this paper, we propose a framework for studying the effect of adopting KDD in the banking sector in Egypt. We present the results of the field survey, which support our belief in the validity of our proposal. The outline of this paper is as follows.

Please use the following format when citing this chapter:

Khedr, A., Kok, J.N., 2006, in IFIP International Federation for Information Processing, Volume 218, Professional Practice in Artificial Intelligence, eds. J. Debenham, (Boston: Springer), pp. 201–208.

Section 2 is about the adoption of new technology whereas section 3 presents a description of problems with adopting KDD in the banking sector in Egypt. Section 4 presents the results of a survey that we conducted in the Egyptian banking sector, to identify the causes and the solutions for the main problem. Section 5 describes the conceptual framework for adopting KDD and the ways of measuring the framework's variables. Section 6 concludes and points at future work.

2 Adoption of new technology

Stoneman [4] integrated the idea that adopting a new technology like KDD is similar to or the same as any other kind of investment under uncertainty and therefore can be analyzed and measured [5]. The investment decision of adopting the new technology is characterized by 1) uncertainty of the prospect profit, 2) irreversibility that creates at least some sunk costs, and 3) the opportunity of the delay. The primary implication of the way of looking at the adoption of any new technology' problem is that there is "option value" to waiting: that is, adoption should not take place the instant that benefits equal costs, but should be delayed until benefits are somewhat above costs [6].

Adoption of a new technology is often expensive for many reasons [6]. The observable determinants of the new technology adoption are the benefits gained by the user and the costs of adoption. These benefits are simply the difference in profits when an organization migrates from an older technology to a newer. In the case of customers, the benefits are the increased utility from the new product or service, but may also include such "non-economic" factors as the satisfaction of being the first on the block with a new product or service [6].

3 The banking sector in Egypt

During the last thirty-five years, two important changes have taken place in the Egyptian banking sector; one in the 1970s and one in the 1990s.

The first important change happened in the 1970s, when competition among and between banks and financial service firms increased considerably. The increased competition has placed the new emphasis on the value of the customer retention. In relation to this phenomenon, Vitria [7] states, "the cost of acquiring the new customers continues to rise as the competition forces providers to offer increasingly better incentives. This encourages customers to move from service to service, without giving the banks a chance to recover their acquisition costs".

The second important change happened in 1991, when Egypt introduced an extensive Economic Reform and Structural Adjustment Program (ERSAP). The economy changed from an inward-looking centrally planned economy, dominated by the public sector, to an outward-looking economy led by the private sector. Liberalization and privatization of the financial sector in general and of the banking system in particular, were crucial to the intended transformation of the economy [8].

Egypt's transforming economy was following the same path as the globalization processes across the world. This worldwide globalization of financial markets has led to create strong relationships among financial institutions [9]. As a result, the financial institutions today face a fast-paced, dynamic, and competitive environment at a global scale. Given such a competitive environment, the financial services sector, as well as the financial institutions, is required to examine their performance because their survival depends on their productive efficiencies with their customers. Early studies (see, for example, Berger and Humphrey [10]; Berger, Hunter, and Timme [11]) demonstrated that in particular, in the banking sector, inefficiencies are more important than scale and scope issues.

The introduction of adoption new technology such as KDD in the Egyptian banking sector would require a different approach than the approach used in other countries because of the cultural, economic, and social differences as outlined in Figure 1 [12]. The provisional problem statement is as follows:

"There is a need for the banking sector in Egypt to adopt the new technologies to use available data in a more efficient way in order to manage customer relations; the present systems are time consuming and unreliable; knowledge discovery in databases could improve the customer relationship management and the customer retention in the banking sector in the country. Given the unique characteristics of the country a new approach will be needed for the introduction of KDD".

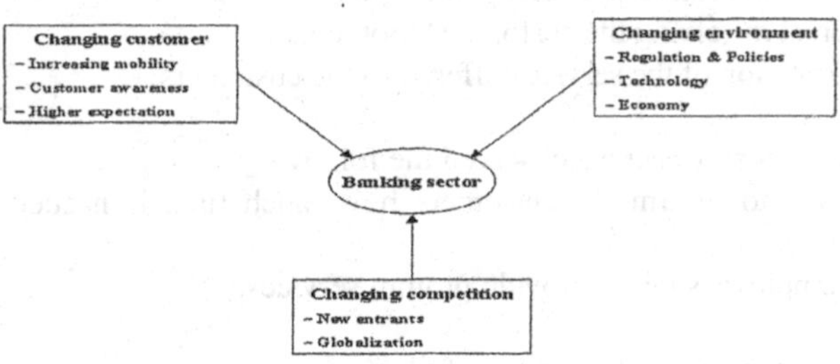

Figure 1: Factors influencing the Egyptian banking sector
Source: Adopted from Tina Harrison, 2000

4 Survey

To identify the problems of the Egyptian banks, and which issues need to be resolved to remove the problem, we conducted a survey to study the current tools used by the Egyptian banking sector to achieve their strategies, and the main obstacles that this sector is facing to adopt KDD techniques. The survey was conducted among customers, CRM specialists, and IT specialists of one of the largest banks in Egypt:

- CRM department: All staff in the main building in Cairo branch, 28 samples.

- Information technologies and computer centre department: All staff in the main building in Cairo branch, 30 samples.
- Employees (front end employees): All staff in the main branch in great Cairo, 172 samples.
- Customers/clients: 560 samples.

In the customer survey questionnaire (560 samples), the respondents were 472 samples divided into two groups, namely, the control group (236 samples) and the experimental group (236 samples).

Next, we will describe the survey results, focusing on the current situation in the bank, and the obstacles to adopt KDD techniques.

The customers' point of view: The survey analysis for the customers considered five aspects, namely interior design, reliability, responsiveness, assurance, and empathy.

For the interior design aspect we observed the following:
- Most of the customers are not satisfied with the interior design of their bank.
- Neither the bank's facilities and materials, nor the bank's employees, look representative for their bank.

For the reliability aspect we observed the following:
- The bank does not keep its promises to keep the customers.
- Lack of provided services with acceptable speed.
- Lack of interest in solving the customers' problems.
- Lack of information of the services offered to the customers.

For the responsiveness aspect we observed the following:
- The bank fails to inform the customers how much time is needed to perform certain services.
- The bank's employees fail to provide prompt services.

For the assurance aspect we observed the following:
- The bank's employees do not instill confidence.
- Customers feel safe and behave courteously when dealing with the bank.

For the empathy aspect we observed the following:
- The bank does not give individual attention to the customers.
- The bank's opening hours are inconvenient to the customers.
- The customers do not feel that their interests are at their banks' heart.
- The bank's employees do not always understand the customers' needs.

The CRM department's point of view: The CRM staff has complaints about the inaccuracy of the systems they use, the lack of user-friendliness of said systems, and the constant need for assistance from the IT staff.

The IT department's point of view: The systems and applications currently in use are unable to provide all the necessary customer data and information in an adequate and accurate way.

Next, we present the survey results on the obstacles of adoption of KDD from the point of view of the CRM and IT departments. The CRM department is, in general, not acquainted with KDD. The IT department is not satisfied with the current level of service they deliver. The IT department strongly supports the application and use of modern techniques to improve their service level. Both departments listed the following seven obstacles to the incorporation of KDD:

- the lack of information on expected profitability;
- the lack of capital;
- the lack of information on customer needs and requirements;
- the lack of information on all services offered and accepted by customers;
- the lack of information on service quality standards and new markets;
- the lack of information on modern technologies; and
- the lack of qualified engineers, DW experts, managers, and consultants.

In summary, from the survey the following three conclusions can be drawn:

- Most of the bank's customers are neither satisfied in dealing with the bank, nor have any loyalty towards the bank. However, they feel safe in dealing with the bank.
- The CRM department employees are not satisfied with the existing service systems.
- The IT department is not satisfied with the existing service level they offer to other employees' bank. They fully support the new proposed techniques.

5 Framework

After identifying the main obstacles, a framework is proposed to investigate the effect of adopting KDD that can help the banking sector in Egypt to improve CRM, in particularly by increasing customer retention. The framework has the following three objectives:

1. To study the current status of methods and tools for analyzing and providing information through the existing system in Egyptian banks, to find the degree of adaptability to state-of the- art technology.
2. To explore how CRM may benefit from KDD.
3. To discuss how successful KDD can be measured.

We focus in detail on the effect of KDD on customer satisfaction in customer retention. The conceptual framework for customer retention as shown in Figure 2, investigates KDD as independent: by considering adaptation and impact of implementing KDD, as well as customer retention as dependent variable.

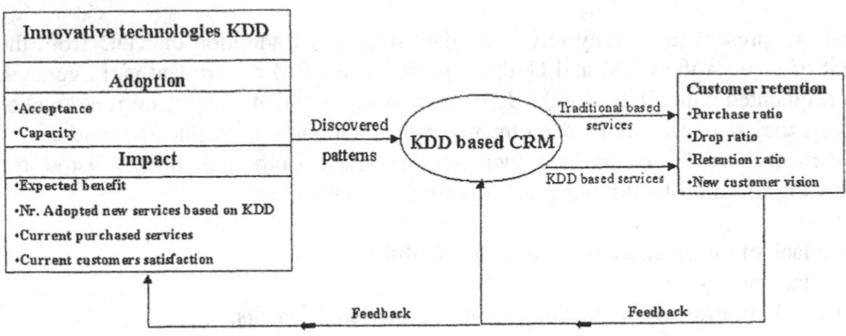

Figure 2: Conceptual framework

Adoption

The adopted technology is the way of how the users accept and use a technology. When users are presented with a new technology, two main factors influence their decision about how and when they will use it [13]:

- ***Acceptance***: Acceptance measure is defined by Fred Davis as "the degree to which a person believes that using a particular system would enhance his or her job performance" and "the degree to which a person believes that using a particular system would be free from effort" [13]. Also it can be defined as a "perceived usefulness, perceived ease of use, and user acceptance of information technology" [13]. The acceptance measure considers two different groups of opinions: CRM staff department and IT staff department.

- ***Capacity***: Capacity measure is defined in the present research as the bank capacity or ability to apply the new technology techniques (obstacles to the new techniques by CRM & IT departments) from different aspects such as time effort consuming, fund, lack of information, and expertise. The acceptance factor considers two different groups opinions CRM staff department and IT staff department.

Impact

To measure the impact of implementing KDD, four different measurements are considered as following:

- ***Expected benefits***: This measure describes the benefits gained by adopting KDD from different view of points CRM and IT staffs.

- *New services based on KDD*: This measure describes the characteristics of the new services that offered by bank based on KDD.
- *Current purchased services*: This measure describes the characteristics of the current/exiting services that offered by bank according to the previous bank' CRM strategy.
- *Customers' satisfaction*: To measure the customer satifaction level in the bank the study investigate the customer satisaction from five differernt customer' views:
  - the physical appearance,
  - service level and reliability,
  - employees' behaviour and attitude,
  - assurance, and
  - empathy.

Customer retention

We use five measurements of the dependent variable customer retention:

- *Competitive advantage factors*: This measure describes CRM and IT staffs' views of competitive advantage factors.
- *Purchase/ active ratio*: This ratio is also known as the next buy or the opening of a new service and calculated by (number of buying new services purchased/ number of buying existing services purchased) in the last 12 months.
- *Drop ratio*: The ratio expresses the percentage of the customer's decision to cancel a product that is characterized by a non-ending status and calculated by (number of drop/cancelled services/ existing services offered by bank) in the last 12 months.
- *Retention ratio*: The ratio expresses the percentage of the respond or active customer to buy the new services in the last 12 months and calculated by (the number of active customers/ number of total customers).
- *New customer vision*: The experimental study will be used to measure the difference between the customer vision towards the bank's services and the products after introducing KDD techniques and the customer opinion in the services that offered based on implementing KDD results.

6 Conclusions and Further work

In this paper, we proposed a framework for studying the effect of KDD on CRM in the Egyptian banking sector. We believe that the KDD process and the applications may perform a significant role in Egyptian banks to improve CRM, in particular for customer retention. Our belief is supported by the results of a field survey at the largest Egyptian bank that indicated that:

- most of the bank's customers are neither satisfied in dealing with the bank, nor have any loyalty towards the bank, but do feel safe in dealing with the bank;
- the bank's CRM department is not satisfied with the existing service systems; and
- the IT department is not satisfied with the existing service level they offer to other employees' bank through all services, and supports the introduction of the new techniques.

These problems are could typically be solved by the adoption of KDD. The next step is to analyze the effect of adopting KDD in the banking sector in Egypt according to the conceptual framework. We expect the first results to be available when the bank has implemented KDD by the end of 2006.

References

[1] OECD, A New Economy?- The Role of Innovation and Information Technology in Recent OECD Economic Growth, *DSTI/ IND/ STP/ ICCP, No.1*, 2000.
[2] Porter, M. and S. Stern, Innovation: Location Matters, Sloan Management Review, 2001, pp. 28-37.
[3] Devedzic, V., Knowledge Discovery and Data Mining, School of Business Administration, University of Belgrade, Yugoslavia, 1998, pp.1-24.
[4] Stonman, Paul, Financial Factors and the Inter Firm Diffusion of New Technology: A Real Option Model, *University of Warwick EIFC Working Paper No.8*, 2001.
[5] Dixit, Avinah, and Robert Pindyck, Investment Under Uncertainty, (Princeton, New Jersey: Princeton University Press, 1994).
[6] Hall, Bronwyn H. and Khan, Beethika, Adoption of New Technology, University of California, Berkeley, Department of Economics, *UCB, Working Paper No. E03-330*, 2003, pp. 1-16.
[7] Vitria, Technology, Inc., Maximizing the Value of Customer Information Across Your Financial Services Enterprise, White Paper, 2002, pp.1-10.
[8] El-Shazly, Alaa, Incentive-Based Regulations and Bank Restructuring in Egypt, Cairo University, Egypt, 2001, pp.1-24.
[9] Ragunathan, V., Financial Deregulation and Integration: An Australian Perspective, *Journal of Economics and Business*, 1999, pp. 505-514.
[10] Berger, A. N. and D. B. Humphrey, The dominance of inefficiencies over scale and product mix economies in banking, *Journal of Monetary Economics, Vol.28*, 1991 pp.117-148.
[11] Berger, A. N., W. C. Hunter, and S. G. Timme, The Efficiency of Financial Institutions: A Review and Preview of Research Past, Present, and Future, *Journal of Banking and Finance Vol.17*, 1993, pp. 221-249.
[12] Harrison Tina, *Financial Service Marketing*, (Pearson Education Limited, 2000).
[13] Davis, F. D., Perceived Usefulness, Perceived Ease of Use and User Acceptance of Information Technology, *MIS Quarterly, Vol.13 (3)*, 1989, pp. 319-340.

Pattern Discovery and Model Construction: an Evolutionary Learning and Data Mining Approach

Harry Zhou
Department of Computer and Information Sciences, Towson University.
Baltimore, MD, USA
WWW home page: http://www.towson.edu/~zhou

Abstract. In the information age, knowledge leads to profits, power and success. As an ancestor of data mining, machine learning has concerned itself with discovery of new knowledge on its own. This paper presents experiment results produced by genetic algorithms in the domains of model construction and event predictions, the areas where data mining systems have been focusing on. The experiment results have shown that genetic algorithms are able to discover useful patterns and regularities in large sets of data, and to construct models that conceptualize input data. It demonstrates that genetic algorithms are a powerful and useful learning algorithm for solving fundamental tasks data mining systems are facing today.

1 Introduction

In the information age, knowledge leads to profits, power and success. Thus, the demand for information in our society makes discovery of useful patterns and regularities in large sets of data a necessity, while the fast growth of CPU speeds and memory sizes makes it possibility. In the past decade, it gave a birth to data mining, a technology that discovers meaningful new correlations and trends by shifting through large amounts of data[4]. As an ancestor of data mining, machine learning has concerned itself with making computers that learn things for themselves. Since the birth of data mining, it provides many algorithms and techniques for data mining systems to explore large sets of data and discover new knowledge[2]. This paper presents experiment results produced by genetic algorithms in the domains of model building and event predictions, the areas where data mining systems have been focusing on. The purpose of this paper is to demonstrate that genetic algorithms are a powerful and useful tool for solving fundamental tasks data mining systems are facing today. In what follows, a brief description of genetic algorithms is described, followed by a discussion of genetic learning and data mining. Genetic learning

Please use the following format when citing this chapter:

Zhou, H., 2006, in IFIP International Federation for Information Processing, Volume 218, Professional Practice in Artificial Intelligence, eds. J. Debenham, (Boston: Springer), pp. 209–218.

experiments conducted in two different domains along with their results are presented. It concludes with future research topics.

2 Outline of Genetic Algorithms

Genetic algorithms are known as an evolutionary approach designed to reflect the idea of "Survival of the fittest". These algorithms encode a potential solution to a specific problem on a simple chromosome-like data segment and apply genetic operators, such as mutation and crossover, to these segments so as to preserve critical information.

A general sketch of a genetic algorithm is given below:

```
t = 1
Initialization P(t) // P(t) is the population at time t
Evaluation P(t);
While (termination condition is not true)
   t = t + 1;
      Selection P(t)
   Offspring Generation P(t)
   Replacement P(t)
   Evaluation P(t)
```

It begins with a population of candidate solutions, usually generated randomly in the Initialization phase. In the Evaluation phase each candidate solution is evaluated and assigned a score indicating how well it performed with respect to the target problem. In the Selection phase better candidate solutions are selected and given more chances to "reproduce" than poorer candidate solutions. The offspring generation is accomplished by applying the genetic operators Mutation and Crossover. The idea is that some good genes from their parents should be inherited by their offspring. The genetic operators produce new instances in such a way that offspring still resemble, but not identical to, their parents. Since the population is limited in size, some poor candidate solutions are replaced by the newly produced children. This process is repeated until termination conditions are met.

3 Descriptive Genetic Learning

A model is a high-level, global description of a data set summarizing the main features. The goal of descriptive data mining is to construct a model that describes all of the data from limited observations. The fundamental objective is to produce insight and understanding about the structure of the data, and to enable us to see its important characteristics. Examples are models(segmentation) used in marketing to divide customers into groups based on purchasing patterns, and cluster analysis used in psychiatric research to describe illness. In this section, a genetic learning approach is presented along with its experimental results in the domain of model construction and descriptive learning. More specifically, a set of training instances are given to the genetic algorithm, and the expected output from the genetic learning system is a model that describes all positive instances and rejects all negative instances in the domain of regular expressions and finite automata[1,5].

A finite automaton can be described by a 5-tuple (Q, S, δ, q_0, F), where Q is a finite set of states, S is a finite input alphabet, q_0 in Q is the initial state, $F \subseteq Q$ is the set of final states, and δ is the transition function mapping the cartesian product of Q and S into Q. That is, δ(q, a) is a state for each state q and an input symbol a. An example X is said to be accepted by a finite automaton M = (Q, S, δ, q_0, F) if δ(q_0, X) = p for some p in F. The language accepted by M, designated L(M), is the set {x | δ(q_0, X) is in F}. A language is a regular expression if it is a set of input symbols accepted by some finite automata.

In out experiments, a concept to be learned is a language over {0,1} where the grammar is described either by a finite automaton, English, or a regular expression. It is assumed that the teacher uses either English or a regular expression to specify a concept while the genetic algorithm, based on a set of examples, searches for a finite automaton that represents the concept. In other words, the learning task is not simply to construct a finite automaton but rather to find a finite automaton that must be equivalent to the regular expression the teacher has in mind. The input to the genetic algorithm consists of one set of positive examples that must be accepted by the finite automaton and one set of negative examples that must be rejected by the finite automaton. The output from the genetic algorithm is a finite automaton which is expected to be equivalent to the described concept.

In the following experiments, the process of constructing a finite automaton based on a set of data can be viewed as a search in the space of all possible finite automata. With the maximum number of states limited to 8, each candidate solution in the population is denoted by the following form:

$$((X_1, Y_1, F_1)\ (X_2, Y_2, F_2)\ \ldots\ (X_8, Y_8, F_8))$$

where each (X_i, Y_i, Z_i) represents the state i. X_i and Y_i correspond to the destination states of the 0 arrow and the 1 arrow respectively. F_i is represented by three bits. The first two bits of Fi are used to indicate whether there exists an arrow coming from state i. The third bit of Fi shows whether the state i is a final state.

3.1 Finite Automata Construction

The learning task can be summarized as follows. Given a list of positive examples and a list of negative examples, the learning system is expected to construct an abstract description in the form of a model. The produced model should not only accept all the positive examples, and reject all the negative examples, it also is expected to characterize these examples conceptually. It is known that the problem of finite automata construction based on examples is a NP-complete problem, and the hill-climbing has been applied to it with limited success [1,5]. As a global search algorithm by nature, the capabilities of genetic algorithms are tested in the following experiments.

3.2 Experiment Design

Good examples must characterize the main features of the concept the teacher has in mind. It is reasonable to assume that neither humans nor learning algorithms are able to abstract a concept from a set of poorly selected examples. The following experiment shows how a set of examples are selected and how an experiment is designed. The concept the teacher has in mind is: (10)*, which is a sequence consisting of any number pairs of 1 and 0.

The positive example set:
(10) (1010) (101010) (10101010101010) (1010101010101010)

The negative example set:
(101) (000) (1001010) (10110) (1) (0)

The output produced by the genetic algorithm based on the above examples is shown below:
where the letter F in a box indicates the state is a final state.

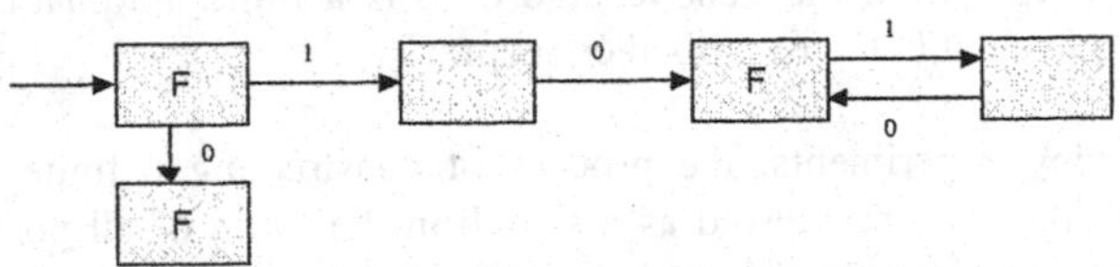

The finite automaton produced by the genetic algorithm agrees with the given positive examples and negative examples. It is, however, not the one specified by the regular expression (10)*. A close look reveals that the learning algorithm did not understand that an input of 0 should be rejected. Once the training set is modified with a 0 added to the negative example set, the genetic algorithm was able to produce the following two finite automata:

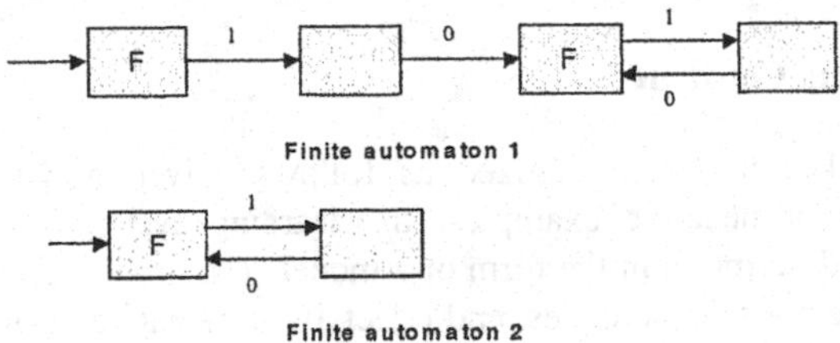

Finite automaton 1

Finite automaton 2

As shown in this experiment, there are many finite automata which are a valid generalization of a given training set. A typical way of solving this problem is to require that the hypothesis be the shortest or the most economical description consistent with all examples[1]. In the context of constructing finite automata, the goal would be to find a finite automaton with the fewest states which is consistent with all positive examples while rejecting all negative examples. In terms of the implementation, every candidate solution in the population is assigned a score indicating how well it matches the input data. Given two equally performing finite automata, the one with fewer states would receive a higher score. This would increase its chance of survival and of generating offspring in the next generation.

3.3 Experiment Results

This section lists the experiments along with their results produced by the genetic algorithm

Experiment 1

Positive examples:
(0) (01) (11) (00) (100) (110) (111) (000) (100100)
(110000011100001) (11011100100)

Negative examples:
(101) (010) (1010) (1110) (1011) (10001) (111010)
(1001000) (11111000) (01110011101) (1101110010) (10)

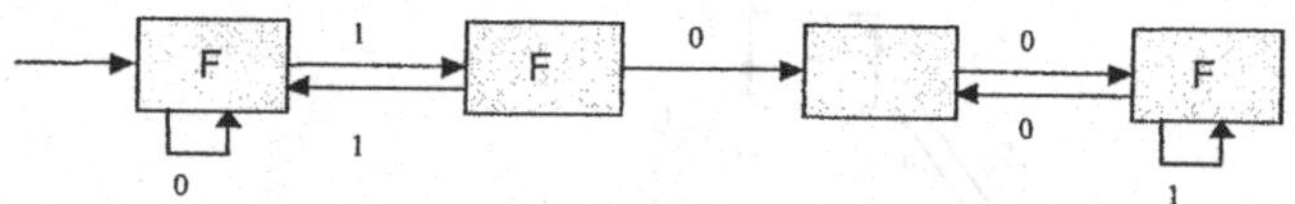

Output: (after 2532 generations)

The regular expression described by English and represented by the above finite automaton is:

any string without an odd number of consecutive 0's following an odd number of consecutive 1's.

Experiment 2

Positive examples:
(00) (11) (00) (1111) (1001) (0110) (1000001011100010)
(0000000011) (111111001010) (01010011)

Negative Examples:
(0) (111) (000) (101) (010) (0000000) (11111) (111000000)

(1111110) (000001111) (11001) (00000011100)

Output (after 2820 generations):

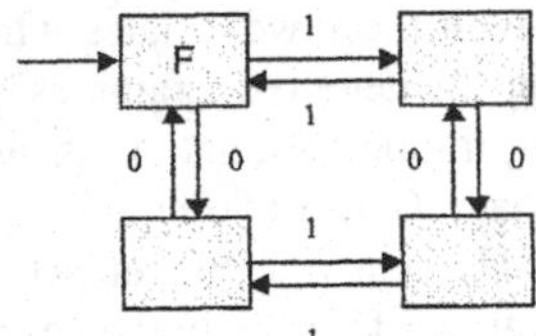

The regular expression represented by the above finite automaton is:

Any string consists of an even number of 0s and an even number of 1s

<u>Experiment 3</u>

Positive examples:
(10) (01) (1100) (101010) (111) (000) (10000) (01000)
(1100000) (100100100) (0000000011) (1111111110)

Negative examples:
(0) (1) (11) (00) (101) (011) (1101) (1111) (00000)
(00000000) (1111111) (100100) (00000111) (1)

Output: (after 2971 generations)

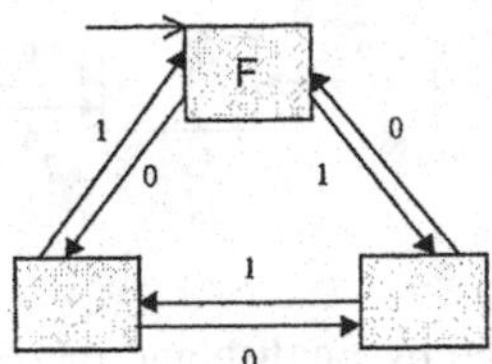

The regular expression represented by the above finite automaton is:

Any string such that the difference between the number of 0s and 1s is 3 times n (n is an integer).

The above experiments demonstrate the power of genetic algorithm in descriptive learning. It is able to construct a model based on incomplete and imprecise data. By looking at a small set of examples, the genetic algorithm impressively conceptualizes the input data and produces a model that summarizes the important common properties shared by the input examples.

4 Predicative Genetic Learning

In contrast to the global nature of descriptive data mining, predictive data mining searches for local patterns and relationships in the data set. It makes statements only about restricted regions. For example, a search through a database of mail order purchases may reveal that people who buy certain combinations of items are also likely to buy others. The key distinction between prediction and description is that prediction has a unique variable as its objective, such as the value of the a stock at some future date, or which horse will win a race. Letter prediction learning is one form of predicative learning.

4.1 Letter Prediction Learning

This section describes letter prediction learning, a research topic both in psychology research and machine learning research. Letter prediction learning is an instance of concept learning, which is concerned with forming a concept characterizing given facts. It involves observing a collection of examples of some regularity, identifying the essential properties common to these examples, and then making a predication. The underlying methodology of concept learning is an inductive inference, a process whereby one acquires general and high-level knowledge from specific observations of a given phenomenon.

4.2 Human Performance

Simon and Kotovsky used the following 12 learning tasks on two groups of human subjects [3].

Letter Sequence	Expected Prediction
(1) cdcdcd ...	cd
(2) aaabbbccc ...	ddd
(3) abmcdmefmghm ...	ijm
(4) defgefghfghi ...	ghij
(5) mabmbcmcd ...	mde
(6) urtustutt ...	uut
(7) abyabxabw ...	abv
(8) rscdstdetuef ...	uvfg
(9) wxaxybyzczad ...	abe
(10) jkqrklrslmst ...	mntu
(11) pononmnmlmlk ...	lkj
(12) npaoqapraqsa ...	rta

The first group consists of 12 people from different walks of life. The second group consists of 67 subjects comprising an entire class of high school seniors. In an experiment a tested human subject is given a sequence of letters, called a training sequence, and then is asked to make a prediction for a plausible continuation of the sequence. In their experiments, a total of 79 human subjects were given these tasks.

Surprisingly, none of these tasks was solved by all human subjects. The performance of these two groups is summarized below[3]:

Task number	Correct Group of 12	Answers Group of 67
1	12	65
2	12	61
3	12	57
4	2	45
5	9	49
6	5	43
7	9	51
8	4	39
9	7	43
10	6	48
11	5	34
12	5	42

4.3 Experiment Design and Results

Initially, the genetic algorithm learns the English alphabets and their relationship from scratch, produces a list of rules, and then stores them in its knowledge base. Some of the constructed rules are listed below:

The concept of "NEXT":

if <var> A then <var> B
if <var> B then <var> C
.
.
if <var> Y then <var> Z

The concept of "PRIOR":

if <var> B then <var> A
if <var> C then <var> B
.
.
if <var> Z then <var> Y
.

where <var> stands for a variable that can take any value

Similarly, the genetic algorithm learned and constructed other concepts (rules) such as "double next letter", "double prior letter", "vowel", and "consonant". In the learning phrase, the genetic algorithm applies these building blocks to make a new rule based on the letter sequence, and therefore, is able to make prediction .

For each concept, the genetic is given a set of randomly generated letters. Whenever the genetic algorithm constructs a rule generating a correct prediction with respect to the concept, it is rewarded. Otherwise, the genetic algorithm is punished by given a negative reward. Other than these rewards, the entire learning process is conducted by the genetic algorithm without any human assistance.

A letter learning task consists of two phases: a training phase and a predicting phase. In the training phase, a sequence of letters are provided. The genetic algorithm conducts predicative learning by detecting the periodicity in the letter sequence and then applies the rules it has already constructed to make predictions. At the end of a training phase, the genetic algorithm is able to construct a set of rules specifically tailored to the given learning sequence, and then uses it to make a prediction for the continuation of the letter sequence.

Given the 12 learning tasks designed by Simon and Kotovsky[3], the genetic algorithm tested under the same experimental conditions was able to predict the logical continuation of the these sequence correctly without a single error. It is worth repeating that the genetic algorithm was not programmed. Instead, it learned the basic concepts of English from scratch and applied the knowledge to solve these letter prediction learning tasks.

To make learning more challenging, another kind of sequence learning, known as "regularity learning" is also conducted. In regularity learning, the genetic algorithm is given several groups of letters separately. These sequences appeared quite different at first, but a closer look reveals that they are governed by same regularities.

To illustrate, consider the following example:

Group 1: a c e
Group 2: i k m
Group 3: u ? ?

Given the first two groups, the group 3 is expected to be predicted and completed. The following regularity learning tasks have been used in our experiments.

	Group 1	Group 2	Group 3	Predicted
(1)	cc	tt	s?	s
(2)	rrs	aab	x??	xy
(3)	afeh	osuu	id??	of
(4)	abc	stu	m??	no

(5) ae	ou	i?	o
(6) cdf	rst	t??	vw
(7) dfh	bdf	u??	wy
(8) cade	vowu	je??	ki
(9) xghyig	vrnwtm	aab???	bca
(10) ihbojc	atrevs	omm???	unn

In our experiments, the genetic algorithm is able to solve all the above problems correctly using the knowledge it acquired. The results show the potentials of genetic algorithms in the field of predicative learning.

5 Conclusion

This research shows the feasibility and effectiveness of genetic algorithms in both pattern discovery and model construction. Experimental evidence presented in this paper show that the genetic algorithm exhibits forms of intelligent behaviors and learning capabilities, such as knowledge adaptation, rule construction, and conceptual reasoning, which are not yet seen in many other learning systems and data mining systems. As a powerful learning algorithm, genetic algorithms promise potential for many challenging descriptive and predicative learning many data mining systems are facing today.

References

1. A. Birkendorf, Boker and Simon. Learning Deterministic Finite Automata from Smallest Counterexamples. In SIAM Journal on Discrete Mathematics Vol. 13, Number 4:465-491. 2000.

2. J. Han and M. Kamber, Data Mining: Concepts and Techniques. Morgan Kaufmann Publishers. 2001.

3. H. A. Simon and K. Kotovsky, Human Acquisition of Concepts for Sequential Patterns, Psychological Review, 70: 534-536, 1963.

4. Ryszad S. Michalski, "Machine Learning and Data Mining: Methods and Applications". 1998

5. Tomita, M, Learning of construction of finite automata from examples using hill-climbing. Thesis. Carnegie-Mellon University, 1982.

Towards a Framework for Knowledge Discovery:

An Architecture for Distributed Inductive Databases

Jeroen S. de Bruin, Joost N. Kok
Universiteit Leiden, Leiden Institute of Advanced Computer Science (LIACS), Niels Bohrweg 1, 2333 CA Leiden, The Netherlands,
jdebruin@liacs.nl

Abstract. We discuss how data mining, patternbases and databases can be integrated into inductive databases, which make data mining an inductive query process. We propose a software architecture for such inductive databases, and extend this architecture to support the clustering of inductive databases and to make them suitable for data mining on the grid.

1 Introduction

The size and variety of machine-readable data sets have increased dramatically and the problem of *data explosion* has become apparent. Scientific disciplines are starting to assemble primary source data for use by researchers and are assembling data grids for the management of data collections. The data are typically organized into collections that are distributed across multiple administration domains and are stored on heterogeneous storage systems. Recent developments in computing have provided the basic infrastructure for fast data access as well as many advanced computational methods for extracting patterns from large quantities of data.

These collections provide excellent opportunities for *data mining*. Data mining refers to the process of analyzing data in databases hoping to find patterns that are novel, interesting, and useful. In a way it is comparable to statistics since it uses techniques based on statistics, but takes it a bit further in the sense that where statistics aims at validating given hypotheses, in data mining often millions of potential patterns are generated and tested, aiming at potentially finding some that are prove to be useful. This is however a much more computationally intensive process. Examples of well-known data mining techniques are discovery of association rules (which properties of individuals are typically associated with each other?); building predictive models (decision trees, rules, neural nets) that can be used to predict unknown properties of individuals; building probabilistic models that summarize the statistical properties of a database, etc.

Please use the following format when citing this chapter:

de Bruin, J.S., Kok, J.N., 2006, in IFIP International Federation for Information Processing, Volume 218, Professional Practice in Artificial Intelligence, eds. J. Debenham, (Boston: Springer), pp. 219–228.

The enormous amount of data generated from scientific experiments, together with the developments in data mining and data warehousing, have led to a paradigm-shift in scientific research from hypothesis-driven science to discovery-driven science. No longer need experiments be conducted in a hypothesis-driven fashion, where the experimenter has an idea, and tries to validate by experimenting. Rather, the trend is to collect as much data as possible on a specific function or system, look for emerging *patterns*, interpret those patterns, and relate them to the current knowledge.

The *challenge* is to provide a persistent and consistent environment for the discovering, storing, organizing, maintaining, analyzing *patterns,* possibly across *distributed* environments.

2 Inductive Databases

With respect to such pattern bases, the important question arises how the existing methods and algorithms can be elegantly integrated into current database management systems. In order to meet this reqirement, Imielinsky and Mannila proposed the concept of so-called inductive databases [3]. In an inductive database it is possible to get answers about the collected data in the database as well as answers to questions about inductively gathered "knowledge" in the form of patterns concerning that data.

Inductive databases have been studied extensively within the European cInQ project and also play a central role in its recently founded successor IQ (acronym for: Inductive Queries for Mining Patterns and Models, EU IST-FET). In order to efficiently and effectively deal with patterns, researchers from scientific domains would greatly benefit from adopting a Pattern-Base Management System (PBMS) in which patterns are made first-class citizens. This provides the researcher with a meaningful abstraction of the data.

The general idea is to modify existing databases to support efficient pattern storage, and extend databases with an implementation of an inductive query language and in this manner transforming a DataBase Management System (DBMS) into a DataBase Knowledge Discovery System (DBKDS). Since inductive databases provide architecture for pattern discovery as well as a means to discover and use those patterns through the inductive query language, data mining becomes in essence an interactive querying process. Some of these queries, however, will not be efficient despite query optimizations. Therefore, some data mining primitives must be built into the database system itself, and must serve as primitive functions within the inductive query language.

The efficiency of the data mining process also depends on the way that data is represented within the database, so a compromise must be made between efficient storage and efficient discovery. Since a gigabyte is becoming cheaper and cheaper every day, we are inclined to prioritize a representation that facilitates efficient discovery over efficient storage.

Over the past few years much research has been done on (efficient) pattern representation and pattern storage issues [2, 5]. The studies in the PANDA project (http://dke.cti.gr/panda/) have shown that the relational way of storing patterns is very inefficient, and proves to be too rigid to efficiently and effectively store patterns, since patterns often have a more semi-structured nature. To be able to support a wide variety of patterns and pattern classes, XML or variations have been explored and the results were encouraging. [6, 7]

3 Distributed Knowledge Discovery

Over the last few years grid computing – the use of the memory and/or processing resources of many computers connected with each other by a network to solve computation problems – has received much attention, and not without reason. The research community - universities, academic research institutes, and industrial research laboratories - is becoming ever more dependent on previous research outcomes from third parties. The complexity of modern experiments, usually requiring the combination of heterogeneous data from many fields (physics, astronomy, chemistry, biology, medicine), requires multidisciplinary efforts. This implies that this community is becoming increasingly dependent on the quality of the *e-Science infrastructure.* Such an infrastructure allows scientists to collaborate with colleagues world-wide and to perform experiments by utilizing resources of other organizations. A common infrastructure for experimentation also stimulates community building and the dissemination of research results. These developments apply to pure as well as applied sciences, including data mining.

Data used in knowledge discovery is often distributed over a multiple of resources, which in their turn can be spread among several different logical or physical places. Of course, the same can be true for patterns over that data. It is therefore important to see how standard data mining algorithms can be adapted to cope with these distributions to make *data mining on the grid* possible.

The problem stated above can be addressed in two ways. One way is to adapt current mining algorithms to cope with distributed data and pattern sources. Current data mining algorithms usually address problems on a single resource, and require a somewhat rigid structure for the data. Relational mining algorithms, thus mining algorithms specifically developed for relational databases and thus able to work with several tables within such a database could prove to be a good basis for such adaptation.

The second way is through an architecture that supports a distributed environment, allowing the database or patternbase itself to support and internalize remote connections to other databases and patternbases. In this case, the client is unaware of the fact that is mining in fact scheduled and executed on different databases or patternbases, since to the user there appears to be only one location of data storage. It is the task of the database or patternbase itself to keep track of all connections and remote access protocols.

Another advantage of data mining on the grid is the ability to process data mining requests on a location other than the client or the data server(s). This poses some implications on the inductive query language supported by the inductive database, since it must be able to evaluate and segment queries into subqueries that can be simultaneously processed by multiple (distinct and/or remote) processing locations.

To be able to support such remote query processing, it should be addressed and internalized in the architecture of the inductive database itself. The architecture should support load balancing algorithms that are efficient enough to dynamically and continuously check whether or not a (sub)query should be handled locally or be outsourced to another grid node.

4 Knowledge Discovery Architecture

In this section we propose an architecture that addresses the challenges posed in sections 2 and 3. We have based this architectural design on component technology, which is commonly seen as the evolution of object oriented technology. The reason for choosing the component-oriented paradigm lies in the fact that it is well suited for the description of architectures and that it decentralizes the development effort. Especially the last property is important for an inductive database, since a user must be able to outfit the inductive query language with its own custom developed data mining algorithms. Component software i.e. software made out of software components, is designed for extensibility, and therefore the use of component technology seems an obvious one.

The remainder of this section will be used to discuss four different architectural levels that together form the Distributed Inductive Database Architecture. These levels are:

- The Fusion level
- The Query level
- The DataNet level
- The Delegate level

The Fusion level

At the heart of our architecture lies the inductive database. As stated earlier, we view an inductive database as a traditional (relational) database extended with a patternbase. Of course, for the sake of simplicity and security, the user should remain oblivious of the separation between patternbase and database, creating the need for automatic, transparent updating of patterns whenever changes are made in the patternbase or database.

In order to explain the fusion architecture, we first need to specify some constraints on a pattern, and define the relationship between patterns and their related underlying data. A *pattern* is a semantically rich representation of a collection of data. A pattern, as defined in this architecture, has at least the following properties: A unique id or name, the data collection that it applies to, a set of measurements, and the component and function that calculates these measurements.

Now consider the (simplified) architecture in Figure 1, which functions as a fusion component between patternbase and database, thereby using the component catalog of data mining primitives that are supported by the inductive query language. Notice that there is a notifier present in the fusion architecture, namely *Notify_Table_Update*, which is used by the database to signal that a certain table has changed. The fusion component is a passive component that listens for update notifications, and remains idle if there are none.

To illustrate what happens when an update notification is received, let us consider the case that the data in a set of tables *T* has changed. In this case, the database sends a notification to the Fusion component specifying *T*. The Fusion component then requests the pattern collection *P*, which consists of all patterns in the patternbase that have $t \in T$ in their data collection specification. At the same time, the Fusion component requests all the data from *T*, and specifies both sets *P* and *T* in a call to a component in the Data Mining Primitives catalog. It knows exactly what components and routines to call, since this is part of the pattern's specification. After the calculations have been completed, the Fusion component returns the updated patterns to the patternbase via the *Update_Patterns* interface.

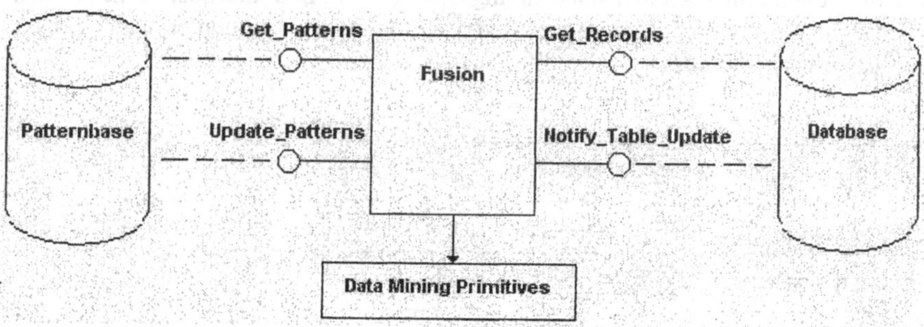

Figure 1: The Fusion Level

The situation described above shows how updating of patterns can be done in an automatic, transparent way without interference from the client.

The Query level

The Query architecture addresses the issues related to the inductive query language built on top of the inductive database. Currently, a number of inductive query languages that have been implemented, i.e. MSQL [4] and MINE RULE [1]. For now, we will not address their individual properties, advantages and disadvantages, nor the effects they might have on the proposed architecture. Instead, we will present a global architectural framework, where the choice of query language could be considered an implementation detail that becomes an issue when the architecture becomes a blueprint for a more application-specific design as part of the product family that the architecture constitutes.

As is illustrated in Figure 2, this architecture provides a layered approach to the analysis, optimization and execution of a query. This is pretty straightforward if the query concerns only patterns or only data, but it becomes complex if both are addressed in the same query, via so called crossover operations.

The top layer of the architecture consists of the query parser, which parses the entire query and assigns meaning to each identifier in the query string. It subsequently passes these tokens on to the query analyzer and the query optimizer. Both operate closely together, and have an almost synergetic relationship: The query analyzer checks what parts of the query can be handled in parallel or can be handled more efficiently, and passes this on to the optimizer. The optimizer, in turn, optimizes these queries, which may yield in a new set of (sub)queries, which are passed back to the query analyzer for further analysis, until no more optimizations are possible. We are fortunate that lately inductive query decomposition and optimizing such (sub)queries have been given a great deal of attention [8] [9].

After the query has been analyzed and optimized, it is passed on to the query scheduler, which schedules the subqueries for execution, either locally or remotely. The query scheduler is also responsible for parallel or sequential scheduling of queries.

At the lowest level of the Query architecture the query executor is found. This layer is responsible for delegating the queries to the correct data storage facility at the fusion level and performing the correct data mining primitives on them, such as crossover operations or other data mining operations. After the queries have been executed their individual results are passed back to the query scheduler, which passes the final result to the client.

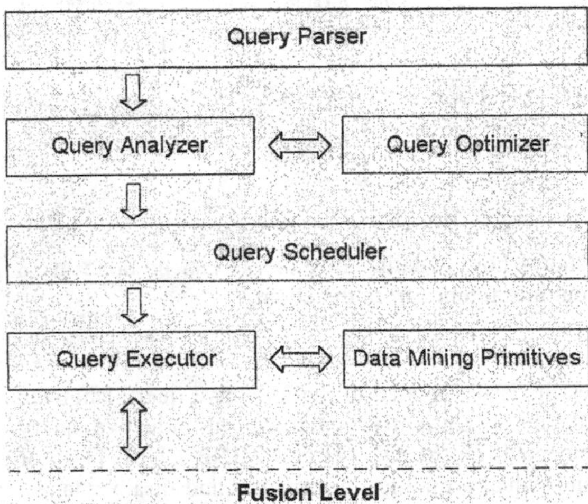

Figure 2: The Query Level

The DataNet level

Up to this point we have modeled a database and a patternbase as a single entity. However, we mentioned earlier that data mining over multiple data sources could be accomplished in an architectural manner by having databases keep track of remote connections with other databases. The architecture we foresee here is based on a peer2peer network architectural style; each data server also functions as a router in a private data net.

The use of an internal data net could have many advantages. For the user, it appears that there is only one database that they can query, and depending on the user permissions, the database dispatches his or her requests to the right database or patternbase in the data net, resulting in a greater ease of use and increased security.

There are some drawbacks to this method as well, especially in the area of overhead management. For each user of the database his or her status must be checked for access rights, operational rights, etc. It is a huge challenge to solve this in an efficient and scalable way.

The DataNet architecture in Figure 3 addresses some of the issues and functionalities discussed above. Each database (or patternbase) contains three catalogs: the Data Catalog, which is used by the database to specify which tables it contains; the User Catalog, which specifies which users or user groups have access to (part of) its content; and finally, the Connection catalog, which contains (private) information on all the other databases that are part of the data net. The DataNet architecture is built on top of the Query architecture, but the separation is not strict: After all, the query analyzer and scheduler check whether or not the data queried is available in the database. If not, the subquery addressing that data will be forwarded by the query scheduler via the DataNet level to the database that does contain the data, which can be found out by broadcasting a request on all data catalogs in the data net.

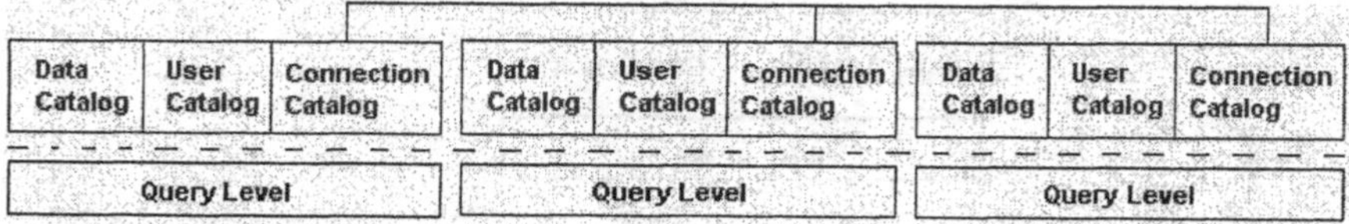

Figure 3: The DataNet Level

The Delegate level

The Delegate Architecture is the part of the architecture that interacts with the data grid to which the database is possibly attached. This architectural part concerns itself with intelligent structures and components that perform load-balancing algorithms, remote method invocations and procedure migration to processing nodes.

The Delegate architecture, as depicted in Figure 4, displays a possible framework for implementation. Notice that this architectural level is also connected to the Query level, since the query scheduler needs the routines the Delegate level to make a decision whether or not the (sub)query execution should be performed locally, or on a remote processing node in the grid.

As can be seen, there are two major parts in this layer. The first part is the load-balancer, which contains algorithms that check whether the task should be performed locally or on a grid node. The decision depends on a range of factors, such as the type of query, the load of the local node, the load of the external nodes, etc. Apart from providing the optimal solutions at any given time, these algorithms must also be fast enough to provide the solution in a reasonable amount of time.

The second part of the Delegate architecture is the grid driver, which wraps the remote method invocation requests of the database so they are compatible with the grid software. To execute the query on a remote location, that remote location will need the data and the procedure code of the query, which are delivered in one package by the grid driver.

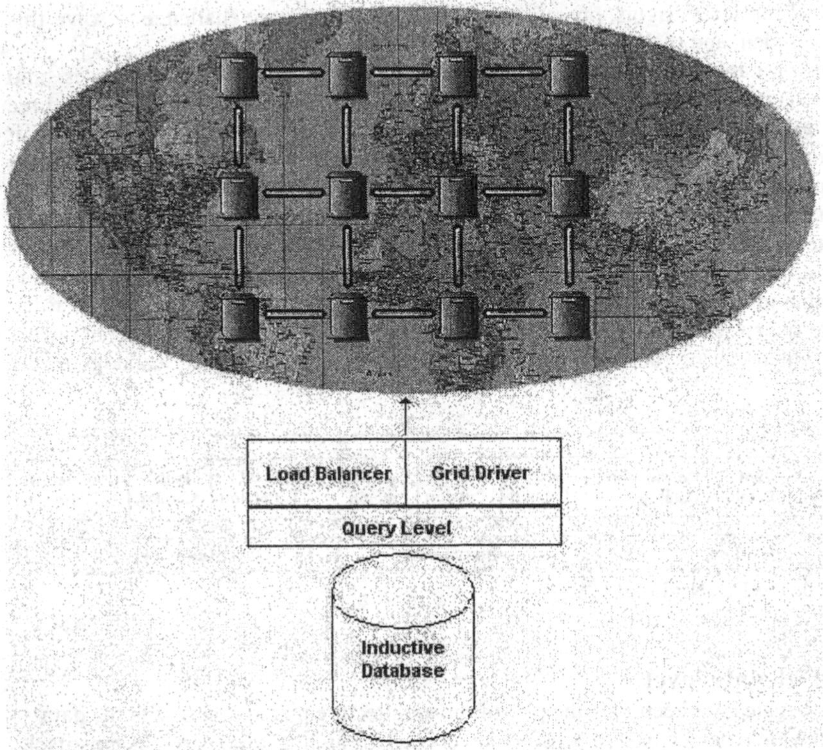

Figure 4: The Delegate Level

5 Use Case

In this section we will present a use case scenario that illustrates the workings of the diverse parts of the architecture. Suppose we have a database that contains transaction information on product sales for a supermarket and we want to perform some market-basket analysis. Normally we would use the *apriori-algorithm* to uncover frequent item sets and association rules in the data collection. In this example we will illustrate how this can be done in an inductive database.

First, consider a query that tries to find frequent patterns in the transaction data using a data mining primitive *FREQ_ITEM*. When the user poses this query to the inductive database, the query scheduler uses the query analyzer and optimizer to receive an optimized set of (sub)queries.

The next task of the query scheduler is to verify whether the tables addressed in the (sub)queries are available locally or if it's somewhere else in the data net.. When they are available locally, the query scheduler uses the data mining primitives to execute the (sub)queries using the data retrieved from the tables. If some of the data is not available locally, the (sub)queries involving those data are forwarded to the DataNet level, where it sends out a broadcast to discover the location of the required data. After the location has been received and the user has been verified, the subquery is sent to the query scheduler at that location. In this example, let the required data be available locally, so the query scheduler executes the query using the data mining primitive *FREQ_ITEM*, which results in a collection *P* containing frequent patterns over the transaction data set.

Let the collection *P* be stored in a pattern table *T*. Now that we have all frequent patterns over the data set, we can use those patterns to find association rules in them using a second data mining primitive *ASSOC_PATTERN*. This example illustrates the benefits of storing patterns as well as data. The reuse of patterns could prove to be an enormous optimization in data mining.

Now consider the case where we want to check if the same frequent item sets hold for another transaction database. To do this, we could either formulate the same query again over the second dataset, or we can use patternset *P* of the last query and apply a *CHECK_PATTERN* crossover data mining primitive operation to it. This illustrates the potential power of the inductive database: intuitively, the patternset *P* describes a subset of the data and thus it is intuitively more efficient to operate on those patterns instead of the whole dataset. While it is true that you can derive all patterns from the underlying data, but sometimes it might be more efficient to gain patterns from the patterns already available, as is the case in the example described above.

6 Conclusions and Future Work

In this paper we have discussed the topics of inductive databases and distributed knowledge discovery. We introduced a global architecture for the implementation of an inductive database that is suited for distributed computing and querying over the grid and discussed its various components. We have also described how a query would be handled by the architecture.

Our plan is to implement this architecture using the inductive database SINDBAD (acronym for: structured inductive database development) [10] which has been developed by Stefan Kramer and his team. By using an existing inductive database we can see how modifications in the architecture affect the efficiency of storage and querying, allowing us to maximize its performance.

Another goal is to provide a complete set of data mining primitives which are suitable for distributed data mining. However, research needs to be done on how existing algorithms can be modified for distributed computing. Furthermore, a thorough investigation must be done on which algorithms should be in this set.

Acknowledgements

This work is part of the BioRange programme of the Netherlands Bioinformatics Centre (NBIC), which is supported by BSIK grant BSIK03013 through the Netherlands Genomics Initiative (NGI). The authors also gratefully acknowledge support from the Leiden Universiteits Fonds. Finally, the authors would like to thank Stefan Kramer for allowing us to get involved in the SINDBAD project, and Dr. Fons Verbeek for proofreading this paper.

References

[1] J-F Boulicaut, M. Klemettinen, H. Mannila, *Querying Inductive Databases: A Case Study on the MINE RULE Operator*. PKDD 1998: 194-202

[2] L. de Raedt, *A perspective on inductive databases*. SIGKDD Explorations 4, pp. 69–77, 2003.

[3] T. Imielinski, H. Mannila, *A database perspective on knowledge discovery*, Communications of the ACM, v. 39 n. 11, pp. 58-64, Nov. 1996

[4] T. Imielinski, A. Virmani, MSQL: *A Query Language for Database Mining*, Data Mining and Knowledge Discovery, Vol. 2(4), pp. 373-408, 1999.

[5] R. Meo, *Inductive Databases: Towards a New Generation of Databases for Knowledge Discovery*, invited paper at First International Workshop on Integrating Data Mining, Database and Information Retrieval (IDDI), at DEXA, Copenhagen, Denmark, August, 22, 2005.

[6] R.Meo, G.Psaila, *Toward XML-Based Knowledge Discovery Systems*, Proc. of the IEEE International Conference on Data Mining, pp. 665-668, 9-12 December, 2002, Maebashi City, Japan.

[7] E. Bertino, B. Catania, E. Kotsifakos, A. Maddalena, I. Ntoutsi, Y. Theodoridis, *PBMS Querying and Storage Issues*, PANDA Technical Report PANDA-TR-2004-02, Feb. 2004

[8] C. Masson, C.Robardet, J-F. Boulicaut: *Optimizing subset queries: a step towards SQL-based inductive databases for itemsets*. SAC 2004: pp. 535-539

[9] L. de Raedt , M. Jaeger , S. D. Lee , H. Mannila, *A Theory of Inductive Query Answering*, Proceedings of the 2002 IEEE International Conference on Data Mining (ICDM'02), p.123, December 09-12, 2002

[10] S. Kramer, V. Aufschild, A. Hapfelmeier, A. Jarasch, K. Kessler, S. Reckow, J. Wicker, L. Richter: *Inductive Databases in the Relational Model: The Data as the Bridge*. In Knowledge Discovery in Inductive Databases: 4th International Workshop, KDID 2005, Porto, Portugal, October 3 , 2005.

Prototype Of Speech Translation System For Audio Effective Communication

Richard Rojas Bello[1], Erick Araya Araya[2] and Luis Vidal Vidal[2]
[1]Escuela de Ingeniería Civil en Informática, Universidad Austral de Chile, Valdivia, Chile
rrojas1@inf.uach.cl
[2]Instituto de Informática, Universidad Austral de Chile
Valdivia, Chile
{earaya,lvidal}@inf.uach.cl

Abstract. The present document exposes the development of a prototype of translation system as a Thesis Project. It consists basically on the capture of a flow of voice from the emitter, integrating advanced technologies of voice recognition, instantaneous translation and communication over the internet protocol RTP/RTCP (Real time Transport Protocol) to send information in real-time to the receiver. This prototype doesn't transmit image, it only boards the audio stage. Finally, the project besides embracing a problem of personal communications, tries to contribute to the development of activities related with the speech recognition, motivating new investigations and advances on the area.

1 Introduction

At present internet offers almost instantaneous different and efficient ways of communication without considering the distance among people. The current technology allows the access to e-mail, news services, instant messaging services (for example *MSN Messenger*) and applications for video conference. Nevertheless, in the topic of video-conference and specifically in voice conversations there are still obstacles that hinder a full communication; one of them is the difference of languages. This is the point on which the proposed solution is focused on; solution that approaches the problem integrating technologies of recognition and speech synthesis, together with technologies of transmission of voice on IP networks (VoIP) (Rojas Bello 2005).

Please use the following format when citing this chapter:

Bello, R.R., Araya, E.A., Vidal, L.V., 2006, in IFIP International Federation for Information Processing, Volume 218, Professional Practice in Artificial Intelligence, eds. J. Debenham, (Boston: Springer), pp. 229–236.

1.1 State of the art

In contrast to the traditional biometric recognition - as it can be fingerprint - the speech recognition is neither fixed nor static, there is only dependent information of the act.

The state of the art of the automatic verification of the speech proposes the construction of the speaker's stochastic model based on its own characteristics and extracted from carried out trainings.

Bergdata Biometrics GmbH®, for example, differs between high and low level of information for speech recognition (Graevenitz 2001). Inside the high level of information is the dialect, accent, the speech style and the context, all characteristics that at present are recognized only by human beings. The low level of information contemplates rhythm, tone, spectral magnitude, frequencies and bandwidth of the individual's voice; characteristics that are being used in recognition systems. Bergdata finally states that the speech recognition will be complementary to the biometric techniques.

On December 23, 1999, Science Daily made public the information that scientifics at Carnegie Mellon University and its colleagues of C-STAR (Consortium for Speech Translation Advanced Research) would drive an international videoconference. They showed a system web of planning of journeys. The system used translation speech to speech, interpreting six different languages in six different locations around the world. The demonstration was successful; however, they faced problems characteristic of the spontaneous speech: interruptions, doubts and stutterers (ScienceDaily 1999). The software to communicate and to make references to web documents was *JANUS*. *JANUS* has evolved in its own version III. It manages spontaneous spoken dialogues, of conversation, and with a opened up vocabulary in several speech domains (Waibel 2004).

A similar project, where Carnegie Mellon University is also part is *NESPOLE*. *NESPOLE* is a system applied directly to the world of the electronic trade; it allows to the internet users to visit websites and to be connected transparently with a human agent of the company that provides the service (Cattoni y Lazzari 2005).

2 Prototype

2.1 Design

The figure 1 represents the recognition system prototype, translation and transport over RTP proposed as solution (Rojas Bello 2005). The diagram shows the stream sent by a user A (Spanish language) toward a user B (of English language). The user B executes a far prototype's instance.

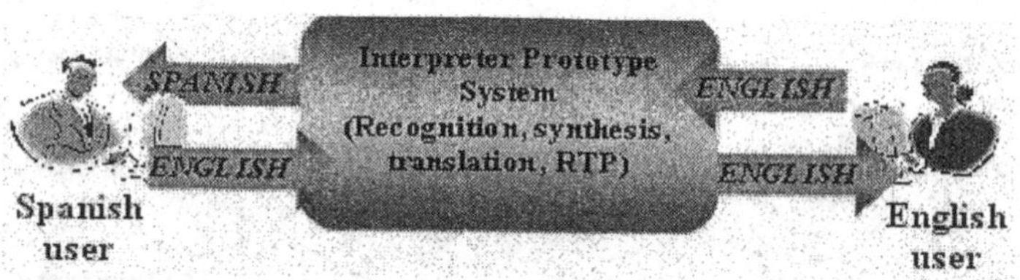

Fig. 1. Interpreter Prototype System

The libraries used to develop the recognition and speech synthesis modules were *Microsoft® SAPI SDK* version 4.0. These libraries add the advantage that the application not only uses the engine included in *SAPI*, but rather engines of other developers can also be recognized by the application if they are compatible with SAPI.

To enable the speech recognition in Spanish the engine *Dragon NaturallySpeaking® Spanish* was used.

The recognition in English was achieved in two different ways, with English Continuous of *Microsoft® SAPI SDK* (included in the libraries) and with *Dragon NaturallySpeaking® English.*

The Spanish synthesis was implemented making use of the *TTS3000 Lernout & Hauspie®* masculine and feminine voices engine; the English synthesis with *Microsoft® SAPI 4.0* voices.

The variety of available voices for speech synthesis offer users different forms of being identified. The prototype has masculine and feminine voices with varied tones and in diverse environments.

The translation was achieved using the service of translation *Google™ Language Tools*, which provides quick translations with appropriate semantics.

Libraries RTP that constitute the base of the audio transmission and reception are *WinRTP* those are open source and are inside present technologies in the market as part of solutions *Cisco AVVID®*.

To view in more detail the figure 2 shows the system's components interaction. In this figure a user speech a phrase which is captured as text using the libraries *SAPI SR* and speech recognitions engines installed previously on the system. Next, the text is send to *Google™ Language Tools* to translate it into Spanish or English according to the case. *Language Tools* returns the text translated and this is synthesized into a WAV file by the libraries *SAPI TTS* and text to speech engines. The WAV files are read by *WinRTP* libraries and sent through internet as RTP packages to the remote user.

The RTP packages that become from the remote user (his/her WAV file synthesized) are received by *WinRTP* and played directly on speakers.

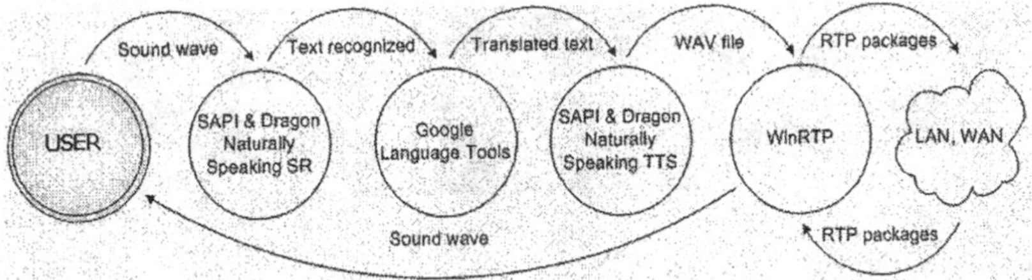

Fig. 2. Interpreter Prototype System's components

2.2 Implementation

The application begins with the dialogue of the figure 3. The user must enter a name and choose the mode of speech recognition that needed.

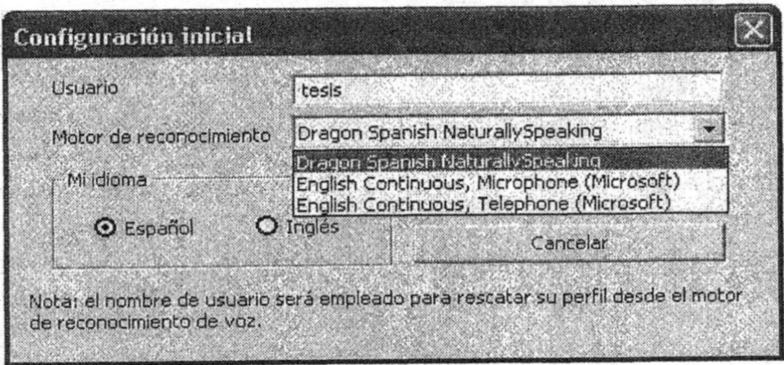

Fig. 3. Users configuration

Next, the user must choose a voice that represents it (fig. 4). The chosen voice will be the one that the second participant of the session will listen. Every time that the user selects a type of voice of the menu the selected character will be introduced itself and told that from that moment it will be the output synthesized voice.

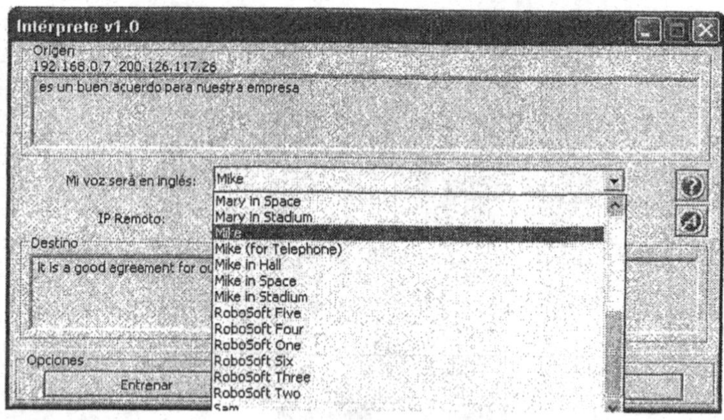

Fig. 4. Main dialogue

For the speaker is necessary to know the IP number of the second computer that executes an application's instance (fig. 5). The communication for this prototype is unicast and begins when pressing the "Transmitir" (Transmit) button. This button has a double purpose: to begin, and to finish the transmission and reception.

Fig. 5. Transmission to remote IP

Every time that the user speaks a sentence the system takes charge of translating it, to synthesize it in the remote participant's language and to send it in real time. Two text boxes show for separate the original text and the translation to synthesize obtained from *Google™ Language Tools.*

2.3 Performance

The best performance obtained by the prototype was using *Dragon NaturallySpeaking® Spanish*. It obtained a high accuracy to 96% just by 5 sessions of training.

The behavior of the bandwidth (BW) was analyzed executing a prototype's instance. The input/output traffic was observed in intervals of 1 second between a 320/128 Kbps and 512/128 Kbps node. On 320/128 Kbps node the behavior is in figure 6.

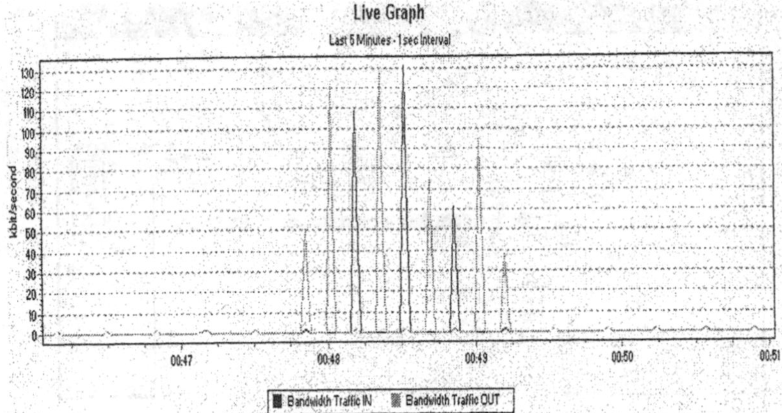

Fig. 6. BW on 320/128 Kbps node

The consumption of BW on the 320/128 Kbps node didn't overcome the 128 Kbps, and the input stream reached the 131 Kbps. The transmitted phrases were received with an approximate retard of 1 sec. and without perceptible jitter.

From the 320/128 Kbps node was carried out the transmission of phrases with different sizes. In the table 1 the sizes are observed (in words and characters) of eleven sentences. Each phrase has associate the necessary time to synthesize it and the maximum consumption of output BW measured in intervals of 1 sec.

Table 1. Performance for characters in 320/128 Kbps connection

Phrase number	Characters	Words	Kbps	Seconds
1	500	77	400	35
2	450	66	400	31
3	400	60	400	27
4	350	50	400	25
5	300	46	385	21
6	250	38	380	18
7	200	32	370	14
8	150	26	350	10
9	100	19	230	7
10	50	9	140	4
11	25	5	75	2

The received audio quality at node 512/256 Kbps was not perceived with jitter until the reception of phrases of 100 characters. The use of BW registered 230 Kbps at node 320/128.

The necessary time to generate the synthesis of the translation behaved in a lineal way (fig. 7), this is, the extension of the phrase results to be proportional at the time used to synthesize it.

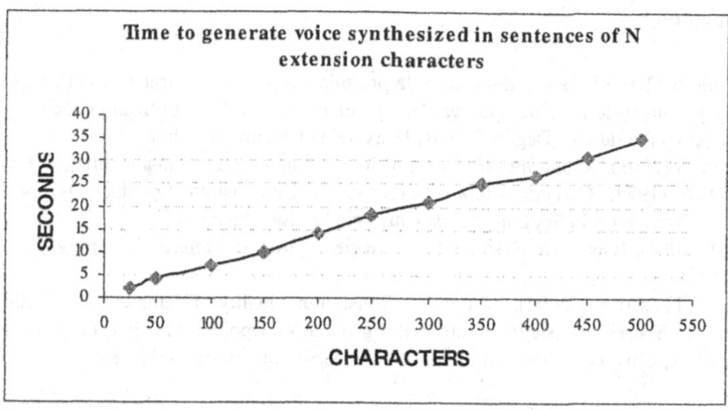

Fig. 7. Time to generate synthesized speech in phrases of N extension characters

3 Conclusions

This project was focused on as an engineering work that seeks for solution to a communicational and social restrictive, the difference of languages. Processes of technological packages opening were faced as and integration of speech recognition, speech synthesis, VoIP and the web service functions.

The designed software can synchronize with the user's needs. The election of compatible libraries with solutions unaware to Microsoft® made the final user to have in his hands the possibility to acquire engines (recognition or synthesis) which are within the user economic reach and adjusted to his specific requirements.

The implemented translation module fulfills the functionality required for the prototype. The connection to *Google™ Language Tools* provided sentences translated successfully in both ways (English/Spanish, Spanish/English) and with a correct syntax and semantics.

The proposed prototype design possesses an expandable connectivity. To incorporate a SIP module to approach the IP and traditional telephony would not represent a radical change in the proposed architecture. Also, SIP uses RTP to transmit information in real time.

The information of the table 1 indicates that the optimum would be to synthesize translations smaller than 50 characters (10 words approx.). An extension of 50 characters doesn't overcome the 4 seconds in synthesizing. The implementation of an algorithm that divides extensive sentences in new of smaller size could reduce even more the time of synthesis.

The use of recognitions engines with high percentages of precision - like *Dragon NaturallySpeaking®* - reduces the occurrence of erroneous recognitions. This directly benefits the efficiency of the recognition module and of the whole system.

References

Rojas Bello R (2005) Diseño y desarrollo de prototipo de sistema de traducción instantánea de habla y transmisión en tiempo real, sobre el protocolo RTP utilizando tecnologías de reconocimiento de voz. Degree Thesis, Universidad Austral de Chile

Graevenitz G (2001). About Speaker Recognition Technology. Bergdata Biometrics GmbH

ScienceDaily (1999). Carnegie Mellon Scientists To Demonstrate Spontaneous Speech-To-Speech Translation In Six Languages. Carnegie Mellon University

Waibel A (2004). Interactive Systems Laboratories. Carnegie Mellon University, Universität Karlsruhe

Cattoni R, Lazzari G (2004). Not only Translation Quality: Evaluating the NESPOLE! Speech-to-Speech Translation System along other Viewpoints. ITC-irst, Carnegie Mellon University, Universität Karlsruhe, CLIPS, University of Trieste, AETHRA

A Knowledge Representation Semantic Network for a Natural Language Syntactic Analyzer Based on the UML

Alberto Tavares da Silva[1], Luis Alfredo V. Carvalho[2]

1 Escuela Politecnica del Ejército del Ecuador
atsfc@espe.edu.ec
WWW home page:
http://www.espe.edu.ec/espe_portal/portal/main.do?sectionCode=91
2 Universidade Federal do Rio de Janeiro,
COPPE - Instituto Alberto Luiz Coimbra
de Pós-graduação e Pesquisa de Engenharia - Brasil
LuisAlfredo@ufrj.br
WWW home page: http://www.cos.ufrj.br/~alfredo

Abstract. The need for improving software processes approximated the software engineering and artificial intelligence areas. Artificial intelligence techniques have been used as a support to software development processes, particularly through intelligent assistants that offer a knowledge-based support to software process' activities. The context of the present work is a project for an intelligent assistant that implements a linguistic technique with the purpose of extracting object-oriented elements from requirement specifications in natural language through two main functionalities: the syntactic and semantic analyses. The syntactic analysis has the purpose of extracting the syntactic constituents from a sentence; and the semantic analysis has the goal of extracting the meaning from a set of sentences, i.e., a text. This paper focuses on the syntactic analysis functionality and applies the UML to its core as a semantic network for knowledge representation, based on the premise that the UML is *de facto* a standard general modeling language for software development.

1 Introduction

In the software engineering area, object-oriented technology use has increased to the point of becoming a currently dominant technology in software development [1]. In spite of the advantages that object-oriented technology can provide in the software development community, the fundamental problems associated with the

Please use the following format when citing this chapter:

da Silva, A.T., Carvalho, L.A.V., 2006, in IFIP International Federation for Information Processing, Volume 218, Professional Practice in Artificial Intelligence, eds. J. Debenham, (Boston: Springer), pp. 237–246.

identification tasks of the object-oriented elements, i.e., classes, attributes, relationship and multiplicities, remain; these tasks are easily handled manually and guided by heuristics that the analyst acquires through experience, whose results are posteriorly transferred to a CASE tool characterizing an automation gap between natural language requirement specifications and the respective conceptual modeling [2]. The automatic support to requirement analysis processes can better reflect the *problem solve* behavior of experienced analysts [3].

The need for improving software processes approximated the software engineering and artificial intelligence areas. A growing number of researches have used artificial intelligence techniques as a support to software development processes, particularly through intelligent assistants that offer a knowledge-based support to software process' activities [4].

The context of the present work is a project for an intelligent assistant that implements a linguistic technique with the purpose of extracting object-oriented elements from requirement specifications in natural language, enabling the generation of a conceptual model based on the UML class diagram notation. The referred approach includes three main linguistic requirements: a grammar, a knowledge representation structure and a knowledge representation language. The linguistic technique for the proposed intelligent assistant adopts, from computational linguistics (which automatically analyses natural language in terms of software programs called parsers), two main functionalities: the syntactic and the semantic analyses [5]. The syntactic analysis has the purpose of extracting the syntactic constituents that include the lexicon syntactic structures, like verb phrases; and the grammatical categories, like nouns. The semantic analysis has the goal of extracting the meaning from a text. Fig. 1 illustrates a general schema of the problem solution for the referred assistant.

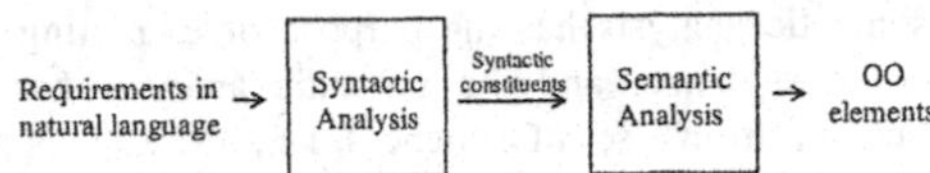

Fig. 1. The problem solution in a pipeline style.

This paper focuses on the syntactic analysis functionality and applies the UML to its core as a semantic network for knowledge representation based on the premise that the UML is *de facto* a standard general modeling language for software development [1]. Based on the referred structure, a knowledge base (KB) can be generated, enabling the syntactic analysis. The proposed semantic network realizes two more logical representations for the intelligent assistant: the static structure and the database conceptual model.

The present article is structured in the following way: the second section presents the three linguistic requirements for the proposed syntactic analyzer; the third section presents the proposed UML semantic network with a case study; and the fourth section presents the conclusions.

2 Linguistic Requirements

2.1 Grammar

There are three basic approaches to a grammar: the traditional, the phrase structure and the transformational. The *traditional grammar* denominates as subject and predicate the essential parts of any construction whose core is the verb. The *phrase structure grammar* includes the syntactic description based on the identification of all kinds of syntactic constituents and the formulation of rules that order the words inside a sentence. The *transformational grammar* has the transformational rules as its basis, making it possible to convert the deep structures, identified in the constituent grammar analysis, into surface structures that correspond to the real form of the enunciation, i.e., the kernel sentence [6-8].

This work adopts the *phrase structure grammar* because it allows the representation of the knowledge to be modeled by the proposed UML semantic network as well as the extraction of the syntactic constituents from the sentences. The cited grammar permits to specify a language with an infinite number of sentences as the natural language, being well-founded on a formalism based on production with four components [5, 9]:

T – terminal vocabulary: language words and symbols being defined;
N – non-terminal vocabulary: symbols used to specify the grammar;
P – set of production;
S – start symbol.

2.2 Knowledge Representation Language

The language enables the formulation of knowledge through symbolic representations that will capacitate a system to reason [10]. First-order logic (FOL) is the most widely used, studied and implemented version of logic [11]. It is important to note, from [10], that whatever other features a knowledge representation language may have ought to comprise a well-defined notion of entailment because the so-called *job reasoning* here means to compute the entailments of a KB.

Many modern logicians limit the expressive power of FOL to a more easily computable subset, like Horn Clauses [10, 11]. In Horn clause representation, a KB can often be separated in two types of clauses: facts and rules. The facts are used to determine the basic truth from a domain, whereas the rules are used to understand the vocabulary and express new relationships. The propositions considered as true arguments are denominated *hypotheses or axioms*, and the propositions that search the logical consequences from the reported axioms are denominated *theorems*. Based on the abovementioned concepts, there appears the activity denominated *a theorem proof*, whose objective is to derive the logical consequences from the given propositions [12, 13]. The logical reasoning, or logical inference, involves the logical consequence concept. Logic is the inference science which is based on two basic hypotheses: in a correct inference the premises must be true and the inferred conclusion must have a logical relation with the premises in a way that guarantees the transference of the truth contained in these premises to the conclusion; the relation between the premises and conclusion, which guarantees the transference of the truth, is a formal relation denominated logical consequence or logical entailment, which can be analyzed as a relation between logical forms [14]. The Resolution Procedure permits to automate the deductive reasoning in a FOL knowledge base, in a complete and consistent way, with the objective of determining whether a sentence α, or a formula, is true or not in a *KB*, i.e., if $KB \models \alpha$ (whether α is a logical consequence of KB). The resolution procedure is more manageable when applied to a Horn clause KB [10], being called a *SLD* resolution (Selected literals, Linear pattern, over Definite clause).

There are two languages that allow a high level symbol manipulation in NLP: Lisp and Prolog. This work emphasizes Prolog, which syntax is in FOL logic with clauses written in Horn clause [10-12, 15]. Prolog clauses include facts and rules that are accepted as a set of axioms and the user's question as the presumed theorem. The Prolog inference mechanism tries to prove the theorem, as it is a theorem prover based on the SLD resolution procedure [12, 13]. Prolog is also a suitable language to implement the phrase structure grammar [12, 13, 16]. A large number of Prolog implementations provide a notational extension called *Definite Clause Grammar (DCG)*, that facilitates the formal grammars' implementation in Prolog and it is directly executed as a syntactic analyzer, which enables sentence decomposition in its constituents. DCG allows implementing the *context dependence*, where a sentence depends on the context where it happens, like a concordant number [13].

Based on the abovementioned considerations, this work adopts the Horn clause in DCG notation as the knowledge representation language, based on the premise that DCG was developed as a linguistic modeling tool that permits the depiction of any sentential structure that can be represented by a phrase structure grammar and, also, that has a well-defined notion of entailment based on an SLD resolution procedure.

2.3 Knowledge Representation Structure

Semantic network is a structure for representing knowledge as a pattern of interconnected nodes and arcs, in a way that the nodes represent concepts of entities, attributes, events and states; and the arcs represent the connections among the concepts [17]. Stuart Shapiro, who implemented the first semantic network with integral support for FOL, believes that a network structure can actually support important types of "subconscious" reasoning that are not directly representable in a linear logical form [17]. Shastri affirms that, in a general way, it is possible to translate a semantic network into a non-graphic language and vice versa [18]. Russel and Norvig [15] consider the semantic network a system specially projected to organize and to reason about/upon categories, offering graphic help to visualize a KB, being also a logical form. To Sowa [19], the semantic network is a declarative graphic depiction which can be used to represent knowledge as an automated reasoning support for it.

Sowa [19] classifies UML diagrams as a semantic network and justifies it by saying that central to the UML exists a network definition of object types and another one like a relational graph that permits the representation of metalevel information. The UML semantic understanding demands to comprehend the UML specification through a four-layer metamodel hierarchy [1]. The meta-metamodeling layer, called M3 in Fig. 2, defines the metamodeling specification language. The metamodeling layer, called M2, defines the model specification language as the UML. The model layer, called M1, has the primary responsibility of describing semantic domains, i.e., it allows the generation of user models as UML metamodel instances. The lowest layer, called M0, includes run-time instances of the model elements. The UML semantic refers to the run-time interpretation from the generated models [20].

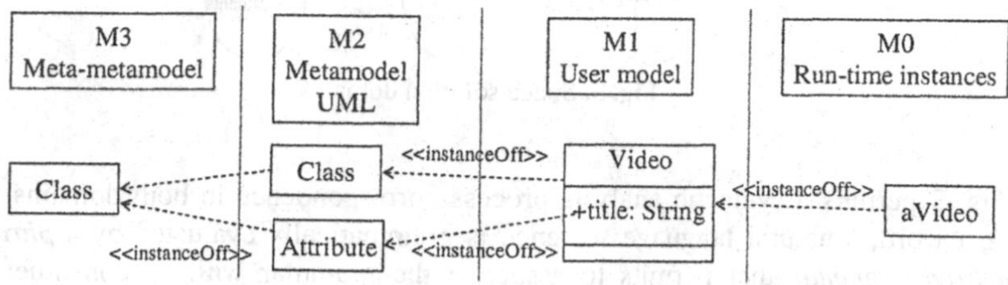

Fig. 2. The UML layer hierarchy

The present work adopts the UML class diagram notation, from the metamodel layer in Fig. 2, as the knowledge representation structure, i.e., the semantic network. The justification considers that a UML class diagram model, in the user model layer of Fig. 2, is a static structure composed by nodes and arcs interconnected, where the nodes represent classes and the arcs, associations [17]. The referred model is a system projected to organize and to reason with object instances, e.g., from UML run-time instance layers, objects representing axioms can be instantiated and asserted in a KB in accordance to the adopted knowledge representation language syntax, i.e., a Horn clause in DCG notation. The Prolog inference engine enables the reasoning through a logical consequence among the referred axioms.

3 Semantic Network for the Syntactic Analyzer

3.1 Knowledge Representation Structure

The linguistic requirements for the proposed syntactic analyzer include: the phrase structure grammar as the grammar, the Horn clause in DCG notation as the knowledge representation language and the UML class diagram as the knowledge representation structure, being this last requirement the core of the present work.

Two domains are defined based on a general problem-solution vision: real world aspects and symbolic representations, as illustrated in Fig. 3. Both domains were defined based on three representation concepts. The first defines representation as a relationship between two domains, where the first is meant to stand for or take the place of the second [10]. The second defines representation as the correspondence between the real world and the symbolic representation [15]. In the third one, the symbols serve as surrogates for external things [11].

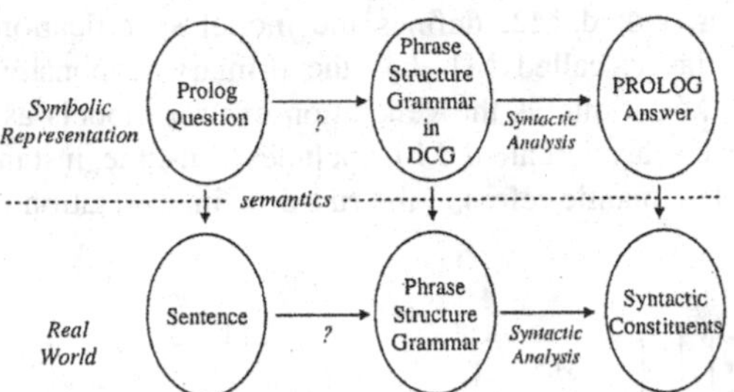

Fig. 3. Space solution domains

Fig. 3 permits a syntactic analysis process correspondence in both domains. In the real word, a natural language sentence is grammatically evaluated by a *phrase structured grammar* that permits to associate the grammar with its constituents' analysis; the results are the syntactic constituents. In the symbolic representation world, the sentence corresponds to a question in Prolog notation, or a theorem to be proved by the Prolog theorem prover; the sentence is processed by the KB inference engine, which axioms implement the *phrase structure grammar* from the respective real world in DCG notation; the result is a Prolog clause as the answer to the goal. There is a semantic relationship between both domains as illustrated in Fig. 3.

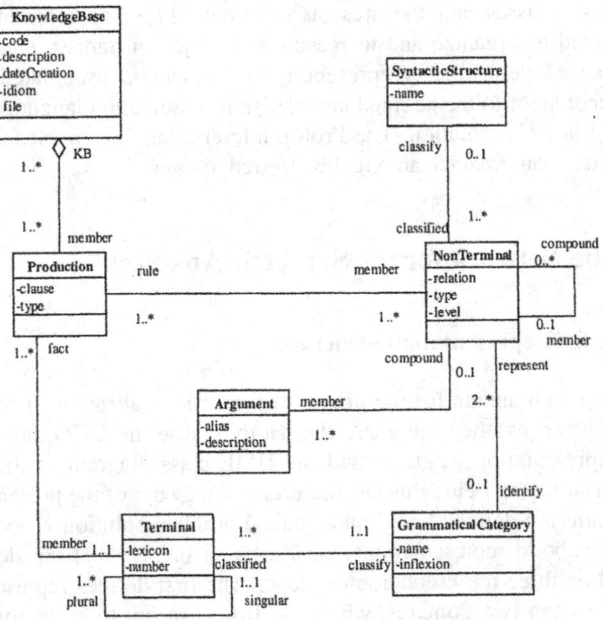

Fig. 4. Semantic network for the syntactic analyzer

Based on the premise that the knowledge kernel of the syntactic analyzer is the grammar, Fig. 4 illustrates a knowledge representation structure of a *phrase structure grammar.* The proposed semantic network works like a bridge between the other two linguistic requirements, i.e., the phrase structure grammar as the grammar and the Horn clause in DCG notation as the knowledge representation language. The knowledge represented by the referred network is the phrase structure grammar and the knowledge generated is a set of axioms from the cited grammar represented symbolically through the Horn clause. This confirms Shastri's affirmation that it is possible to translate a semantic network into a non-graphic language [18].

Based on the premise that the *job of reasoning* is to compute the entailments of a KB [10], the Horn Clause knowledge representation language adopted has a well defined notion of logical entailment. The reasoning occurs through the theorem prover inference mechanism, i.e., Prolog. The reasoning in the proposed syntactic analyzer includes examining whether a sentence has the grammatical sequence in accordance to the phrase structure grammar implemented and, based on the correct analysis, generating the syntactic constituents.

3.2 Case Study

This case study adapts a short example implemented in [13] and illustrates a production instantiation from the proposed UML semantic network, i.e., it shows the composition of an axiom enabling its own assertion in a KB. The following grammar is based on the phrase structure grammar, the knowledge language is Horn clause in DCG notation, implementing the context dependence based on a concordant number [13]:

T: { the, hates, hate, cat, mouse, cats, scares }.
N: { noun_phrase, verb_phrase, determiner, noun, verb,NP, VP, Verb, Det, Noun, Number, Number1}.
P: { (sentence, (Number,sentence(NP, VP)) --> noun_phrase(Number, NP), verb_phrase(Number, VP).,
verb_phrase(Number, verb_phrase(Verb, NP)) --> verb(Number1,Verb), noun_phrase(Number, NP).,
noun_phrase(Number, noun_phrase(Det, Noun)) --> determiner(Det), noun(Number,Noun).,
determiner(determiner(the)) --> [the].,
verb(singular,verb(hates)) --> [hates].,
verb(plural,verb(hate)) --> [hate].,
noun(singular,noun(cat)) --> [cat].,
noun(singular,noun(mouse)) --> [mouse].,
noun(plural,noun(cats)) --> [cats].,
verb --> [scares].,
verb --> [hates]. }.
S: { sentence }

The non-terminal symbols (N) represent the grammar and include the grammatical category symbols, the syntactic structure symbols and the argument symbols. The NonTerminal class enables the generation of the relations based on the referred symbols; these relations are, incidentally, the ones that compose the productions. As an example, the following relations compose the above second production:

- *verb_phrase(Number, verb_phrase(Verb, NP)).*
- *verb_phrase(Verb, NP).*
- *verb(Number1,Verb).*
- *noun_phrase(Number, NP).*

Fig. 5 illustrates a run-time interpretation, i.e., layer M0 in Fig.2, which corresponds to an instantiation of the object oProduction from the Production class, which *clause* attribute has the following state: "verb_phrase(Number, verb_phrase(Verb, NP)) --> verb(Number1, Verb), noun_phrase(Number, NP)". The object oProduction is composed by three instantiations from the NonTerminal class.

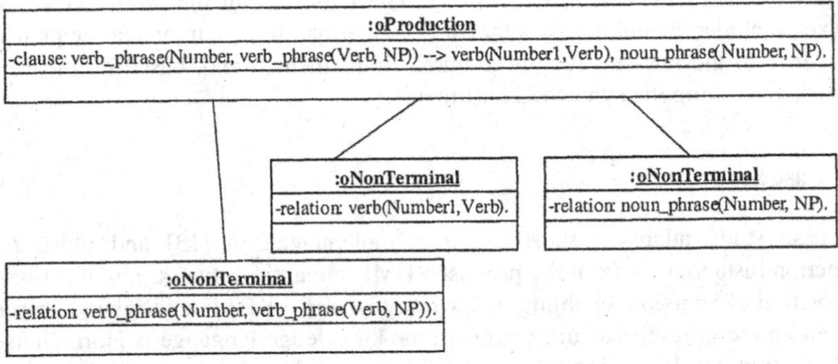

Fig. 5. A run-time interpretation for a production

Fig. 6 shows the instantiation of the oNonTerminal object, also in layer M0 in Fig. 2, whose *relation* attribute has the following state: "noun_phrase(Number, NP)". The referred object composition depends on other three object instantiations, i.e., one object from the SyntaticStructure class and two objects from the Argument class.

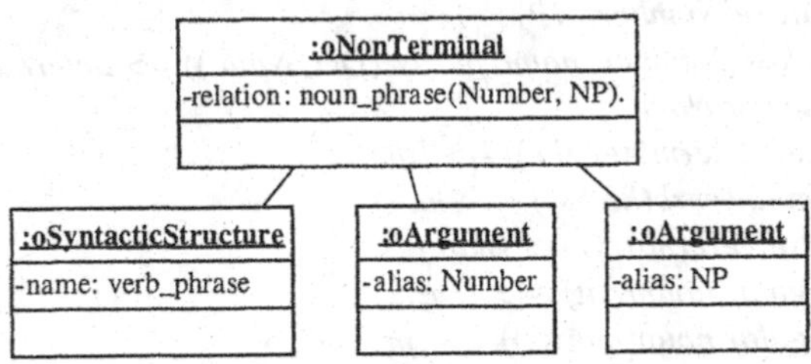

Fig. 6. A run-time interpretation for a relation

As abovementioned, the purpose of the Syntactic Analyzer is extracting the syntactic constituents from a sentence. The prototype, illustrated in Fig. 7, instantiates all the productions of the present case study from the proposed UML semantic network, permitting to extract the syntactic constituents, e.g., from the sentence "the mouse hates the cat", the word "mouse" belongs to the grammatical category "noun" and is inside the syntactic structure "noun phrase".

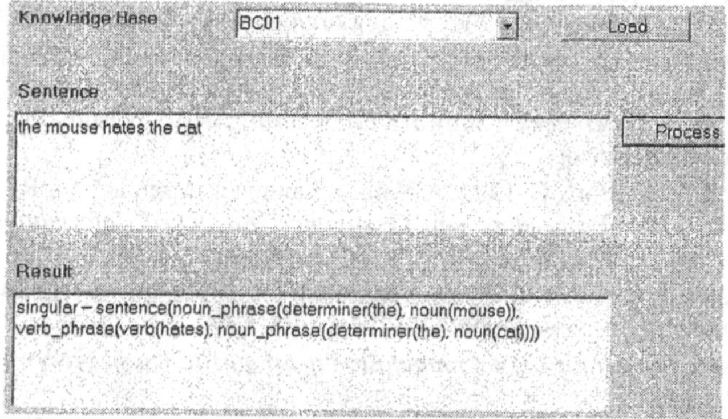

Fig. 7. Syntactic analyzer output

4 Conclusion

The linguistic requirements for the proposed syntactic analyzer include: the phrase structure grammar as the grammar, the Horn clause in DCG notation as the knowledge representation language and the UML class diagram as the knowledge representation structure, i.e., the semantic network, being this last requirement the core of the present work. The referred semantic network works like a bridge between the other two linguistic requirements, i.e., the knowledge represented by the semantic network is the phrase structure grammar and the knowledge generated by the same network is a set of axioms from the cited grammar, represented symbolically through the Horn clause. This confirms Shastri's affirmation that it is possible to translate a semantic network into a non-graphic language [18].

The semantic network based on the UML class diagram complies with some important concepts. Firstly, its structure is equivalent to a model made by nodes and arcs interconnected [17]. Secondly, it is a system projected to organize and to reason with categories that offer graphical help to visualize the KB, being a kind of logic [15]. Moreover, it is a surrogate for external things, i.e., the phrase structure grammar [11]. In addition to that, it gives support to automation reasoning by means of the theorem prover inference mechanism proposed, which includes examining whether a sentence has the grammatical sequence in accordance to the phrase structure grammar implemented and, based on the correct analysis, generating the syntactic constituents. Finally, inside an object-oriented view from the UML model, the semantics occurs through the object run-time interpretations, as illustrated in Fig. 5.

Briefly, the meaning of the semantic network proposed is a KB whose axioms are able of reasoning under a question, i.e., a theorem to be proved.

References

1. OMG 2004. Object Management Group: UML 2.0 Infrastructure. OMG document ptc/04-10-14, http://www.omg.org/cgi-bin/doc?ptc/2004-10-14.
2. Overmyer, S. P.; Lavoie, B.; and Rambow O. 2001. Conceptual Modeling through Linguistic Analysis Using LIDA. In *Proceedings of the 23rd International Conference on Software Engineering*, 0401. Washington, DC: IEEE Computer Society.
3. Rolland, C., and Proix, C. 1992. A Natural Language Approach for Requirements Engineering. In *Proceeding on Conference Advanced Information Systems Engineering* 257-277. Manchester: Springer-Verlag.
4. R. A. Falbo, Integração de Conhecimento em um Ambiente de Desenvolvimento de Software. Ph.D. Dissertation, COPPE, UFRJ, 1998.
5. R. Hausser, *Foundations of Computational Linguistic* (Springer-Verlag, Berlin, 2001).
6. N. Chomsky, *Syntactic Structures* (Mouton de Gruyter, Berlin, 2002).
7. J. C. Azevedo, *Iniciação à Sintaxe do Português* (Jorge Zahar Editor, Rio de Janeiro, 2003).
8. M. C. P. Souza e Silva and I. V. Koch, *Lingüística Aplicada ao Português: Sintaxe* (Cortez Editora, São Paulo, 2004).
9. R. Grishman, *Computational Linguistics: An Introduction* (Cambridge University Press, 1999).
10. R. Brachman, and H. J. Levesque, *Knowledge Representation and Reasoning* (Morgan Kaufmann Publishers, San Francisco, 2004).
11. J. F. Sowa, *Knowledge Representation. Logical, Philosophical and Computational Foundations* (Brooks/Cole, California, 2000).
12. W. F. Clocksin and C. S. Mellish, *Programming in Logic* (Springer-Verlag Berlin Heidelberg, 2003).
13. I. Bratko, *PROLOG – Programming for Artificial Intelligence* (Addison-Wesley Publishers, 2001).
14. H. Kamp, and U. Reyle, *From Discourse to Logic. Introduction to Modeltheoretic Semantics of Natural Language, Formal Logic and Discourse Representation Theory* (Kluwer Academic Publishers, Netherlands, 1993).
15. S. Russel, Stuart and P. Norvig, *Inteligência Artificial* (Editora Campus, Rio de Janeiro, 2004).
16. A. Gal, G. Lapalme, P. Saint-Dizier and H. Somers, *Prolog for Natural Language Processing* (John Wiley & Sons, 1991).
17. J. F. Sowa, *et al.*, *Principles of Semantic Networks. Explorations in the Representation of Knowledge* (Morgan Kaufmann Publishers, 1991), pp 1-3.
18. L. Shastri, Why Semantic Networks? In: *Principles of Semantic Networks. Explorations in the Representation of Knowledge* (Morgan Kaufmann Publishers, 1991), pp. 109-136.
19. J. F. Sowa, Semantic Networks (August, 12, 2002); http://www.jfsowa.com/pubs/semnet.htm.
20. B. V. Selic, On the Semantic Foundations of Standard UML 2.0, *LNCS 3185*, (Springer-Verlag Berlin Heidelberg, 2004), pp. 181-199.

Fast simulation of animal locomotion: lamprey swimming

Matthew Beauregard, Paul J. Kennedy, and John Debenham

Faculty of IT, University of Technology, Sydney, PO Box 123, Broadway, NSW 2007, AUSTRALIA,
paulk@it.uts.edu.au

Abstract. Biologically realistic computer simulation of vertebrate locomotion is an interesting and challenging problem with applications in computer graphics and robotics. One current approach simulates a relatively simple vertebrate, the lamprey, using recurrent neural networks for the spine and a physical model for the body. The model is realized as a system of differential equations. The drawback with this approach is the slow speed of simulation. This paper describes two approaches to speeding up simulation of lamprey locomotion without sacrificing too much biological realism: (i) use of superior numerical integration algorithms and (ii) simplifications to the neural architecture of the lamprey.

1 Introduction

Vertebrate locomotion – walking, swimming, crawling, hopping – is a complex process that is difficult to imitate in simulated environments. Arms, legs, and spinal columns have many degrees of freedom that must be controlled in a coordinated way for stable locomotion to occur. This complexity has limited the use of biologically realistic locomotion in computer graphics and robotics, despite its considerable advantages.

Some characteristics common to locomotion in all vertebrates suggest a fruitful approach. The key to vertebrate locomotion is not the brain but the spinal cord, which contains all the structures necessary for coordinated movement. All types of motion, whether by legs or slithering muscles, on land or through water, are driven by oscillations between the left and right sides of small segments in the spinal cord. This suggests that an approach to the problem is to study a simple vertebrate and design a simulation that successfully imitates it. The findings will illuminate locomotion in higher vertebrates.

Let us introduce that simplest vertebrate. The lamprey is a jawless eel-shaped fish. Primitive in an evolutionary sense, its major distinguishing feature is a large rounded sucker surrounding the mouth [1]. Its spinal cord is a continuous column of neurons made up of around 100 clusters. Each cluster projects motoneurons to the surrounding muscles [2]. Lampreys swim by propagating a wave along the body from head to tail by phased muscular contraction. Normally the wavelength of this traveling wave is constant and approximately corresponds to body length; its frequency determines the speed of swimming.

Please use the following format when citing this chapter:

Beauregard, M., Kennedy, P.J., Debenham, J., 2006, in IFIP International Federation for Information Processing, Volume 218, Professional Practice in Artificial Intelligence, eds. J. Debenham, (Boston: Springer), pp. 247–256.

The lamprey has been studied thoroughly over several decades. See [3] for a clear introduction to some of the modeling and other papers in the same volume (e.g. [4]) for further details. A variety of simulations has been implemented (see Section 2) but in the pursuit of absolute faithfulness to biology they run very slowly, which is a hindrance to their practical use in computer graphics.

In this paper we develop an understanding of the neural structure, demonstrate an implementation of swimming, and introduce a simplification resulting in reduced execution time while retaining biological realism. Sections 2 and 3 describe our model and the implementation and numerical strategies for increasing simulation speed. In section 4 we describe typical behavior of the model and, in section 5, give results for increasing simulation speed by simplifying the neural structure. Finally, section 6 gives a conclusion.

2 Model

Ijspeert [2] groups neural models of the lamprey into three classes: biophysical, connectionist and mathematical. Biophysical models most closely replicate the biological systems of the lamprey. Their main intent is to investigate whether enough is understood of lamprey neurobiology to produce models whose results agree with physiological observations. Connectionist models are less realistic and seek to capture only the main feature of biological neurons: a changing frequency of action potential spikes according to input. The main interest here is in connections between neurons. Mathematical models are more abstracted again and view the neural controller as a chain of oscillators, the focus being on examining the couplings between them. Connectionist models are very similar to dynamical recurrent neural networks. They compute the mean firing rate of biological neurons depending on input and time constants. They can be discrete in time or continuous using *leaky integrators*. Ekeberg presents a sophisticated connectionist model that formed the basis for our work [5] as well as that of [2].

The model presented here simulates both the lamprey's neural activity and the results of that activity when applied to a physical body in water. In contrast to previous work, the neural and physical aspects of simulation are combined into a single model, rather than two separate but interacting models.

2.1 Neural model

While biologically the spinal cord is a continuous column of neurons without clear boundaries, it can be considered as roughly 100 discrete but interconnected oscillators (or segmental networks). The combined assembly is known as a central pattern generator (CPG). The main types of neuron involved in the process are: motoneurons (MN) projecting to muscles, excitatory interneurons (EIN) projecting to ipsilateral neurons (ie. those on the same side of the segment), lateral inhibitory interneurons (LIN) projecting to ipsilateral neurons, contralateral inhibitory interneurons (CIN) projecting to contralateral neurons (ie. the other side of the segment) and excitatory brain stem (BS) that project from the brain. The controller consists of 100 segmental networks. Each model neuron represents a population of functionally similar neurons. Actual connections between segments are not well known. Ekeberg chose a simplified, symmetric coupling (except for connections from the CINs which are longer tailward). Parameters for both inter– and intrasegmental connections and extents are given in Table 1. In order to limit output from neurons and to compensate neurons in segments near ends of the body (and have fewer intersegmental inputs), synaptic weights are scaled by dividing by the number of input segments.

Ekeberg [5] advocated supplying extra excitation to the first few segments of the spinal column to help generate a phase–lagged oscillation down the spine. However, we found in our simulations that this is not necessary to generate phase–lagged oscillation and actually impaired the speed of the lamprey. Arrangement of segmental coupling is sufficient to cause a traveling wave towards the tail. Accordingly, extra excitation was not applied.

Table 1. Neural connection configuration. From [2] with additions from [5] and separately–controllable left– and right–side excitation. Negative weights indicate inhibitory connections. Extents of connections to neighbor segments are given in brackets (headward and tailward, respectively).

To ↓	From: EIN_L	CIN_L	LIN_L	EIN_R	CIN_R	LIN_R	BS_L	BS_R
EIN_L	0.4 [2, 2]	-	-	-	-2 [1, 10]	-	2	0
CIN_L	3 [2, 2]	-	-1 [5, 5]	-	-2 [1, 10]	-	7	0
LIN_L	13 [5, 5]	-	-	-	-1 [1, 10]	-	5	0
MN_L	1 [5, 5]	-	-	-	-2 [5, 5]	-	5	0
EIN_R	-	-2 [1, 10]	-	0.4 [2, 2]	-	-	0	2
CIN_R	-	-2 [1, 10]	-	3 [2, 2]	-	-1 [5, 5]	0	7
LIN_R	-	-1 [1, 10]	-	13 [5, 5]	-	-	0	5
MN_R	-	-2 [5, 5]	-	1 [5, 5]	-	-	0	5

Each neuron is modeled as a leaky integrator with a saturating transfer function. u is the mean firing frequency of the population of neurons:

$$\dot{\xi}_+ = \frac{1}{\tau_D}\left(\sum_{i\in\psi_+} u_i w_i - \xi_+\right)$$

$$\dot{\xi}_- = \frac{1}{\tau_D}\left(\sum_{i\in\psi_-} u_i w_i - \xi_-\right)$$

$$\dot{\vartheta} = \frac{1}{\tau_A}(u - \vartheta)$$

$$u = 1 - e^{(\Theta-\xi_+)\Gamma} - \xi_- - \mu\vartheta \text{ if positive}$$

$$0\text{, otherwise,} \qquad (1)$$

where ξ_+ and ξ_- are the delayed 'reactions' to excitatory and inhibitory input and ϑ represents the frequency adaptation (decrease in firing rate over time given a constant input) observed in some real neurons. w are the synaptic weights of excitatory and inhibitory presynaptic neuron groups ψ_+ and ψ_-, τ_D is the time constant of the dendritic sums, τ_A the time constant of frequency adaptation, μ a frequency adaptation constant, Θ the threshold and Γ the gain. The parameters for the constants given in Table 2 are hand-tuned to produce output that matches physiological observations.

Table 2. Neuron parameters. From [5]. See text for an explanation of symbols.

Neuron type	Θ	Γ	τ_D	μ	τ_A
EIN	-0.2	1.8	30 ms	0.3	400 ms
CIN	0.5	1.0	20 ms	0.3	200 ms
LIN	8.0	0.5	50 ms	0.0	-
MN	0.1	0.3	20 ms	0.0	-

2.2 Physical model

We model the body similarly to [5] and [2]. It is represented by ten links (so ten neural segments act on one body segment) and nine joints between them with one degree of freedom. Each link is modeled as a right elliptic cylinder with the major axes of the ellipses aligned vertically. All links have length l of 30 mm and are 30 mm high. Their width is a maximum of 20 mm, decreasing towards the tail. Muscles appear on both sides of the body, attached to the centers of each segment. They are modeled with a spring–and–damper arrangement, where the force exerted by the muscle is set using the spring constant. Thus the local body curvature varies linearly with muscle length. Body and neural network are linked by having motoneuron excitation drive the muscular spring constants. For the purposes of modeling, the body is represented in two dimensions as rectangles with joints at the midpoints of their sides. The position of a link i can be described by (x_i, y_i, φ_i), where x_i and y_i are the coordinates of the rectangle centre and φ_i is the angle of a line through the centre and the joint with respect to the x–axis (see Fig. 1). This simulation strategy gives a maximal representation of the body position, so constraint forces are used to keep links together. Physical parameter values of the links are the same as those of [2].

Body movement is a result of three forces: torques T generated by the muscles, forces W_i from the water and constraint forces F_i and F_{i-1}. These forces determine the acceleration of the links according to Newton's law of motion. Change in position for links $i \in \{1, \ldots, N\}$ is determined by integration.

$$m_i \ddot{x}_i = W_{i,x} + F_{i,x} - F_{i-1,x}$$
$$m_i \ddot{y}_i = W_{i,y} + F_{i,y} - F_{i-1,y}$$

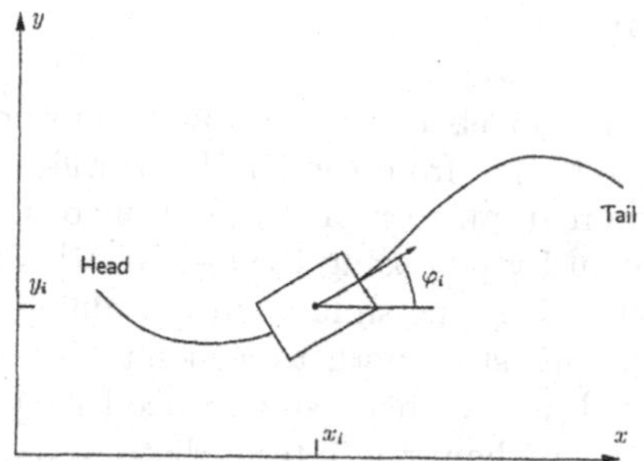

Fig. 1. Co-ordinates describing the position of a link. From [5].

$$I_i\ddot{\varphi}_i = T_i - T_{i-1} - (F_{i-1,x} + F_{i,x})\,\frac{l_i}{2}\sin\varphi_i \\ +(F_{i-1,y} + F_{i,y})\,\frac{l_i}{2}\cos\varphi_i \quad (2)$$

Muscles are modeled as springs directly connected to the sides of the links. In an adaptation of Hooke's law, the force exerted by each spring on its associated joint is determined not only by the local curvature of the body but also linearly by the output of the motoneurons in the associated segments. As in [5], torque is defined as

$$T_i = \alpha\,(M_L - M_R) + \beta\,(M_L + M_R + \gamma)\,(\varphi_{i+1} - \varphi_i) + \delta\,(\dot{\varphi}_{i+1} - \dot{\varphi}_i)$$

where M_L and M_R are left and right motoneuron activity and the parameters α (=3 N mm), β (=0.3 N mm), γ (=10) and δ (=30 N mm ms) are set as in [5].

Speed of motion through water in our case is sufficiently high that we only account for inertial water force which is proportional to the square of the speed:

$$W = \rho v^2 \frac{A}{2} C$$

where ρ is the fluid density, v object speed, A area parallel to movement and C drag coefficient. The abbreviation $\lambda = \rho\frac{A}{2}C$ is made in [5], together with the simplification $W = W_\perp + W_\parallel = v_\perp^2\lambda_\perp + v_\parallel^2\lambda_\parallel$ and values of $\lambda_\perp$ and $\lambda_\parallel$ for links.

Body segments are constrained such that for adjacent segments, joints for the facing sides must be in the same position (ie., the links stay joined together). Joint position is expressed in terms of x_i, y_i and φ_i for $i \in \{1, \ldots, n-1\}$, so

$$x_i + \frac{l_i}{2}\cos\varphi_i = x_{i+1} - \frac{l_{i+1}}{2}\cos\varphi_{i+1} \\ y_i + \frac{l_i}{2}\sin\varphi_i = y_{i+1} - \frac{l_{i+1}}{2}\sin\varphi_{i+1} \quad (3)$$

Equations (2) and (3) form a differential–algebraic equation (DE) system [5] typical of non-minimal coordinate systems that can be numerically integrated.

3 Implementation

The neural and physical models described above were implemented in C++. The numerical solver collection from the GNU Scientific Library [6] integrated the DEs. A rendering program, to represent output of the simulation graphically, was implemented in Python using PyOpenGL [7]. The program accepted an output logfile generated by the simulation containing system state at 5 ms intervals, and rendered this state both to a monitor window and to file. The files were later combined into a video using mencoder [8]. While the simulator and renderer can be run without the intermediate step of a logfile, keeping a permanent record of simulations is advantageous, as are the abilities to run the simulation without rendering overhead and to re–render simulations.

Embedded 8th order Runge–Kutta Prince–Dormand method with 9th order error estimate (rk8pd) was selected as the numerical solver for the DE system. Also, rather than selecting a fixed step size an adaptive solving controller was used, that takes a variable number of smaller substeps, with backtracking, to keep solution error under a set maximum error limit. We set the error limit to 10^{-3}, which is the largest error rate resulting in acceptable precision for simulations of 100000 ms. This error limit should be decreased for longer simulations.

The physical and neural models were combined into one system of DEs for solution, a departure from Ijspeert [2] where the systems were separate. Ijspeert's physical solver used a step length of 0.5 ms, 1/10th that of the step length of his neural solver, presumably because the neural system behaves in a more regular way and is thus less subject to accumulated error, allowing larger solving steps to be taken and thus reducing runtime. But when an adaptive step–size controller is used this arrangement is detrimental to performance. Input from the neural system is constant for 10 steps of the physical system, then abruptly changes, resulting in "sawtooth" input. At every "tooth", the adaptive controller responds to the sudden change by backtracking and taking extremely small solving steps. For this reason a combined system was constructed, so the neural and physical models are solved at the same rate. This is faster, although more steps are taken through the neural system than are perhaps required.

4 Typical model behavior

We describe a typical simulation in which left and right brainstem inputs are set to 0.67, a suitable level for forward movement. Quantitative results vary with excitation level but general system behavior is the same. A 10 s simulation takes 620 s to run on an AMD 1800 CPU.

As simulation begins, both ends of the lamprey curl inward to the left (Fig. 2). As they start to uncurl at 100 ms, a wave forms along the body and is evident at 150 ms. This wave mirrors in place, then at 300 ms starts to propagate down the body. For the first 750 ms the wave propagates without causing forward motion, but then the lamprey begins to move and at 1000 ms has travelled

70 mm. At 2000 ms, the lamprey travels at 385 mm s^{-1}, 80% of its steady–state speed. It reaches 466 mm s^{-1} at 6000 ms and maintains this indefinitely (Fig. 3).

The body is about 1.5 wavelengths long as the initial propagation forms, but at steady state this becomes two wavelengths as segment co–ordination improves. Amplitude of the tailward wave peak is about three times that of the headward, partly because of the lesser mass in the tailward segments, and partly because they are at the end of the fish. Steady–state undulation frequency resulting from the given brainstem excitation is just over 6 Hz. Swimming speed and characteristics observed are similar to those observed by [2].

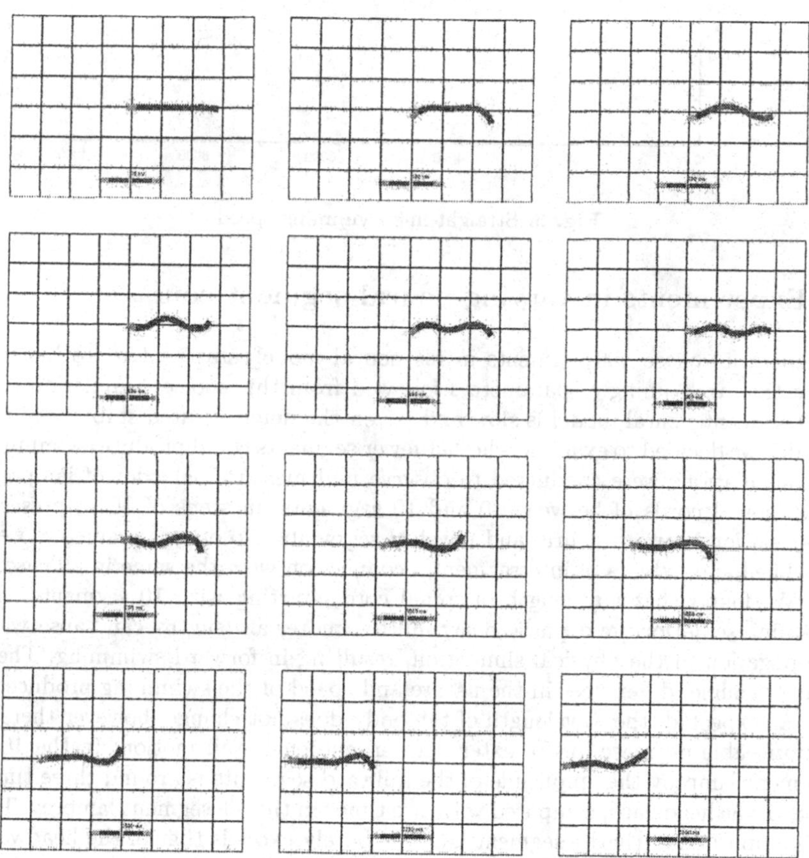

Fig. 2. Straight-line swimming behavior. Gridlines are 100 mm apart. Lamprey is in middle of each image with (fixed) input from left and right brainstem below. Images taken at 10, 100, 150, 200, 300, 500 ms, then every 250 ms.

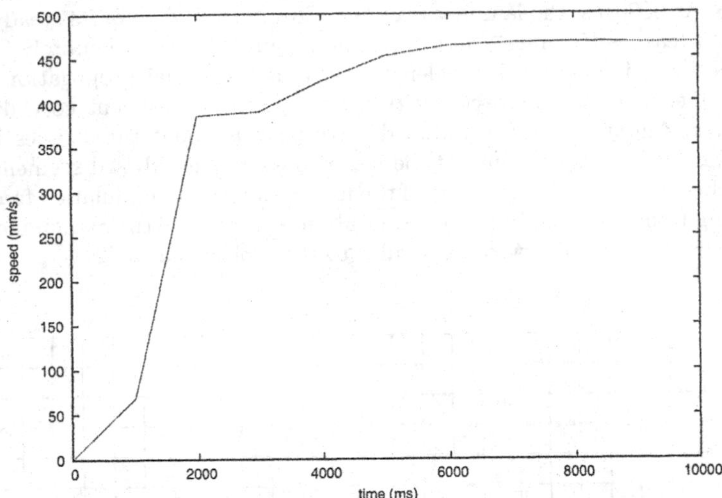

Fig. 3. Straight-line swimming speed

5 Experiments in varying neural segment count

Ekeberg [5] chose 100 segments in his neural model, staying true to biology. Selection and tuning of parameters followed from this choice. Simulation of a 100 segment neural model is slow and, given the demonstrated stability of the model, we decided to examine whether fewer segments could produce swimming. So, simulations were conducted to observe and measure behavior of lampreys with spinal cords of between 90 and 10 segments, in steps of 10 to preserve the relation between neural and physical segments. No other parameters were modified and extents of intersegmental connection were the same in all cases.

We found that any length of spinal cord, starting with 10 segments, can sustain oscillations and phase delay. Furthermore, all lengths can cause wave propagation in the physical simulation, resulting in forward swimming. There are, of course, differences in the nature and speed of the swimming produced.

As expected, the wavelength of the body does not change; however there is a noticeable decrease in the extent of perpendicular tail motion. In the 100–segment lamprey the amplitude of the tailward segments is around three times that of the headward, compared with two times in the 50–segment lamprey. The tail amplitude of the 10–segment lamprey barely exceeds that of the headward segments. At this length propagation of a traveling wave is only just perceptible, with most of the activity being the standing–wave inversion characteristic of the startup behavior of the 100–segment lamprey.

Shortening the lamprey spine causes a proportional decrease in swimming speed. Because the simulation exhibits different behaviors at startup before reaching steady state, swimming speed was measured by recording the time taken for the lamprey to swim 15, 30, 50, 200 and 400 mm. The 50 mm milestone represents significant forward motion and can be regarded as the boundary between initial conditions and steady state. The 400 mm milestone gives a reasonable measure of steady swimming speed independent of starting conditions.

Fig. 4 shows the time for lampreys of different segments to reach the distance milestones. With one exception, the swimming speed of each lamprey is reasonably proportional to the reduction in segments. Regarding the startup behavior of the lampreys, it can be seen that while the 30–segment lamprey reaches the 15 mm milestone earlier than expected, and the 40– and 50–segment lampreys reach it later, this early lead has almost vanished by 50 mm.

The graph clearly shows the unexpectedly small length of time for the 20–segment lamprey to reach steady state. It passes the 15 mm and 30 mm marks ahead of the 100–segment lamprey, and reaches 50 mm in equal time. And while it takes 2.5 times as long to pass 400 mm, this is twice as fast as we would estimate from the behavior of the other lampreys. A 20–segment spine seems very compatible with the 10–segment body, for reasons not yet fully understood. Investigation of this high affinity has the potential to yield significant insight into the relationship between the neural system and the body, and bears exploration.

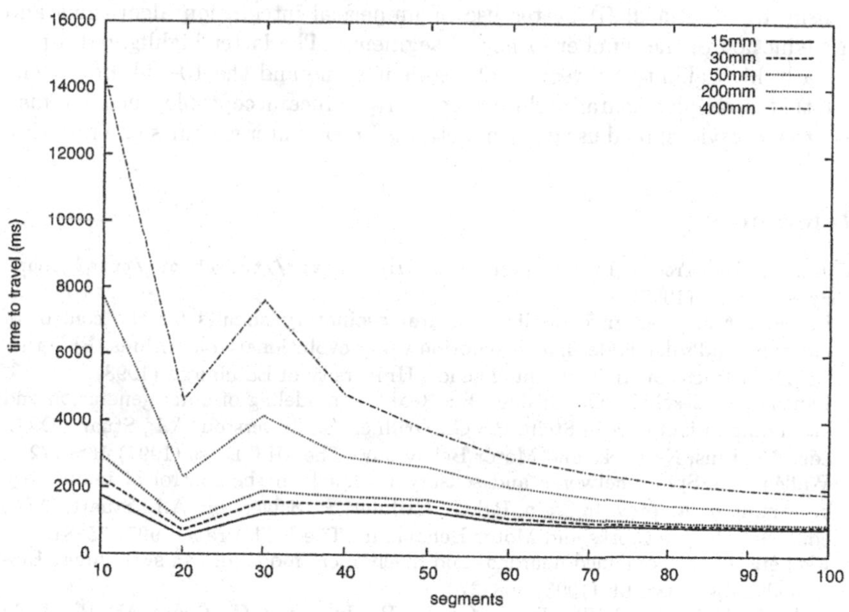

Fig. 4. Time for 10- to 100- segment lampreys to reach distance milestones

Most of the execution time is spent in the neural simulation and is essentially linear with the number of segments. This is because there are 24 DEs per neural segment compared with 3 per body link giving a total of $24s + 3b$ DEs for a lamprey with s neural segments and b body links. Thus, reducing the number of neural segments results in a corresponding reduction in execution time. A 1000 ms simulation takes 78 CPU seconds for the 100–segment lamprey and 16 s for the 20–segment. Execution time for the 10–segment lamprey is 13 s, allowing us to estimate the time spent in the physical simulation as around 9 s.

The number of neural segments, and the intersegmental connectivity scheme, in Ekeberg's original simulation are well–chosen and result in a model that is both similar in layout to the biological lamprey and in behavior. By reducing the number of segments while keeping the same connection scheme and the same physical parameters, we are simulating a shorter lamprey stretched into a longer, more flexible body. That this arrangement can propagate a traveling wave and generate forward motion is additional confirmation of the model stability.

6 Conclusion

We describe the design and implementation of a simulation of the neural pathways and physical body of a lamprey realized in a system of DEs. Two approaches for increasing simulation speed with graceful degradation of biological realism are identified: (i) better use of numerical integration algorithms and (ii) reduction of the number of neural segments. The latter highlighted a particularly high affinity between a 20–segment spine and the 10–link body. The fact that a simpler neural architecture can produce acceptable behavior may lead to more widespread use of such methods in computer graphics and robotics.

References

1. Janvier, P.: Tree of Life: Hyperoartia. URL: `http://tolweb.org/tree?group=Hyperoartia` (1997)
2. Ijspeert, A.J.: Design of artificial neural oscillatory circuits for the control of lamprey- and salamander-like locomotion using evolutionary algorithms. PhD thesis, Department of Artificial Intelligence, University of Edinburgh (1998)
3. Lansner, A., Ekeberg, Ö., Grillner, S.: Realistic modeling of burst generation and swimming in lamprey. In Stein, P.S.G., Grillner, S., Selverston, A.I., Stuart, D.G., eds.: Neurons, Networks and Motor Behaviour. The MIT Press (1997) 165–172
4. Wallén, P.: Spinal networks and sensory feedback in the control of undulatory swimming in lamprey. In Stein, P.S.G., Grillner, S., Selverston, A.I., Stuart, D.G., eds.: Neurons, Networks and Motor Behaviour. The MIT Press (1997) 75–81
5. Ekeberg, Ö.: A combined neuronal and mechanical model of fish swimming. Biological Cybernetics **69** (1993) 363–374
6. Galassi, M., Davies, J., Theiler, J., Gough, B., Jungman, G., Booth, M., Rossi, F.: GNU Scientific Library Reference Manual. 2nd edn. Network Theory Ltd. (2003)
7. Fletcher, M.C., Liebscher, R.: PyOpenGL – the Python OpenGL binding. URL: `http://pyopengl.sourceforge.net/` (2005)
8. Bérczi, G.: Encoding with MEncoder. URL: `http://www.mplayerhq.hu/DOCS/HTML/en/mencoder.html` (2005)

Towards a case-based reasoning approach to analyze road accidents

Valentina Ceausu[1]
Sylvie Desprès[1]

René Descartes University
45 rue des Saints Pres
75270 Paris cedex 06
valentina.ceausu@math-info.univ-paris5.fr
sd@math-info.univ-paris5.Fr

Abstract. In this paper the prototype of a system designed to analyze road accidents is presented. The analysis is carried out in order to recognize within accident reports general mechanisms of road accidents that represent prototypes of road accidents. Case Based Reasoning (CBR) is the chosen problem solving paradigm. Natural language documents and semi-structured documents are used to build the cases of our system, which creates a difficulty. To cope with this difficulty we propose approaches integrating semantic resources. Hence, an ontology of accidentology and a terminology of road accidents are used to build cases. The alignment of two resources supports the retrieval process. A data processing model, based on models of accidentology, is proposed to represent the cases of the system. This paper presents the architecture of ACCTOS (ACCident TO Scenarios), a case based reasoning system prototype. The model to represent the cases is introduced and the phases of the case based reasoning cycle are detailed.

1 Introduction

In this paper the prototype of a system designed to analyze road accidents is presented. The analysis is carried out in order to recognize, within accident reports, general mechanisms of road accidents that represent prototypes of road accidents.
Case based reasoning is the chosen problem solving paradigm. Cased based reasoning solves a new problem by re-using a collection of already solved problem. The problem to be solved is called the target case. The collection of already solved problems make up the case base, an important feature of any case based reasoning system. The reasoning cycle of a case based reasoning system is composed of phases aiming to: (i)create the target case; (ii) retrieve cases of the case base which are similar to the target case; (iii) adapt solutions of some of these cases in in order to propose a solution for the target case.
Natural language documents and semi-structured documents are used to build our system cases. To cope with the difficulty of natural language, we proposed

Please use the following format when citing this chapter:

Ceausu, V., Desprès, S., 2006, in IFIP International Federation for Information Processing, Volume 218, Professional Practice in Artificial Intelligence, eds. J. Debenham, (Boston: Springer), pp. 257–264.

approaches integrating semantic resources. An ontology of accidentology and a terminology of road accidents are used to build descriptions of cases. The alignment of two resources supports the retrieval process. Based on accidentology models, a data-processing model is proposed to represent the cases of the system.
The outline of this paper is as follows: first, the architecture of ACCTOS (ACCident TO Scenarios) is presented and the model proposed to represent cases of the system is introduced. Then, phases of the case based reasoning cycle are detailed. Finally, conclusions are drawn and future works are suggested.

2 Architecture and resources of the system

To present the architecture, we use a division into modules, where each of the module addresses a different phase of the reasoning cycle (see Fig. 1).

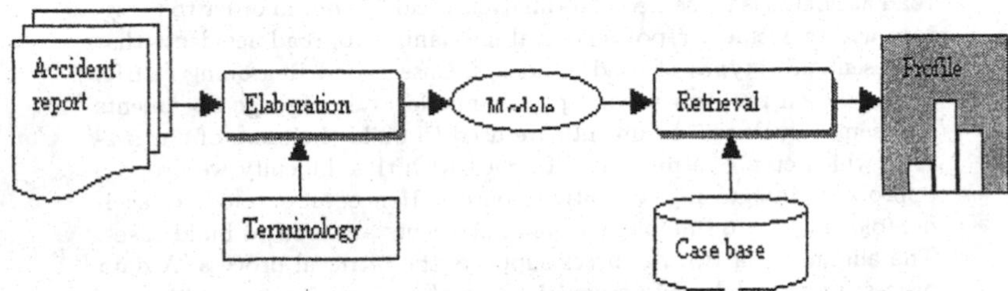

Fig. 1. System architecture

Resources of the system
ACCTOS exploits two types of documents -accident reports and accident scenarios -to create cases.
Accident reports are documents written by the police. They include structured paragraphs describing An accident actors and context and natural language paragraphs explaining what happened in the accident (written with the help of witnesses, people involved in the accident or policemen). Accident scenarios are documents created by road safety researchers. They are prototypes of road accidents and present in a general way facts and causal relations between different phases leading to collision. An accident scenario describes an accident as a sequence of four situations (or phases): the driving situation, the accident situation, the emergency situation and the shock situation. Prevention measures aiming to improve road safety are provided for each accident scenario. A first study led by the department *Mechanisms of accidents* of INRETS (Institut national de recherche sur les Transport et leur Sécurité) established a first collection of accident scenarios involving pedestrians. These scenarios and

assigned proposals will be used to build the case base.
The input of the system is a set of reports of accident that occurred on the same road section. Accidents are analyzed from electronic accident reports. The *PACTOL* tool (Centre d'Etudes Techniques de l'Equipement de Rouen) made the reports anonymous. An electronic accident report is a semi-structured document containing structured paragraphs and natural language paragraphs. Structured paragraphs contain variables describing the accident. The variables correspond to humans and vehicles involved in the accident.The accident context is also specified by variables. Text paragraphs describe what happened in the accident according to several points of view: the police (synthesis of the facts), the people involved (declarations) and the witnesses.
From each accident report, a model is built by the *Elaboration* module. This model is used by the *Retrieval* module of the system in order to query the case base. The initial case based of ACCTOS is created from accident scenarions. As a result, correspondences between the initial accident report and accident scenarios are established. A correspondence is constituted by an assignment (*accident report, accident scenario*) and a trust assessment.
The output of the system is a profile of scenarios. A profile of scenarios is composed of several scenarios, where a coefficient is assigned to each scenario of the profile, reflecting its weighting within the profile.
The first module implements the authoring the case phase. Retrieval phase is done by the second module. Further on the model proposed to represent cases of the system and phases of case based reasoning cycle are presented.

3 Description of cases

A data-processing model is proposed, based on accidentology models (see [5]), to represent cases of the system. A case is described by two types of elements: global variables and agents.
Global variables specify the number of agents involved in an accident, the environment in which the accident occurred - such as main road or secondary road - and the accident context (by day, in intersection, etc.).
A human involved in an accident and his vehicle represent an agent (see tab.1). This representation allows us to cope with difficulties related to metonymy between the human involved in the accident and his vehicle. It also allows us to treat the particular case of pedestrians. Each agent is defined by two components - human and vehicle - and by his evolution in the accident. A domain term (*ie: driver, car*) and attributes (*ie: age*) are assigned to each component of an agent. Agent evolution is specified by a set of relations describing interactions: between an agents' components; between an agent and other agents involved in the accident.

Table 1. Components of an agent

Agent	Human	Vehicle	Attributes	Evolution
Agent 1	Pedestrian	no vehicle	age: 60	crossing; running
Agent 2	Driver	Car	age: 35	moving; turning to

4 Authoring the case

The scope of this phase is to create the problem to be solved, also called the target case.The model presented above is used to represente the target case. Each target case is created from an accident report. Both the structured and the natural language paragraphs of an accident report are exploited to create the target case.

Environnement identification

An accident report is a semi-structured document. Data about people and vehicles involved in an accident and about the environment and context of the accident are stored in specific structures. Based on these structures we have designed automatic procedures to retrieve valuable information.

Identification of agents

To describe agents involved in accidents we need to :

- Identify the terms assigned to their components;
- Identify the values of their attributes;
- Identify the agents'evolution;

Terms of components and values of attributes are identified automatically thanks to the accident report structure.
Agents' evolution is identified thanks to natural language paragraphs of accident reports: declarations, testimonies, police syntheses. Agent evolution is expressed by a set of domain verbs identified within these paragraphs.
Text mining techniques and a terminology of road accidents are used jointly to identify the evolution of each agent.
A terminology represents terms of a given field and relations between those terms. Relations are expressed by verbs and, usually, accepts two arguments: *Relation(domain, range)*, where *Relation* is a verb of the field, and *domain* and *range* are terms of the field.
For instance, *diriger-vers(véhicule, direction)* is a relation of the domain. We used a terminology created from 250 reports of accidents that occurred in and around the Lille region. This terminology is expressed in OWL (see [15]).
Text mining techniques are also employed to identify agent evolution. An approach based on information extraction using pre-defined patterns is adopted.

We used lexical patterns to extract information. A lexical pattern is a set of lexical categories. For example *Noun, Noun* or *Verb, Preposition, Noun* are lexical patterns. In order to identify instances of patterns, natural language paragraphs are tagged using TreeTagger ([10]). A pattern recognition algorithm (see [2]) allows us to identify associations of words matching predefined patterns. The output of this algorithm is shown below :

Lexical Patterns and Corresponding word regroupings :
Noun, Preposition, Noun: groupe de piéton (group of pedestrians)
Noun, Preposition, Adjective: trottoir de droite (right hand side pavement)
Verb, Preposition, Noun: diriger vers place (direct to square)

We defined a set of verbal patterns able to highlight relations of the domain. A set R of verbal relations is extracted. Instances of those patterns could represent relations of the field, such as *diriger-vers (direct to)*, but also meaningless word regroupings, such as *diriger 306 (direct 306)*. They need to be validated and attached to agents of the accident. To do so, each agent $a(t_h, t_v)$, having t_h and t_v as components, queries the terminology in order to identify relations that have one of his components as arguments. The result is:

$$R_{agent}(t_h, t_v) = R_{resource}(t_h) \bigcup R_{resource}(t_v)$$

where $R_{resource}(t_h)$ and $R_{resource}(t_v)$ are relations of terminology having t_h, respectively t_v as arguments. By intersecting R_{agent} and R the evolution of an agent is identified as:

$$Evolution_{agent} = R_{agent} \bigcap R$$

Relations of R that are not modeled by the terminology are ignored. For each agent, the evolution is identified as a set of verbal relations extracted from the accident report and validated by the terminology of road accidents.

5 Building the initial case base

The case base is an important feature of a case based reasoning system. the case base is composed of couples *Problem, Solution*, that are called source cases.
A set of accident scenarios is used to build the initial case base of the system. The accident scenario represents the *Problem*; measures of preventions assigned to the scenario represent the *Solution*.
An **ontology of accidentogoly**(see [4]) supports descriptions of source cases. This ontology was built from expert knowledge, texts of the field and accident scenarios. It models the concepts of the field and the relations that hold between them. Ontology concepts are structured in thre main classes: the human, the vehicle and the environment. A domain term and attributes are assigned

to each concept. Concepts are connected by different types of relations. IS-A relations build the hierarchy of domain concepts. Verbal relations that describe interactions between concepts are also modeled.
An editor of scenarios was developed to build source cases. The editor integrates the ontology of accidentology. It allows users to describe each accident scenario by choosing the appropriate concepts and relations of the ontology. The editor also allows users to assign to each concept or relation a coefficient indicating its importance. Importance coefficients are established thanks to linguistic markers. Homogeneous descriptions of cases are created by integrating the ontology.

6 Retrieval process

The retrieval process aims to retrieve source cases similar to the target case. Already solved problems similar to the target case are identified. Therefore, a solution to the target case can be proposed by adapting solutions of those problems. We propose a retrieval approach supported by the alignment of two semantic resources : the terminology and the ontology.
Ontology alignment can be described as follows: given two resources each describing a set of discrete entities (which can be concepts, relations, etc.), find correspondences that hold between these entities. In our case, a function $Sim(E_o, E_t)$ is used allowing us to estimate similarity between entities of the ontology, E_o, and entities of the terminology, E_t, where an entity could be either a concept or a relation. Based on this, for T, a target case, two steps are needed to retrieve similar source cases.
(1) The first step is based on case base indexation. Global variables are used to index the case base. The values of the global variables of the target case are taken into account to identify a set of source cases. The result is a set of source cases having the same context as the target case and involving the same number of agents.
(2)A voting process is used to improve this first selection. The vote is done by each target case agent to express the degree of resemblance between himself and agents of a source case. A note is given by each target case agent to every source case. This note is given by taking into accounts agents' components and theirs evolution. A first similarity measure proposed is given by:

$$Sim(a_i, a_j) = SimComponent(a_i, a_j) + SimEvolution(a_i, a_j)$$
$$\text{if } SimComponent(a_i, a_j) \neq 0 \text{ , otherwise } Sim(a_i, a_j) = 0$$

where a_i is an agent of the target case and a_j is an agent of a source case.

$SimComponent(a_i, a_j)$ expresses the similarity among the agents taking into account component similarities :

$$SimComponent(a_i, a_j) = ch_j * sim(H_i, H_j) + cv_j * sim(V_i, V_j)$$

, where ch_j and cv_j are importance coefficients established for the source case, and values of $sim(H_i, H_j)$ and $sim(V_i, V_j)$ are given by the alignment of the two resources.
Evolution similarity expresses resemblances between of two agents' evolutions :

$$SimEvolution(a_i, a_j) = \frac{\sum_r c_r * sim(rSource_r, rTarget_r)}{\sum_r c_r}$$

Coefficients c_r expresses the importance of $rSource_r$ relation for the considered source case. Values of $sim(rSource_r, rTarget_r)$ are given by alignment of the two resources.
Each agent of the target case evaluates his resemblance to agents of the source case by using the presented approach. A similarity vector is obtained. The note $note_i$ given by the $agent_i$ to the source case is the maximum value of this similarity vector. Based on notes given by agents, the similarity between he target case and a source case is estimated by the average value:

$$Sim(target, source) = \frac{\sum_{i=1}^{N_a} note_i}{N_a}$$

where $note_i$ is the note granted by the agent $agent_i$, and N_a is the number of agents of the considered target case. Indexing the case base allows a fast identification of source cases that are similar to the target case. By voting, the most similar cases are selected among the cases retrieved by the first selection. The retrieval process is driven by the description of source cases whose importance coefficients are taken into account by similarity measures.

7 Conclusion and future work

This paper presents the prototype of a system designed to analyze road accidents. Case based reasoning is the adopted problem solving paradigm. Cases of the system are created from semi-structured documents provided by two different communities : accident reports written by the police and accident scenarios created by road safety researchers. Semantic resources are used to cope with heterogeneity and natural language representations. A terminology of road accidents supports the authoring the case phase. Description of source cases is supported by the ontology of road accidents. The alignment of a road accident terminology and ontology enables the retrieval process.
This system is under development. There now remains to implement the proposed approaches, evaluate the system and make it better.
To do so, a few lines of research are already considered, as for example : enriching the text mining techniques so as to improve the authoring the case phase ant obtain more precise descriptions of target cases.

References

1. R. Bergmann , On the use of Taxonomies for Representing Case Features and Local Similarity Measures, 6th German Workshop on Case-Based Reasoning, 1998
2. V. Ceausu and S. Després , Towards a Text Mining Driven Approach for Terminology Construction, 7th International conference on Terminology and Knowledge Engineering, 2005
3. Cherfi and A. Napoli and Y. Toussaint, Vers une méthodologie de fouille de textes s'appuyant sur l'extraction de motifs fréquents et de règles d'association, onférence francophone sur l'apprentissage automatique, 2003
4. S. Després, Contribution la conception de méthodes et d'outils pour la gestion des connaissances, Université René Descartes, Paris, October, 2002
5. D. Fleury, Sécurité et urbanisme. La prise en compte de la sécurité routière dans l'aménagement urbain, Presses de l'Ecole Nationale des Ponts et chaussées, Paris, November, 1998
6. K.M. Gupta and D.W. Aha and N. Sandhu, Exploiting taxonomic and causal relations in conversational case retrieval, Sixth European Conference on Case-Based Reasoning, 2002
7. M. Klein, Combining and relating ontologies: an analysis of problems solutions, Workshop on ontologies and Information sharing, IJCAI , 2001
8. U. Hahn and K. Schnattinger, Towards text knowledge engineering, American Association for Artificial Intelligence Conference , 1998
9. P. Seguela, Adaptation semi-automatique d'une base de marqueurs de relations sémantiques sur des corpus spécialisés, Terminologie et Intelligence Artificielle, 1999
10. , H. Schmid, Probabilistic part-of-speech tagging using decision trees, International Conference on New Methods in Language Processing, 1994
11. B. Smyth and P. McClave, Similarity vs. diversity, 4th International Conference on Case-Based Reasoning, 1994
12. R. Weber and D.W. Aha and N. Sandhu and H. Munoz-Avila, A textual case-based reasoning framework for knowledge management applications, 4th Ninth German Workshop on Case-Based Reasoning, 2001
13. N. Wiratunga and S. Craw and S. Massie, Index Driven Selective Sampling for CBR, 5th International Conference on Case-Based Reasoning, 2003
14. N. Wiratunga and I. Koychev and S. Massie, Feature Selection and Generalisation for Retrieval of Textual Cases, 7th European Conference on Case-Based Reasoning, 2004
15. World Wide Web Consortium (W3C), OWL - Web Ontology Language,

Solving the Short Run Economic Dispatch Problem Using Concurrent Constraint Programming

Juan Francisco Díaz F.[1], Iván Javier Romero[1], and Carlos Lozano[2]

[1] Universidad del Valle, Cali, Colombia
Escuela de Ingeniería de Sistemas y Computación
{jdiaz,ivromero}@univalle.edu.co
[2] Escuela de Ingeniería Eléctrica y Electrónica
clozano@univalle.edu.co

Abstract. This paper shows a description of an application for solving the Short-Run Economic Dispatch Problem. This problem consists of searching the active power hourly schedule generated in electrical networks in order to meet the demand at minimum cost. The solution cost is associatted to the inmediate costs of thermal units and the future costs of hydropower stations. The application was implemented using Mozart with real-domain constraints and a hybrid model among real (XRI) and finite domains (FD). The implemented tool showed promising results since the found solution costs were lower than those found in the literature for the same kind of problems. On the other hand, in order to test the tool against real problems, a system with data from real networks was implemented and the solution found was good enough in terms of time efficiency and accuracy. Also, this paper shows the usability of Mozart language to model real combinatory problems.

1 Introduction

The Hydrothermal Economic Dispatch Problem has as one of its purposes to generate the active power supply schedule for generating units in an electrical system in order to meet the demand at minimum cost. This can be seen as an optimization constraint satisfaction problem (*OCSP*) with a combinatory space of solutions.

An OCSP is defined by a set of variables, their domains, a series of constraints among them and an objective function to be optimized. The general objective is to assign values to all variables in such a way that they meet all the constraints among them and the objective function evaluated for these values be optimized. The Concurrent Constraint Programming (CCP) approach is widely used for solving this type of problems.

Solving an OCSP using CCP languages, consists of two steps: modeling the problem (logical specification) and specifying the search strategy for finding its solutions. Modeling involves basically writing in the con-

Please use the following format when citing this chapter:

Díaz F., J.F., Romero, I.J., Lozano, C., 2006, in IFIP International Federation for Information Processing, Volume 218, Professional Practice in Artificial Intelligence, eds. J. Debenham, (Boston: Springer), pp. 265–274.

current constraint programming language the variables, their domains and the constraints among them.

In the CCP paradigm a procedure, called a propagator, is associated to each constraint. This procedure tries to reduce the domain of the variables associated to it (i.e. it discards values of the domains of the variables that can not be part of any solution.)

The collection of propagators acting on the variables may cause a domain to become empty. This means that the problem specification is contradictory and so, there is no solution. A propagator is considered solved when any combination of values in their domains is a solution. Propagators may instead reach a fixed point state in which nothing new about the variables can be deduced (i.e. the domains cannot be further reduced). In that case, a search stage is necessary.

Specifying the search strategy consists in defining the criteria for the search when the propagation has taken computation to a fixed point state in which undetermined variables (i.e. those having domains with more than one value) remain. The main idea is to add to the current fixed point state one or more constraints that allow the propagation process to advance a little bit more (i.e. allowing it to reduce some domain of some variable). Since these constraints are not part of the problem constraints, it is also necessary to explore what happens if the opposite constraints are added to the fixed point state. In that way all possibilities are taken into account and no solution is missed. The process of adding these new constraints is called distribution.

The search strategy specifies the constraints that must be added and the order in which the searching process is carried out; whatever they are, adding them creates two new search states. In each of them, the propagation process is applied again until a new fixed point state is reached and the procedure is repeated.

If all variables are determined, a solution (not necessarily optimal) has been found. The latter is taken, a constraint saying that the next solution must be better than the last solution found is added, and a searching process for a new solution is started. This procedure is repeated until the optimal (or near optimal) solution is found or the systems resources, time, memory be exhausted. Otherwise, if, after exploring all possibilities, all states are contradictory states, then the problem does not have a solution.

The efficiency of the search is directly linked to the number of explored states. The more the domains of the variables in the propagation stage are efficiently reduced, the less states are generated and, therefore the problem is solved more quickly. The number of generated states also depends on the distribution strategy.

Searching for the best solution in the CCP model uses a branch and bound technique. A valuation (in this case, the cost of generation) of a previously found solution provides an upper bound. A constraint asserting that the next solution must have a better valuation than the upper bound is then added. This constraint has also an associated propagator that further reduces the search tree.

Using the CCP paradigm thus in general leads to smaller search trees. Furthermore, the tree rarely has to be traversed exhaustively, even when all possible solutions must be computed.
In this work, the Concurrent Constraint Programming (CCP) technique is used to search for approximate solutions to the *Economic Dispatch Problem* by using Mozart, a concurrent constraint programming language.
Mozart language was used because the specification of the search strategy can be done by the programmers in a very high level reflecting easily the intuition of the expert in the subject or problem to be solved. This makes Mozart suitable for programming the intelligent, reasonable strategies defined by the experts.
The developed application was used to solve problems found in both the literature and real life, with excellent perspective related to time efficiency. However, the application shows a high use of RAM memory. The results found allows to be optimistic about real problems being solved by this technique.
This paper is organized as follows: Section 2 makes an introduction to the economic dispatch problem; in Section 3, the proposed model in natural lenguage and its implementation in Mozart are described. In Section 4 the implemented distribution strategies are described. In Section 5 the solved problems results given by the developed application are shown, and finally, in Section 6 the conclusions and future work are ennumerated.

2 The Economic Dispatch Problem

The purpose of the power system economic operation is to use the energy resources (thermal, hydro, solar, wind, among others) available for energy generation in an optimal manner such that the electricity demand is met at minimum cost and under certain degree of reliability, quality and security [1]. Among the generating power units that we might find in a power system are: thermal power plants that work with fossil fuel, run-of-river power plants, hydro power plants and chain plants.

Solution Cost. The solution cost is due mainly to the sum of all dams future costs at the end of the study and, the inmediate costs of the thermal power plants for each of the study analisys stages. When the stored water rises, less water is used for energy production in the correspondig stage; as a consequence, more thermal generation is required, and the inmediate costs are higher. In turn, the future cost functions are associated to the thermal generation costs from the following stage until the final stage of planning[2, 3]. When the systems thermal power plants operate at the same incremental costs, the power production cost is the lower [5].

3 The Model and its implementation in Mozart

This section shows a general model description in natural language as well as the transformations of some of the mathematical equations into Mozart.

3.1 Modelling in natural language

Objective Function. The objective function is composed by a sum of all inmediate costs for each of the period study stages; these inmediate costs are composed by the thermal units production costs in each of the operating areas, plus curtailment plant costs, plus the water releases costs for each of the areas with hydropower plants. Also, the dam's future costs from each area is added to the objective function.
Demand Constraint. The power demand for each area should be met. The amount of power that cannot be met in an area is represented by a curtailment plant. The produced power by an area to meet its demand, plus the transmission line losses is composed by the amount of power generated by its power plants, plus the imported power from other areas, less the exported power to other areas. The curtailment plants are ficticious plants used to guarantee the solution feasibility when it is not possible to meet the demand.
Units Operating Constraint. The power produced by both hydroplants with dams and run-of-river power plants is limited by the generator turbine efficiency. The thermal power plants can only operate between upper and lower boundaries.
Dams Dynamics. The storage volume of water in a dam at the end of each study period stage should be equivalent to the stored volumen at beggining, plus the water inflows due to tributary rivers and the discharges from upstream reservoirs, less the flow rate through the turbine, less the spillage discharge rate, less the leakages and evaporations.
Constraints over Run-of-River Power Plants. The power produced by this kind of power plant is due mainly to the water inflows due to both the tributary rivers and the discharges from upstream reservoirs. There must be a correpondence between the amount of inflows and the amount of produced power, with the discharges and spillages from the upstream power plants.
Importing and Exporting Constraints. The main constraint imposed over the interarea transactions is related to the limitation on the transmission lines. What an importing is for one area, it is exporting for other and so, there is a limit on exporting due to the transmission line limitations. Also, the amount of power imported by an area a_1 should be equal to the exported power from area a_2.

3.2 Implementation of the model in the Mozart language

Figure 1 shows the implementation of the dam storage volume Equation (2) at the end of a specific period of time, using Mozart language. The description of both model decision variables and variables with known values for Equation (2) are presented in Table 1. It is possible to notice the expresivity of the Mozart language for easily translating this kind of formula.

Table 1. Elements of the Equation (2)

$UCH_{t,r,m}$	Undammed water done by the hydro plant m in area r during stage t (decision variable)
$SCH_{t,r,m}$	Releases done by hydro plant m in area r during stage t (decision variable)
$PCH_{r,i}$	Set of hydro plants upstream directly connected with hydroelectric plant i in area r (known value)
$V_{t,i,r}$	Volume of stored water in the hydroelectric plant dam i from area r to the final period of time t (decision variable)
$A_{t,r,i}$	Water streams per hour entering to the dam in hydro plant i in area r in stage t (known value)
$S_{t,i,r}$	Volume of released water per hour by hydro plant with dam i in area r during stage t (decision variable)
$Ph_{t,r,i}$	Delivered Power per hour by Hydro Power Plant with Dam i from area r in stage t (decision variable)
$\rho_{r,i}$	Hydro Power Plant i production coefficient in area r
$f_{t,i,r}$	Leakings in dam per hour by hydro plant i in area r (known value)
$e_{t,i,r}$	Steaming in dam per hour by hydro plant i in area r (known value)
dur	Duration of the stage in hours

$$IU = \sum_{m \in PCH_{r,i}} [UCH_{t,r,m} + SCH_{t,r,m}] \tag{1}$$

$$V_{t,r,i} = V_{(t-1),r,i} + \left(A_{t,r,i} + IU - \frac{Ph_{t,r,i}}{\rho_{r,i}} - S_{t,r,i} - f_{r,i} - e_{r,i} \right) \cdot dur \ \forall t \forall r \forall i \tag{2}$$

4 Distribution Strategies Implementation

All the distribution strategies are based mainly on two functions, *Order* and *Value*. The function *Order* decides which is the next variable to be distributed, comparing among pairs of variables from a list of those that have not been determined yet. The function *Value* decides what value to assign to the chosen variable in *Order*. Distribution strategies for both thermal units and hydro units were developed.

Distribution strategies for thermal units Two distribution strategies were developed for thermal units. The first deals with the first-order

```
for T in 2..NPeriods do
   CArea={MakeTuple c NAreas} in
   for R in 1..NAreas do
      ConstHydro={MakeTuple c RArea.R.nHydroPlant} in
      for I in 1..RArea.R.nHydroPlant do
         Spill HydroPower VolDam IU
      in
         %%Domain declaration for Spill HydroPower
         %%VolDam ...
         IU = {InflowUpstream T R I}
         {XRI.Consistency
          eq(VolDam
             plus(
                CPeriod.(T-1).area.R.rHydro.I.volDam
                times(
                   sub(plus(RArea.R.rHydro.hydrol.I.T
                            IU)
                       plus(
                          divide(HydroPower
                                 RArea.R.rHydro.cf.I)
                          Spill RArea.R.rHydro.filt.I
                          RArea.R.rHydro.evap.I)
                      ) Dur ) ) ) }
         ConstHydro.I =
         constHydro(volDam:VolDam
                    spill:Spill hidroPower:HydroPower)
      end CArea.R = c(rHydro:ConstHydro)
   end CPeriod.T = c(area:CArea) end
```

Fig. 1. Representation of the dam dynamics equation in Mozart

cost functions. This strategy selects first the thermal units in order of priority (lower coefficients in the cost function). The value of the variable to distribute will be the nearest to the upper boundary. The second strategy was designed to deal with second-order cost functions. This strategy chooses first by stage order, then by area, then by incremetal costs between the limits and at last, it chooses the incremental costs below lower boundary. If the chosen variable by the function *Order* generates incremental costs considering the power constraint, then it distributes by the nearest value to the generated power at the same incremental costs. If the chosen variable has its ideal power to operate at the same incremental costs under the lower boundary, then it will distribute by the lower limit of the variable. If the chosen variable has its ideal power to operate at the same incremental costs over the upper limit, then it will distribute by the upper limit of the variable.
If the selected variable to distribute can generate incremental costs among the limits then, it chooses the nearest value. Both distribution

strategies for thermal units were implemented for the variables within FD and XRI domains.

Distribution strategies for hydroelectric units Three distribution strategies were developed for hydroelectric units in the XRI domain. The first chooses the variable in order of priority: the power from an hydro plant, the spillage from the dam, and the level of the dam. The second strategy, considers not only the order of the first, but gives priority to the variables that represent the power from hydro plants with dam with the greater amount of outflows power plants that benefit from its discharges and spillages; then, it gives the priority to the plant with the greater dam. The third strategy gives priority to the plant with the greater dam. These strategies were also implemented in the finite domain but only considering the distribution of the variables representing the power from hydro power plants.

In Figures 2 and 3, the implementation in Mozart language of the first strategy in the finite domain is shown. Again, from these figures it can be seen the expresivity of the language for coding these strategies. In addition, as it can be seen in Figure 4, higher order programming gives the possibility for easily changing from one strategy to another.

The function *Value* is the same for the six strategies. For the variables representing the hydropower plants with dam, the value of the power with which the distribution will be done, will be according to a percentage of power at which the plants are required to operate. For variables representing the run-of-river power plants, the distribution will be done always over its upper limit. For variables representing the discharges and the levels of the dam, the distribution will be carried out using their lower limits and upper limits, respectively, in order to keep their discharges to the minimum possible value and the level of the dam at the highest possible limit, respectively.

5 Tests

The tests were carried out in a PC with Linux Operating System, Debian 3.1, with two Xeon processors at 2.8 GHz each and 2 GB RAM memory. Some of the problems were taken from the literature, others were considered using the data found in [4]. The future cost curves of the solved problems from [4] were taken by multiplying the future cost curves from the Laja lake found in the same factor.

The conventions BSCL,BSC,STBS and MUBS used in Table 2 mean cost of the best solution found in literature, cost of the best solution found by the application, time employed in searching the best solution, and used memory in the best solution time, respectively. The best solution found by the application uses a notation *xri(<limInfCosto limSupCosto>)*, which is a variable in the *XRI* domain.

As it can be seen in Figure 5 (Problem 8 in Table 2), the solution (generation costs) of the implemented tool chooses hydropower generation over thermal generation so the cost is minimized. It is also seen that the

```
Order =
proc{$ V1 V2 C}
   if V1.idPeriod < V2.idPeriod then
      C = true
   else
      if V1.idPeriod > V2.idPeriod then
         C = false
      else
         if V1.MaxLevDam > 0.0 then
            if V2.MaxLevDam > 0.0 then
               if V1.nConRiverDown >
                  V2.nConRiverDown then
                  C = true
               else
                  if V1.nConRiverDown <
                     V2.nConRiverDown then
                     C = false
                  else
                     C = V1.MaxLevDam >=
                     V2.MaxLevDam
                  end
               end else C = true end
         else C = V2.MaxLevDam <= 0.0
         end end end end
```

Fig. 2. Representation of function order in Mozart.

```
Value =
proc{$ V R}
   VAux VAux2
in
   {FD.reflect.max V.hydroPowerPlantFinit VAux}
   VAux2 =
   {Float.toInt {Float.´/´
                {Number.´*´ Nivel V.maxPower} 100.0}}
   if VAux < VAux2 then
      R = VAux
   else
      {FD.reflect.nextLarger
       V.hydroPowerPlantFinit VAux2 R}
   end end
```

Fig. 3. Representation of function value in Mozart.

```
proc {Strategy Data}
   . . .
   R=generic(order:      Order
             filter:     Filter
             select:     Select
             value:      Value
             procedure:  Proc)
in
   %%This call the distributor
   {Distribuidor.distribute R Data} end
```

Fig. 4. Calling the distributor with a especific strategy.

hydropower generation follows closely the demand behaviour, allowing to flatten the thermal generation and keeping it at its lowest levels.

Table 2. Found Solutions

Problem	BSCL	BSC	STBS(ms)	MUBS(MB)
1 [6, p. 32-33]	8194,36	xri(8165.01 8165.08)	10	2,5
2 [6, p. 32-33]	7008,32730	xri(6998.98 6999.06)	60000	30
3 [5, p. 504]	86657,0736	xri(86621.3 86621.3)	8000	6
4 [6, p. 368]	32246.44	xri(32242.5 32242.5)	85000	40
5 [6, p. 368]	31984.82	xri(32005.7 32005.8)	25000	12
6 [4]	–	xri($3.91541e^8$ $3.91541e^8$)	116000	250
7 [4]	–	xri($2.79907e^8$ $2.79907e^8$)	100000	1600
8 [4]	–	xri($4.03688e^8$ $4.03688e^8$)	35000	900
9 [1, p. 93]	−21662.4	xri(−21662.4 −21662.4)	198000	90
10 [1, p. 98]	−12660	xri(−11394.9 − 11393.9)	3000	2
11 [4]	–	xri($2.90519e^8$ $2.90519e^8$)	200000	800

As it can be seen in Table 2, in many problems the generation costs found with the application were lower than in the literature and in a few, the solution found was a little higher than in literature. Furthermore, it is good to notice that it was possible to solve problems with real data, i.e., the problems with data taken from [4].

6 Conclussions and Future Work

In the development of this work, it was possible to show that the Concurrent Constraint Programming is applicable to the Short-term Hydrothermal Economic Dispatch Problem. The Economic Dispatch Problem is a combinatory, non linear problem, that offers real challenges for searching the solution.
Also, it is evident the possibility to develop intelligent strategies in a very high level and modular form using Mozart language.

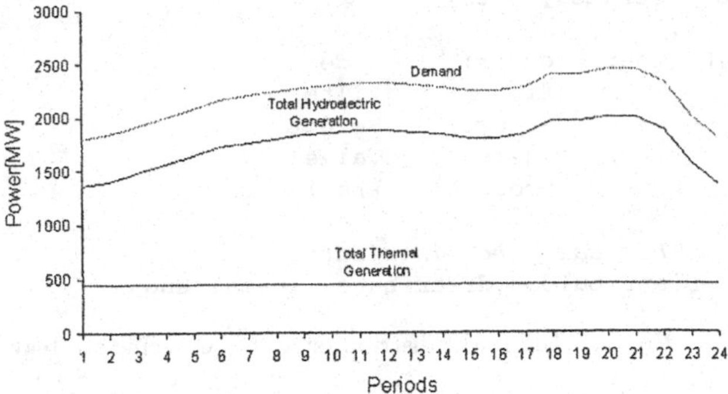

Fig. 5. Hydro Power and thermal generation for the problem 8 of Table 2

In the implemented model, the obtained results (generation costs) were better than those reported in literature. In several problems, the solution found had lower costs and in others, the results were very closed to those in the literature. At the same time, the model was applied for solving problems with real data, representing a real electrical energy supply system.

A hybrid model was implemented for distribution in both real and finite domains. In the future, it would be interesting to solve the *Economic Dispatch* along with the *Unit Commitment Problem.*

References

1. Pablo Hernán Corredor. *Operación Económica de Sistemas de Potencia.* Universidad Potinficia Bolivariana, 1992.
2. Mario Pereira, Nora Campodonico, and Rafael Kelman. Long-term Hydro Scheduling based on Stochastics Models. *EPSOM*, 1998.
3. Mario Pereira, Nora Campodonico, and Rafael Kelman. Application of Stochastic Dual DP and Extensions to Hydrothermal Scheduling. Research Report 012-99, PSRI, 1999.
4. Esteban Manuel Gil Sagás. Programación de la generación de corto plazo en sistemas hidrotérmicos usando algoritmos géneticos, tesis para optar al grado de magister en ingeniería eléctrica, 2001.
5. William Stevenson. *Análisis de Sistemas Eléctricos de Potencia.* Mc Graw Hill, 1996.
6. Allen Wood. *Power generation, operation and control.* Mc Graw Hill, 1996.

Micromechanics as a Testbed for Artificial Intelligence Methods Evaluation

Ernst Kussul[1], Tatiana Baidyk[1], Felipe Lara-Rosano[1], Oleksandr Makeyev[2], Anabel Martin[1] and Donald Wunsch[3]

1 Center of Applied Sciences and Technological Development, National Autonomous University of Mexico, Cd. Universitaria, Circuito Exterior s/n, Coyoacán, 04510, México, D.F., Mexico
ekussul@servidor.unam.mx; tbaidyk@aleph.cinstrum.unam.mx; lararf@servidor.unam.mx; anabelmartin@lycos.com

2 Dept. of Electrical and Computer Engineering, Clarkson University, 5720, Potsdam, NY 136992, USA
mckehev@hotmail.com

3 Applied Computational Intelligence Lab, Dept. of Electrical and Computer Engineering, University of Missouri-Rolla, 1870 Miner Circle, Rolla MO 65409, USA
dwunsch@ece.umr.edu

Abstract. Some of the artificial intelligence (AI) methods could be used to improve the performance of automation systems in manufacturing processes. However, the application of these methods in the industry is not widespread because of the high cost of the experiments with the AI systems applied to the conventional manufacturing systems. To reduce the cost of such experiments, we have developed a special micromechanical equipment, similar to conventional mechanical equipment, but of a lot smaller overall sizes and therefore of lower cost. This equipment can be used for evaluation of different AI methods in an easy and inexpensive way. The methods that show good results can be transferred to the industry through appropriate scaling. This paper contains brief description of low cost microequipment prototypes and some AI methods that can be evaluated with mentioned prototypes.

1 Introduction

The development of AI technologies gives one an opportunity to use them not only for conventional applications (expert systems, intelligent databases [1], technical diagnostics [2, 3] etc.) but also for automation of mechanical manufacturing. Such AI methods as adaptive critic design [4, 5], adaptive fuzzy Petri networks [6, 7],

Please use the following format when citing this chapter:

Kussul, E., Baidyk, T., Lara-Rosano, F., Makeyev, O., Martin, A., Wunsch, D., 2006, in IFIP International Federation for Information Processing, Volume 218, Professional Practice in Artificial Intelligence, eds. J. Debenham, (Boston: Springer), pp. 275–284.

neural network based computer vision systems [8-12], distributed knowledge representation based on assembly neural networks [13-15] among others can be used to solve the automation problems. To introduce these methods into the industry it is necessary to examine them first in real industry environment. Such examination is very expensive. It is possible to reduce the examination cost by using cheaper environment that simulates all the processes of mechanical manufacturing. Such environment can be created on the basis of the micromechanical equipment. We have been developing micromechanical equipment for many years [16-18] and since this idea was proposed for the first time in [19] we have developed adaptive systems based on this idea and performed some experiments that prove the efficiency of the proposed approach. In this paper we describe the results that were obtained during last two years. Our adaptive systems for micromechanical equipment control are based on image recognition with neural networks.

This paper is organized in the following way: the second section contains the brief description of micromechanical devices that have been developed and used in our work. In the third section we describe image recognition systems based on neural networks and their applications in micromechanical equipment automation. The fourth section contains description of a new problem in micromechanical manufacturing that can be solved by the methods based on neural networks.

2 Development of micromechanical equipment

The main idea of low cost micromechanical equipment manufacturing is the following: each new micro device should be manufactured by micromachine tools and micro assembly devices which have the overall sizes comparable with the overall sizes of work pieces to be manufactured. For example, if new microdevice contains the shaft of 0.2mm diameter and of 0.8mm length then this shaft is to be manufactured with the lathe with the overall sizes of 4mm * 4mm * 4mm. In most cases the lathe of such overall sizes will automatically have tolerances that coincide with the shaft specifications. The main errors of machine tools that originate from thermal expansions, vibrations, elastic deformations etc. are proportional to the overall sizes of the machine tool [20]. So if we manufacture the micro shaft with the lathe that has 25 times smaller overall sizes than the overall sizes of the conventional lathe then we can decrease the tolerances 25 times. The low end lathe of conventional overall sizes has tolerances of about 0.05mm, so our micro lathe should have tolerances of about 0.002mm. It is sufficient for most applications of said micro shaft. Low end conventional lathe has low cost. Our micro lathe should have even lower cost due to low consumption of materials, work area and energy.

To examine the possibility of production of micromachine tools that have low cost components we have developed 2 prototypes of micromachine tools with the cost of components of less than $100. One of these prototypes is shown in Fig. 1.

The experiments with these prototypes have proved that they permit manufacturing of micro work pieces similar to ones produced with expensive Japanese micro lathe. Some examples of micro work pieces manufactured by our micromachine tools are presented in Fig. 2 and Fig. 3.

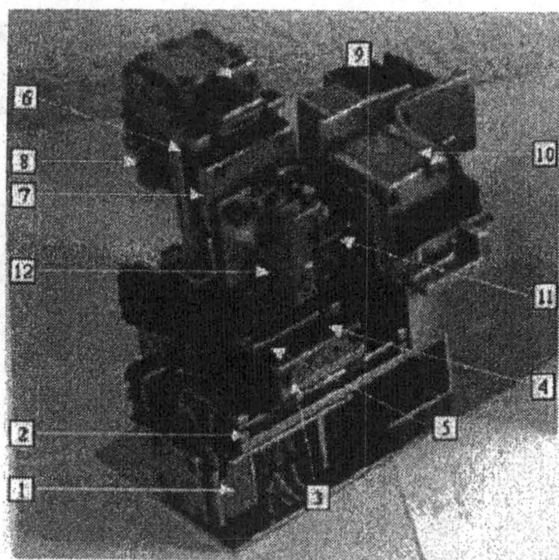

Fig. 1. Micromachine tool prototype: 1 – Y-direction drive; 2 - Y-direction guides; 3 – X-direction guides; 4 – X-direction carriage; 5 – X-direction drive; 6 – Z-direction guides; 7 – Z-direction carriage; 8 – Z-direction drive motor; 9 – Z-direction drive gearbox; 10 – chuck support; 11 – chuck; 12 – cutter and measurement tool support

Japanese researchers turned the brass needle of 0.05mm diameter to show the possibility of micro turning [21]. They used micro lathe which has expensive components (some thousands dollars). We repeated their results (Fig. 2) with micromachine tool that has very cheap components (less than $100).

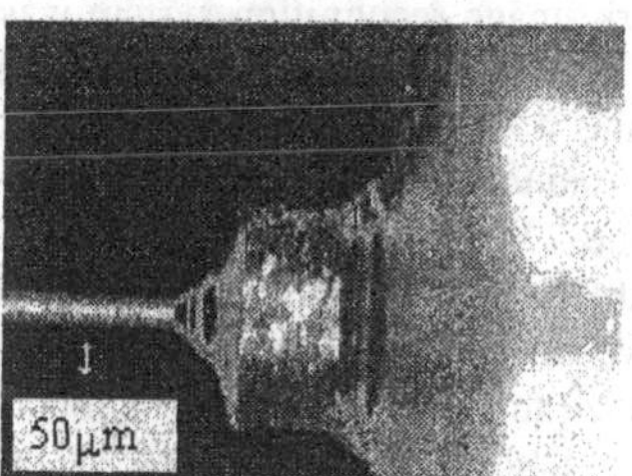

Fig. 2. Brass needle of 50 μm diameter manufactured with the first micromachine tool prototype

In Fig. 3 two examples of micro work pieces manufactured with our micromachine tool prototype are presented. The first work piece is the gear with the worm that can be used in micro transmissions. The second work piece is the screw that can be used in gas filters of "micro cyclone" type.

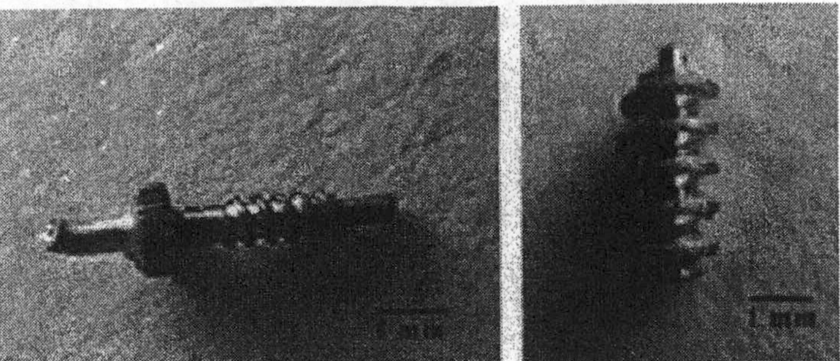

Fig. 3. Examples of micro work pieces manufactured with the first micromachine tool prototype

3 Computer vision systems for micromechanical applications

To obtain high precision in low cost microequipment we use adaptive algorithms based on computer vision systems.

3.1 Image recognition in micro assembly

The first problem which we dealt with was the problem of micro assembly. To introduce the pin into the hole it is necessary to collocate them with close tolerances. Low cost microequipment does not permit such collocation without adaptive algorithms. Neural network image recognition system was created to recognize the mutual pin-hole position. To investigate the potential of this system we created the image database that contains 441 images with different mutual positions of pin and hole. For this purpose we used the prototype shown in Fig. 4.

In our system we used one TV camera for teleconferences and four light sources [11]. The shadows from different light sources (Fig. 5) permit us to obtain the 3-D position of the pin relative to the hole. We use a neural classifier LIRA (Limited Receptive Area) to recognize this position [12]. The input of our neural classifier is an image that is a combination of four images of one pin-hole position that correspond to different light sources. This image is processed and the contours are extracted (Fig. 6). The output of the neural classifier gives the *X* and *Y* coordinates of pin relative to the hole.

If this position is recognized with the precision of 0.1mm then the recognition rate is sufficiently high: 99.5% for *X* coordinate and 89.9% for *Y* coordinate.

3.2 Shape recognition

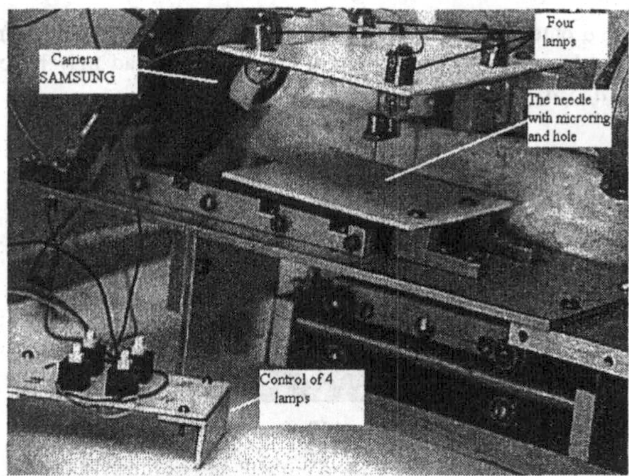

Fig. 4. Micro assembly system controlled by the vision system

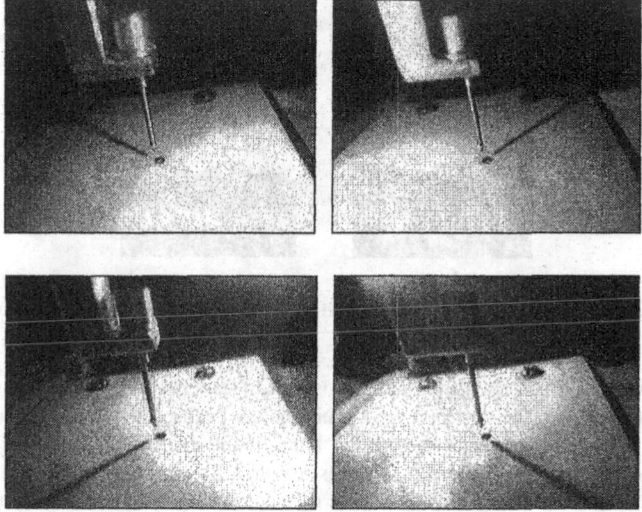

Fig. 5. An example of four images of the same pin-hole position obtained with different light sources

The other task where we used neural networks was the task of shape recognition [22]. Low cost microequipment does not permit precise allocation of the cutters in CNC lathe. The errors of cutter allocation produce erroneous shape of manufactured work piece. An example of such erroneous shape is shown in Fig. 7. Two cutters are used for manufacturing of the screws shown in Fig. 7. One cutter is used for the treatment of the outer diameter and the other one is used for the treatment of the thread. If mutual position of cutters is not correct the thread may have erroneous shape (Fig. 7, *a*, *c*, *d*).

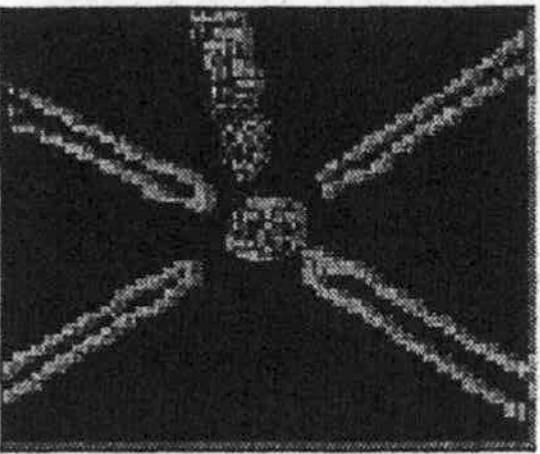

Fig. 6. An example of the input image of the LIRA neural classifier

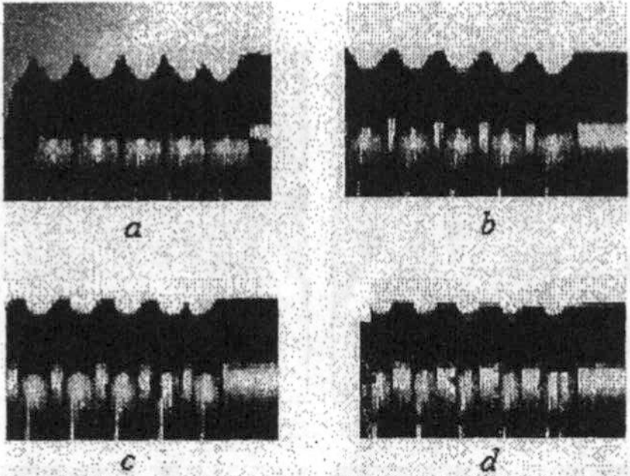

Fig. 7. Examples of micro screws manufactured with different mutual positions of cutters

It is difficult to evaluate the mutual position of cutters directly. That is why we propose to evaluate the correctness of their mutual position using the shape of the first screw that is manufactured with the lathe. If the distance between the second cutter and the lathe axis is less than necessary then the shape of the thread will be like the one presented in Fig. 7, *a*. If this distance is larger than necessary then the shape of the thread will be like ones in Fig. 7, *c*, *d*.

We have produced 40 screws of 3mm diameter with the CNC-lathe Boxford. Ten screws were produced with correct position of the thread cutter (Fig. 15, *b*). Thirty screws were produced with erroneous positions of the cutter.

Ten of them (Fig. 15, *a*) had the distance between the cutter and the screw axis 0.1mm smaller than necessary. Ten screws (Fig. 15, *c*) were produced with the distance 0.1mm larger than necessary and the remaining ten (Fig. 15, *d*) with the distance 0.2mm larger than necessary. We created an image database of these screws using web camera Samsung mounted on an optical microscope. Five randomly selected images from each group were used for the neural classifier's training and the other five were used for the neural classifier's testing.

The best recognition rate in shape recognition obtained with the PCNC neural classifier (Permutation Coding Neural Classifier) was 92.5% [22].

3.3 Texture recognition

The third task was the recognition of surface textures. This is the issue of the day for the quality inspection systems and sometimes for work piece orientation recognition in the assembly process. For this task we developed the texture recognition system based on the RSC (Random Subspace) neural classifier [23].

To test our texture recognition system we created our own image database of metal surface images. Four texture classes correspond to metal surfaces after: milling, polishing with sandpaper and turning with lathe (Fig. 8).

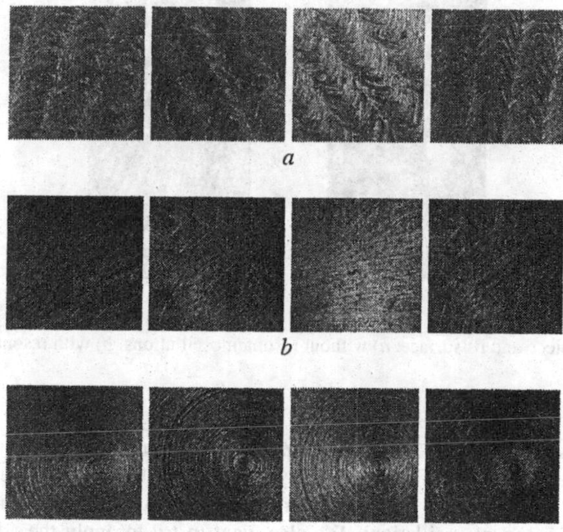

Fig. 8. Examples of metal surfaces after: *a*) milling, *b*) polishing with sandpaper, *c*) turning with lathe

It can be seen that different lighting conditions affect greatly the grayscale properties of the images. The textures may also be arbitrarily oriented and not centered perfectly. Metal surfaces may have minor defects and dust on it. All this image properties correspond to the conditions of the real industrial environment and make the texture recognition task more complicated. Scanning square window was used to extract texture features for neural classifier's training and testing. The numbers of images in training and recognition sets were 3 and 17 correspondingly. The best recognition rate of 80% was obtained in this task.

4 Future work: Avoiding the resonance oscillations in cutting process

Mechanical treatment of metal surfaces frequently suffers from resonant oscillations of either work piece or cutting tool. Such oscillations result in decrease of both surface quality and work piece precision. The resonant oscillations appear when the rigidity of the system Machine tool – Tool – Work piece is insufficient. In Fig. 9, *a* an example of the work piece that was manufactured without resonant oscillation is presented.

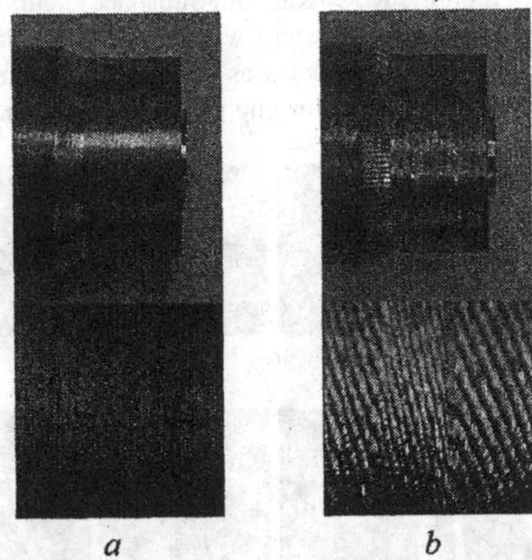

Fig. 9. Work piece and its surface: *a*) without resonant oscillations, *b*) with resonant oscillations

For comparison, an example of the work piece that was manufactured with resonant oscillation is presented in Fig. 9, *b*. Many factors affect the resonance oscillations appearance. We intent to prove the connectionist neural network approach for prediction of resonant oscillations. We also want to try to apply the adaptive critic design methods to the optimal control of cutting process under resonant oscillations condition [24].

Acknowledgements

This work was supported by projects PAPIIT IN108606-3, PAPIIT IN116306-3.

References

1. Eberhart, R.: Overview of computational intelligence [and biomedical engineering applications]. Proceedings od the 20-th Annual International Conference of the IEEE Engineering in Medicine and Biology Society **3** (1998) 1125-1129
2. Hui, T., Brown, D., Haynes, B., Xinxian Wang: Embedded e-diagnostic for distributed industrial machinery. IEEE International Symposium on Computational Intelligence for Measurement Systems and Applications (2003) 156-161
3. Awadallah, M., Morcos, M.: Application of AI tools in fault diagnosis of electrical machines and drives-an overview. IEEE T Energy Conver **18**, Issue 2 (2003) 245-251
4. Werbos, P.: Advanced Forecasting Methods for Global Crisis Warning and Models of Intelligence. In: General Systems Yearbook **22** (1977) 25-38
5. Prokhorov, D., Wunsch, D.: Adaptive Critic Designs. IEEE T Neural Networ **8**, N 5 (1997) 997-1007
6. Xiaoou Li, Lara-Rosano, F.: A weighted fuzzy Petri net model for knowledge learning and reasoning. International Joint Conference on Neural Networks, IJCNN '99 **4** 2368 –2372
7. Xiaoou Li, Wen Yu, Lara-Rosano, F.: Dynamic Knowledge Inference and Learning under Adaptive Fuzzy Petri Net Framework. IEEE T Syst Man Cy **39**, N4 (2000) 442-450
8. Bottou, L., Cortes, C., Denker, J., Drucker, H., Guyon L., Jackel L., LeCun J., Muller U., Sackinger E., Simard P., Vapnik V.: Comparison of Classifier Methods: a Case Study in Handwritten Digit Recognition. In: Proceedings of 12th IAPR International Conference on Pattern Recognition **2** (1994) 77-82
9. Fukushima, K. Neocognitron: A hierarchical neural network capable of visual pattern recognition. Neural Networks **1** (1988) 119-130
10. Roska, T., Rodriguez-Vazquez, A.: Toward visual microprocessors. Proceedings of the IEEE **90**, Issue 7 (July 2002) 1244-1257
11. Baidyk, T.: Application of Flat Image Recognition Technique for Automation of Micro Device Production. Proceedings of the International Conference on Advanced Intelligent Mechatronics "AIM'01", Italy (2001) 488-494
12. Baidyk, T., Kussul, E., Makeyev, O., Caballero, A., Ruiz, L., Carrera, G., Velasco, G.: Flat image recognition in the process of microdevice assembly. Pattern Recogn Lett **25/1** (2004) 107-118
13. Kussul E.M., 1992, Associative Neural Structures. Kiev, Naukova Dumka, 144p. (in Russian).
14. Amosov N.M., Baidyk T.N., Goltsev A.D., Kasatkin A.M., Kasatkina L.M., Kussul E.M., Rachkovski D.A., 1991, Neurocomputers and Intelligent Robots. Kiev, Naukova Dumka, 272 p. (in Russian).
15. Baidyk T.N., 2001, Neural Networks and Artificial Intelligence Problems. Kiev, Naukova Dumka, 264 p. (in Russian).
16. Kussul, E., Rachkovskij, D., Baidyk, T., Talayev, S.: Micromechanical Engineering: a Basis for the Low-cost Manufacturing of Mechanical Microdevices Using Microequipment. J Micromech Microeng **6** (1996) 410-425
17. Kussul, E., Baidyk, T., Ruiz-Huerta, L., Caballero, A., Velasco, G., Kasatkina, L.: Development of Micromachine Tool Prototypes for Microfactories. J Micromech Microeng **12** (2002) 795-812.
18. Kussul E., Baidyk T., Ruiz L., Caballero A., Velasco G., 2002, Development of Low-cost Microequipment. 2002 International Symposium on Micromechatronics and Human Science, IEEE, Nagoya, Japan, Oct. 20-23, pp.125-134.
19. Lara-Rosano F., Kussul E., Baidyk T., Ruiz L., Caballero A., Velasco G., 2004, Artificial Intelligence Systems in Micromechanics. In: Artificial Intelligence Applications and Innovations (IFIP 18th Computer Congress), Ed. By Max Bramer, Vladan Devedzic Boston/Dordrecht/London, Kluwer Academic Publishers, pp.1-10

20. Kussul E., Baidyk T., Ruiz-Huerta L., Caballero-Ruiz A., Velasco G., 2006, Scaling down of microequipment parameters, Precis Eng (to be published).
21. Yuichi Okazaki, and Tokio Kitahara, Micro-lathe equipped with closed-loop numerical control, 2nd International Workshop on Microfactories IWMF2000, Fribourg, Switzerland, October 9-10, 2000, pp.87-91.
22. Baidyk T., Kussul E., 2004, Neural Network Based Vision System for Micro Workpieces Manufacturing. WSEAS T Syst, Issue 2, Volume 3, April 2004, pp.483-488.
23. Baidyk T., Kussul E., Makeyev O. Texture Recognition with Random Subspace Neural Classifier, WSEAS T Circuits Syst, Issue 4, Volume 4, April 2005, pp.319-325.
24. Werbos P. Approximate Dynamic Programming for Real-Time Control and Neural Modeling. Chapter 13 in Handbook of Intelligent Control: Neural, Fuzzy and Adaptive Approaches, (White & Sofge, eds.), Van Nostrand Reinhold, New York, NY, 1992.

Burst Synchronization in Two Pulse-Coupled Resonate-and-Fire Neuron Circuits

Kazuki Nakada[1], Tetsuya Asai[2] and Hatsuo Hayashi[1]

[1] Kyushu Institute of Technology nakada@brain.kyutech.ac.jp
[2] Hokkaido University asai@sapinens-ei.eng.hokudai.ac.jp

The present paper addresses burst synchronization in out of phase observed in two pulse-coupled resonate-and-fire neuron (RFN) circuits. The RFN circuit is a silicon spiking neuron that has second-order membrane dynamics and exhibits fast subthreshold oscillation of membrane potential. Due to such dynamics, the behavior of the RFN circuit is sensitive to the timing of stimuli. We investigated the effects of the sensitivity and the mutual interaction on the dynamic behavior of two pulse-coupled RFN circuits, and will demonstrate out of phase burst synchronization and bifurcation phenomena through circuit simulations.

1 Introduction

Functional networks of silicon spiking neurons are shown to be useful in a wide variety of applications [5]-[10]. Recent research efforts have concentrated on real-time event-based computation, so-called temporal cording, in which coincidence or synchrony detection plays essential roles in neural information processing, such as auditory perception [6], onset detection [8], and learning and memory [9]-[10]. Temporal filtering properties are also significant to extract temporal structure of spike sequences in which information may be encoded.

Computational performance of such functional networks of silicon spiking neurons will be limited if their components are quite simple. For instance, the Axon-Hillock circuit [3], widely known as an electronic analogue of the integrate-and-fire neuron (IFN) model, can only act as a low-pass filter for a sequence of pulses. For increasing their performance, alternative silicon spiking neurons [14]-[21], such as a low-power IFN circuit with frequency adaptation [17] and asynchronous chaotic spiking neuron circuits [19], [20], have been previously developed. These circuits increase selectivity to inputs into a silicon spiking neuron due to synchrony detection and temporal filtering properties. Synaptic circuits with short-term plasticity [8], [10]-[12] and spike-timing-dependent plasticity [10], [13] can also increase computational performance of silicon spiking neural networks. However, they can work effectively only at network level.

In this context, we designed an analog integrated circuit for a resonate-and-fire neuron (RFN) model [1] using complementary metal-oxide-semiconductor (CMOS) technology [21]. The RFN model is a spiking neuron model that has second-order membrane dynamics and exhibits damped subthreshold oscillation

---

Please use the following format when citing this chapter:

Nakada, K., Asai, T., Hayashi, H., 2006, in IFIP International Federation for Information Processing, Volume 218, Professional Practice in Artificial Intelligence, eds. J. Debenham, (Boston: Springer), pp. 285–294.

of the membrane potential. Due to such membrane dynamics, the RFN model is sensitive to the timing of stimuli, and thus it exhibits nonlinear phenomena observed in biological neurons, such as coincidence detection, post-inhibitory rebound, and frequency preference [1]. The RFN circuit acts as a coincidence detector and a band-pass filter at circuit level since it inherits the sensitivity of the RFN model. Thus, it is expected to be useful for large-scale implementation of functional silicon spiking neural networks.

In the present work, we focus on dynamic behavior of a system of two pulse-coupled RFN circuits. It is expected that pulse-coupled RFN circuits exhibit different behavior as compared to pulse-coupled IFN circuits because of the peculiar sensitivity to the timing of inputs of the RFN circuit. As a first step toward understanding of collective behavior of the coupled RFN circuits, we investigated how effective the sensitivity and the mutual interaction were to the behavior of the two pulse-coupled RFN circuits. Through circuit simulations using the simulation program with integrated circuit emphasis (SPICE), we will demonstrate out of phase synchronization of periodic and quasi periodic bursts, and bifurcation phenomena.

2 Burst Synchronization in Two Pulse-Coupled Resonate-and-Fire Neuron Models

Let us here summarize a resonate-and-fire neuron (RFN) model [1], and burst synchronization in out of phase observed in two pulse-coupled RFN models.

2.1 Resonate-and-fire neuron model

The RNF model is a spiking neuron model that has second-order subthreshold membrane dynamics and a firing threshold [1]. The dynamics of the RFN model are described by:

$$\dot{x} = bx - wy + I \tag{1}$$

$$\dot{y} = wx + by \tag{2}$$

or by an equivalent complex form:

$$\dot{z} = (b + iw)z + I \tag{3}$$

where $z{=}x + iy$ is a complex variable. The real and imaginary parts, x and y, are the current- and voltage-like variables, respectively. The constants b and w are parameters, and I is an external input. If the variable y exceeds a certain threshold a_{th}, the variable z is reset to an arbitrary value z_o, which describes activity-dependent after-spike reset. This model has second-order membrane dynamics, and thus it exhibits dynamic behavior, such as fast subthreshold oscillation, resulting in the coincident detection, post-inhibitory-rebound, and frequency preference [1].

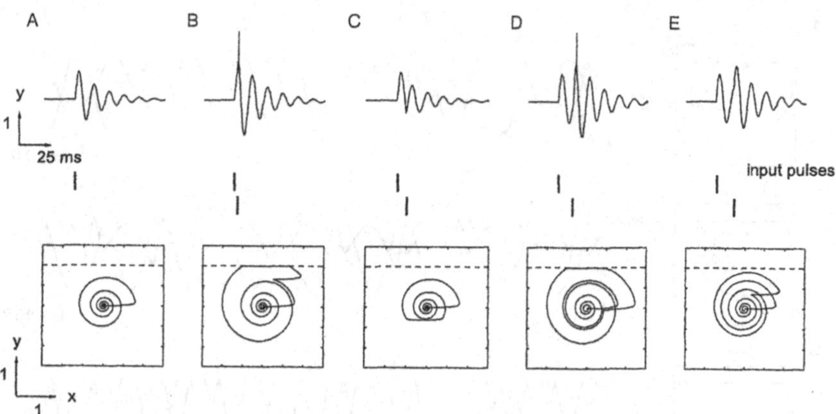

Fig. 1. Behavior of the resonate-and-fire neuron model in response to (A) a single pulse, (B) a coincident doublet, (C) a non-resonant doublet, (D) a resonant doublet, and (E) a non-resonant doublet, where output pulses are manually written.

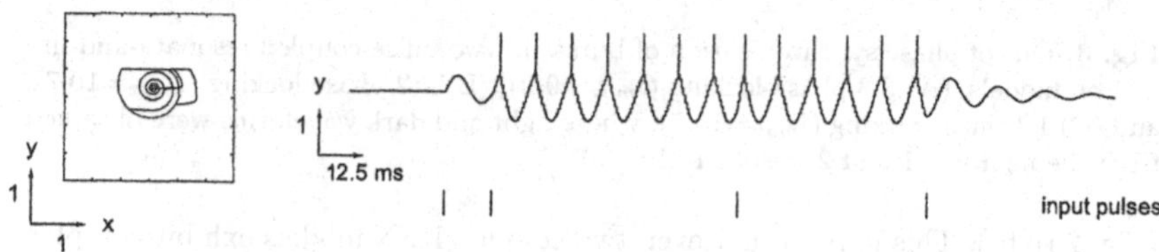

Fig. 2. Pacemaker activity of the resonate-and-fire neuron model as a bias current is injected. Output pulses are manually written. The last pulse cancels out the pacemaker activity.

Figure 1 shows typical behavior of the RFN model in response to input pulses. In this case, we used the following parameters: $b = -0.1$, $w = 1$, $a_{th} = i$, $z_o = -0.5 + i$, and the input pulses were given by: $I = i_{\max}(t/\tau)\exp(1-t/\tau)$, where the time constant $\tau = 0.05$ ms, the maximal amplitude $i_{\max} = 12$, and t was an elapsed time since a pulse was given. When a pulse that cannot evoke an action potential alone arrives at an RFN model, a damped subthreshold oscillation occurs, as shown in Fig. 1A. When a pair of pulses arrives at the RFN model at a short interval (a coincident doublet, e.g. 2.5 ms, Fig. 1B), or at an interval nearly equal to the intrinsic period of the subthreshold oscillation (a resonant doublet, 12.5 ms, Fig. 1D), the RFN model fires a spike. However, the RFN model does not fire a spike in response to a doublet with an interval in other ranges, e.g. 7.5 ms (Fig. 1C) or 15.0 ms (Fig 1E).

The RFN model fires a sequence of spikes in response to inputs when a bias current is injected (pacemaker activity), as shown in Fig. 2, where the bias current $i_{bias} = 0.68$ and the maximal amplitude of the input pulses $i_{max} = 5$. Depending on the timing of input pulses, the pacemaker activity disappears

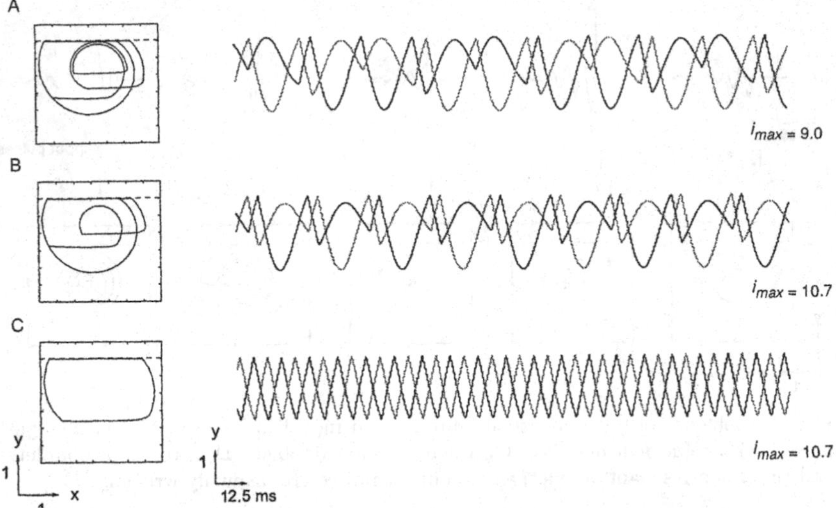

Fig. 3. Out of phase synchronization of bursts in two pulse-coupled resonate-and-fire neuron models. (A) 3:3 phase-locking (i_{max}=9.0), (B) 2:2 phase locking (i_{max}=10.7), and (C) 1:1 phase locking (i_{max}=10.7), where light and dark waveforms were obtained from the neurons, 1 and 2, respectively.

(Fig. 2 right). This implies that even two coupled RFN models exhibit complex phenomena due to the sensitivity to the input timing and mutual interaction.

2.2 Burst synchronization in two pulse-coupled RFN models

We here consider a system of two pulse-coupled RFN models, which is given by the following equation:

$$\dot{z}_j = (b + iw)z_j + i_{bias} + i_{\max}(t_k/\tau)\exp(1-t_k/\tau)\ (j, k = 1, 2) \tag{4}$$

where $z_j = x_j + iy_j$ is a complex state variable of the j-th neuron. The real and imaginary parts, x_j and y_j, are the current- and voltage-like variables, respectively. The constants b and w are parameters, and i_{bias} is a bias current. The time constant $\tau = 0.05$ ms and the maximal amplitude i_{max}, and t_k is an elapsed time since the arrival of the latest spike from another neuron k. In the following, the threshold a_{th}, and the constants b and w have the same values as those used in the previous section, respectively.

The system of two pulse-coupled RFN models has been previously analyzed in view of anti-phase synchronization and its stability [2]. However, the effects of the reset value z_o on such synchronization were not considered in the previous work. The reset value may affect the sensitivity to the timing of input to the RFN model. Although any positive input given on the right side of the phase

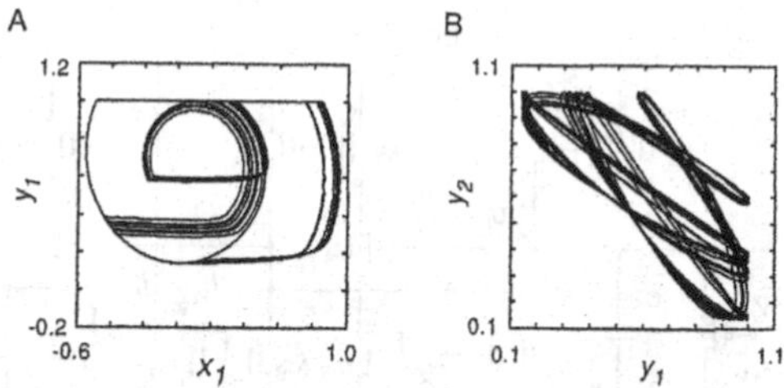

Fig. 4. Out of phase synchronization of quasi periodic bursts in two pulse-coupled resonate-and-frie neuron models.

plane act as excitatory, it is determined whether a positive input given on the left side of the phase plane act as excitatory or not depending on the strength and the phase of the input, as shown in Fig. 1. The reset value determines the trajectory of the RFN model after firing, resulting in changing the sensitivity to the timing of input.

For increasing the effects on the sensitivity to the timing of inputs to the RFN model, we set the reset value at $z_o = -0.5 + i$. Furthermore, we set the bias input at i_{bias}=0.68 so that each RFN model became a pacemaker. Under such conditions, we investigated the behavior of two pulse-coupled RFN models and the effects of the sensitivity and the mutual interaction between the two RFN models. We changed the maximal amplitude of the pulse input i_{max} as a parameter. Consequently, out of phase burst synchronization and bifurcation phenomena were observed. In the range of the amplitude i_{max} between 6.25 and 9.0, bursts of RFNs are stably out of phase, such as shown in Fig. 3A, where $i_{max} = 9.0$ and each burst contains three spike. In this case, the trajectory in the phase plane is very close to the threshold (Fig. 3A left), and thus this burst synchronization becomes unstable and a bifurcation occurs when i_{max} is increased slightly further. When i_{max} is around 10.7, each burst contains two spikes through bursts of RFNs are still out of phase (Fig. 3B). In this range of I_{max}, $1:1$ out of phase synchronization coexists (Fig. 3C); when the initial phase difference between two RFN models is nearly π, the out of phase synchronization occurs. At $i_{max} = 14.0$, the trajectory in the phase plane is very close to the threshold, and thus another bifurcation occurs at this point. When i_{max} exceeds 14.0, $1:1$ out of phase synchronization becomes stable. In addition, bursts of RFNs are roughly out of phase in the range of i_{max} from 9.1 to 10.6 through the bursts are quasi periodic.

Figure 4 shows trajectories in the x_1-y_1 and y_1-y_2 phase planes, and the symmetry we can find in Fig. 4B indicates the out of phase synchronization of quasi periodic bursts. The stability of such out of phase synchronization could be analyzed by a similar method presented in [2].

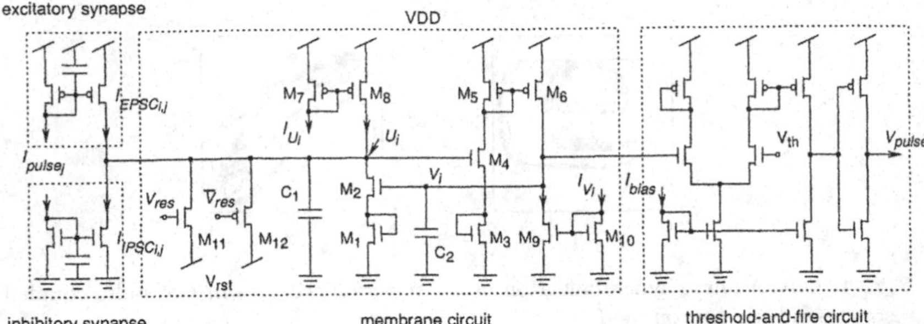

Fig. 5. Schematic of the resonate-and-fire neuron circuit. The circuit consists of a membrane circuit, a threshold-and-fire circuit, and excitatory and inhibitory synaptic circuits. The membrane circuit has the second-order dynamics containing two state variables U_i (a current-like variable) and V_i (a voltage-like variable), and it shows oscillatory behavior mediated and modulated by synaptic inputs.

3 Circuit Implementation of the RFN model

We designed the RFN model as an analog integrated circuit in our previous work [21]. Figure 5 shows the schematic of the RFN circuit, which consists of a membrane circuit, a threshold-and-fire circuit, and current-mirror integrators as excitatory and inhibitory synaptic circuits [4].

The membrane circuit was derived from the Volterra system for modeling prey-predator interactions to mimic the membrane dynamics of the RFN model by using the current-voltage relationship of subthreshold MOS FETs [21]. The dynamics of the membrane circuit are described as follows:

$$C_1\frac{dU_i}{dt} = -g(U_i - V_{rst}) + I_{in} + \bar{I}_{U_i} - I_o\exp\left(\frac{\kappa^2}{\kappa+1}\frac{V_i}{V_T}\right) \tag{5}$$

$$C_2\frac{dV_i}{dt} = I_o\exp\left(\frac{\kappa^2}{\kappa+1}\frac{U_i}{V_T}\right) - \bar{I}_{V_i} \tag{6}$$

where the voltages U_i and V_i are state variables, C_1 and C_2 the capacitance, g the total of the conductance of transistors, M_{11} and M_{12}, V_{rst} the reset voltage, κ the capacitive coupling ratio from the gate to the channel, V_T the thermal voltage, and I_o the pre-exponential current [4]. I_{in} represents the summation of synaptic currents:

$$I_{\text{in}} = \sum_j I_{\text{EPSC}_{i,j}} - \sum_j I_{\text{IPSC}_{i,j}} \tag{7}$$

where $I_{\text{EPSC}_{i,j}}$ and $I_{\text{IPSC}_{i,j}}$ represent the i-th post-synaptic currents through the j-th excitatory and inhibitory synaptic circuits. The currents, $\bar{I}_{U_i}$ through M_8 and $\bar{I}_{V_i}$ through M_9, are approximately described as follows:

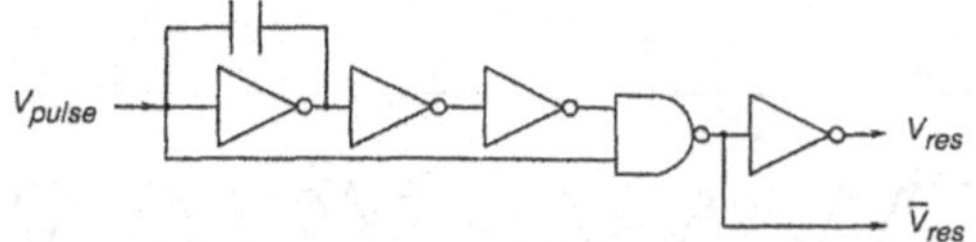

Fig. 6. Schematic of the delay-and-inverter circuit.

$$\bar{I}_{U_i} = \alpha I_{U_i}(1 + \frac{\text{VDD} - U_i}{V_{E,p}}) \tag{8}$$

$$\bar{I}_{V_i} = \beta I_{V_i}(1 + \frac{V_i}{V_{E,n}}) \tag{9}$$

where $I_{U_i}$and $I_{V_i}$are bias currents, VDD the power-supply voltage, $V_{E,p}$ and $V_{E,n}$ the Early voltage [4] for an nMOS FET and a pMOS FET, respectively, and α and β the fitting constants.

The equilibrium point of the RFN circuit, (U_o, V_o), can easily be obtained, and the stability of the point can also be analyzed by the eigenvalues of the Jacobian matrix of the circuit,

$$J = \begin{bmatrix} -\frac{\alpha I_{U_i}}{V_{E,p}} & -\frac{\kappa^2}{\kappa+1}\frac{I_{V_o}}{V_T} \\ \frac{\kappa^2}{\kappa+1}\frac{I_{U_o}}{V_T} & -\frac{\beta I_{V_i}}{V_{E,n}} \end{bmatrix} \tag{10}$$

where I_{U_o} and I_{V_o} represent the equilibrium current at the equilibrium point. It is assumed that the leak conductance g is zero. We used diode-connected transistors M_1 and M_3 to obtain small coefficients for I_{U_o} and I_{V_o}, and short transistors having small Early voltages for M_7-M_{10} to obtain large coefficients for I_{U_i} and I_{V_i}. Consequently, the equilibrium point becomes a focus, and the membrane circuit exhibits damped oscillation in response to an input. In this case, the circuit dynamics is qualitatively equivalent to the membrane dynamics of the RFN model near the equilibrium point.

Inputs thorough synaptic circuits change the trajectory of the oscillation of the membrane circuit. If V_i exceeds a threshold voltage V_{th}, the threshold-and-fire circuit that consists of a comparator and an inverter generates a spike, i.e. a pulse voltage V_{pulse}, and the spike is fed into a delay-and-inverter circuit [9] with a mirror capacitance shown in Fig. 6. The delay-and-inverter circuit converts V_{pulse} to reset voltages V_{res} and $\bar{V}_{res}$ for reseting U_i to a bias voltage V_{rst}. Pulse current, $I_{pulse,i}$, is generated as a result of switching by V_{res}, and given into the synaptic circuits. The behavior of the RFN circuit described above is qualitatively the same as that of the RFN model.

4 Burst Synchronization in Pulse-Coupled RFN circuits

We here demonstrate burst synchronization in two pulse-coupled RFN circuits using the circuit simulator, T-Spice Pro, with the model parameters for the

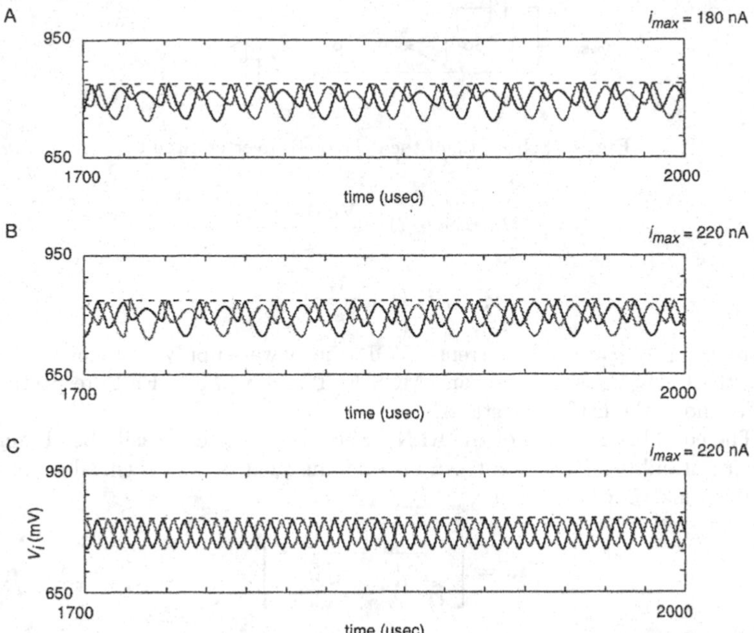

Fig. 7. Out of phase synchronization in two pulse-coupled resonate-and-fire circuits.

AMI 0.35-μm CMOS process. Through following simulations, we set the supply voltages at VDD = 1.5 V, $V_{\rm th}$ = 835 mV, and $V_{\rm rst}$ = 730 mV, the bias current at I_{U_i} = 14 nA, I_{V_i} = 10 nA, and $I_{\rm bias}$ = 250 nA, and the capacitance of the membrane circuit, the delay-and-inverter circuit, and the synaptic circuits, at $C_1 = C_2 = 0.5$ pF, $C_3 = 0.5$ pF. $C_{\rm p} = 0.02$ pF, respectively.

Figure 7 shows out of phase synchronization of the two pulse-coupled RFN circuits. We determined circuit parameters so that the subthreshold behavior of the RFN circuit became qualitatively same as that of the RFN model with the parameters used in the previous section, and the period of the subthreshold oscillation was set at about 18.3 μs. We changed the maximal amplitude of the synaptic current i_{max} from 150 nA to 250 nA. The synaptic currents were injected into each RFN circuit through five excitatory synaptic circuits for each firing. When i_{max} = 180 nA, 3 : 3 out of phase burst synchronization was observed (Fig. 7A). Such 3 : 3 burst synchronization became unstable around i_{max} = 193 nA. Figure 7B shows 2 : 2 out of phase burst synchronization at i_{max} = 220 nA. Such 2 : 2 out of phase burst synchronization coexists with 1 : 1 synchronization depending on the initial conditions (Fig. 7C). Figure 8 shows phase plane portraits of the RFN circuit during two types of the burst synchronization at a steady state. In spite of disturbance due to reseting pulse noise, both types of burst synchronization were maintained. These results show

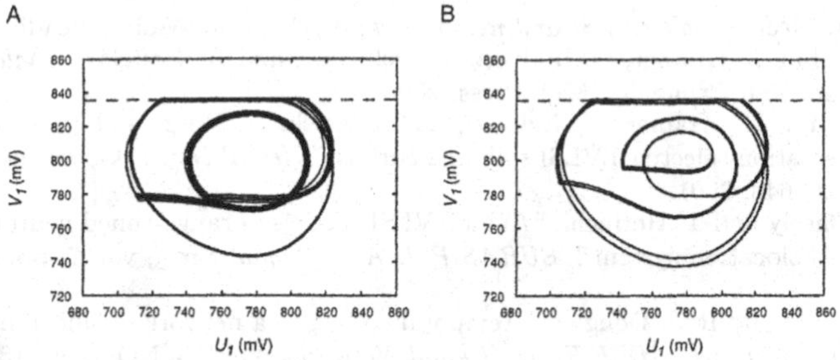

Fig. 8. Phase plane portraits of the RFN circuit at a steady state. (A) 3:3 out of phase burst synchrnozation. (B) 2:2 out of phase burst synchronization.

the stability of the out of phase burst synchronization in the two pulse-coupled RFN circuits. When out of phase burst synchronization became unstable, quasi periodic burst synchronization occurred. During autonomous firing, the firing frequency is larger than the natural frequency of the subthreshold oscillation of the RFN circuit. This induces the out of phase burst synchronization. Thus, the location of the reset value affects the stability of the out of phase burst synchronization since the reset value determines the firing frequency during autonomous periodic firing. In the above simulations, we fixed the parameters except for the maximal amplitude of the synaptic current. If we change the parameters, such as the threshold value and the bias currents, the stability of burst synchronization may change greatly. It should be noted that the bias currents change the equilibrium point and the natural frequency of the RFN circuit; consequently they also change the stability of the burst synchronization.

5 Conclusions

We have shown the out of phase burst synchronization in two pulse-coupled RFN model and its analog integrated circuit implementation. Through circuit simulations using SPICE, we have confirmed the stable region for out of phase burst synchronization. Such burst synchronization is of peculiar in the system of two pulse-coupled RFN circuits. As further considerations, we are going to study collective behavior in a large scale of coupled RFN circuits in view of both theoretical analysis and practical implementation.

References

1. E. M. Izhikevich, "Resonate-and-fire neurons," *Neural Networks*, vol. 14, pp. 883-894, 2001.
2. K. Miura and M. Okada, "Pulse-coupled resoante-and-fire neurons," *Phys. Rev. E*, vol. 70, 021914, 2004.

3. C. A. Mead, *Analog VLSI and neural systems*, Addison-Wesley, Reading, 1989.
4. S.-C. Liu, J. Kramer, G. Indiveri, T. Delbruck, and R. Douglas, *Analog VLSI: Circuits and Principles*, MIT Press, 2002.
5. S.-C. Liu, J. Kramer, G. Indiveri, T. Delbruck, T. Burg, and R. J. Douglas, "Orientation-selective aVLSI spiking neurons," *Neural Networks*, vol. 14, no. 6-7, pp. 629-643, 2001.
6. M. Cheely and T. Horiuchi, "Analog VLSI models of range-tuned neurons in the bat echolocation system," *EURASIP J. Appl. Signal Proc.*, vol. 7, pp. 649-658, 2003.
7. S.-C. Liu and R. J. Douglas, "Temporal coding in a network of silicon integrate-and-fire neurons," *IEEE Trans. Neural Networks*, Vol. 15, NO.5, pp. 1305-1314, 2004.
8. Y. Kanazawa, T. Asai, M. Ikebe, and Y. Amemiya, "A novel CMOS circuit for depressing synapse and its application to contrast-invariant pattern classification and synchrony detection," *Int. J. Robotics and Automation*, vol. 19, no. 4, pp. 206-212, 2004.
9. H. Tanaka, T. Morie, K. Aihara, "Associative memory operation in a Hopfield-type spiking neural network with modulation of resting membrane potential," presented at *Int. Symp. on Nonlinear Theory and its Applications,* Bruges, Belgium, 2005.
10. G. Indiveri, E. Chicca and R. J. Douglas, "A VLSI array of low-power spiking neurons and bistable synapse with spike-timing dependent plasticity," *IEEE Trans. Neural Networks,* vol. 17, no. 1, pp. 211-221, 2006.
11. C. Rasche and R. H. R. Hahnloser, "Silicon synaptic depression," *Biol. Cybern.*, vol. 84, pp. 57-62, 2001.
12. S.-C. Liu, "Analog VLSI circuits for short-term dynamic synapses," *EURASIP J. Appl. Signal Proc.*, vol. 7, pp 620-628, 2003.
13. A. Bofill-i-Petit and A. F. Murray, "Synchrony detection and amplification by silicon neurons With STDP synapses, *IEEE Trans. Neural Networks*, Vol. 15, NO.5, pp. 1296- 1304, 2004.
14. S. R. Schultz and M. A. Jabri, "Analogue VLSI integrate-and-fire neuron with frequency adaptation," *Electronic Letters,* vol. 31, no. 16, pp. 1357-1358, 1995.
15. K. A. Boahen, *Retinomorphic Vision Systems: Reverse Engineering the Vertebrate Retina*, Ph.D. thesis, California Institute of Technology, Pasadena CA, 1997.
16. A. van Schaik, "Building blocks for electronic spiking neural networks," *Neural Networks*, vol. 14, no. 6-7, pp. 617-628, 2001.
17. G. Indiveri, "A low-power adaptive integrate-and-fire neuron circuit," in *proc. IEEE Int. Symp. Circ. Syst.*, 2003.
18. T. Asai, Y. Kanazawa, and Y. Amemiya, "A subthreshold MOS neuron circuit based on the Volterra system," *IEEE Trans. Neural Networks*, vol. 14, no. 5, pp. 1308-1312, 2003.
19. H. Nakano and T. Saito, "Grouping synchronization in a pulse-coupled network of chaotic spiking oscillators," *IEEE Trans. Neural Networks,* vol. 15, no. 5, pp. 1018-1026, 2004.
20. Y. Horio, T. Taniguchi and K. Aihara, "An Asynchronous Spiking Chaotic Neuron Integrated Circuit," *Neurocomputing*, Vol. 64, pp. 447-472, 2005.
21. K. Nakada, T. Asai, H. Hayashi, "A silicon resotate-and-fire neuron on the Volterra system," presented at *Int. Symp. on Nonlinear Theory and its Applications,* Bruges, Belgium, 2005.

Ant Colonies using Arc Consistency Techniques for the Set Partitioning Problem

Broderick Crawford[1,2] and Carlos Castro[2]

[1] Escuela de Ingeniería Informática, Pontificia Universidad Católica de Valparaíso, Chile
[2] Departamento de Informática, Universidad Técnica Federico Santa María, Chile
broderick.crawford@ucv.cl Carlos.Castro@inf.utfsm.cl

Abstract. In this paper, we solve some benchmarks of Set Covering Problem and Equality Constrained Set Covering or Set Partitioning Problem. The resolution techniques used to solve them were Ant Colony Optimization algorithms and Hybridizations of Ant Colony Optimization with Constraint Programming techniques based on Arc Consistency. The concept of Arc Consistency plays an essential role in constraint satisfaction as a problem simplification operation and as a tree pruning technique during search through the detection of local inconsistencies with the uninstantiated variables. In the proposed hybrid algorithms, we explore the addition of this mechanism in the construction phase of the ants so they can generate only feasible partial solutions. Computational results are presented showing the advantages to use this kind of additional mechanisms to Ant Colony Optimization in strongly constrained problems where pure Ant Algorithms are not successful.

1 Introduction

Set Covering Problem (SCP) and Set Partitioning Problem (SPP), or Equality Constrained Set Covering, are two types of problems that can model different real life situations [2, 3, 11, 21]. In this work, we solve some benchmarks of them with Ant Colony Optimization (ACO) algorithms and some hybridizations of ACO with Constraint Programming based on Arc Consistency.

There exist problems for which ACO is of limited effectiveness, among them the very strongly constrained problems. They are problems for which neighborhoods contain few solutions, or none at all, and local search is of very limited use. Probably, the most significant of such problems is the SPP [18]. A direct implementation of the basic ACO framework is incapable of obtaining feasible solutions for many standard tested instances of SPP. The best performing metaheuristic for SPP is a genetic algorithm due to Chu and Beasley [5, 6]. There exist already some first approaches applying ACO to the SCP. In [1, 16] ACO has been used as a construction algorithm and the approach has only been tested on some small SCP instances. Others works [15, 17] apply Ant Systems to the SCP and use techniques to remove redundant columns and local search to improve solutions. In [14] there is a very interesting work of ACO solving the related problem Set Packing.

In this paper we explore the addition of a mechanism, usually used in complete techniques, in the construction phase of ACO algorithms in a different

Please use the following format when citing this chapter:

Crawford, B., Castro, C., 2006, in IFIP International Federation for Information Processing, Volume 218, Professional Practice in Artificial Intelligence, eds. J. Debenham, (Boston: Springer), pp. 295–301.

way of the used form in [20] where was proposed a lookahead function evaluating pheromone in a supersequence problem, and in [13] where was introduced a lookahead mechanism to estimate the quality of the partial solution.

The remainder of the paper is organised as follows: Section 2 is devoted to the presentation of the problems and their mathematical models. In Section 3, we describe the applicability of the ACO algorithm for solving SPP and SCP. In Section 4, we present the basic concepts to adding Constraint Programming techniques to the two basic ACO algorithms: Ant System and Ant Colony System. In Section 5, we present results when adding Constraint Programming techniques to the two basic ACO algorithms to solve some benchmarks from ORLIB. Finally, in Section 6 we conclude the paper and give some perspectives for future research.

2 Equality Constrained Set Covering Problem

Equality Constrained Set Covering Problem, or Set Partitioning Problem, is the NP-complete problem of partitioning a given set into mutually independent subsets while minimizing a cost function defined as the sum of the costs associated to each of the eligible subsets. SPP importance derives from the fact that many combinatorial optimization problems (such as, crew scheduling, vehicle routing, project scheduling, and warehouse location problems, to name a few) can be modeled as SPP with maybe some additional constraints. In SPP we are given a $m \times n$ matrix $A = (a_{ij})$ in which all the matrix elements are either zero or one. Additionally, each column is given a non-negative cost c_j. We say that a column j can cover a row i if $a_{ij} = 1$. Let J denotes a subset of the columns and x_j a binary variable which is one if column j is chosen and zero otherwise. The SPP can be defined formally as follows:

$$Minimize \;\; f(x) = \sum_{j=1}^{n} c_j \times x_j$$

Subject to

$$\sum_{j=1}^{n} a_{ij} \times x_j = 1; \forall i = 1, \ldots, m$$

These constraints enforce that each row is covered by exactly one column. The SCP is a SPP relaxation. The goal in the SCP is to choose a subset of the columns of minimal weight which covers every row. The SCP can be defined formally using constraints to enforce that each row is covered by at least one column as follows:

$$\sum_{j=1}^{n} a_{ij} \times x_j \geq 1; \forall i = 1, \ldots, m$$

3 Ant Colony Optimization for Set Covering Problems

ACO can be applied in a very straightforward way to the SCP and SPP. The columns are chosen as the solution components and have associated a cost and a pheromone trail [10]. Each column can be visited by an ant once and only once and that a final solution has to cover all rows. A walk of an ant over the graph representation corresponds to the iterative addition of columns to the partial solution obtained so far. Each ant starts with an empty solution and adds columns until a cover is completed. A pheromone trail and a heuristic information are associated to each eligible column j. A column to be added is chosen with a probability that depends of pheromone trail and the heuristic information. In the application of ACO to other problems, such as the TSP, there are some differences. For example, the SPP/SCP solution construction of the individual ants does not necessarily end after the same number of steps of each ant, but only when a cover is completed. One of the most crucial design decisions to be made in ACO algorithms is the modeling of the set of pheromones. In the original ACO implementation for TSP the choice was to put a pheromone value on every link between a pair of cities, but for other combinatorial problems often can be assigned pheromone values to the decision variables (first order pheromone values) [10]. In this work the pheromone trail is put on the problems componentes (each elegible column J) instead of the problems connections. And setting good pheromone quantity is a non trivial task too. The quantity of pheromone trail laid on columns is based on the idea: *the more pheromone trail on a particular item, the more profitable that item is* [16]. Then, the pheromone deposited in each component will be in relation to its frequency in the ants solutions. In this work we divided this frequency by the number of ants obtaining better results. We use a dynamic heuristic information that depends on the partial solution of an ant. It can be defined as $\eta_j = \frac{e_j}{c_j}$, where e_j is the so called cover value, that is, the number of additional rows covered when adding column j to the current partial solution, and c_j is the cost of column j [10]. In other words, the heuristic information measures the unit cost of covering one additional row. An ant ends the solution construction when all rows are covered. Figure 1 describe the pure ACO algorithm to solve SCP and SPP.

In this work, we use two instances of ACO: Ant System (AS) and Ant Colony System (ACS) algorithms, the original and the most famous algorithms in the ACO family [9, 8, 10]. ACS improves the search of AS using: a different transition rule in the constructive phase, exploting the heuristic information in a more rude form, using a list of candidates to future labeling and using a different treatment of pheromone. ACS has demostrated better performance than AS in a wide range of problems.

Trying to solve larger instances of SPP with the original ACO implementation derives in a lot of unfeasible labeling of variables, and the ants can not obtain complete solutions. In this paper we explore the addition of a mechanism in the construction phase of ACO in order to that only feasible partial solutions are generated.

```
Procedure ACO_for_SCP_and_SPP
 Begin
  InitParameters();
   While (remain iterations) do
    For k := 1 to nants do
     While (solution is not completed) do
      AddColumnToSolution(election)
      AddToTabuList(k);
     EndWhile
    EndFor
    UpdateOptimum();
    UpdatePheromone();
   EndWhile
 Return best_solution_founded
End.
```

Fig. 1. Pure ACO algorithm for SCP and SPP

4 ACO with Constraint Programming

Recently, some efforts have been done in order to integrate Constraint Programming techniques to ACO algorithms [19, 12].An hibridization of ACO and CP can be approached from two directions: we can either take ACO or CP as the base algorithm and try to embed the respective other method into it. A form to integrate CP into ACO is to let it reduce the possible candidates of the not yet instantiated variables participating in the same constraints that the actual variable. A different approach would be to embed ACO within CP. The obvious point at which ACO can interact with CP is during the labeling phase, using ACO to learn a value ordering that is more likely to produce good solutions.

In this work, ACO uses CP in the variable selection (when adding columns to partial solution). The CP algorithm used in this paper is Arc Consistency Technique and Chronological Backtracking [7]. In the construction phase ACO performs Arc Consistency between pairs of a not yet instantiated variable and an instantiated variable, i.e., when a value is assigned to the current variable, any value in the domain of a future variable which conflicts with this assignment is removed from the domain.

Adding Arc Consistency Technique and Backtracking to ACO for SPP means that columns are chosen if they do not produce any conflict with respect to the next column to be chosen, trying to assure the possibilities of ants in order to complete the solutions. Figure 2 describe the hybrid ACO with CP.

5 Experiments and Results

Table 1 presents results when adding Forward Checking to the basic ACO algorithms for solving standard benchmarks taken from the ORLIB [4]. The first four columns of the Table 1 present the problem code, the number of rows (constraints), the number of columns (decision variables), and the best known solution for each instance, respectively. The next two columns present the cost obtained when applying AS and ACS, and the last two columns present the results combining AS and ACS with Forward Checking. Considering several tests

```
Procedure ACO+CP_for_SPP
 Begin
  InitParameters();
  While (remain iterations) do
     For k := 1 to nants do
        While (solution is not completed) and TabuList <> J do
           Choose next Column j with Transition Rule Probability
           For each Row i covered by j do                /* j constraints          */
             feasible(i):= Posting(j);                   /* Constraint Propagation */
           EndFor
           If feasible(i) for all i then AddColumnToSolution(j)
                                    else Backtracking(j); /* set j uninstantiated  */
           AddColumnToTabuList(j);
        EndWhile
     EndFor
    UpdateOptimum();
    UpdatePheromone();
  EndWhile
  Return best_solution_founded
 End.
```

Fig. 2. Hybrid ACO+CP algorithm for SPP

and published experimental results [16, 17, 10] we use the following parameters values for the algorithms: evaporation rate = 0.4, number of iterations = 160, number of ants = 120, influence of pheromone (alpha) = 1.0, influence of heuristic information (beta) = 0.5, for ACS the list size = 500 (in scp41, scp42, scp48, scp61, scp62, and scp63), for ACS Qo = 0.5.

Algorithms were implemented using ANSI C, GCC 3.3.6, under Microsoft Windows XP Professional version 2002.

Problem	Rows	Columns	Optimum	AS	ACS	AS + FC	ACS + FC
sppnw39	25	677	10080	11670	10758	11322	10545
sppnw34	20	899	10488	13341	11289	10713	10797
sppnw26	23	771	6796	6976	6956	6880	6880
sppnw23	19	711	12534	14304	14604	13932	12880
scp41	200	1000	429	473	463	458	683
scp42	200	1000	512	594	590	574	740
scp48	200	1000	492	524	522	537	731
scp51	200	1000	253	289	280	289	464
scp61	200	1000	138	157	154	155	276
scp62	200	1000	146	169	163	170	280
scp63	200	1000	145	161	157	161	209

Table 1. ACO with Forward Checking

The effectiveness of ACO improved with Arc Consistency is shown to the SPP, the strongly constrained characteristic of this problem does the stochastic behavior of pure unsuitable for solve it. In the original ACO implementation the SPP solving derives in a lot of unfeasible labeling of variables, and the ants can not complete solutions. For SCP, the huge size of the search space and the relaxation of the constraints does ACO algorithms work better than ACO+CP considering the same execution conditions.

6 Conclusions and Future Directions

The concept of Arc Consistency plays an essential role in Constraint Programming as a problem simplification operation and as a tree pruning technique during search through the detection of local inconsistencies among the uninstantiated variables. We have shown that it is possible to add Arc Consistency to any ACO algorithms. The computational results confirm that the performance of ACO is possible to improve with some types of hibridization.

Our goal was to demonstrate that ACO is possible to improve with CP in some kind of problems. Future versions of the algorithm will study the pheromone treatment representation and the incorporation of available local search techniques in order to reduce the input problem (Pre Processing) and improve the solutions given by the ants (Post Processing). The ants solutions may contain redundant components which can be eliminated by a fine tuning after the solution, then we will explore Post Processing procedures, which consist in the identification and replacement of the columns of the ACO solution in each iteration by more effective columns.

References

1. D. Alexandrov and Y. Kochetov. Behavior of the Ant Colony Algorithm for the Set Covering Problem. In *Proc. of Symp. Operations Research*, pp 255–260. Springer Verlag, 2000.
2. E. Andersson, E. Housos, N. Kohl and D. Wedelin. Crew Pairing Optimization. *In Yu G.(ed.)Operations Research in the Airline Industry*,Kluwer Academic Publishing, 1998.
3. E. Balas and M. Padberg. Set Partitioning: A Survey. *SIAM Review*, 18:710–760, 1976.
4. J. E. Beasley. OR-Library:Distributing test problem by electronic mail. *Journal of Operational Research Society*, 41(11):1069–1072, 1990.
5. J. E. Beasley and P. C. Chu. A genetic algorithm for the set covering problem. *European Journal of Operational Research*, 94(2):392–404, 1996.
6. P. C. Chu and J. E. Beasley. Constraint handling in genetic algorithms: the set partitoning problem. *Journal of Heuristics*, 4:323–357, 1998.
7. R. Dechter and D. Frost. Backjump-based Backtracking for Constraint Satisfaction Problems. *Artificial Intelligence*, 136:147–188, 2002.
8. M. Dorigo, G. Di Caro, and L. M. Gambardella. Ant Algorithms for Discrete Optimization. *Artificial Life*, 5:137–172, 1999.
9. M. Dorigo and L. M. Gambardella. Ant colony system: A cooperative learning approach to the traveling salesman problem. *IEEE Transactions on Evolutionary Computation*, 1(1):53–66, 1997.
10. M. Dorigo and T. Stutzle. *Ant Colony Optimization*. MIT Press, USA, 2004.
11. A. Feo, G. Mauricio, and A. Resende. A Probabilistic Heuristic for a Computationally Difficult Set Covering Problem. *OR Letters*, 8:67–71, 1989.
12. F. Focacci, F. Laburthe and A. Lodi. Local Search and Constraint Programming. *Handbook of metaheuristics*,Kluwer, 2002.

13. C. Gagne, M. Gravel and W.L. Price. A Look-Ahead Addition to the Ant Colony Optimization Metaheuristic and its Application to an Industrial Scheduling Problem. In J.P. Sousa et al., eds., *Proceedings of the fourth Metaheuristics International Conference MIC'01*, July 16-20, 2001. Pages 79-84.
14. X. Gandibleux, X. Delorme and V. T'Kindt. An Ant Colony Algorithm for the Set Packing Problem. In M. Dorigo et al., editor, *ANTS 2004*, vol 3172 of *LNCS*, pp 49–60. SV, 2004.
15. R. Hadji, M. Rahoual, E. Talbi, and V. Bachelet. Ant colonies for the set covering problem. In M. Dorigo et al., editor, *ANTS 2000*, pp 63–66, 2000.
16. G. Leguizamón and Z. Michalewicz. A new version of Ant System for subset problems. In *Congress on Evolutionary Computation, CEC'99*, pp 1459–1464, Piscataway, NJ, USA, 1999. IEEE Press.
17. L. Lessing, I. Dumitrescu, and T. Stutzle. A Comparison Between ACO Algorithms for the Set Covering Problem. In M. Dorigo et al., editor, *ANTS 2004*, vol 3172 of *LNCS*, pp 1–12. SV, 2004.
18. V. Maniezzo and M. Milandri. An Ant-Based Framework for Very Strongly Constrained Problems. In M. Dorigo et al., editor, *ANTS 2002*, vol 2463 of *LNCS*, pp 222–227. SV, 2002.
19. B. Meyer and A. Ernst. Integrating ACO and Constraint Propagation. In M. Dorigo et al., editor, *ANTS 2004*, vol 3172 of *LNCS*, pp 166–177. SV, 2004.
20. R. Michel and M. Middendorf. An Island model based Ant system with lookahead for the shortest supersequence problem. *Lecture notes in Computer Science, Springer Verlag*, 1498:692–701, 1998.
21. R. L. Rardin. *Optimization in Operations Research.* Prentice Hall, 1998.

Automatic Query Recommendation using Click-Through Data

Georges Dupret[1] and Marcelo Mendoza[2]

[1] Yahoo! Research Latin America
Blanco Encalada 2120, Santiago, Chile
gdupret@yahoo-inc.com

[2] Department of Computer Science, Universidad de Valparaíso,
Gran Bretaña 1091, Playa Ancha, Valparaíso, Chile
marcelo.mendoza@uv.cl

Abstract. We present a method to help a user redefine a query suggesting a list of similar queries. The method proposed is based on click-through data were sets of similar queries could be identified. Scientific literature shows that similar queries are useful for the identification of different information needs behind a query. Unlike most previous work, in this paper we are focused on the discovery of better queries rather than related queries. We will show with experiments over real data that the identification of better queries is useful for query disambiguation and query specialization.

1 Introduction

Besides the practical difficulties inherent to the manipulation of a large number of pages, the difficulty of ranking documents based on generally very short queries and the fact that query needs are often imprecisely formulated, users are also constrained by the query interface, and often have difficulty articulating a query that could lead to satisfactory results. It happens also that they do not exactly know what they are searching for and select query terms in a trial and error process.

Better formulation of vague queries are likely to appear in the query logs because experienced users tend to avoid vague formulation and issue queries specific enough to discard irrelevant documents. Different studies sustain this claim: [7] report that an independent survey of 40,000 web users found that after a failed search, 76% of users try rephrasing their query on the same search engine. Besides, the queries can be identical or articulated differently with different terms but they represent the same information needs as found and reported in [6, 9].

We propose in this work a simple and novel query recommendation algorithm. While most methods recommend queries related to the original query, this method aims at improving it.

Please use the following format when citing this chapter:

Dupret, G., Mendoza, M., 2006, in IFIP International Federation for Information Processing, Volume 218, Professional Practice in Artificial Intelligence, eds. J. Debenham, (Boston: Springer), pp. 303–312.

1.1 Related Work

A well known query reformulation strategy is *relevance feedback* [1]. The main idea is to present to a user a list of documents related to an initial query. After examining them, the user selects those which are relevant. Using important terms attached to the selected documents, it is possible to reformulate the original query adding terms to it and *reweighting* the query representation in the document vector model. Recent work also incorporate logs as a useful source data for this strategy [2]. For example, in [5], large query logs are used to construct a surrogate for each document consisting of the queries that were a close match to that document. It is found that the queries that match a document are a fair description of its content. They also investigate whether query associations can play a role in query expansion. In this sense, in [8], a somewhat similar approach of summarizing document with queries is proposed: Query association is based on the notion that a query that is highly similar to a document is a good descriptor of that document. One of the main differences of *relevance feedback* strategies with our approach is that relevance feedback is focused on the improvement of the quality of the documents retrieved. We propose a more flexible strategy, focused on the identification of alternate queries allowing the specialization or generalization of the original query. Finally, we are interested in the identification of better queries more than related queries.

The literature also shows related work based on clustering techniques. For example, Wen et al. [10] suggest a method for recommend queries using clustering techniques over data generated from query logs. Given a particular query, it utilizes the previous session logs of the same query to return pages that most users visit. To get a statistically significant result, it is only applied on a small set of popular queries. Because the engine is a commercial one, more details on the method are uneasy to obtain. On the other hand, Baeza-Yates et al. [4] recommend queries building a term-weight vector for each query. Each term is weighted according to the number of document occurrences and the number of selection of the documents in which the term appears. Then they use clustering techniques to identify related queries. Unfortunately, the method is limited to queries that appears in the log and is biased by the search engine.

Finally, some interesting applications such as *Electronic Roads* [3] use concepts related to query specialization in order to offer to the user better navigation choices. Considering user profile information and meta-data, the application creates dynamic links in each new navigation step to new information units. One of the main differences between *Electronic Roads* and our approach is that the creation of the meta-data is performed by experts, so the proposed method is semi-automatic. Also the system needs a user profile to improve their recommendations. Is our aim to propose an automatic query recommendation method based only in the information registered in the logs, without the user cooperation.

1.2 Contribution

The simple method we propose here aims at discovering alternate queries that improve the search engine ranking of documents: We order the documents selected during past sessions of a query according to the ranking of other past queries. If the resulting ranking is better than the original one, we recommend the associated query.

1.3 Outline

The remainder of this paper is organized as follows. In Sect. 2 we present our query recommendation method. We apply this method in Sect. 3 on the query logs of `TodoCL`, an important Chilean search engine. Finally we conclude in Sect. 4.

2 Query Recommendation Framework

2.1 Preliminaries

First, we need to introduce some definitions. We understand by `keyword` any unbroken string that describes the query or document content. A `query` is a set of one or more keywords that represent an information need formulated to the search engine. The same query may be submitted several times. Each submission induces a different `query instance`. A `query session` consists of one query and the URLs the user clicked on, while a `click` is a Web page selection belonging to a query session. We also define a notion of consistency between a query and a document:

Definition 1 (Consistency). *A document is* `consistent` *with a query if it has been selected a significant number of times during the sessions of the query.*

Consistency ensures that a query and a document bear a natural relation in the opinion of users and discards documents that have been selected by mistake once or a few time. Similarly, we say that a query and a set of documents are consistent if each document in the set is consistent with the query.

2.2 Query Recommendation method

Many identical queries can represent different user information needs. Depending on the topic the user has in mind, he will tend to select a particular subgroup of documents. Consequently, the set of selections in a session reflects a sub-topic of the original query. We might attempt to assess the existing correlations between the documents selected during sessions of a same query, create clusters and identify queries relevant to each cluster, but we prefer a simpler, more direct method where clustering is done at the level of query sessions.

Let $D(s_q)$ be the set of documents selected during a session s_q of a query q. If we make the assumption that $D(s_q)$ represents the information need behind q, we might wonder if other queries are consistent with $D(s_q)$ and better rank the documents of $D(s_q)$. If these queries exist, they are potential query recommendations. We then repeat the procedure for each session of the original query, select the potentially recommendable queries that appear in a significant number of sessions and propose them as recommendations to the user interested in q.

We need to introduce a criteria in order to compare the ranking of a set of documents for two different queries. Firstly, we define the rank of a document in a query as follows:

Definition 2 (Rank of a Documents). *The rank of document u in query q, denoted $r(u, q)$, is the position of document u in the answer list returned by the search engine.*

We extend this definition to sets of documents:

Definition 3 (Rank of a Set of Documents). *The rank of a set U of documents in a query q is defined as:*

$$r(U, q) = \max_{u \in U} r(u, q) \ .$$

In other words, the document with the worst ranking determines the rank of the set. Intuitively, if a set of documents achieves a better rank in a query q_a than in a query q_b, then we say that q_a ranks the documents better than q_b. We formalize this as follows:

Definition 4 (Ranking Comparison). *A query q_a ranks better a set U of documents than a query q_b if:*

$$r(U, q_a) < r(U, q_b) \ .$$

This criteria is illustrated in Fig. 1 for a session containing two documents.

Now, it is possible to recommend queries comparing their rank sets. We can formalize the method as follows:

Definition 5 (Recommendation). *A query q_a is a recommendation for a query q_b if a significant number of sessions of q_a are consistent with q_b and are ranked better by q_a than by q_b.*

The recommendation algorithm induces a directed graph between queries. The original query is the root of a tree with the recommendations as leaves. Each branch of the tree represents a different specialization or sub-topic of the original query. The depth between a root and its leaves is always one, because we require the recommendations to improve the associated document set ranking.

Finally, we observe that nothing prevents two queries from recommending each other:

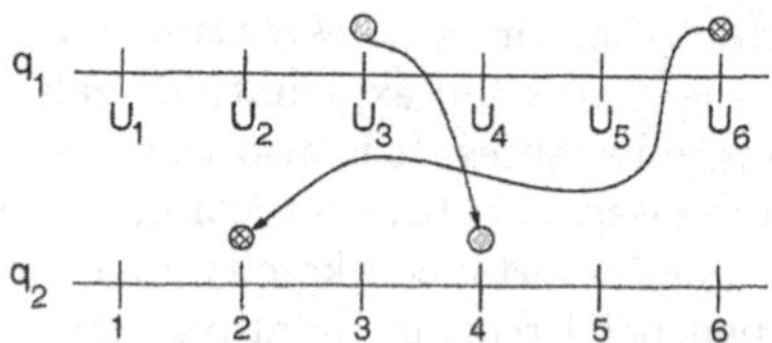

Fig. 1. Comparison of the ranking of two queries. A session of the original query q_1 contains selections of documents U_3 and U_6 appearing at position 3 and 6 respectively. The rank of this set of document is 6 by virtue of Def. 3. By contrast, query q_2 achieves rank 4 for the same set of documents and therefore qualifies as a candidate recommendation.

Definition 6 (Quasi-synonyms). *Two queries are quasi-synonyms when they recommend each other.*

We will see in the following section that this definition leads to queries that are indeed semantically very close.

3 Experimental Results

In this section we present the evaluation of the method introducing a brief descriptive analysis of the results and showing a user evaluation experiment. Firstly we will describe the data used for the experiments.

3.1 Data

The algorithm implied by Def. 5 was easy to implement using log data organized in a relational database. We used the logs of the TodoCL search engine (www.todocl.cl) for a period of three months. TodoCL is a search engine that mainly covers the .cl domain (Chilean web pages) and some pages included in the .net domain that are related with Chilean ISP providers. It indexed over 3,100,000 Web pages and has currently over 50,000 requests per day.

Over three months the logs gathered 20,563,567 requests, most of them with no selections: Meta search engines issue queries and re-use the answer of *TodoCL* but do not return information on user selections. A total of 213,540 distinct queries lead to 892,425 registered selections corresponding to 387,427 different URLs. There are 390,932 query sessions. Thus, in average users clicked 2,28 pages per query session and 4,17 pages per query.

3.2 Descriptive Analysis of the Results

We intend to illustrate with two examples that the recommendation method has the ability to identify sub-topics and suggest query refinement. Fig. 2 shows the recommendation graphs for the queries `Valparaiso` and `Fiat`. The query `Valparaiso` requires some contextual explanation. Valparaiso is an important harbor city, with various universities. It is also the home for the *Mercurio*, the most important Chilean newspaper. It also recommends some queries that are typical of any city of some importance like city hall, municipality and so on. The more potentially beneficial recommendations have a higher link number. For example $9/33 \simeq 27\%$ of the users would have had access to a better ranking of the documents they selected if they had searched for `university` instead of `Valparaiso`. This also implicitly suggests to the user the query `university Valparaiso`, although we are maybe presuming the user intentions. A more complex recommendation graph is associated to the query `Fiat`. The user who issued the query `Fiat` is recommended essentially to specify the car model he is interested in, if he wants spare parts, or if he is interesting in selling or buying a fiat. Note that such a graph also suggests to a user interested in – say – the history or the profitability of the company to issue a query more specific to his needs.

We already observed that two queries can recommend each other. We show in Table 1 a list of such query pairs found in the logs. We reported also the number of original query sessions and number of sessions enhanced by the recommendation so as to have an appreciation of the statistical significance of the links. We excluded the mutual recommendation pairs with less than 2 links. For example, in the first row, out of the 13 sessions for `ads`, 3 would have been better satisfied by `advert`, while 10 of the 20 sessions for `advert` would have been better satisfied by `ads`.

→	query	query	←
3/13	ads	advert	10/20
3/105	cars	used cars	2/241
34/284	chat	sports	2/13
2/21	classified ads	advertisement	2/20
4/12	code of penal proceedings	code of penal procedure	2/9
3/10	courses of english	english courses	2/5
2/27	dvd	musical dvd	2/5
2/5	family name	genealogy	2/16
3/9	hotels in santiago	hotels santiago	2/11
5/67	mail in Chile	mail company of Chile	2/3
7/15	penal code	code of penal procedure	2/9
8/43	rent houses	houses to rent	2/14
2/58	van	light truck	3/25

Table 1. Examples of "Quasi-synonym" queries recommend each other.

We can see that the proposed method generates a clustering *a posteriori* where different sessions consisting of sometimes completely different sets of

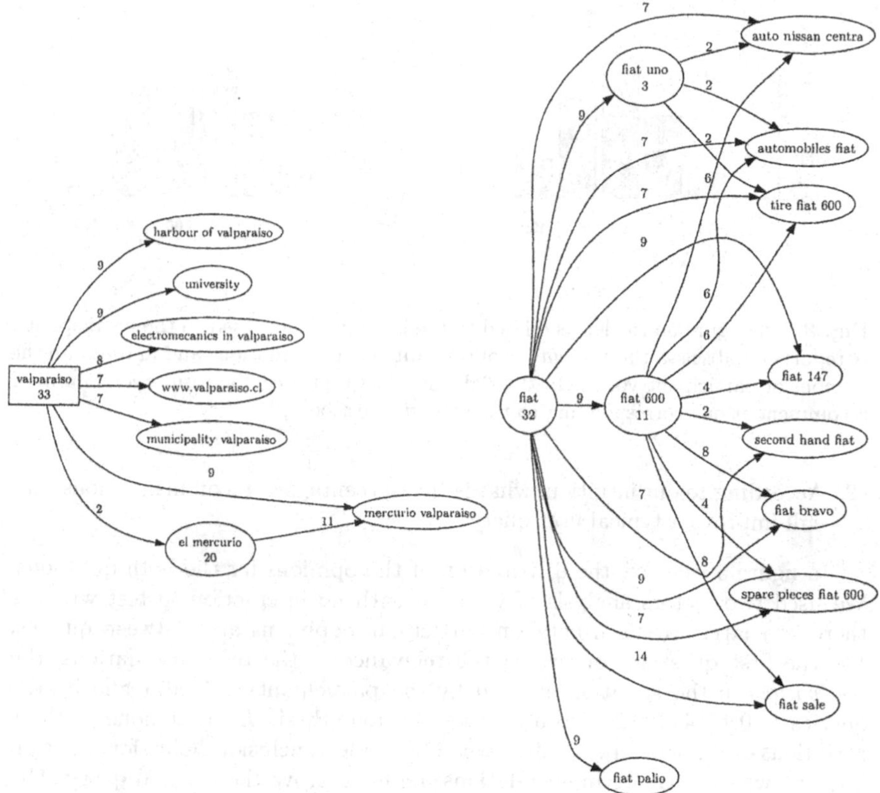

Fig. 2. Queries Valparaiso, Fiat and associated recommendations. The node number indicate the number of query session. The edge numbers count the sessions improved by the pointed query.

documents end up recommending a same query. This query can then label this group of session.

3.3 User Evaluation

We will analyze user evaluations of the quality of query recommendations. We presented to a group of 19 persons of different backgrounds ten recommendation trees similar to Fig. 2, selected randomly from all the trees we extracted from the logs. Obviously we discarded queries with a small number of sessions and queries with a too large number of recommendations. We asked two questions to the participants:

1. What percentage of recommendations are relevant to the original query?

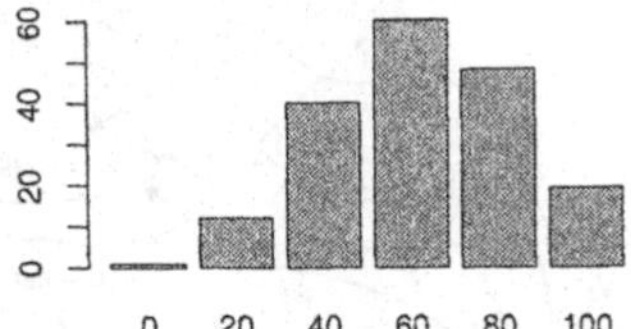

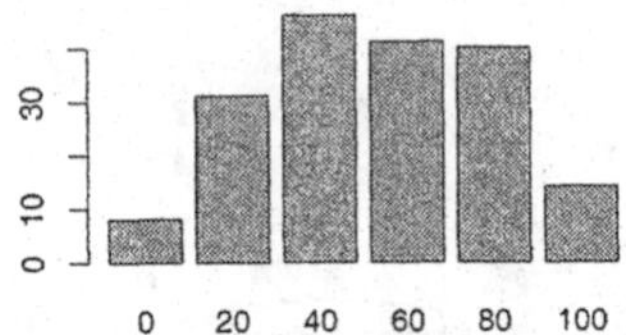

Fig. 3. The figure on the left is related to the first question raised to the participants. It reports on abscissa the percentage of relevant recommendations and in ordinate the number of participant votes. On the right figure, we plotted the results for improved recommendations corresponding to the second question.

2. According to our intuition, what is the percentage of recommendations that will improve a typical user query?

In figure 3 we show the distribution of the opinions for the both questions. We used two factors analysis of variance with no interaction to test whether there is a large variation between participants opinions and between queries. For the first question concerning the relevance of the recommendations, the $p - values$ of the variation induced by the participants is 0.5671 and by the queries is 0.1504, leading to accepting the hypothesis H_0 that none of these variations is statistically significative. The same conclusion holds for question 2 about whether the recommendations might improve the original query. The $p - values$ in this case are 0.9991 and 0.2130. This shows that no participant was over or under estimating the relevance and the improvement percentages systematically, and that no query is particulary worse or better than the other.

The recommendations along with the mean of participants answer can be found in Table 2. Some queries and recommendations in this table are specific to Chile: "El Mercurio" is an important national newspaper, "Colmena" is a private health insurance company but the term "colmena" in Spanish also means beehive. It seems that people searching for honey producers where fooled by a link to the "Colmena" health insurance company. Some sessions of the query for "health insurance company" contained links to "Colmena" that appear high in the ranking for "honey bees". This problem should disappear if we fix a higher consistency threshold 1, which would be possible with larger logs. Folklore and Biology are important activities in the "University of Chile" that users might look for. "Wei" is a computer store.

Query	Relevance	Improvement	Recommended queries
people finders	52%	45%	Chilean finder Argentinian finder OLE search Finder of Chilean people
used trucks	70%	53%	cars offers used cars sales used trucks rentals trucks spare parts
naval battle of Iquique	78%	76%	Arturo Prat biography J. Prieto government treaty of Ancon Chilean navy
computers	74%	61%	*sky Chile* **Wei** motherboards notebook
dictionary	41%	34%	English dictionary dictionary for technology look up words in a dictionary tutorials
El Mercurio	62%	52%	**El Mercurio of December** *currency converter* **El Mercurio de Valparaiso** **El Mercurio de Antofagasta**
health insurance companies	58%	55%	**Banmedica** **Colmena** *honey bees* contralory of health services
map of Santiago	81%	68%	map of Chile Santiago city city map of Santiago street map of Santiago
Universidad de Chile	41%	25%	**Universidad Catolica** university folklore biology
wedding dresses	61%	55%	dress rentals wedding dress rentals party dresses bachelor party

Table 2. Queries used for the experiments and recommendations with strong levels of consistency. Average relevance value is shown in column 2. Average improvement value is shown in column 3. Wrong recommendations are in cursive fonts. Trademarks are in bold fonts.

4 Conclusion

We have proposed a method for query recommendation based on user logs that is simple to implement and has low computational cost. The recommendation method we propose are made only if users are expected to improve. Moreover, the algorithm does not rely on the particular terms appearing in the query and documents, making it robust to alternative formulations of an identical information need. Our experiments show that query graphs induced by our method identify information needs and relate queries without common terms.

Acknowledgements

Marcelo Mendoza was supported by CONICYT Chile, project FONDECYT 1061201.

References

1. J.J. Rochio (1971) Relevance feedback in information retrieval. The SMART Retrieval System - Experiments in Automatic Document Processing, Prentice Hall Inc.
2. Ian Ruthven and Mounia Lalmas and C. J. van Rijsbergen (2003) Incorporating user search behavior into relevance feedback. JASIST 54(6):529-549.
3. Georgios Fakas and Antonis C. Kakas and Christos Schizas (2004) Electronic Roads: Intelligent Navigation Through Multi-Contextual Information. Knowledge Information Systems 6(1):103-124, Springer.
4. Baeza-Yates, R. and Hurtado, C. and Mendoza, M. (2004) Query Recommendation Using Query Logs in Search Engines. Current Trends in Database Technology - EDBT 2004 Workshops, LNCS 3268:588-596, Heraklion, Greece.
5. Bodo Billerbeck and Falk Scholer and Hugh E. Williams and Justin Zobel (2003). Query expansion using associated queries. CIKM 03, 2-9, ACM Press, New Orleans, LA, USA.
6. Jansen, M. and Spink, A. and Bateman, J. and Saracevic, T. (1998). Real life information retrieval: a study of user queries on the web. ACM SIGIR Forum, 32(1):5-17.
7. NPD (2000). Search and Portal Site Survey, Published by NPD New Media Services.
8. Falk Scholer and Hugh E. Williams (2002). Query association for effective retrieval. CIKM 02, 324-331, ACM Press, McLean, Virginia, USA.
9. Silverstein, C. and Henzinger, M. and Hannes, M. and Moricz, M. (1999). Analysis of a Very Large Alta Vista Query Log. SIGIR Forum 33(3):6-12, ACM Press.
10. Wen, J. and Nie, J. and Zhang, H. (2001). Clustering User Queries of a Search Engine. Proc. of the 10th WWW Conference, Hong Kong.

A Shared-Memory Multiprocessor Scheduling Algorithm

Irene Zuccar[1], Mauricio Solar[1], Fernanda Kri[1], Víctor Parada[1]
1 Departamento de Ingeniería Informática, Universidad de Santiago de Chile. http://www.diinf.usach.cl

Abstract. This paper presents an extension of the Latency Time (LT) scheduling algorithm for assigning tasks with arbitrary execution times on a multiprocessor with shared memory. The Extended Latency Time (ELT) algorithm adds to the priority function the synchronization associated with access to the shared memory. The assignment is carried out associating with each task a time window of the same size as its duration, which decreases for every time unit that goes by. The proposed algorithm is compared with the Insertion Scheduling Heuristic (ISH). Analysis of the results established that ELT has better performance with fine granularity tasks (computing time comparable to synchronization time), and also, when the number of processors available to carry out the assignment increases.

1 Introduction

Real-world applications of scheduling is a complex problem in which a large quantity of research have been done in the fields of computer science, artificial intelligence and operational research. Some recently examples are a real application in a printing company shown in [1] and a solution to the Single-Track Railway Scheduling Problem presented in [2]. On the other hand, a comparison of parallel models of genetic algorithm and tabu search to schedule concurrent processes into a parallel machine with homogeneous processors is shown in [3].

In parallel computing there is the problem of finding the best use of the available computer resources of the objective machine with which one is working. After a literature review we could not find any work related that presents a solution that takes into consideration the synchronization time, which is a characteristic of systems with shared memory, in the execution of applications. These applications are usually divided into tasks of different duration that are executed in the available processors. The Latency Time (LT) algorithm [4] approaches this reality, but it has the restriction that the tasks must be of unit duration. This paper presents the

---

Please use the following format when citing this chapter:

Zuccar, I., Solar, M., Kri, F., Parada, V., 2006, in IFIP International Federation for Information Processing, Volume 218, Professional Practice in Artificial Intelligence, eds. J. Debenham, (Boston: Springer), pp. 313–321.

extension of the LT algorithm removing this restriction, allowing tasks with arbitrary duration to be assigned efficiently.

The paper is organized as follows: section 2 introduces the theoretical background of the scheduling problem. Section 3 details the LT algorithm and the extension proposed. Section 4 shows the analysis of the results. Finally, section 5 presents the conclusions.

2 Theoretical Framework

It is always possible to represent a parallel computer application as a task graph. A task graph is a DAG (Directed Acyclic Graph) defined by a tuple (V, E, C, T), where $V = \{n_i, i \in [1, n]\}$ $(n = |V|)$ is the set of nodes that represent the tasks that must be itinerated; $E = \{e_{ij}, i, j \in [1, n]\}$ $(e = |E|)$ is the set of directed edges that indicated the precedence between tasks i and j; $C=\{c_{ij}, i, j \in [1, n]\}$ is the cost associated with each edge of the DAG, and $T=\{t_i, i \in [1, n]\}$ is the computing time for each task. The granularity of a graph is the ratio of the average duration of the tasks and the average of the communications within the DAG (Equation 1).

$$Gr = \frac{\sum_{i \in V} t_i}{n} \Bigg/ \frac{\sum_{i,j \in V} c_{ij}}{e} \qquad (1)$$

Communication is considered when it takes at least 20% of the time occupied in computing. If it is less than that value, it is considered negligible. Therefore, if $(0 < Gr < 5)$, the granularity is said to be *fine*, and if $Gr \geq 5$, the granularity is said to be coarse [4].

2.1 Scheduling Algorithms

Normally, the inputs to the scheduling algorithms are a task graphs (representing an applications), and the number of processors p of the system. The output is a Gantt chart of the assignment found. The algorithms can consider or not consider the cost of communication between the tasks, and in that way it is determined whether they work on machines with shared or distributed memory. Those algorithms that consider arbitrary communication between the tasks are oriented to the exchange of messages. Those that do not consider communication have in general been proposed for machines with shared memory. This is because it is considered that the time necessary for synchronization between the tasks, Δt, is negligible compared to the duration, t_i, of the tasks (therefore, c_{ij} is ignored). It can even be applied to machines with distributed memory, but with the concept of coarse granularity. There are different approaches to solve the scheduling problem: Meta-Heuristic algorithms [5], Clustering algorithms [6], Lists algorithms [7].

Meta-heuristic algorithms [5] are defined in a general way and must be modeled according to the nature of the problem to be solved. Their main advantage is that, even though they do not deliver an optimum solution, they provide solutions close to the optimum.

List algorithms have a special case of assignment heuristic which consists in assigning a priority to each task, and creating a priority list. Then, every enabled task from the list (its predecessors have already been assigned) it is assigned to an available processor. Among the algorithms that consider communication the following can be mentioned: *ISH* (*Insertion Scheduling Heuristic*) [8], *MCP* (*Modified Critical Path*) [9] and *LT* [4]. The *ISH* algorithm operates as a classical list algorithm, but when choosing the processor for the next assignment it looks if the processor has empty time spaces. If so it will consider the rest of the enabled tasks on the list and use, if possible, those spaces.

A *clustering* algorithm maps the nodes of the DAG into disjoint groups of tasks called *clusters*, which correspond to the sets that group tasks. All the tasks of a given *cluster* are executed on the same processor. The main difference between these algorithms is the heuristic that they have to generate the *clusters*. Examples are *DSC* (*Dominant Sequence Clustering*) [10] and *RC* (*Reverse Clustering*) [6].

3 Extended Latency Time Scheduling Algorithm (ELT)

3.1 Latency Time Scheduling Algorithm (LT)

LT is a list algorithm that operates on DAGs with tasks of unit duration. It assumes a multiprocessor system with identical processing elements where each processor carries out only one task at a time until it is completed. This algorithm considers communication in parallel machines with shared memory, using as input parameter the synchronization time, Δt, when accessing the shared memory, which belongs to the system. That time is considered comparable to the duration of the tasks, t_i, by means of the proportionality constant k (Equation 2).

$$\Delta t = k \cdot t_i \tag{2}$$

LT is designed to operate with DAGs of fine granularity, where $t_i < \Delta t$ or $t_i \approx \Delta t$. It is a two-step algorithm: first, it calculates the priority of each task, which aims at maximizing the number of enabled tasks and decreasing the latency time used for synchronization, and second, it generates the Gantt chart corresponding.

3.2 Priority Function of Extended Latency Time Extended (ELT)

The priority function defined for ELT is based on the one used by LT, but more information is added. To choose the most adequate priority function, nine combinations of possible ways of prioritizing the information of each node were defined. Tests were carried out on the sets of DAGs defined in this paper, and the best priority function found, for each node, was based on the following calculations:

$l(n_i)$: Size of the longest path starting from the input nodes of the DAG, up to node n_i. To this size must be added the duration of the tasks and the system's time Δt.
$L(n_i)$: Size of the longest path from node n_i to the output nodes. To this size must be added the duration of the tasks and the system's time Δt.
L_i: Size of the longest path that goes through node n_x (Equation 3).

$$L_i = l(n_i) + L(n_i) - 1 - t_i \tag{3}$$

CP: Set of nodes that make up the critical path.
L_{CP}: Size of the DAG's longest path, called Critical Path.
Out_i: Number of immediate successors of node n_i.
$Hang_i$: Number of tasks achievable by node n_i.
T_i: Duration of each node n_i.
SP_i: priority of the node n_i (*Static Priority*).

Calculation of the priority is done as follows:

1. Determine L_i, $\forall\, i \in [1, n]$ (according to equation 3). Group the tasks that have the same L_i and arrange them in decreasing order: every new ordered group is labeled as L_q with q: 0, 1, 2, ...
2. Determine Out_i, $\forall\, i \in [1, n]$. Group the tasks that have the same out_i and arrange them in decreasing order: every new ordered group is labeled as OUT_r with r: 0, 1, 2, ...
3. Determine $Hang_i$, $\forall\, i \in [1, n]$. Group the tasks that have the same $hang_i$ and arrange them in decreasing order: every new ordered group is labeled as $HANG_s$ with s: 0, 1, 2, ...
4. Determine T_i, $\forall\, i \in [1, n]$. Group the tasks that have the same T_i and arrange them in decreasing order: every new ordered group is labeled as T_u with u: 0, 1, 2, ...
5. Determine $priority_i$, $\forall\, i \in [1, n]$. To do this, add the subscripts of the subsets (L_q, OUT_r, $HANG_s$, T_u) to which each task belongs. Group the tasks that have the same $priority_i$ and arrange them in decreasing order: every new ordered group is labeled as PG_v con v: 0, 1, 2, ...
6. Determine $SP_i = \{v \,/\, n_i \in PG_v\}$, $\forall\, i \in [1, n]$.

3.3 Assignment's Extended Latency Time (ELT)

ELT [11] is capable of operating with tasks of arbitrary duration, using the same assignment policy as LT. It should be noted that the relation shown in Equation 2 does not represent this new instance. However, Δt remains constant and is an input parameter to the algorithm. Every task has a time window of a size corresponding to its duration. For every time unit that goes by, the window of the task at the moment processed, are reduced by one unit until they reach zero, at which time the tasks that are enabled can be updated, and the corresponding assignments can be made on the processors that are no longer busy.

The ELT algorithm, whose computing complexity is $O(n^2)$, is shown below.

ELT Algorithm

```
t=0
Calculate priority for each node nx.
For each node, define a Time Window equal to the size of the task.
Put into Unsched all DAG nodes.
Put into Enable all nodes with entry level tlevel = 1*.
Put into groupp+1 all Enable nodes.
EnabledTasks := TRUE
WHILE Unsched is not empty DO
  IF EnabledTasks THEN Schedule(t)
                       Update Enable with recently assigned nodes.
  Displace the Time Window for each task in Schedj(t)
  IF any task assigned completed its Time Window THEN
        EnabledTasks:= TRUE
  ELSE EnabledTasks:= FALSE
        UpdateOldTasks(), UpdateGroupTasks()
        IF EnabledTasks THEN
          Update Unsched removing recently assigned nodes.
            Update-Enable(t)
  t := t + 1
ENDWHILE
Return Sched
```

4 Tests and Results

A comparison was made with seven scheduling algorithms obtained from the literature. To save space, the only comparison shown is that with the ISH algorithm, which is the algorithm that gave the best results with respect to ELT. The performance of the ELT algorithm was compared with the ISH algorithm by means of the average of the percentage difference between the results obtained by both algorithms for sets of test DAGs. If the value is positive, it means that the ELT algorithm delivers a best solution in its total parallel time (*PT*), and therefore it is better.

The set of tests used consists of 226 DAGs which are divided into three categories: 180 “random structure” DAGs, 60 of which have tasks with random duration (**CR**), 60 have tasks with duration between 1 and 2 time units (**$CR_{1\text{-}2}$**), and 60 have tasks with duration between 1 and 5 time units (**$CR_{1\text{-}5}$**); and 46 DAGs of “known structure” (obtained from the literature for comparison purposes), of which 23 have tasks with arbitrary duration (**CC**) and 23 have the same structure of the previous ones, but the tasks have durations between 1 and 2 time units (**$CC_{1\text{-}2}$**). All the results obtained are found in [11].

Figures 1, 2 and 3 show the comparison between ELT and ISH for differents values of Δt and of p. Figure 1 shows the result of the average of the percentages of

* Nodes without predecessors.

the *PT* when both algorithms, were applied to the $\mathbf{CR}_{1\text{-}5}$ set. The graph of Figure 2 shows the result of the average of the percentages in the *PT* when ELT and ISH were applied on the $\mathbf{CR}_{1\text{-}2}$ set. And finally, that of Figure 3, the same result obtained on the **CC** set.

The best results of the ELT algorithm were obtained, in general, for granularity less than 3 (Figures 1-3). On the other hand, increasing the number of processors available to carry out the assignment of the DAG improves the results obtained by the ELT algorithm in relation to the ISH algorithm. This is explained because the ELT algorithm has a priority function whose purpose is, among other things, to maximize the number of enabled tasks, so having more processors means executing these tasks and decreasing the total parallel time. However, as the number of processors increases, the performance of the ELT improves, but more slowly because ELT is in charge of executing the enabled tasks, and not of balancing the load among the processors. Therefore, as more processing elements appear, there is a point at which some of them are not being occupied, making it possible to minimize the number of processors required for the solution.

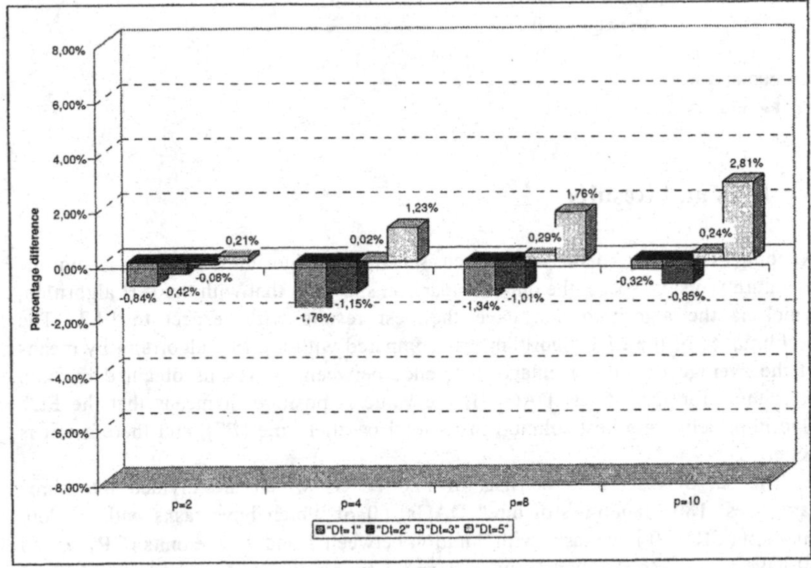

Fig. 1. Comparison of the average percentage in the *PT* between ELT and ISH for $CR_{1\text{-}5}$ (Dt = Δt).

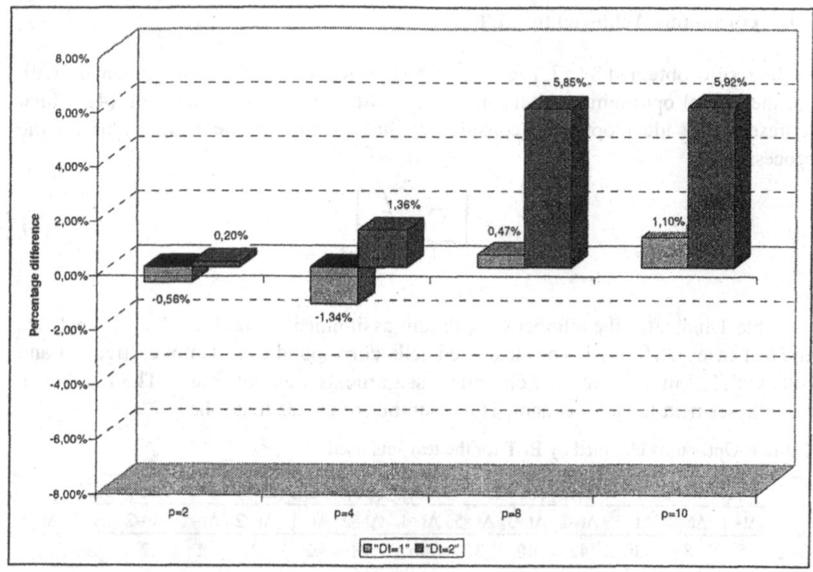

Fig. 2. Comparison of the average percentage in the PT between ELT and ISH for $CR_{1\text{-}2}$ (Dt = Δt).

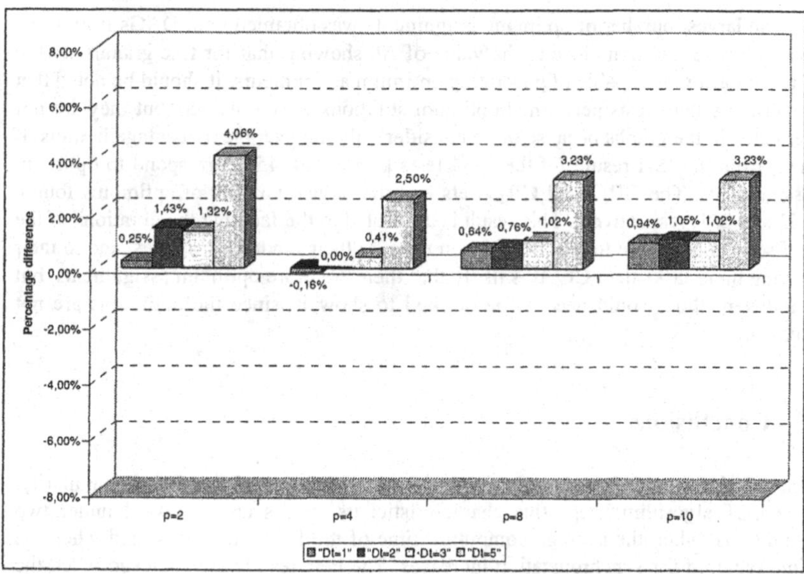

Fig. 3. Comparison of the average difference in *TP* between ELT and ISH for CC (Dt = Δt).

4.1 Optimums Achieved by ELT

In the results obteined by ELT, optimum assignments were found in agreement with the theoretical optimum parallel time (PT_{opt}) value indicated in equation (4), which represents the ideal optimum considering that maximum use is made of all the processors.

$$PT_{opt} = \left\lceil \sum_{i=1}^{n} t_i \Big/ p \right\rceil \tag{4}$$

Table 1 indicates the number of optimum assignments found for the different sets and test cases performed. The shadowed cells correspond to tests not carried out and cells with "-" indicate that an optimum assignments was not found. The number in parentheses next to each set name is the number of DAGs that it has.

Table 1. Optimums obtained by ELT for the test sets used.

	CR (60)		CR_{1-5} (60)				CR_{1-2} (60)		CC (23)		CC_{1-5} (23)			
	Δt=1	Δt=2	Δt=1	Δt=2	Δt=3	Δt=5	Δt=1	Δt=2	Δt=1	Δt=2	Δt=1	Δt=2	Δt=3	Δt=5
p=2	8	8	36	42	40	36	46	38	2	2	1	2	2	2
p=4	4	4	22	21	19	13	21	23	-	-	1	-	-	-
p=6	-	6												
p=8	-	-	10	6	6	1	14	8	-	-	-	-	-	-
p=10	-	-	6	2	1	-	2	-			-	-	-	-
p=16	-	-												

The largest number of optimum assignments was obtained with DAGs from tasks with average duration close to the value of Δt, showing that for fine granularity the ELT algorithm is capable of generating optimum assignments. It should be noted that in all the sets of tests performed optimum solutions were obtained, but they are not reflected in the graphs because these consider only the average percentage in units of time from the ISH result. Of the 2334 tests performed, 455 correspond to optimum assignments. The $\mathbf{CR_{1-2}}$ and $\mathbf{CR_{1-5}}$ sets had the largest number of optimums found, 152 and 261, respectively. This result is attributed to the fact that the durations of the tasks are comparable to synchronization time, to their random structures, and to their having more tasks than **CC**. It is likely that there are more optimum assignments, but another method would need to be defined to show it, since the optimums are not known.

5 Conclusions

The LT algorithm is based on the idea of working using DAGs with fine granularity. The ELT algorithm keeps this characteristic: its results are improved under two conditions, when the average computing time of the DAG decreases, and when the time required for synchronization increases. The best results are achieved when the synchronization time takes the value of the greatest duration of the tasks (granularity less than 3).

Like ELT aims at maximizing the number of enabled tasks, when number of processors for carrying out the assignment increases, the performance of the ELT algorithm improves. However, if exist more processors than enabled tasks, the rest of the processors are ignored.

Acknowledgements

This research was partially supported by CONICYT Grant FONDECYT 1030775, Chile.

Bibliographical References

1. M.J. Geiger and S. Petrovic, An Interactive Multicriteria Optimisation Approach to Scheduling In M. Bramer and V. Devedzic (Eds.), *Artificial Intelligence Applications and Innovations*. Kluwer Academic Publishers, 475-484, (2004).
2. L. Ingolotti, P. Tormos, A. Lova, F. Barber, M. A. Salido, and M. Abril, A Decision Support System (DSS) for the Railway Scheduling Problem. *Artificial Intelligence Applications and Innovations*. Kluwer Academic Publishers, pp. 465-474, (2004).
3. P. Pinacho, M. Solar, M. Inostroza, and R. Muñoz, Using Genetic Algorithms and Tabu Search Parallel Models to Solve the Scheduling Problem. In M. Bramer and V. Devedzic (Eds.). *Artificial Intelligence Applications and Innovations*. Kluwer Academic Publishers, 343-358, (2004).
4. M. Solar and M. Feeley, A Scheduling Algorithm considering Latency Time on a shared Memory Machine, *16th IFIP World Computer Congress 2000*, Beijing, China (Aug., 2000).
5. Y. Kwok and I. Ahmad, Benchmarking and Comparison of the Task Graph Scheduling Algorithms, *Journal of Parallel and Distributed Processing*, 381- 422 (Dec., 1999).
6. H. Zhou, Scheduling DAGs on a Bounded Number of Processors. *Int. Conf. on Parallel and Distributed Processing, Techniques and Applications*, Sunnyvale (Aug. 1996).
7. T. Yang and A. Gerasoulis, List Scheduling with and without Communication Delays, *Parallel Computing*, vol. 19 (1993).
8. B. Kruatrachue and T. Lewis, Duplication Scheduling Heuristics: A New Precedence Task Scheduler for Parallel Processor Systems, Technical Report, Oregon State University (1987).
9. M. Wu and D. Gajski, Hypertool: A Programming Aid for Message-Passing Systems, IEEE Trans. Parallel and Distributed Systems, vol. 1, no. 3 (July, 1990).
10. T. Yang and A. Gerasoulis, DSC: Scheduling Parallel Tasks on an Unbounded Number of Processors, *IEEE Trans. Parallel and Distributed Systems*, vol. 5, no. 9 (Sept. 1994).
11. I., Zuccar; M. Solar, V. Parada, A scheduling algorithm for arbitrary graphs on a shared memory machine, Chilean Computing Week, Punta Arenas, Chile, November, (2001).

Web Attack Detection Using ID3*

Víctor H. García, Raúl Monroy, and Maricela Quintana

Computer Science Department
Tecnológico de Monterrey, Campus Estado de México
Carretera al lago de Guadalupe, Km 3.5, Atizapán, 52926, Mexico
{A00471866,raulm,mquintana}@itesm.mx

Abstract. Decision tree learning algorithms have been successfully used in knowledge discovery. They use induction in order to provide an appropriate classification of objects in terms of their attributes, inferring decision tree rules. This paper reports on the use of ID3 to Web attack detection. Even though simple, ID3 is sufficient to put apart a number of Web attacks, including a large proportion of their variants. It also surpasses existing methods: it portrays a higher true-positive detection rate and a lower false-positive one. The ID3 output classification rules that are easy to read and so computer officers are more likely to grasp the root of an attack, as well as extending the capabilities of the classifier.

1 Introduction

In order to stay in business, many companies have a Web site, through which they promote or offer their products and let a candidate customer compute prices, compare product features, and so on. While profitable, these kinds of Web sites come along with a serious security problem, which is often approached via a standard protection schema: a firewall allowing HTTP(S) traffic. This schema is certainly not enough. According to S21SEC, 1320 public security vulnerabilities, out of the 2113 found only from June to November 2003, 62.5%, had their root in a Web application.

To better protect their resources, companies have strengthened their security mechanisms by incorporating clear and force-able security policies and by including other mechanisms such as an Intrusion Detection System (IDS). Intrusion is any action that puts on risk the integrity, confidentiality and availability of the company information. An IDS is a system that aims to detect intrusions on the fly while identifying the source of the attack.

Depending on its characterisation of intrusion, an IDS is of either of two types: i) misuse, and ii) anomaly. A Misuse IDS (MIDS) annotates as an attack any known pattern of abuse. MIDSs are very effective in detecting known

* We are grateful to the anonymous referees for their useful comments on an earlier draft of this paper. This research was supported by three grants: FRIDA, CONACYT 47557 and ITESM CCEM-0302-05.

Please use the following format when citing this chapter:

Garcia, V.H., Monroy, R., Quintana, M., 2006, in IFIP International Federation for Information Processing, Volume 218, Professional Practice in Artificial Intelligence, eds. J. Debenham, (Boston: Springer), pp. 323–332.

attacks; they exhibit a high true positive detection rate. Yet, they are bad at detecting novel attacks. An Anomaly IDS (AIDS) annotates as an attack any activity that deviates from a profile of ordinary behaviour. Unlike MIDSs, AIDSs are capable of detecting novel attacks. However, they frequently tag ordinary behaviour as malicious, yielding a high false positive detection rate.

Depending on the activity it observes, an IDS can be placed at either of three points: a host, a network or an application. A host IDS usually audits the functionality of the underlying operating system, but can also be set to watch critical resources. An application IDS scrutinises the behaviour of an application. It commonly is designed to raise an alarm any one time the application executes a system call that does not belong to a pre-defined set of system calls, built by some means, an object-code analysis. An network IDS analyses network traffic in order to detect mischievous activities within a computer network. A denial of service attack resulting from flooding a network with packets can be pinpointed only at this level.

Current IDSs are easy to bypass: there is a number of means to get full access to a Web service. Tools have even been developed to go around IDSs, e.g. nikto, fragroute, ADMutate. The main problem of existing IDSs is that they cannot detect new kinds of attacks or even variations of existing ones (so-called *mimicry* attacks). This problem prevails in well known IDSs, like snort. To get around this problem, IDS researchers have turned their attention to machine learning techniques, including classification rules and neural networks.

Current IDSs are also easy to overrun, due to the staggering amount of information they must analyse. The root of the problem is that in a computer site there usually is one IDS: the omnipotent, global sensor. For example, it is a standard practise to have only one NIDS to analyse all the traffic generated over a company network, yielding an increase in the false positive detection rate. To get around this problem, IDS researchers have recently suggested one should have one sensor for each company site service, such as HTTPS, making an application IDS more specialised. Service-oriented IDS have the advantage of specialisation: they produce a low rate of both false positives and false negatives, but at the expense of having a number of small IDSs, possibly working without any coordination. So far, there are only a few publicly available service-oriented IDS [10].

In this paper, we introduce an IDS for protecting a Web application with a low missing alarm and false alarm rates. This IDS makes use of ID3, a well-known classifier that builds a decision tree from a fixed set of examples. Each input example is a Web application query; it has several attributes and belongs to a class, either attack or normal. As we shall see later on in this paper, ID3 requires only that the Web application queries be slightly pre-processed before application. Unlike a neural network, ID3's decision tree can be easily explored to find out the rules applied by the classifier. In our experiments, ID3 was able to successfully classify unseen Web application queries as an attack. If the data base training is growing up because of new vulnerabilities, ID3's performance does not change at all. Unlike neural networks, ID3's output is easy to read by computer officers without having previous knowledge about decision trees techniques. Our hypothesis is that ID3 suffices to generalise on specifying a wide range of Web attacks, provided it is given a sufficiently large set of attack examples.

Paper Overview In what follows, we briefly describe related work, §2, and then characterise the kinds of attacks we want to detect, §3. Then, after outlining ID3 and the requirements it imposes on input data, §4, we show how to apply ID3 to build a decision tree for intrusion detection, §5. We recap and assess the results obtained throughout our experiments on validating our intrusion detection method, §6. Finally, we discuss the conclusions withdrawn from this research work.

2 Related Work

There are many IDSs currently available, ranging from commercial products to unprofitable ones. We briefly describe some of them below.

Rule Induction The application of inductive learning to intrusion detection has a long history in computer security. In 1990, e.g., Teng et al. [11] applied a time-based induction machine in order to characterise an audit trail as chunks of temporally co-related entries, yielding rule-based sequential patterns suitable for anomaly detection.

Cohen's RIPPER [4] is the crux for intrusion detection in JAM [10]. JAM is a distributed IDS that uses a collection of agents to form a number of intrusion detection models. These models are all merged into one, from which a meta-classifier is extracted. This meta-classifier is then used to detect intrusions; it can be combined with the meta-classifiers built in other sites and can migrate along them.

MADAM ID [5] is a framework that applies induction techniques (classifiers, association rules, frequent episodes, etc.) to build models for intrusion detection. It builds two kinds of models; one is about normal behaviour and the other about intrusions. Data is first pre-processed in order to find a representation where each event is normalised to a fixed number of attributes. Techniques are then used to find patterns of frequent occurrence, represented via association rules (connecting event features) and frequent episodes (connecting events).

Bayesian Classifiers Bayesian networks have proved to be very powerful to build decision models that operate under uncertainty conditions. When they are used to approach intrusion detection, an IDS amounts to a set of relations of conditional probabilities, as opposed to a set of classification rules. EMERALD [13], an IDS developed at SRI, includes a module, called eBayes TCP, that applies Bayesian networks to analyse traffic explosions.

ADAM [2] also uses a Bayesian network to build a profile of normal network activity. On operation, ADAM uses a sliding window to take observations from the last D connections. These observations are then compared against the profile of normal behaviour, filtering-out items taken to be normal. The remaining data is then passed onto the misuse, naïve Bayes classifier. ADAM performs especially well with denial of service and probe attacks.

Amor et al. [1] compared naïve Bayes against decision tree algorithms at detecting intrusions at a host level, using the DARPA attack repository as a testbed. Both methods showed a similar detection rate (the latter technique being slightly better than the former one.) As expected, the construction of a naïve Bayes classifier is much faster than the construction of a decision tree one.

Support Vector Machines A Support Vector Machine (SVM) is a technique that has been used widely for both supervised and unsupervised learning. Mukkamala et al. [6] used 5 SVMs to approach intrusion detection. One SVM was used for separating normal traffic and the other ones for identifying each of the 4 attacks involved in the data test set of the 1999 KDD cup. Mukkamala et al. showed that SVMs surpass neural networks on this classification task.

Neural Networks More related to ours is Torres's work on Web intrusion detection [12]. His method, IDS-ANN, which uses an Ellman neural network, analyses data using a layered approach and, thus, it is very time-consuming. A neural network is a black box and so it is difficult to extract general knowledge about intrusion detection.

In this paper, we aim to test how well standard data mining techniques are up to characterise malicious Web application queries. We propose to use ID3, a decision tree technique, instead of a Bayesian network. This is because, according to Amor et al's results (see above), in this problem decision tree techniques perform slightly better at the expense of requiring more computational efforts. This extra cost is an issue when the objects to be classified are large, which is not our case (Web application queries are rather short sequences of symbols.) So we have chosen to favour ID3.

As we shall see later on in this paper, ID3 needs only that the Web application queries be pre-processed before being used. ID3 is able to correctly classify unseen Web application queries as an attack. If the data base training is growing up because of new vulnerabilities, ID3's performance does not change at all. Unlike neural networks, ID3's output is easy to read by computer officers without having previous knowledge about classification techniques. ID3 is widely available and is not difficult to implement.

In the next section we survey the flaws commonly exploited in a Web attack.

3 Web Attacks

SecurityFocus[2] analysed 3,000 security incidents related with Web servers, CGIs and other Web applications. They concluded that the exploits or other tech-

[2] `http://www.securityfocus.com`

niques used to perpetrate these attacks took often advantage of security vulnerabilities already published. This was either because the vulnerabilities were never fixed through a patch, or because the patch was not able to detect small variations of the exploits.

Thus, there are no radically new types of vulnerabilities that the exploits take advantage of. The exploits we want to detect are of four kinds: i) SQL Injection; Cross Site Scripting (XSS); iii) Code injection; and Directory Traversal.

3.1 SQL Injection

SQL injection is a kind of vulnerability where the attack tries to manipulate data base applications by issuing crafted SQL queries. The source usually is an incorrect escaping of dynamically-generated string-literals embedded in SQL statements.[3] The effect is that the SQL statement may do more than the application author intended.

For example, in a Web site, a user usually needs to type in his login and his password in order to get access to some application. With SQL injection, it is possible to send a crafted SQL query in order to bypass this kind of authentication:

```
http://localhost/login.cgi?id_user=vh';%20--
```

The fault exploited by this attack query has to do with the double hyphen (--). SQL ignores anything following a double hyphen, and thus the application, if not properly written, may take the user as valid, granting him full access.

3.2 Cross Site Scripting

Cross site scripting (XSS) is a vulnerability of Web applications that can be used by an attacker to compromise the *same origin policy* of client-side scripting languages, like JavaScript.[4] XSS occurs when a Web application unknowingly gathers malicious data on behalf of a user, usually in the form of a hyperlink. Usually the attacker will encode the malicious portion of the link to the site so the request looks less suspicious. After the data is collected by the Web application, it usually creates an output page for the user containing the malicious data that was originally sent to it, but in a manner to make it appear valid content from the website.[5]

Using XSS and social engineering, an attacker could steal information about credit cards numbers or other personal data. The following link is for public use when testing for XSS:

```
http://www.vuln-dev.net/<script>document.location='http://www.repository.
com/cgi-bin/cookie.cgi? '%20+document.cookie </script>
```

[3] http://en.wikipedia.org/wiki/SQL_injection

[4] http://en.wikipedia.org/wiki/Cross-site_scripting

[5] http://199.125.85.46/articles/xss-faq.shtml

3.3 Code Injection

Code injection is a kind of vulnerability of Web server applications that can be used by the attacker to make the Web application execute arbitrary code. It is a cracking technique used to obtain confidential information or get unauthorised access to a system. These are two example code injection queries:

1. `http://localhost/scripts..%c0%afwinnt/system32/cmd.exe?/c+dir`
2. `http://host/index.asp?something=..\..\..\..\WINNT\system32\cmd.exe?/c+DIR+e:\WINNT\*.txt`

3.4 Directory Traversal

Directory traversal is one of the most common attacks. It aims to traverse the directory structure of a Web server to access files that may not be public. Directory traversal exploits insufficient security validation of user supplied input file names, so that special characters used to traverse to a parent directory are passed through to the file APIs.[6] Two examples of directory traversal attacks are:

1. `http://host/cgi-bin/vuln.cgi?file=../../../../etc/motd`
2. http://host/cgi-bin/vuln.cgi?page=../../../../bin/ls%20-al%20/etc|

The second query, for example, requests for a full directory listing of the "`etc`" directory within a Unix system. It is possible to make different variations on these attacks in order to fool conventional IDSs.

These kinds of attacks are all Web application queries. They take the form of well defined strings. In what follows, we briefly describe the ID3 algorithm and, in the next section, we show how to apply it in order to recognise attack queries.

4 ID3

ID3 is a simple inductive, non-incremental, classification algorithm [7]. Using a top-down, greedy search through a fixed set of examples, it builds a decision tree, which is then applied for classifying future samples. Each example has several attributes and belongs to a class. Each non-leaf node of the decision tree is a decision node, while each leaf node corresponds to a class name.

ID3 extends the concept learning system algorithm adding a feature selection heuristic. Feature selection is used to identify the attribute that best separates the set of input examples, called the *training set*. If the selected attribute completely classifies the training set, then we are done. Otherwise, ID3 is recursively applied, in a greedy fashion, to identify the next best attribute.

When deciding which attribute is the best, ID3 uses a measure called information gain. Information gain is defined in terms of the amount of information portrayed by an attribute, called entropy in information theory. This attribute selection method is very powerful. ID3 is well-established in both industry and academia.

[6] `http://en.wikipedia.org/wiki/Directory_traversal`

ID3, however, operates only on examples described by the same attributes. Attributes must take values from a fixed, finite set. ID3 is not tolerant to noisy or missing attributes. Classes must be sharply defined.

4.1 Other Inductive Classification Algorithms

CN2 [3] is other inductive, classification algorithm, which outputs an (un)ordered list of classification rules, instead of a decision tree. When first proposed, CN2 also used information entropy as a feature selection heuristic. Later, the use of the Laplacian error estimate was suggested as an alternative evaluation function.

C4.5 is a decision tree generating algorithm [8]. It extends ID3 in two main respects: i) it handles training data with missing attribute values; and ii) it handles attributes that take values from an infinite, continuous range.

We ruled out the application of C4.5 to detecting attacks in Web application queries. This is both because Web application queries have no missing attribute values, and because attributes take values from a discrete range. CN2 is just as good as a choice for our problem. Indeed, one advantage of using CN2 over ID3 is that a computer officer would not have to explore the ID3 decision tree in order to obtain the rules applied by the intrusion detection method. In what follows, we show how to apply ID3 (or CN2) to our intrusion detection problem.

5 Generating a Decision Tree for Intrusion Detection

In this section, we describe how to build a decision tree for Web attack detection using ID3.

5.1 Normalisation of URL Locations

Given that they do not fulfil the ID3 data requirements, Web application queries need to be transformed, prior to the application of ID3. A Web application query involves a specific Uniform Resource Locator (URL) and a collection of reserved symbols. An URL is a string, conforming to a standardised format, that is used for referring to resources on the Internet, by their location.[7] The location is irrelevant from an attack formation perspective.

Thus, our first step is to transform every Web application query so that each of its attributes takes a value from a fixed, finite set. This is accomplished by parsing every input query so as to divide it into substrings, using "." and "/" as terminal symbols. Then, for each substring, if it does not match one string that we have previously marked as **reserved**, we replace it with the string "@". Otherwise, the substring is left unmodified. For example, the following Web requirement:

```
B?variableB=something&variableB2=../dir
```

is transformed to:

```
@?@=@&@=../@
```

Here, ?, &, = and .. are assumed to be reserved symbols.

[7] http://en.wikipedia.org/wiki/URL

5.2 Handling Queries of Different Size Using a Sliding Window

The resulting Web application queries cannot yet be input to ID3 since they are not specified by the same attributes. Queries, as illustrated in Section 3, are of different size. We get around this problem using a sliding window. The sliding window is slided one by one, thus this way we get examples with the same number of attributes. After experimenting with a window of different sizes (5, 8, 10, 12, 15), we chose to use a sliding window of size 10, since it proved to build a decision tree that more precisely captured a subset of our examples.

5.3 The Training Data Set

We gathered 400 Web application attack queries from three security vulnerability lists: i) Securityfocus, iii) Unicode IIS Bugtraq,[8] and iii) Daily's Dave vulnerability disclosure list.[9] We also gathered 462 Web application non-attack queries. Non-attack queries were gathered from the Apache log files of 3 servers.[10] Each query was then given one of five classes: i) SQL injection, ii) cross site scripting, iii) code injection, iv) directory transversal and v) normal.

We apply the sliding window strategy to the 862 example training set. Then, the resulting objects were input to ID3 and so we built a decision tree. The decision tree was made classify a number of not previously considered Web application queries. The results of this validation step are reported below.

6 Validation Stage: Experimental Results

Once built, the ID3 decision tree was used as an intrusion detection method, we call *ID3-ids*. We tested Id3-ids against a collection of real Web application queries. The attacks were output by two attack generation engines: i) nikto and ii) nessus. The attacks were input to ID3-ids via a Web proxy cache, Squid. Squid accepts any kind of Web query and then redirects it to a custom Web server. We compared ID3-ids with snort and IDS-ANN.

Tables 1—4 summarise the results obtained throughout experimentations. They indicate both the false alarm rate and the missing alarm rate, considering two sets of attacks. One set of attacks, generated by nikto, contains 1771 examples. The other, generated by nessus, contains 14594 examples. ID3-ids surpasses snort. IDS-ANN is slightly better than ID3-ids at distinguishing the kind of attack under consideration. However, the detection rate of ID3-ids (considering only attack or non-attack) is slightly better.

These results show that ID3 is a competitive alternative for detecting Web application attack queries.

---

[8] http://www.securityfocus.com

[9] http://www.immunitysec.com

[10] http://www.zionn.org,http://www.ganexx.org,http://www.badc0d3d.org.ar/

Table 1. ID3-ids vs snort performance on attacks generated by Nikto

Method name	1771 Nikto generated attacks			Detection rate
	detected	undetected		
		missing alarms	false alarms	
snort	1282	329	160	72.3%
ID3-ids	1650	77	44	93.2%

Table 2. ID3-ids vs snort performance on attacks generated by Nessus

Method name	14594 Nessus generated attacks			Detection rate
	detected	undetected		
		missing alarms	false alarms	
snort	10256	2789	1549	70.27%
ID3-ids	13668	686	240	93.65%

Table 3. ID3-ids vs IDS-ANN performance on attacks generated by Nikto

Method name	1771 Nikto generated attacks			Identification rate	Detection rate
	detected	undetected			
		missing alarms	false alarms		
IDS-ANN	1680	41	50	83.8%	94.86%
ID3-ids	1650	77	44	77.25%	93.2%

Table 4. ID3-ids vs IDS-ANN performance on attacks generated by Nessus

Method name	14594 Nessus generated attacks			Identification rate	Detection rate
	detected	undetected			
		missing alarms	false alarms		
IDS-ANN	13200	989	405	78.5%	90.44%
ID3-ids	13668	686	240	77.25%	93.65%

7 Conclusions and Further Work

ID3 is an effective means for detecting and classifying web application attack queries. It yields a 4.7% missing alarm (false positive detection) rate and a 1.6% false alarm (false negative detection) rate. One major drawback of ID3-ids is that it is non-incremental. So the decision tree has to be built on a regular basis, using an updated attack signature database. Unlike a neural network, the ID3 decision tree can be easily explored and so intrusion detection rules can be further refined by a computer officer. CN2 is as applicable as ID3 to this problem. Actually, we also conducted these experiments using the CN2 toolbox.[11] As expected, we obtained similar results using the information

[11] `http://www.cs.utexas.edu/users/pclark/software.html`

gain feature selection. The false negative and false positive detection rate, however, worsen when the Laplacian error estimate was selected.

Further work involves applying CN2 or ID3 to masquerader detection [9]. We plan on further validating ID3-ids with other attack generating frameworks, like canvas and core impact.

The attack database, the decision tree and the code developed within this research work are at available at `http://webdia.cem.itesm.mx/ac/raulm/pub/id3-ids/`.

References

1. Amor NB, Benferhat S, Elouedi Z (2004) Naive bayes vs decision trees in intrusion detection systems. In Omicini A, Wainwright RL (eds) *Proceedings of the 2004 ACM symposium on Applied computing*, pages 420–424. ACM Press
2. Barbará D, Couto J, Jajodia S, Wu N (2001) ADAM: A testbed for exploring the use of data mining in intrusion detection. *SIGMOD Record*, 30(4):15–24
3. Clark P, Niblett T (1989) The CN2 induction algorithm. *Machine Learning*, 3:261–283
4. Cohen WW (1995) Fast effective rule induction. In Prieditis A, Russell SJ (eds) *Proceedings of the Twelfth International Conference on Machine Learning*, pages 115–123. Morgan Kaufmann
5. Lee W, Stolfo SJ (1999) Combining knowledge discovery and knowledge engineering to build idss. In *Recent Advances in Intrusion Detection (RAID'99)*
6. Mukkamala S, Janoski GI, Sung AH (2000) Monitoring system security using neural networks and support vector machines. In Abraham A, Köppen M (eds) *Proceedings of the First International Workshop on Hybrid Intelligent Systems*, Advances in Soft Computing, pages 121–137. Physica-Verlag
7. Quinlan JR (1986) Induction of decision trees. *Machine Learning*, 1(1):81–106
8. Quinlan JR (1987) Simplifying decision trees. *International Journal of Man-Machine Studies*, 27(3):221–234
9. Schonlau M, DuMouchel W, Ju WH, Karr AF, Theus M, Vardi W (2001) Computer Intrusion: Detecting Masquerades. *Statistical Science*, 16:58–74
10. Stolfo SJ, Prodromidis AL, Tselepis S, Lee W, Fan DW, Chan PK (1997) JAM: Java agents for meta-learning over distributed databases. In Heckerman D, Mannila H, Pregibon D (eds) *Proceedings of the Third International Conference on Knowledge Discovery and Data Mining (KDD-97)*, pages 74–81. AAAI Press
11. Teng H, Chen S, Lu S (1990) Adaptive real-time anomaly detection using inductively generated sequential patterns. In *Proceedings of the 1990 IEEE Computer Society Symposium on Research in Security and Privacy*, pages 278–284. IEEE Computer Society Press
12. Torres E (2003) *Sistema inmunológico para la detección de intrusos a nivel de protocolo HTTP*. PhD thesis, Pontificia Universidad Javeriana
13. Valdes A, Skinner K (2000) Adaptive, model-based monitoring for cyber attack detection. In Debar H, Mé L, Wu SF (eds) *Proceedings of the Third International Workshop on Recent Advances in Intrusion Detection, RAID 2000*, volume 1907 of *Lecture Notes in Computer Science*, pages 80–92. Springer

A Statistical Sampling Strategy for Iris Recognition

Luis E. Garza Castañon[1], Saul Montes de Oca[2], and Rubén Morales-Menéndez[1]

[1] Department of Mechatronics and Automation, ITESM Monterrey Campus, {legarza,rmm}@itesm.mx
[2] Automation Graduate Program Student, ITESM Monterrey Campus, saul_montesdeoca@yahoo.com.mx
Av. Eugenio Garza Sada Sur No. 2501
Monterrey, N.L. 64849 México

Abstract. We present a new approach for iris recognition based on a random sampling strategy. Iris recognition is a method to identify individuals, based on the analysis of the eye iris. This technique has received a great deal of attention lately, mainly due to iris unique characterics: highly randomized appearance and impossibility to alter its features. A typical iris recognition system is composed of four phases: image acquisition and preprocessing, iris localization and extraction, iris features characterization, and comparison and matching. Our work uses standard integrodifferential operators to locate the iris. Then, we process iris image with histogram equalization to compensate for illumination variations.The characterization of iris features is performed by using accumulated histograms. These histograms are built from randomly selected subimages of iris. After that, a comparison is made between accumulated histograms of couples of iris samples, and a decision is taken based on their differences and on a threshold calculated experimentally. We ran experiments with a database of 210 iris, extracted from 70 individuals, and found a rate of succesful identifications in the order of 97 %.

1 INTRODUCTION

Iris recognition is an specific area of biometrics. The main intention of biometrics is to provide reliable automatic recognition of individuals based on the measuring of a physical characteristic or personal trait. Biometrics can be used for access control to restricted areas, such as airports or military installations, access to personal equipments such as laptops and cellular phones, and public applications, such as banking operations [11]. A wide variety of biometrics systems have been explored and implemented with different degrees of success. Resulting systems include different physiological and/or behavioral human features such as: gait, DNA, ear, face, facial thermogram, hand thermogram, hand vein, fingerprint, hand shape, palmprint, signature, voice and iris [7,8]. The last one may provide the best solution by offering a much more discriminating power than others

Please use the following format when citing this chapter:

Castañon, L.E.G., de Oca, S.M., Morales-Menéndez, R., 2006, in IFIP International Federation for Information Processing, Volume 218, Professional Practice in Artificial Intelligence, eds. J. Debenham, (Boston: Springer), pp. 333–341.

biometrics. Specific characteristics of iris such as a data-rich structure, genetic independence, stability over time and physical protection, makes the use of iris as biometric well recognized.
In last years, there have been very successful implementations of iris recognition systems. Differences between them are mainly in the features characterization step. The golden standard is set by Daugman's system, with a performance of 99.9 % of matching [3]. Daugman used multiscale quadrature wavelets (Gabor filters) to extract texture phase structure information of the iris to generate a 2,048-bit iriscode and compared the difference between a pair of iris representations by their Hamming distance. In [10] iris features are extracted by applying a dyadic wavelet transform with null intersections. To characterize the texture of the iris, Boles and Boashash [1] calculated a one dimension wavelet transform at various resolution levels of a concentric circle on an iris image. In this case the iris matching step was based on two dissimilarity functions. Wildes [13] represented the iris texture with a Laplacian pyramid constructed with four different resolution levels and used the normalized correlation to determine whether the input image and the model image are from the same class. A Similar method to Daugman's is reported in [9], but using edge detection approach to localize the iris, and techniques to deal with illumination variations, such as histogram equalization and feature characterization by average absolute deviation. In [5] iris features are extracted by using independent component analysis. Zhu et al [14] uses statistical features, mean and standard deviations, from 2D wavelets transforms and Gabor filters, to make the system more robust to rotation, translation and illumination variations of images. In [6] a new method is presented to remove noise in iris images, such as eyelashes, pupil, eyelids and reflections. The approach is based on the fusion of edge and region information. In [4] an iris recognition approach based on mutual information is developed. In this work couples of iris samples are geometrically aligned by maximizing their mutual information and subsequently recognized. The mutual information was calculated with the algorithm proposed by Darbellay and Vajda. The decision whether two compared images belong to the same eye depends on a chosen threshold of mutual information.
In our approach we work directly with the iris information, instead of using a bank of filters or making a mathematical transformation. These approaches can be very computationally demanding. We claim than our approach will conduct to a fast approach for iris recognition, where just a few samples will be needed to discard many samples in database and allow a more focused sampling in a reduced set of candidate samples.
In our work, a database with colored high resolution eye images, is processed to lower the size and transform to a grey levels image. After this, the iris is located by using integrodifferential operators and extracted by using a transformation from cartesian to polar coordinates. The result of this operation is a rectangular strip containing just the iris area features. To compensate for illumination variations, iris strip is processed by histogram equalization. The feature extraction step is done by randomly sampling square subimages, and building

an acummulated histogram for each subimage. Every iris is represented by a set of accumulated histograms. The optimal size of square areas and the number of features were calculated experimentally. The comparison between iris sample and database is done by computing the Euclidean distance between histograms, and according to a threshold calculated also experimentally, we take the decision to accept o reject the iris sample.
We ran experiments in a database containing 210 samples coming from 70 individuals and found a rate of succesful matching in the order of 97 %.

2 THE PROPOSED APPROACH

The implementation of our approach relies on the use of eyes images from a database. These images use a format with color and high resolution, which can give us some problems with the management of memory. In our database, images can contain more than 6 Mbytes of information. Then, the first step consists in down sizing the image (we use 1024x758 bytes), and transform from color representation to just grey level pixels. This process is sufficient to reveal the relevant features of iris. Eyes images include samples where iris is free from any occlusion, as is shown in figure 1, and others with moderate obstruction from eyelids and eyelashes (Fig. 2).

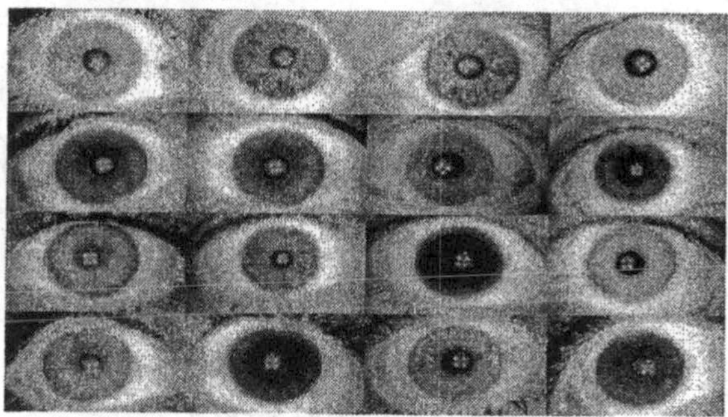

Fig. 1. Eyes samples without noise

2.1 Iris Localization

The finding of limbic and pupilar limits is achieved with the use of the standard integrodifferential operator shown in eqn 1.

$$\max_{(r,x_0,y_0)} = \left| \frac{\partial}{\partial r} G(r) * \oint_{r,x_c,y_c} \frac{I(x,y)}{2\pi r} ds \right| \tag{1}$$

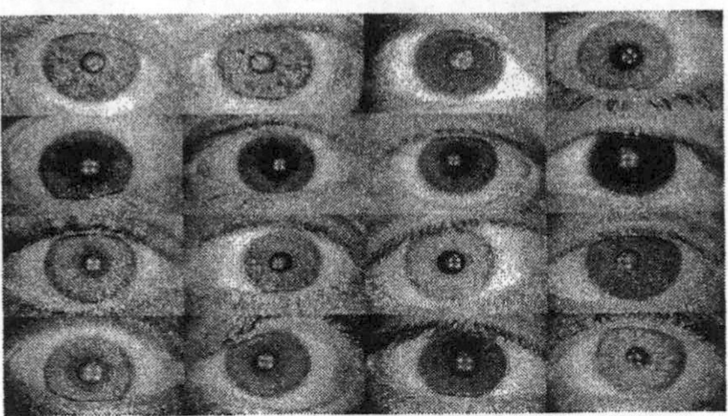

Fig. 2. Eyes samples with noise (moderate obstruction)

where $I(x, y)$ is an image containing an eye.
The operator behaves as an iterative circular edge detector, and searches over the image domain (x, y) for the maximum in the partial derivative with respect to an increasing radius r, of the normalized contour integral of $I(x, y)$ along a circular arc ds of radius r and center coordinates (x_0, y_0). The symbol $*$ denotes convolution and $G_\sigma(r)$ is a smoothimg function, tipically a Gaussian of scale σ.

This operator behaves well in most cases with moderate noise conditions, but requires some fine tuning of parameters, in order to deal with pupil reflections, obscure eyes and excess of illumination. Heavy occlusion (iris area covered more than 40 %) of iris by eyelashes or eyelids needs to be handled by other methods. The extracted iris image has to be normalized to compensate for pupil dilation and contraction under illumination variations. This process is achieved by a transformation from cartesian to polar coordinates, using equations 2 and 3. The output of this transformation is a rectangular image strip , shown in Fig. 5(a).

$$x(r, \theta) = (1 - r)x_p(\theta) + rx_s(\theta) \tag{2}$$

$$y(r, \theta) = (1 - r)y_p(\theta) + ry_s(\theta) \tag{3}$$

where $x(r, \theta)$ and $y(r, \theta)$ are defined as a linear combination of pupil limits $(x_p(\theta),\ y_p(\theta))$ and limbic limits $(x_s(\theta),\ y_s(\theta))$. r is defined in the interval $[0, 1]$, and θ in the interval $[0, 2\pi]$.

2.2 Features Extraction

The iris image strip obtained in previous step, is processed by using an histogram equalization method, to compensate for differences in illumination conditions.

The main objective in this method is that all grey levels (ranging from 0 to 255) have the same number of pixels. Histogram equalization is obtained by working with the accumulated histogram, shown in eqn 4.

$$H(i) = \sum_{k=0}^{i} h(k) \tag{4}$$

where $h(k)$ is the histogram of the kth grey level.
A flat histogram, where every grey level has the same number of pixels, can be obtained by eqn 5.

$$G(i') = (i' + 1)\frac{N * M}{256} \tag{5}$$

Where N and M are the image dimensions and 256 is the number of grey levels. An example of application of histogram equalization method over the iris strip in figure 5(a), is shown in figure 5(b).

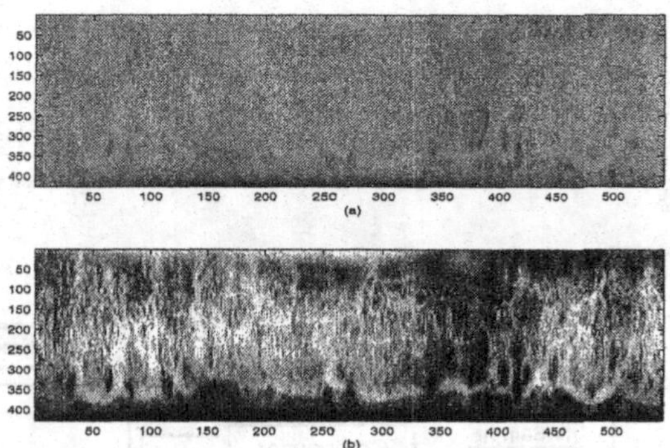

Fig. 3. (a) Extracted iris strip image.(b) Iris strip processed by the histogram equalization method

2.3 Comparison and Matching

In our method, the iris features are represented by a set of accumulated histograms computed from randomly selected square subimages of iris strip (see Fig. 6). An accumulated histogram represents a feature and is built by using equation 4. The complete iris is represented by a set of accumulated histograms, one of them for every subimage. The optimal size of the number of features and subimage size, were determined empirically by experiments. A decision to accept or reject the iris sample is done according to the minimum Euclidean distance calculated from the comparison of iris sample and irises database, and also according to a threshold. Figure 8 shows the structure of this phase.

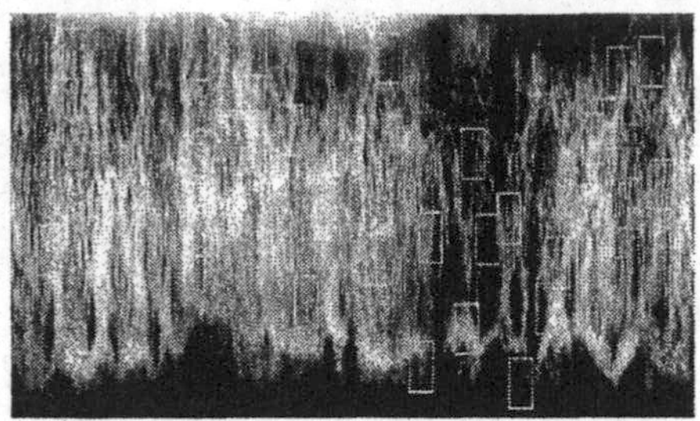

Fig. 4. iris strip image showing a random selection of areas

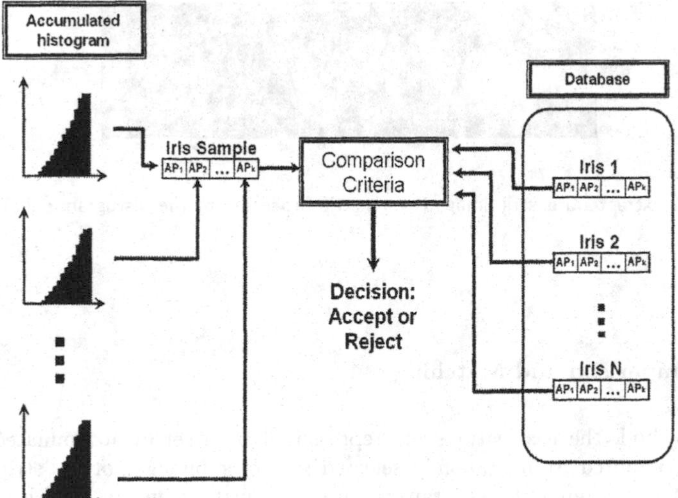

Fig. 5. The process of comparison and matching

3 Experiments

Experiments were ran for a database with 210 samples coming from 70 individuals. In a first step, a set of experiments was scheduled to produce the best acceptance/rejection thresholds (Euclidean distance). In a second step, a set of 10 experiments were conducted by fixing both: the size of subimage area and the number of features or histograms. In every experiment a random iris sample was taken, and a random database of 100 samples was formed without duplicates. The percent of successful identifications reported is the mean of those 10 experiments. The Fig. 8 shows the accuracy on the accept/reject decision taken. The best results of 97.18 % were obtained with an square subimage area of 25 pixels and 210 features. False positive errors were 0.26 % and false negatives errors were 2.56 %.

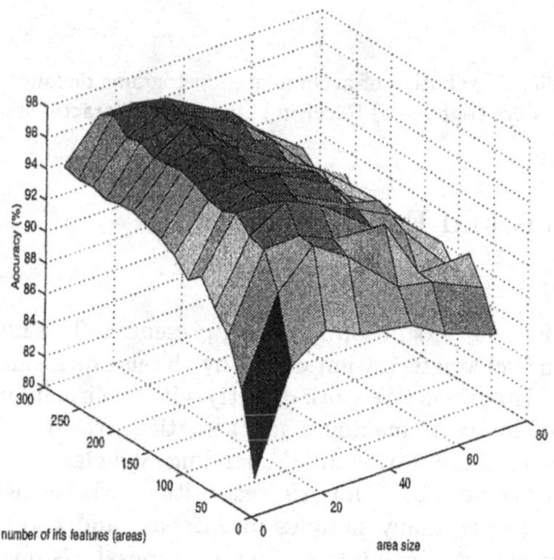

Fig. 6. Results from experiments with different number of features and size of areas

The Fig. 9 (a) shows the distribution observed in function of two types of persons, "authentics" and "impostors". This distribution estimation treats only one-to-one verification mode. We can observe a significant overlapping area, which in turns avoid more accurate scores of recognition. In Fig. 9 (b) is shown the ROC curve that is a plot of genuine acceptance rate against false acceptance rate. Points in the curve denote all possible system operating states in different tradeoffs. Fig. 9 (b) shows an acceptable performance of our method.

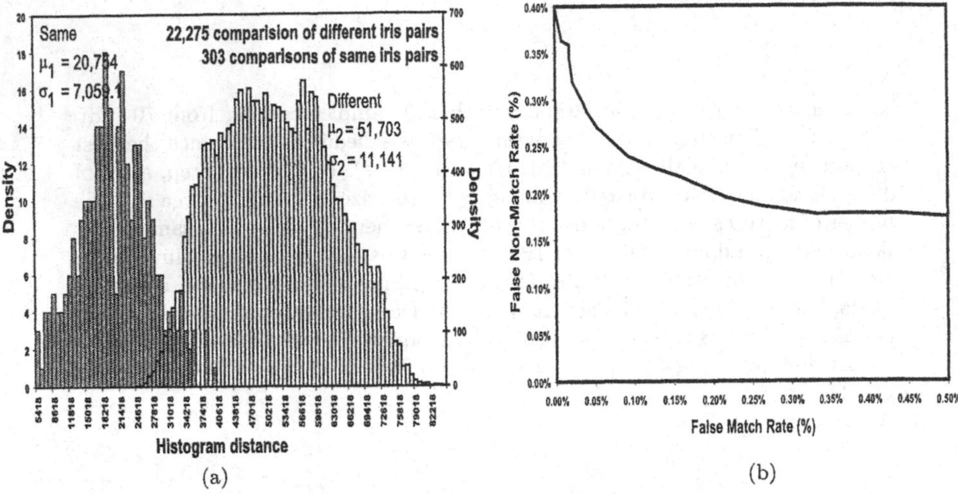

Fig. 7. (a) Probability Distribution of accumulated histograms distance for authentic persons (left) and impostors (right). (b) Receiving Operating Characteristic curve

4 Conclusions and Future Works

A new approach for iris recognition has been presented. The novel contribution relies on the feature characterization of iris by the use of a sampling technique and accumulated histograms. We work directly with the iris information, instead of using a bank of filters or making a mathematical transformation. Both approaches can be very computationally demanding. We claim than our approach will conduct to a fast approach for iris recognition, where just a few samples will be needed to discard many samples in database and allow a more focused sampling in a reduced set of candidates. In our proposal iris image is sampled in a specific number of randomly selected square areas or subimages. From every subimage an accumulated histogram is built, and the whole iris is represented by a set of accumulated histograms. The matching step consists then in a comparison between histograms, and the decision to accept or reject a user is taken based on the minimum difference between iris samples , and a threshold calculated experimentally.

We have found a rate of successful identifications in the order of 97 %.

In future works we will address two aspects: first, the determination of minimal number of samples and the size of samples, to identify accuratelly a person, and second, we are looking a more uniform sampling strategy to avoid redundant information by overlapping of samples.

References

1. W. Boles and B. Boashash, "Iris Recognition for Biometric Identification using dyadic wavelet transform zero-crossing", *IEEE Transactions on Signal Processing*, Vol. 46, No. 4, 1998, pp. 1185-1188.
2. D. Clausi and M. Jernigan, "Designing Gabor Filters for Optimal Texture Separability", *Pattern Recognition*, Vol. 33, 2000, pp. 1835-1849.
3. J. Daugman, "How Iris Recognition Works", *IEEE Transactions on Circuits and Systems for Video Technology*, Vol. 14, No. 1, 2004, pp. 21-30.
4. M. Dobes, L. Machala, P. Tichasvky, and J. Pospisil, "Human Eye Iris Recognition Using The Mutual Information", *Optik*, No. 9, 2004, pp. 399-404.
5. Y. Huang, S. Luo, and E. Chen, "An Efficient Iris Recognition System", In *Proceedings of the First International Conference on Machine Learning and Cybernetics*, 2002, pp. 450-454.
6. J. Huang, Y. Wang, T. Tan, and J. Cui, "A New Iris Segmentation Method for Iris Recognition System", In *Proceedings of the 17th International Conference on Pattern Recognition*, 2004, pp. 554-557.
7. A. Jain, R. Bolle, S. Pankanti, Biometrics: Personal Identification in Networked Society, Kluwer Academics Publishers, 2002.
8. A. Jain, A. Ross, A. Prabhakar, "An Introduction to Biometric Recognition", *IEEE Transactions on Circuits and Systems for Video Technology*, Vol. 14, No. 1, 2004, pp. 4-20.
9. L. Ma, Y. Wang, T. Tan, and D. Zhang, "Personal Identification Based on Iris Texture Analysis", *IEEE Transactions on Pattern Analysis and Machine Intelligence*, Vol. 25, No. 12, 2003, pp. 1519 - 1533.
10. D. de Martin-Roche, C. Sanchez-Avila, and R. Sanchez-Reillo, "Iris Recognition for Biometric Identification using dyadic wavelet transform zero-crossing", In *Proceedings of the IEEE 35th International Conference on Security Technology*, 2001, pp. 272-277.
11. M. Negin, Chmielewski T., Salganicoff M., Camus T., Cahn U., Venetianer P., and Zhang G. "An Iris Biometric System for Public and Personal Use ", *Computer*, Vol. 33, No. 2, 2000, pp. 70-75.
12. Ch. Tisse, L. Martin, L. Torres, and M. Robert, "Person Identification technique using Human Iris Recognition", In *Proceedings of the 15th International Conference on Vision Interfase*, 2002.
13. R. Wildes, "Iris Recognition: An Emerging Biometric Technology", *Proceedings of the IEEE*, Vol. 85, No. 9, 1997, pp. 1348-1363.
14. Y. Zhu, T. Tan, and Y. Wang, "Biometric Personal Identification Based on Iris Patterns", In *Proceedings of the 15th International Conference on Pattern Recognition*, 2000, pp. 801-804.

An Application of ARX Stochastic Models to Iris Recognition

Luis E. Garza Castañón[1], Saúl Montes de Oca[2], and Rubén Morales-Menéndez[1]

[1] Department of Mechatronics and Automation, ITESM Monterrey Campus, {legarza,rmm}@itesm.mx

[2] Automation Graduate Program Student, ITESM Monterrey Campus, saul_montesdeoca@yahoo.com.mx

Av. Eugenio Garza Sada Sur No. 2501
Monterrey, N.L. 64849 México

Abstract. We present a new approach for iris recognition based on stochastic autoregressive models with exogenous input (ARX). Iris recognition is a method to identify persons, based on the analysis of the eye iris. A typical iris recognition system is composed of four phases: image acquisition and preprocessing, iris localization and extraction, iris features characterization, and comparison and matching. The main contribution in this work is given in the step of characterization of iris features by using ARX models. In our work every iris in database is represented by an ARX model learned from data. In the comparison and matching step, data taken from iris sample are substituted into every ARX model and residuals are generated. A decision of accept or reject is taken based on residuals and on a threshold calculated experimentally. We conduct experiments with two different databases. Under certain conditions, we found a rate of successful identifications in the order of 99.7 % for one database and 100 % for the other.

1 Introduction

Iris recognition is related to the area of biometrics. The main intention of biometrics is to provide reliable automatic recognition of individuals based on the measuring of a physical or behavioral characteristic of persons. Biometrics can be used for access control to restricted areas, such as airports or military installations, access to personal equipments such as laptops and cellular phones, and public applications, such as banking operations [13]. A wide variety of biometrics systems have been deployed and resulting systems include different human features such as: face, fingerprint, hand shape, palmprint, signature, voice and iris [8]. The last one may provide the best solution by offering a much more discriminating power than the others biometrics. Specific characteristics of iris such as a data-rich structure, genetic independence, stability over time and physical protection, makes the use of iris as biometric well recognized.

Please use the following format when citing this chapter:

Castañon, L.E.G., de Oca, S.M., Morales-Menéndez, R., 2006, in IFIP International Federation for Information Processing, Volume 218, Professional Practice in Artificial Intelligence, eds. J. Debenham, (Boston: Springer), pp. 343–352.

In last years, there have been different implementations of iris recognition systems. Daugman's system [2] used multiscale quadrature wavelets (Gabor filters) to extract texture phase structure information of the iris to generate a 2,048-bit iris code and compared the difference between a pair of iris representations by their Hamming distance. In [11] iris features are extracted by applying a dyadic wavelet transform with null intersections. To characterize the texture of the iris, Boles and Boashash [1] calculated a one dimension wavelet transform at various resolution levels of a concentric circle on an iris image. In this case the iris matching step was based on two dissimilarity functions. Wildes [15] represented the iris texture with a Laplacian pyramid constructed with four different resolution levels and used the normalized correlation to determine whether the input image and the model image are from the same class. A Similar method to Daugman's is reported in [10], but using edge detection approach to localize the iris, and techniques to deal with illumination variations, such as histogram equalization and feature characterization by average absolute deviation. In [7] a new method is presented to remove noise in iris images, such as eyelashes, pupil, eyelids and reflections. The approach is based on the fusion of edge and region information. In [3] an iris recognition approach based on mutual information is developed. In that work, couples of iris samples are geometrically aligned by maximizing their mutual information and subsequently recognized.

In our work we apply standard techniques as integro-differential operators to locate the iris, and histogram equalization over extracted iris area to compensate for illumination variations. The main contribution in this work is given in the step of characterization of iris features by using stochastic ARX models, commonly used by the automatic control community. In our work every iris in database is represented by an ARX model learned from data. In the comparison and matching step, data taken from an arriving iris sample are substituted in every ARX model and residuals are generated. A decision to accept or reject the sample is taken based on the residuals and on a threshold calculated experimentally. The architecture of the proposed method is shown in Fig. 1.

We conduct experiments with UBIRIS database [14] and MILES database [12]. Under certain conditions we found a rate of successful identifications in the order of 99.7 % and 100 % respectively.

2 THE PROPOSED APPROACH

The implementation of our approach relies on the use of colored eyes images from UBIRIS and MILES databases. Eyes images include samples where iris is free from any occlusion, and others with moderate obstruction from eyelids and eyelashes. Noisy samples from UBIRIS database are shown in Fig. 2. We transform the images color representation to just grey level pixels, because this process is sufficient to reveal the relevant features of iris.

Our iris recognition system consists of four steps: iris localization and extraction, iris features characterization, and comparison and matching.

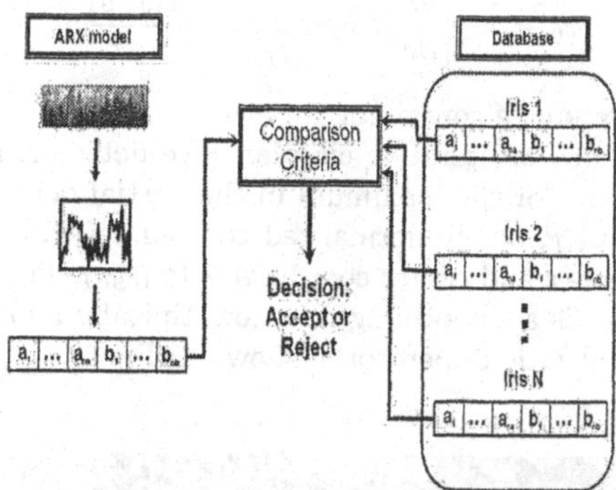

Fig. 1. Architecture of the iris recognition system based on ARX models

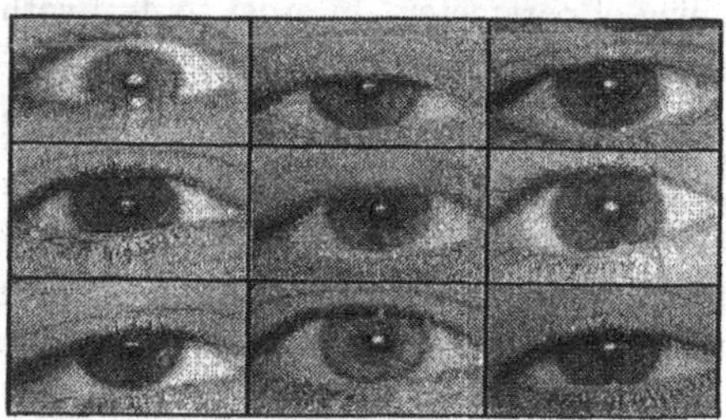

Fig. 2. Eyes samples with noise (moderate obstruction)

2.1 Iris Localization

The search of limbic and pupilar limits is achieved with the use of the integro-differential operator shown in eqn 1.

$$\max_{(r, x_0, y_0)} = \left| \frac{\partial}{\partial r} G(r) * \oint_{r, x_c, y_c} \frac{I(x, y)}{2\pi r} ds \right| \tag{1}$$

where $I(x, y)$ is an image containing an eye.
The operator behaves as an iterative circular edge detector, and searches over the image domain (x, y) for the maximum in the partial derivative with respect to an increasing radius r, of the normalized contour integral of $I(x, y)$ along a circular arc ds of radius r and center coordinates (x_0, y_0). The symbol $*$ denotes convolution and $G_\sigma(r)$ is a smoothimg function, tipically a Gaussian of scale σ. The result of this localization operator is shown in Fig. 3.

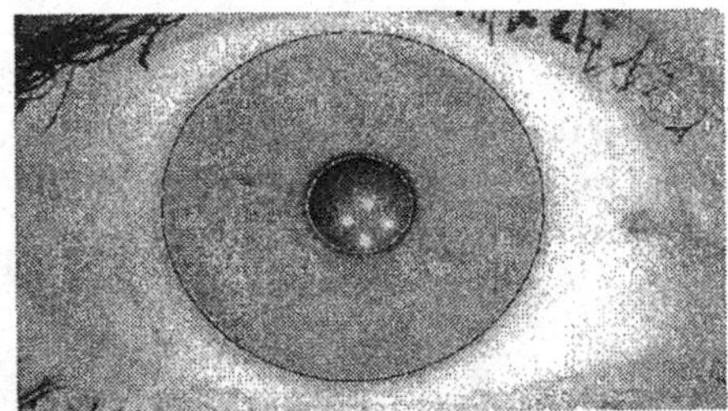

Fig. 3. localization of limbic and pupilar limits with integro-differential operators

This operator behaves well in most cases with moderate noise conditions, but requires some fine tuning of parameters, in order to deal with pupil reflections, obscure eyes and excess of illumination. Heavy occlusion of iris by eyelashes or eyelids needs to be handled by other methods. In our work, eye images with heavy occlusion were discarded.
The extracted iris image has to be normalized to compensate for pupil dilation and contraction under illumination variations. This process is achieved by a transformation from cartesian to polar coordinates, using equations 2 and 3. The output of this transformation is a rectangular image strip , shown in Fig. 4.

$$x(r, \theta) = (1 - r)x_p(\theta) + rx_s(\theta) \tag{2}$$

$$y(r, \theta) = (1 - r)y_p(\theta) + ry_s(\theta) \tag{3}$$

where $x(r, \theta)$ and $y(r, \theta)$ are defined as a linear combination of pupil limits $(x_p(\theta),\ y_p(\theta))$ and limbic limits $(x_s(\theta),\ y_s(\theta))$. r is defined in the interval $[0, 1]$, and θ in the interval $[0, 2\pi]$.

Fig. 4. iris strip image

2.2 Feature Characterization by ARX Models

We propose the representation of iris image by an stochastic ARX model. An ARX model represents the behavior of a dynamic system in discrete time [5], where the output V_k depends on the input U_k and past values of both variables. To represent iris image by an ARX model, we first divide the iris strip image in a rectangular grid, and define output V_k as the mean grey level value of every subarea in the grid. The input U_k is defined as the corresponding row number of subarea on the grid.
In discrete time the ARX model is defined as follows:

$$v_k = a_1 v_{k-1} + a_2 v_{k-2} + \cdots + a_{na} v_{k-na} + b_1 u_{k-1-nd} + \cdots + b_{nb} u_{k-nb-nd} \quad (4)$$

Where $a_1, a_2, \cdots a_{na}$ and $b_1, b_2, \cdots b_{nb}$ are the model coefficients to be learned by a least squares (LS) algorithm, n_d is an integer number representing the number of times steps that output V_k takes to show the effect of a given input U_k. This term usually is called dead time. In our case we assume $n_d = 0$. Former model can be represented as a discrete transfer function in the complex z domain, and is expressed as:

$$\frac{V(z)}{U(z)} = \frac{b_1 z^{-1} + b_2 z^{-2} + \cdots + b_{nb} z^{-nb}}{1 - a_1 z^{-1} - a_2 z^{-2} - \cdots - a_{na} z^{-na}} z^{-nd} \quad (5)$$

The coefficients $a_1, a_2, \cdots a_{na}$ and $b_1, b_2, \cdots b_{nb}$ are learned by a least squares (LS) algorithm. This method minimizes an index based on differences between the real data and the model. We define first the following vectors:

$$\Psi^T = [v_{k-1} \;\; v_{k-2} \;\; \cdots \;\; v_{k-na} \;\; u_{k-1-nd} \;\; \cdots \;\; u_{k-nb-nd}] \quad (6)$$

$$\theta_N = [a_1 \;\; a_2 \;\; \cdots \;\; a_{na} \;\; b_1 \;\; \cdots \;\; b_{nb}] \quad (7)$$

and then we can rewrite eqn. 4 as follows:

$$v_k = \Psi_k^T \theta \quad (8)$$

LS algorithm find the coefficients vector θ that makes the best estimate of output v_k, defined as:

$$\widehat{v}_k = \Psi_k^T \theta + e_k \tag{9}$$

where $k = nm, nm + a, ..., N$ and $nm = max(na, nb + nd)$. difference between real data and model is given by:

$$e_N = V_N - \Psi_N \theta_N \tag{10}$$

The performance index that LS algorithm minimizes is given by:

$$J = \sum_{k=nm}^{N} e_k^2 = e_N^T e_N \tag{11}$$

Iris database then is composed by an ARX model for every iris. When an iris arrives for recognition, the comparison is made by using eqn. (11), and obtaining the error in eqn. (10), where V_N and θ_N belong to iris in database (I^T) and matrix Ψ_N belongs to iris simple (I^S), this lead us to following equations:

$$e_N = V_N^{I^T} - \Psi_N^{I^S} \theta_N^{I^T} \tag{12}$$

where e_N, $V_N^{I^T}$, $\Psi_N^{I^S}$ y $\theta_N^{I^T}$ are defined as:

$$e_N = \begin{bmatrix} e_{nm} \\ e_{nm+1} \\ \vdots \\ e_N \end{bmatrix}, V_N^{I^T} = \begin{bmatrix} v_{nm}^{I^T} \\ v_{nm+1}^{I^T} \\ \vdots \\ v_N^{I^T} \end{bmatrix},$$

$$\Psi_N^{I^S} = \begin{bmatrix} v_{nm-1}^{I^S} & \cdots & v_{nm-na}^{I^S} & u_{nm-1-nd}^{I^S} & \cdots & u_{nm-nb-nd}^{I^S} \\ v_{nm}^{I^S} & \cdots & v_{nm-na+1}^{I^S} & u_{nm-nd}^{I^S} & \cdots & u_{nm-nb-nd+1}^{I^S} \\ \vdots & \ddots & \vdots & \vdots & \ddots & \vdots \\ v_{N-1}^{I^S} & \cdots & v_{N-na}^{I^S} & u_{N-1-nd}^{I^S} & \cdots & u_{N-nb-nd}^{I^T} \end{bmatrix}, \theta_N^{I^T} = \begin{bmatrix} a_1^{I^T} \\ a_2^{I^T} \\ \vdots \\ a_{na}^{I^T} \\ b_1^{I^T} \\ \vdots \\ b_{nb}^{I^T} \end{bmatrix}$$

3 Experiments

Experiments were ran for UBIRIS and MILES databases. Images with too much occlusion and noise were discarded, because the difficulty to locate the iris region with integro-differential operators. Then, our UBIRIS experimental database was built with 1013 samples coming from 173 users, and MILES database consists of

DB Size (%)	# of iris	# Threshold samples	# Test samples
100	1013	52	788
90	912	46	693
80	811	42	596
70	710	36	501
50	507	26	308

Table 1. UBIRIS Databases used for experiments with 173 users. First column refers to the percent of database used. For instance, 90 % means that 10 % of worst user samples were discarded. Second column refers to total number of iris samples, third column refers to the number of samples used to calculate the decision threshold, and fourth column refers to the total number of samples used for testing.

DB Size (%)	# of iris	# Threshold samples	# Test samples
100	36	10	167
75	36	8	116

Table 2. MILES Databases used for experiments with 119 users.

grid size	**100 % DB**	**90 % DB**	**80 % DB**	**70 % DB**	**60 % DB**	**50 % DB**
4 × 4	84.64	85.39	93.42	96.65	97.93	99.7
5 × 5	86.31	87.82	91.69	94.23	97.93	98.8
8 × 8	83.21	84.98	86.68	92.36	94.25	95.51
10 × 10	80.12	80.38	83.54	88.64	86.67	90.12

Table 3. Results of experiments for UBIRIS database (in % of accuracy) with different grid size. Best results are highlighted

grid size	**100 % DB**	**75 % DB**
4 × 4	91.53	100.0
5 × 5	94.35	100.0
8 × 8	93.41	99.19
10 × 10	93.79	99.19

Table 4. Results of experiments for MILES database (in % of accuracy) with different grid size. Best results are highlighted

213 samples from 199 users. With these databases, we perform some experiments with 100 % of samples and others experiments where worst user samples were discarded. Tables 1 and 2 shows the different databases used.

The order of ARX model (number of coeffficients a_i,b_i) was determined empirically by doing differents experiments, and best results were obtained for $n_a = 5$ and $n_b = 5$ in both, UBIRIS and MILES databases. In tables 3 and 4 these results are shown. We can see that best results were obtained for cleaner databases.
In Fig.5 we can see the ROC curves for UBIRIS databases used in experiments. Databases with cleaner iris samples reflects better results. In Fig. 6 we can see the authentic-impostor distribution curves for two UBIRIS databases used. The Overlapping between distribution curves in Fig. 6 (a) leads to worst results. Similar ROC and authentic-impostor curves were obtained for MILES database experiments and are not shown.

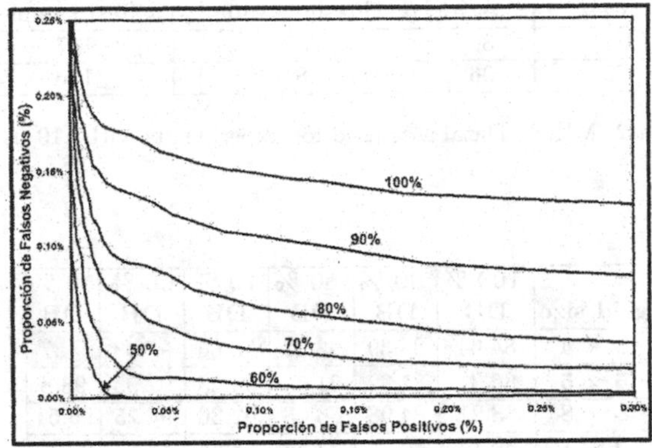

Fig. 5. Receiver operating characteristic (ROC) curve for experiments with different databases.

4 Comparison to Previous Work

Daugman's system [2] has been tested thoroughly with databases containing thousands of samples, and reports of 100 % of accuracy have been given. In [11], the experimental results given are in the order of 97.9 %, by working with a database of 100 samples from 10 persons. Boles and Boashash [1] report best results in the order of 100 % but working with very small sets of images. Wildes [15] report results in the order of 100 % by working with a database of 600 samples coming from 40 individuals. In [10], a report is given about a performance of 99.09 % in experiments with a database of 500 iris images from 25 individuals. In [7] the results are between 98 % and 99 % by working with CASIA database

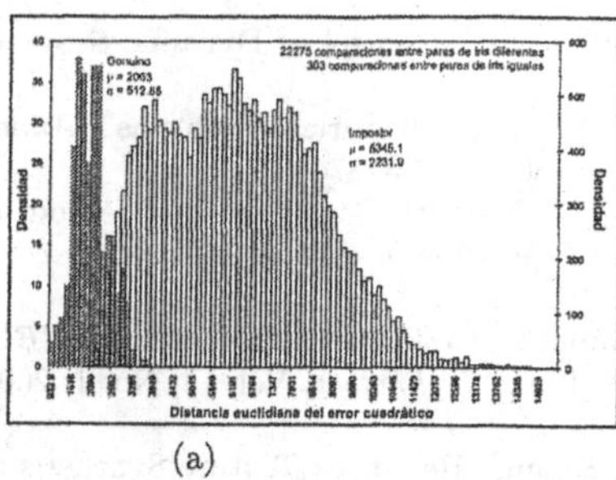

(a)

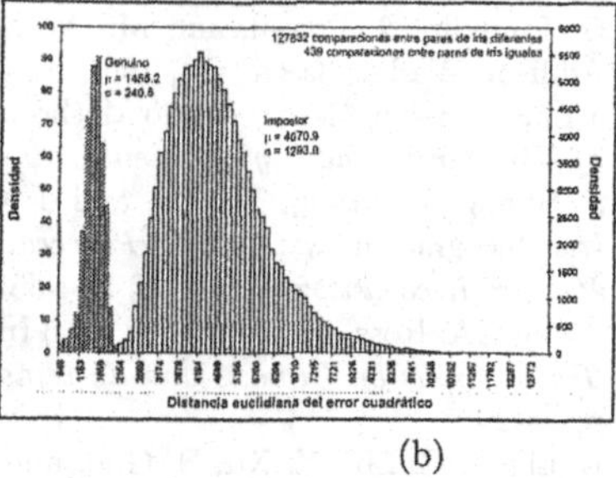

(b)

Fig. 6. authentic-impostor distribution for ARX based system. (a) database with 100% of data. (b) database with 50% of data.

(2255 samples from 213 subjects). In [3] best results are in the order of 99.05 % with a database of 384 images from 64 persons.
None of these works specify the quality of databases, so a direct comparison is not possible. What we can say is that we are competitive with most methods when our method work with clean databases, which means eye images with no obstruction and noise. Our best results were 99.7 % for UBIRIS database and 100 % for MILES database obtained with cleanest databases.

5 Conclusions and Future Works

A new approach for iris recognition has been presented. The novel contribution relies on the feature characterization of iris by the use of stochastic ARX models. Although experimental results show better results for databases with cleaner eyes images, we are looking forward to improve the methodology by combining statistical sampling methods and stochastic models. We believe the combination of best aspects of both approaches will lead us to a more robust and accurate iris identification system.

References

1. W. Boles and B. Boashash, "Iris Recognition for Biometric Identification using dyadic wavelet transform zero-crossing", *IEEE Transactions on Signal Processing*, Vol. 46, No. 4, 1998, pp. 1185-1188.
2. J. Daugman, "How Iris Recognition Works", *IEEE Transactions on Circuits and Systems for Video Technology*, Vol. 14, No. 1, 2004, pp. 21-30.
3. M. Dobes, L. Machala, P. Tichasvky, and J. Pospisil, "Human Eye Iris Recognition Using The Mutual Information", *Optik*, No. 9, 2004, pp. 399-404.
4. A. Efros, and T. Leung, "Texture Synthesis by Non-Parametric Sampling", in *Proceedings of the 7th IEEE International Conference on Computer Vision*, September 1999, Vol. 2, pp. 1033-1038.

5. G. Franklin, J. Powell, and M. Workman, Digital Control of Dynamic Systems, Addison-Wesley, 3a edition, 1997
6. J. Hammersley, "Monte Carlo Methods for Solving Multivariate Problems", *Annals of New York Academy of Science*, 1960, No. 86, pp. 844-874.
7. J. Huang, Y. Wang, T. Tan, and J. Cui, "A New Iris Segmentation Method for Iris Recognition System", In *Proceedings of the 17th International Conference on Pattern Recognition*, 2004, pp. 554-557.
8. A. Jain, A. Ross, A. Prabhakar, "An Introduction to Biometric Recognition", *IEEE Transactions on Circuits and Systems for Video Technology*, Vol. 14, No. 1, 2004, pp. 4-20.
9. L. Liang, C. Liu, Y. Xu, B. Guo, and H. Shum, "Real-time Texture Synthesis by Patch-based Sampling", *ACM Transactions on Graphics*, Vol. 20, No. 3, July 2001, pp. 127-150.
10. L. Ma, Y. Wang, T. Tan, and D. Zhang, "Personal Identification Based on Iris Texture Analysis", *IEEE Transactions on Pattern Analysis and Machine Intelligence*, Vol. 25, No. 12, 2003, pp. 1519 - 1533.
11. D. de Martin-Roche, C. Sanchez-Avila, and R. Sanchez-Reillo, "Iris Recognition for Biometric Identification using dyadic wavelet transform zero-crossing", In *Proceedings of the IEEE 35th International Conference on Security Technology*, 2001, pp. 272-277.
12. Miles Research. Sample iris Pictures. http://www.milesresearch.com/
13. M. Negin, Chmielewski T., Salganicoff M., Camus T., Cahn U., Venetianer P., and Zhang G. "An Iris Biometric System for Public and Personal Use ", *Computer*, Vol. 33, No. 2, 2000, pp. 70-75.
14. H. Proenca, and L. Alexandre,"UBIRIS: A Noisy Iris Image Database", in *Proceedings of the International Conference on Image Analysis and Processing 2005*, Vol. 1, pp. 970-977.
15. R. Wildes, "Iris Recognition: An Emerging Biometric Technology", *Proceedings of the IEEE*, Vol. 85, No. 9, 1997, pp. 1348-1363.